THE INERRANT WORD

THE INERRANT
WORD

BIBLICAL, HISTORICAL, THEOLOGICAL,
AND PASTORAL PERSPECTIVES

John MacArthur

General Editor

FOREWORD BY R. C. SPROUL

WHEATON, ILLINOIS

Library of Congress Cataloging-in-Publication Data
The inerrant word: biblical, historical, theological, and pastoral perspectives / John MacArthur, general editor; foreword by R. C. Sproul.
    pages cm
  Includes bibliographical references and index.
  ISBN 978-1-4335-4861-1 (hc)
  1. Bible—Evidences, authority, etc. I. MacArthur, John, 1939– editor.
BS480.I427   2016
220.1'32—dc23   2015023859

Contents

Part 4
INERRANCY IN PASTORAL PRACTICE:
APPLYING TO LIFE

Foreword

R. C. Sproul

"The Bible is the Word of God, which errs." From the advent of neoorthodox theology in the early twentieth century, this assertion has become a mantra among those who want to have a high view of Scripture while avoiding the academic liability of asserting biblical infallibility and inerrancy. But this statement represents the classic case of having one's cake and eating it too. It is the quintessential oxymoron.

Let us look again at this untenable theological formula. If we eliminate the first part, "The Bible is," we get "The Word of God, which errs." If we parse it further and scratch out "the Word of" and "which," we reach the bottom line:

"God errs."

The idea that God errs in any way, in any place, or in any endeavor is repugnant to the mind as well as the soul. Here, biblical criticism reaches the nadir of biblical vandalism.

How could any sentient creature conceive of a formula that speaks of the Word of God as errant? It would seem obvious that if a book is the Word of God, it does not (indeed, cannot) err. If it errs, then it is not (indeed, cannot be) the Word of God.

To attribute to God any errancy or fallibility is dialectical theology with a vengeance.

Perhaps we can resolve the antinomy by saying that the Bible originates with God's divine revelation, which carries the mark of his infallible truth, but this revelation is mediated through human authors, who, by virtue of their humanity, taint and corrupt that original revelation by their penchant for error. *Errare humanum est* ("To err is human"), cried Karl Barth, insisting that by denying error, one is left with a docetic Bible—a Bible that merely "seems" to be human, but is in reality only a product of a phantom humanity.

Who would argue against the human proclivity for error? Indeed, that proclivity is the reason for the biblical concepts of inspiration and divine superintendence of Scripture. Classic orthodox theology has always maintained that the Holy Spirit overcomes human error in producing the biblical text.

Barth said the Bible is the "Word" (*verbum*) of God, but not the "words" (*verba*) of God. With this act of theological gymnastics, he hoped to solve the unsolvable dilemma of calling the Bible the Word of God, which errs. If the Bible is errant, then it is a book of human reflection on divine revelation—just another human volume of theology. It may have deep theological insight, but it is not the Word of God.

Critics of inerrancy argue that the doctrine is an invention of seventeenth-century Protestant scholasticism, where reason trumped revelation—which would mean it was not the doctrine of the magisterial Reformers. For example, they note that Martin Luther never used the term *inerrancy*. That's correct. What he said was that the Scriptures never err. Neither did John Calvin use the term. He said that the Bible should be received as if we heard its words audibly from the mouth of God. The Reformers, though not using the term *inerrancy*, clearly articulated the concept.

Irenaeus lived long before the seventeenth century, as did Augustine, Paul the apostle, and Jesus. These all, among others, clearly taught the absolute truthfulness of Scripture.

The church's defense of inerrancy rests upon the church's confidence in the view of Scripture held and taught by Jesus himself. We wish to have a view of Scripture that is neither higher nor lower than his view.

The full trustworthiness of sacred Scripture must be defended in every generation, against every criticism. That is the genius of this volume. We need to listen closely to this recent defense.

Dr. R. C. Sproul
Former President, International Council on Biblical Inerrancy
Orlando, Florida
Advent 2014

Introduction

WHY A BOOK ON BIBLICAL

INERRANCY IS NECESSARY[1]

John MacArthur

It was A. W. Tozer who famously stated, "What comes into our minds when we think about God is the most important thing about us." The reason for this, Tozer went on to explain, is that deficient views of God are idolatrous and ultimately damning: "Low views of God destroy the gospel for all who hold them." And again, "Perverted notions about God soon rot the religion in which they appear. . . . The first step down for any church is taken when it surrenders its high opinion of God."[2] As Tozer insightfully observed, the abandonment of a right view of God inevitably results in theological collapse and moral ruin.

Because God has made himself known in his Word, a commitment to a high view of Scripture is of paramount importance. The Bible both *reflects* and *reveals* the character of its Author. Consequently, those who deny its veracity do so at their peril. If the most important thing about us is how we think about God, then what we think about his self-revelation in Scripture

---

[1] In places throughout this introduction, I have adapted material from the following: John MacArthur, "Preach the Word: Five Compelling Motivations for the Faithful Expositor," *The Master's Seminary Journal* 22, no. 2 (Fall 2011): 163–77; John MacArthur, *Nothing But the Truth: Upholding the Gospel in a Doubting Age* (Wheaton, IL: Crossway, 1999); John MacArthur, *Strange Fire: The Danger of Offending the Holy Spirit with Counterfeit Worship* (Nashville: Thomas Nelson, 2013); and John MacArthur, *You Can Trust the Bible* (Chicago: Moody Press, 1988).
[2] A. W. Tozer, *The Knowledge of the Holy* (New York: HarperCollins, 1961), 1, 3–4.

is of the utmost consequence. Those who have a high view of Scripture will have a high view of God. And vice versa—those who treat the Word of God with disdain and contempt possess no real appreciation for the God of the Word. Put simply, it is impossible to accurately understand who God is while simultaneously rejecting the truthfulness of the Bible.

No church, institution, organization, or movement can rightly claim to honor God if it does not simultaneously honor his Word. Anyone who claims to reverence the King of kings must joyfully embrace his revelation and submit to his commands. Anything less constitutes rebellion against his lordship and receives his express displeasure. To disregard or distort the Word is to show disrespect and disdain for its Author. To deny the veracity of the Bible's claims is to call God a liar. To reject the inerrancy of Scripture is to offend the Spirit of truth who inspired it.

For that reason, believers are compelled to treat the doctrine of biblical inerrancy with the utmost seriousness. That mandate is especially true for everyone who provides oversight to the church in positions of spiritual leadership. This book is a call to all Christians, and especially those who lead the church, to handle Scripture in a way that honors the God who gave it to us.

Here are four reasons why believers must stand firm on God's revealed truth.

Scripture Is Attacked, and We Are Called to Defend It

First, the Bible is under constant assault.

Based on Paul's description of false teachers in 2 Timothy 3:1–9, it is clear that the greatest threat to the church comes not from hostile forces without, but from false teachers within. Like spiritual terrorists, they sneak into the church and leave a path of destruction in their wake. They are wolves in sheep's clothing (Matt. 7:15), characterized by hypocrisy and treachery, and motivated by insatiable greed and fleshly desires. Thus, every Christian must defend Scripture and use it properly.

The church has been threatened by savage wolves and spiritual swindlers from its earliest days (cf. Acts 20:29). Satan, the father of lies (John 8:44), has always sought to undermine the truth with his deadly errors (Gen. 3:1–5; 1 Tim. 4:1; cf. 2 Cor. 11:4, 14). It is not surprising, then, that church history has often been marked by seasons in which falsehood and deception have waged war against the pure gospel.

Consider, for example, the havoc created by the following six errors: Roman Catholicism, higher criticism, modern cults, Pentecostalism, clinical psychology, and market-driven church-growth strategies. Though each of these historical developments is very different, all of them share a common rejection of the authority of Scripture.

Roman Catholicism exchanged the authority of Scripture for the authority of religious tradition. One of the earliest deceptions to infiltrate the church on a massive scale was *sacramentalism*—the idea that an individual can connect with God through ritualism or religious ceremony. As sacramentalism gained widespread acceptance, the Roman Catholic Church supposed itself to be a surrogate savior, and people became connected to a system, but not to Christ. Religious ritual became the enemy of the true gospel, standing in opposition to genuine grace and undermining the authority of God and His Word. Many were deluded by the sacramental system. It was a grave danger that developed throughout the Middle Ages, holding Europe in a spiritual chokehold for nearly a millennium. Because they recognized that Christ alone is the head of the church, the Protestant Reformers gladly submitted to his Word as the sole authority within the church. Consequently, they also confronted any false authority that attempted to usurp Scripture's rightful place, and in so doing, they exposed the corruption of the Roman Catholic system.

Higher criticism exchanged the authority of Scripture for the authority of human reason and atheistic naturalism. Not long after the Reformation, a second major wave of error crashed upon the life of the church: *rationalism.* As European society emerged from the Middle Ages, the resulting Age of Enlightenment emphasized human reason and scientific empiricism, while simultaneously discounting the spiritual and supernatural. Philosophers no longer looked to God as the explanation for the world; rather, they sought to account for everything in rational, naturalistic, and deistic terms. As men began to place themselves above God and their own reason over Scripture, it was not long until rationalism gained access to the church. Higher-critical theory—which denied the inspiration and inerrancy of the Bible—infiltrated Protestantism through seminaries in both Europe and the United States. So-called Christian scholars began to question the most fundamental tenets of the faith as they popularized quests for the "historical Jesus" and denied Mosaic authorship of the Pentateuch. The legacy of that rationalism, in the form of theological liberalism and continual attacks on biblical inerrancy, is yet alive and well. As such, it represents a continued threat to the truth.

Modern cults exchanged the authority of Scripture for the authority of self-appointed leaders such as Joseph Smith, Ellen G. White, and Joseph Rutherford. Arising in the nineteenth century, cult groups such as the

Mormons, the Seventh-Day Adventists, and the Jehovah's Witnesses preyed on the biblical ignorance of their spiritual victims. They claimed to represent pure forms of Christianity. In reality, they merely regurgitated ancient errors such as Gnosticism, Ebionism, and Arianism.

Pentecostalism exchanged the authority of Scripture for the authority of personal revelations and ecstatic experiences. Officially beginning in 1901 under the leadership of Charles Fox Parham, the Pentecostal movement was sparked when some of his students reportedly experienced the gift of tongues. In the 1960s and '70s, Pentecostal *experientialism* began to infiltrate the mainline denominations. This movement, known as the charismatic renewal movement, tempted the church to define truth on the basis of emotional experience. Biblical interpretation was no longer based on the clear teaching of the text, but upon feelings and subjective, unverifiable experiences, such as supposed revelations, visions, prophecies, and intuitions. The Third Wave movement of the 1980s continued the growth of mysticism within the church, convincing people to look for signs and wonders and to listen for paranormal words from God rather than seeking out truth in the written Word of God. People began neglecting the Bible, looking instead for the Lord to speak to them directly. Consequently, the authority of Scripture was turned on its head.

Clinical psychology exchanged the authority of Scripture for the authority of Freudian theories and clinical therapies. In the 1980s, the influence of clinical psychology brought *subjectivism* into the church. The result was a man-centered Christianity in which the sanctification process was redefined for each individual and sin was relabeled a sickness. The Bible was no longer deemed sufficient for life and godliness; instead, it was replaced with an emphasis on psychological tools and techniques.

Market-driven churches exchanged the authority of Scripture for the authority of felt needs and marketing schemes. At the end of the twentieth century, the church was also greatly damaged by the Trojan horse of *pragmatism*. Though it looked good on the outside (because it resulted in greater numbers of attendees), the seeker-driven movement of the 1990s quickly killed off any true appetite for sound doctrine. Ear tickling became the norm as "seekers" were treated like potential customers. The church adopted a marketing mentality, focusing on "what works" at the expense of biblical ecclesiology. Pragmatism inevitably gave way to *syncretism*, because popularity was viewed as the standard of success. In order to gain acceptance in a postmodern society, the church became soft on sin and error. Capitulation was masked as tolerance; compromise redefined as love;

and doubt extolled as humility. Suddenly, interfaith dialogues and manifestos—and even interfaith seminaries—began to sprout on the evangelical landscape. So-called evangelicals started to champion the message that "we all worship one God." And those who were willing to stand for truth were dismissed as divisive and uncouth.

As such examples illustrate, whenever the church has abandoned its commitment to the inerrancy and authority of Scripture, the results have always been catastrophic. In response, believers are called to defend the truth against all who would seek to undermine the authority of Scripture. As Paul wrote, "We destroy arguments and every lofty opinion raised against the knowledge of God, and take every thought captive to obey Christ" (2 Cor. 10:5). Jude similarly instructed his readers to "contend earnestly for the faith which was once for all delivered to the saints" (Jude 3 NKJV). In referring to "the faith," Jude was not pointing to an indefinable body of religious doctrines; rather, he was speaking of the objective truths of Scripture that comprise the Christian faith (cf. Acts 2:42; 2 Tim. 1:13–14).

With eternity at stake, it is no wonder that Scripture reserves its harshest words of condemnation for those who would put lies in the mouth of God. The Serpent was immediately cursed in the garden of Eden (Gen. 3:14), and Satan was told of his inevitable demise (v. 15). In Old Testament Israel, to prophesy falsely was a crime punishable by death (Deut. 13:5, 10), a point vividly illustrated by Elijah's lethal encounter with the prophets of Baal on Mount Carmel (1 Kings 18:19, 40). God repeatedly issued strong denunciations against all those who undermined or distorted the truth of his Word (cf. Isa. 30:9–13; Jer. 5:29–31; 14:14–16; Ezek. 13:3–9).

The New Testament repudiates false teachers with equal force (cf. 1 Tim. 6:3–5; 2 Tim. 3:1–9; 1 John 4:1–3; 2 John 7–11). God will not tolerate those who tamper with divine revelation. He takes such an offense personally. It is an affront to his character (cf. Jer. 23:25–32). Accordingly, to sabotage biblical truth in any way—by adding to it, subtracting from it, distorting it, or simply denying it—is to invite the wrath of God (Gal. 1:9; 2 John 9–11). But those who love him and his Word are careful to handle it accurately (2 Tim. 2:15), to teach its doctrines soundly, and to defend the church from those who would distort its truth (Titus 1:9; 2 Pet. 3:16–17).

Scripture Is Authoritative, and We Are Called to Declare It
Second, the Bible comes with God's absolute authority.

The Bible repeatedly testifies to the fact that it is God's Word. The men who wrote Scripture, under the inspiration of the Holy Spirit (2 Pet. 1:19–21), recognized that they were writing God's words under his direction (cf. Amos 3:7). They acknowledge that fact more than thirty-eight hundred times in the Old Testament alone. Speaking of the Old Testament, Paul explained to the believers in Rome, "For whatever was written in former days was written for our instruction, that through endurance and through the encouragement of the Scriptures we might have hope" (Rom. 15:4; cf. 2 Pet. 1:2; Heb. 1:1). The New Testament authors similarly recognized that their writings (cf. 1 Thess. 2:13), along with those of other New Testament writers (cf. 1 Tim. 5:18; 2 Pet. 3:15–16), were inspired by God and thus authoritative.

That the Bible is the very Word of God is spelled out in 2 Timothy 3:16. There Paul explains that "all Scripture is inspired by God" (NASB). The Greek word translated "inspired" is *theopneustos*, a compound word literally meaning "God-breathed." It refers to the entire content of the Bible—that which comes out of his mouth—his Word. The inspiration and sufficiency of Scripture (vv. 16–17) provide the backdrop for the divine charge to *preach the Word* (4:1–2).

Because it is his inspired Word, Scripture perfectly conveys the truth of whatever God has said. The psalmist said, "The law of the LORD is perfect" (Ps. 19:7); "I hope in your word" (119:81); "Your word is very pure" (119:140 NASB); "Your law is true" (119:142); "All your commandments are true" (119:151). As these examples demonstrate, Scripture reflects the trustworthy character of its Author.

God is so closely linked to his Word that, in some passages, the term *Scripture* is even synonymous with the name *God*: "The Scripture . . . preached the gospel beforehand to Abraham, saying 'In you shall all the nations be blessed'" (Gal. 3:8); "Scripture has shut up everyone under sin, so that the promise by faith in Jesus Christ might be given to those who believe" (v. 22 NASB). In these verses, the Bible is said to speak and act as God's voice. The apostle Paul similarly referred to God's speaking to Pharaoh (Ex. 9:16) when he wrote, "For the *Scripture says* to Pharaoh, 'For this very purpose I have raised you up'" (Rom. 9:17). Thus, believers can be confident that whenever they read the Bible, they are reading the very words of God.

Jesus implied that all of Scripture is inspired as a unified body of truth when he declared, "The Scripture cannot be broken" (John 10:35). The entire Bible is pure and authentic; *none* of its words can be nullified, because they are all God's sacred writings (cf. 2 Tim. 3:15). Christ also stressed the divine significance of every detail of Scripture when he said in his Sermon on the Mount, "For truly I say to you, until heaven and earth pass away, not the smallest letter or stroke shall pass from the Law until all is accomplished" (Matt. 5:18).

Importantly, because God is a God of truth who does not speak falsehood, his Word is also true and incapable of error. The Author of Scripture calls himself the essence of truth (Isa. 65:16), and the prophet Jeremiah ascribes the same quality to him: "The LORD is the true God" (Jer. 10:10). The writers of the New Testament also equated God with truth (e.g. John 3:33; 17:3; 1 John 5:20), and both Testaments emphasize that God cannot lie (Num. 23:19; Titus 1:2; Heb. 6:18). Thus, the Bible is inerrant because it is God's Word, and God is a God of truth (Prov. 30:5). Accordingly, those who deny the doctrine of inerrancy dishonor God by casting doubt on the truthfulness and trustworthiness of that which he has revealed.

Scripture Is Accurate, and We Are Called to Demonstrate It

Third, the Bible is demonstrably true.

Despite the attacks of the skeptics and critics, the testimony of Scripture has stood the test of time. It has proven itself to be accurate—historically, geographically, archaeologically, and so on—time and time again.

Though the accuracy of Scripture can be demonstrated in a variety of ways, two of the most compelling involve science and prophecy.

THE BIBLE AND SCIENCE

To any honest observer, the legitimate findings of science (meaning that which can be tested using the scientific method) correspond perfectly to what the Bible reveals. For example, Scripture presents the most plausible understanding of the origins of the universe and the existence of life. The Bible's teaching that God created the world makes far more sense than the notion that everything spontaneously generated from nothing, which is what the atheistic presuppositions of evolution require.

The renowned nineteenth-century philosopher Herbert Spencer was well known for demonstrating the relevance of science to philosophy. He articulated five knowable categories in the natural sciences: time, force, motion, space, and matter. Spencer's insights were applauded when he publicized them. Yet they were hardly innovative. Genesis 1:1, the first verse in the Bible, says, "In the beginning [time], God [force] created [motion] the heavens [space] and the earth [matter]." The Creator made the truth clear in the very first verse of biblical revelation.

The record of Scripture is accurate when it intersects with the fundamental findings of modern science. The first law of thermodynamics, which deals with the conservation of energy, is implied in passages such as Isaiah 40:26 and Ecclesiastes 1:10. The second law of thermodynamics indicates that although energy cannot be destroyed, it is constantly going from a state of order to disorder. This law of entropy corresponds to the fact that creation is under a divine curse (Genesis 3), such that it groans (Rom. 8:22) as it heads toward its ultimate ruin (2 Pet. 3:10–13) before being replaced with new heavens and the new earth (Revelation 21–22). Findings from the science of hydrology are foreshadowed in places such as Ecclesiastes 1:7; Isaiah 55:10; and Job 36:27–28. And calculations from modern astronomy, regarding the countless number of stars in the universe, are anticipated in Old Testament passages such as Genesis 22:17 and Jeremiah 33:22.

The book of Job is one of the oldest books in the Bible, written some thirty-five hundred years ago. Yet it has one of the clearest statements of the fact that earth is suspended in space. Job 26:7 says that God "hangs the earth on nothing." Other ancient religious books make ridiculous scientific claims, including the notion that the earth rests on the backs of elephants. But when the Bible speaks, it does so in a way that corresponds to what scientific discoveries have found to be true about the universe.

Many additional examples could be cited. But this is sufficient to make the point: though the Bible was not written as a technical scientific manual, it is accurate whenever it addresses scientific phenomena. That is precisely what we would expect, since it is the revelation of the Creator himself. When God speaks about this world that he made, he does so in a way that accurately corresponds to reality.

The Bible and Prophecy

Scripture's amazing accuracy can also be seen by looking at the incredible record of biblical prophecy. The Bible's ability to predict the future cannot be explained apart from the recognition that God is its Author. For example, the Old Testament contains more than three hundred references to the Messiah that were precisely fulfilled by Jesus Christ.

Consider the following messianic prophecies from just one Old Testament passage—Isaiah 53. In this chapter, written some seven hundred years before the birth of Christ, the prophet Isaiah explained that:

- the Messiah would not come in the trappings of royal majesty (v. 2); consequently, he would be despised and rejected by the nation of Israel (v. 3);
- he would be a man of sorrows and acquainted with grief (v. 3), yet he would bear the griefs and sorrows of the nation (v. 4);
- he would be pierced through for the sins of others (v. 5);
- he would be scourged (v. 5);
- God would place the iniquity of the people on him (v. 6);
- though oppressed in judgment and falsely accused, he would not open his mouth in self-defense; rather, he would be like a lamb led to slaughter (v. 7);
- he would be killed for the transgressions of the people (v. 8);
- though he would be assigned a grave for wicked men, he would be buried in a rich man's tomb (v. 9);
- he would be crushed by God as a guilt offering for sin (v. 10);
- after his death, he would see the fruit of his labors (implying that he would be raised from the dead) (v. 10);
- he would bring justification to many by bearing their iniquities (v. 11); and
- he would be richly rewarded for his faithfulness (v. 12).

Isaiah 53 clearly describes the Lord Jesus Christ. Yet it was penned seven centuries before the events it describes. It is difficult to imagine a more vivid illustration of the divine quality that Scripture possesses, since only God could know the future with such detailed precision.

The Bible includes many other prophecies as well. For example, Isaiah 44–45 predicted the rise of a Persian ruler named Cyrus who would allow the Jewish people to return from their captivity. That prophecy was fulfilled one hundred and fifty years later, exactly as it had been foretold. Ezekiel 26 foretold the total destruction of the Phoenician city of Tyre. That prediction came true some two hundred and fifty years later, during the conquest of Alexander the Great. The Assyrian city of Nineveh serves as a similar example. Though it was one of the most formidable and feared cities of the ancient world, the prophet Nahum predicted that it would soon be destroyed (Nah. 1:8; 2:6). Its collapse occurred just as the prophet declared.

These and hundreds of other examples prove the Bible to be exactly what it claims to be: revelation from the One who knows the beginning from the end (Isa. 46:10).

Scripture Is Active through the Power of the Spirit, and We Are Called to Deploy It

Finally, the Bible is not a dead letter, but the living and powerful Word of God (Heb. 4:12).

Some books can change a person's thinking, but only the Bible can change the sinner's nature. It is the only book that can totally transform someone from the inside out. When God's Word is proclaimed and defended, it goes forth with Spirit-generated power.

It is the Holy Spirit who empowers the proclamation of the gospel (1 Thess. 1:5; 1 Pet. 1:12), convicting the hearts of unbelievers through the preaching of the Word (cf. Rom. 10:14) so that they respond in saving faith (1 Cor. 2:4–5). As the Lord himself promises, "So shall My word be that goes forth from My mouth; it shall not return to Me void, but it shall accomplish what I please, and it shall prosper in the thing for which I sent it" (Isa. 55:11 NKJV). The apostle Paul similarly describes the Word of God as "the sword of the Spirit" (Eph. 6:17). And the author of Hebrews declares: "For the word of God is living and active, sharper than any two-edged sword, piercing to the division of soul and of spirit, of joints and of marrow, and discerning the thoughts and intentions of the heart" (4:12).

Thus, the proclamation of the Word is far more than empty noise or lifeless oratory. Because it is empowered by the Spirit of God, the truth of Scripture cuts through barriers of sin and unbelief. Yet, God's Word is more than just a sword. It is the means by which the Spirit of God regenerates the heart (cf. Eph. 5:26; Titus 3:5; James 1:18), sanctifies the mind (John 17:17), produces spiritual growth (2 Tim. 3:16–17; 1 Pet. 2:1–3), and conforms believers into the image of Christ (2 Cor. 3:18).

It is the Spirit who makes it possible for "the word of Christ [to] dwell in you richly" (Col. 3:16), a phrase that parallels Paul's instruction to "be filled with the Spirit" (Eph. 5:18), so that believers can manifest the fruit of a transformed life by expressing praise to God and love for others (cf. Eph. 5:19–6:9; Col. 3:17–4:1).

The Holy Spirit not only inspired the Scriptures (2 Pet. 1:21), he also energizes and illumines them, meaning that he enables their life-giving and life-sustaining work. As a result, sinners are rescued from the domain of darkness and transferred into the kingdom of the Savior (Col. 1:13). They become new creatures in Christ, having been born again through the Spirit's power (John 3:1–8). Their lives are changed forever: they are given new desires, motives, and affections. That internal change of heart inevitably manifests itself in an external change of behavior, such that they are no longer characterized by the lusts of the flesh but instead exhibit the fruit of the Spirit (cf. Rom. 8:9–13; Gal. 5:16–23). Only the Bible can effect that kind of change in people's lives, because only the Bible is empowered by the Spirit of God.

Conclusion

In a day when the Word of God is under assault, not just from those outside the church but also from those who profess to be Christians, it is the sacred duty of all who love the Lord to contend earnestly for his revealed truth. As we have briefly discussed in this introduction, we ought to do so because when sound doctrine is attacked, we are duty-bound to defend the faith. We take our stand boldly, knowing that we do so on the basis of God's very authority. Moreover, we advance with confidence, not only because the veracity of Scripture can be convincingly demonstrated, but also because the Word we proclaim is empowered by the Spirit of God. Though God's truth may be unpopular in our modern age, it will never return void, but will always accomplish the purposes for which God designed it.

To preach, teach, and defend the Scriptures is both our sacred privilege and our solemn responsibility. My prayer is that the pages that follow will instill both certainty and courage in your heart and mind—the certainty that comes from knowing God's Word is absolutely true, and the courage that is needed to stand for that conviction.

Part 1

INERRANCY IN
THE BIBLE

Building the Case

1

The Sufficiency of Scripture

PSALM 19

John MacArthur

Psalm 19 is the earliest biblical text that gives us a comprehensive statement on the superiority of Scripture. It categorically affirms the authority, inerrancy, and sufficiency of the written Word of God. It does this by comparing the truth of Scripture to the breathtaking grandeur of the universe, and it declares that the Bible is a better revelation of God than all the glory of the galaxies. Scripture, it proclaims, is perfect in every regard.

The psalm thereby sets Scripture above every other truth claim. It is a sweeping, definitive affirmation of the utter perfection and absolute trustworthiness of God's written Word. There is no more succinct summation of the power and precision of God's written Word anywhere in the Bible.

Psalm 19 is basically a condensed version of Psalm 119, the longest chapter in all of Scripture. Psalm 119 takes 176 verses to expound on the same truths Psalm 19 outlines in just eight verses (vv. 7–14).

Every Christian ought to affirm and fully embrace the same high view of Scripture the psalmist avows in Psalm 19. If we are going to live in obedience to God's Word—especially those who are called to teach the Scriptures—we need to do so with this confidence in mind.

After all, *faith* (not moralism, good works, vows, sacraments, or rituals, but *belief in Christ as he is revealed in Scripture*) is what makes a person a Christian. "Without faith it is impossible to please him, for whoever would draw near to God must believe that he exists and that he rewards those who seek him" (Heb. 11:6); "For by grace you have been saved through faith. And this is not your own doing; it is the gift of God, not a result of works" (Eph. 2:8–9a).

The only sure and safe ground of true faith is the Word of God (2 Pet. 1:19–21). It is "the word of truth, the gospel of [our] salvation" (Eph. 1:13). For a Christian to doubt the Word of God is the grossest kind of self-contradiction.

When I began in ministry nearly half a century ago, I fully expected I would need to deal with assaults against Scripture from unbelievers and worldlings. I was prepared for that. Unbelievers by definition reject the truth of Scripture and resist its authority. "The mind that is set on the flesh is hostile to God, for it does not submit to God's law; indeed, it cannot" (Rom. 8:7).

But from the beginning of my ministry until today, I have witnessed— and had to deal with—wave after wave of attacks against the Word of God coming *mostly from within the evangelical community.* Over the course of my ministry, virtually all of the most dangerous assaults on Scripture I've seen have come from seminary professors, megachurch pastors, charismatic charlatans on television, popular evangelical authors, "Christian psychologists," and bloggers on the evangelical fringe. The evangelical movement has no shortage of theological tinkerers and self-styled apologists who seem to think the way to win the world is to embrace whatever theories are currently in vogue regarding evolution, morality, epistemology, or whatever— and then reframe our view of Scripture to fit this worldly "wisdom." The Bible is treated like Silly Putty, pressed and reshaped to suit the shifting interests of popular culture.

Of course, God's Word will withstand every attack on its veracity and authority. As Thomas Watson said, "The devil and his agents have been blowing at scripture light, but could never prevail to blow it out—a clear sign that it was lighted from heaven."[1] Nevertheless, Satan and his minions are persistent, seeking to derail believers whose faith is fragile or to dissuade unbelievers from even considering the claims of Scripture.

To make their attacks more subtle and effective, the forces of evil disguise themselves as angels of light and servants of righteousness (2 Cor.

---

[1] Thomas Watson, *A Body of Practical Divinity* (T. Wardle, 1833), 23.

11:13–15). That's why the most dangerous attacks on Scripture come from within the community of professing believers. These evil forces are relentless, and we need to be relentless in opposing them.

Over the years, as I have confronted the various onslaughts of evangelical skepticism, I have returned to Psalm 19 again and again. It is a definitive answer to virtually every modern and postmodern attack on the Bible. It offers an antidote to the parade of faulty ministry philosophies and silly fads that so easily capture the fancy of today's evangelicals. It refutes the common misconception that science, psychology, and philosophy must be mastered and integrated with biblical truth in order to give the Bible more credibility. It holds the answer to what currently ails the visible church. It is a powerful testimony about the glory, power, relevance, clarity, efficacy, inerrancy, and sufficiency of Scripture.

In this chapter, I want to focus on a passage in the second half of the psalm—verses 7–9, which speak specifically about the Scriptures.

This is a psalm of David, and in the opening six verses, he speaks of *general revelation.* As a young boy tending his father's sheep, he had plenty of time to gaze at the night sky and ponder the greatness and glory of God as revealed in nature. That's what he describes in the opening lines of the psalm: "The heavens declare the glory of God, and the sky above proclaims his handiwork" (v. 1). Through creation, God reveals himself at all times, across all language barriers, to all people and nations: "Day to day pours out speech, and night to night reveals knowledge. There is no speech, nor are there words, whose voice is not heard. Their voice goes out through all the earth, and their words to the end of the world" (vv. 2–4). God declares himself in his creation day and night, unceasingly. The vastness of the universe, all the life it contains, and all the laws that keep it orderly rather than chaotic are a testimony to (and a manifestation of) the wisdom and glory of God.

As grand and glorious as creation is, however, we cannot discern all the spiritual truth we need to know from it. General revelation does not give a clear account of the gospel. Nature tells us nothing specific about Christ; his incarnation, death, and resurrection; the atonement he made for sin; the doctrine of justification by faith; or a host of other truths essential to salvation and eternal life.

Special revelation is the truth God has revealed in Scripture. That is the subject David takes up in the second half of the psalm, beginning in verse 7. Having extolled the vast glory of creation and the many marvelous ways it reveals truth about God, he turns to Scripture and says the written Word of God is more pure, more powerful, more permanent, more effectual, more telling, more reliable, and more glorious than all the countless wonders written across the universe:

> The law of the LORD is perfect,
>   reviving the soul;
> The testimony of the LORD is sure,
>   making wise the simple;
> The precepts of the LORD are right,
>   rejoicing the heart;
> The commandment of the LORD is pure,
>   enlightening the eyes;
> The fear of the LORD is clean,
>   enduring forever;
> The rules of the LORD are true,
>   and righteous altogether. (Ps. 19:7–9)

In those three brief verses, David makes six statements—two in verse 7, two in verse 8, and two in verse 9. He uses six titles for Scripture: *law, testimony, precepts, commandment, fear,* and *rules*. He lists six characteristics of Scripture: it is *perfect, sure, right, pure, clean,* and *true*. And he names six effects of Scripture: it *revives the soul, makes wise the simple, rejoices the heart, enlightens the eyes, endures forever,* and *produces comprehensive righteousness*.

Thus, the Holy Spirit—with an astounding and supernatural economy of words—sums up everything that needs to be said about the power, sufficiency, comprehensiveness, and trustworthiness of Scripture.

Notice, first of all, that all six statements have the phrase "of the LORD"—just in case someone might question the source of Scripture. This is the law of the Lord—*his* testimony. These are the precepts and commandments of God himself. The Bible is of divine origin. It is the inspired revelation of the Lord God.

By breaking down these three couplets and looking at each phrase, we can begin to gather a sense of the power and greatness of Scripture. Again, the opening verses of the psalm were all about the vast glory revealed in creation. Thus, the central point of this psalm is that *the grandeur and glory of Scripture is infinitely greater than the entire created universe.*

God's Word Is Perfect, Reviving the Soul

David makes his point powerfully yet simply in the first statement he makes about Scripture in verse 7: "The law of the LORD is perfect, reviving the soul." The Hebrew word translated as "law" is *torah*. To this day, Jews use the word *Torah* to refer to the Pentateuch (the five books penned by Moses). Those five books, of course, are the starting point of the Old Testament—but the Psalms and Prophets are likewise inspired Scripture, equally authoritative (cf. Luke 24:44). So when David speaks of "the law of the LORD" in this context," he has the whole canon in mind. "The law," as the term is used here, refers not merely to the Ten Commandments; not just to the 613 commandments that constitute the *mitzvot* of Moses's law; not even to the Torah considered as a unit. David is using the word as a figure of speech to signify all of Scripture.

Throughout Scripture, "the law" often refers to the entire canon. This kind of expression is called *synecdoche*, a figure of speech in which part of something is used to represent the whole. You find this same language in Joshua 1:8, for example. That verse famously speaks of "this Book of the Law," meaning not just the commandments, but all of Scripture as it existed in Joshua's time—Genesis and Job as well as Leviticus and Deuteronomy. Psalm 119 repeatedly uses the same figure of speech (cf. vv. 1, 18, 29, 34, 44, etc.).

When used this way, the language stresses the didactic nature of God's Word. "Blessed is the man whom you discipline, O LORD, and whom you teach out of your law" (Ps. 94:12); "Graciously teach me your law!" (Ps. 119:29). David is thinking of Scripture as a manual on righteous human behavior—*all* Scripture, not merely Moses's law. After all, "All Scripture is breathed out by God and profitable for teaching, for reproof, for correction, and for training in righteousness, that the man of God may be complete, equipped for every good work" (2 Tim. 3:16–17).

And all of it is "*perfect*." Many years ago, I researched that word as it appears in the Hebrew text. It's the Hebrew word *tâmîym*, which is variously translated in assorted English versions as "unblemished," "without defect," "whole," "blameless," "with integrity," "complete," "undefiled," or "perfect." I traced the Hebrew word through several lexicons to try to discern whether there might be some nuance or subtlety that would shade our understanding of it. I spent three or four hours looking up every use of that word in the biblical text. In the end, it was clear: the word means "perfect." It is an exact equivalent of the English word in all its shades of meaning.

David is using the expression in an unqualified, comprehensive way. Scripture is superlative in every sense. Not only is it flawless, but it is also sweeping and thorough. That's not to suggest that it contains everything that can possibly be known. Obviously, the Bible is not an encyclopedic source of information about every conceivable subject. But as God's instruction for man's life, it is perfect. It contains everything we need to know about God, his glory, faith, life, and the way of salvation. Scripture is not deficient or defective in any way. It is perfect in both its accuracy and its sufficiency.

In other words, it contains everything God has revealed for our spiritual instruction. It is the sole authority by which to judge anyone's creed (what they believe), character (what they are), or conduct (what they do).

More specifically, according to our text, Scripture is perfect in its ability to revive and transform the human soul. "For the word of God is living and active, sharper than any two-edged sword, piercing to the division of soul and of spirit, of joints and of marrow, and discerning the thoughts and intentions of the heart" (Heb. 4:12). For believers, the piercing and soul work described in that verse is a wholly beneficial procedure, comparable to spiritual heart surgery. It is that process described in Ezekiel 36:26, where the Lord says: "I will give you a new heart, and a new spirit I will put within you. And I will remove the heart of stone from your flesh and give you a heart of flesh." The instrument God uses in that process is the sword of the Spirit, which is the Word of God. "Of his own will he brought us forth *by the word of truth*" (James 1:18). Jesus said, "The words that I have spoken to you are spirit and life" (John 6:63b). David acknowledges the life-giving principle of God's Word by saying, "The law of the Lord is perfect, reviving the soul" (Ps. 19:7).

In the Hebrew text, the word for "soul" is *nephesh*. As used here, the idea stands in contrast to the body. It speaks of the inner person. If you trace the Hebrew word *nephesh* through the Old Testament, you will find that in the most popular English versions of the Bible, it is translated in a dozen or more ways. It can mean "creature," "person," "being," "life," "mind," "self," "appetite," "desire," or "soul"—but it is normally used to signify the true person, the you that never dies.

So what is the statement saying? Scripture, in the hands of the Holy Spirit, can revive and regenerate someone who is dead in sin. Nothing else has that power—no manmade story, no clever carnal insight, no deep human philosophy. The Word of God is the only power that can totally transform the whole inner person.

God's Word Is Trustworthy, Imparting Wisdom

The second half of Psalm 19:7 turns the diamond slightly and looks at a different facet of Scripture: "The testimony of the Lord is sure, making wise the simple." Here Scripture is spoken of as God's self-revelation. A *testimony* is the personal account of a reliable witness. That word is normally reserved for formal, solemn statements from firsthand sources—usually either in legal or religious contexts. An eyewitness gives sworn testimony in court. A believer relates how he or she came to faith, and we call that a testimony. The word conveys the idea of a formal declaration from a trustworthy source.

Scripture is God's testimony. This is God's own account of who he is and what he is like. It is God's self-disclosure. How wonderful that God has revealed himself in such a grand and voluminous way—sixty-six books (thirty-nine in the Old Testament, twenty-seven in the New), all revealing truth about our God so that we may know him and rest securely in the truth about him.

"The testimony of the LORD is *sure.*" That is its central characteristic. It is true. It is reliable. It is trustworthy.

The world is full of books you cannot trust. As a matter of fact, any book written by man apart from the inspiration of the Holy Spirit will contain errors and deficiencies of various kinds. But the Word of the Lord is absolutely reliable. Every fact, every claim, every doctrine, and every statement of Scripture comes to us in "words not taught by human wisdom but taught by the Spirit" (1 Cor. 2:13a).

And what is the impact of this? Scripture "mak[es] wise the simple." "Simple" is the translation of a Hebrew expression that speaks of naive ignorance. It can be used as a disparaging term, describing people who are callow, gullible, or just silly. It's the same Hebrew word used in Proverbs 7:7, "I have seen among the simple, I have perceived among the youths, a young man lacking sense," and 14:15a, "The simple believes everything." The term signifies someone without knowledge or understanding.

But the derivation of the word suggests the problem is not a learning disability or sheer stupidity. The Hebrew root means "open," suggesting the image of an open door. Many Hebrew words paint vivid images. As a rule, Hebrew is not abstract, esoteric, or theoretical like Greek. This particular expression is a classic example. It embodies the Hebrew idea of what it means to be simpleminded: a door left standing open.

People today like to be thought of as open-minded. To an Old Testament Jew, that would be the essence of half-wittedness. To say that you have an open mind would be to declare your ignorance. It would be very much like modern agnosticism. Agnostics pretend to have an enlightened worldview, and the typical agnostic likes to assume the air and attitudes of an intellectual who is privy to advanced understanding. But the word *agnostic* is a combination of two Greek words meaning "without knowledge." To call oneself an agnostic is to make a declaration of one's ignorance. The Latin equivalent would be *ignoramus*.

It's neither healthy nor praiseworthy to have a constantly open mind with regard to one's beliefs, values, and moral convictions. An open door permits everything to go in and out. This is the attitude that makes so many people today vacillating, indecisive, and double-minded—unstable in all their ways (James 1:8). They have no anchor for their thoughts, no rule by which to distinguish right from wrong, and therefore no real convictions. They simply lack the tools and mental acuity to discern or make careful distinctions. That way of thinking is nothing to be proud of.

If you were able to tell a devout Old Testament believer that you are open-minded, he might say, "Well, close the door." You need to know what to keep in and what to keep out. You have a door on your house, and you close it to keep some things in (children, heat, cooled air, or the family pet) and other things out (burglars, insects, and door-to-door salesmen). You open it only when you *want* to let something or someone in. The door is a point of discretion. It's the place where you distinguish between what should be let in and what should be kept out. In fact, your door may have a peephole that you can look through to help you in discerning who's going to get in and who's not.

Our minds should function in a similar fashion. There's no honor in letting things in and out indiscriminately. We need to close the door and carefully guard what goes in and out (Prov. 4:23).

The Word of God has the effect of making simple minds wise for that very purpose. It teaches us discernment. It trains our senses "to distinguish good from evil" (Heb. 5:14b).

The Hebrew word translated as "wise" in Psalm 19:7 is not speaking of theoretical knowledge, philosophical sophistication, intellectual prowess, smooth speech, cleverness, or any of the other things that define worldly wisdom. Biblical wisdom is about prudent living. The word *wise* describes someone who walks and acts sensibly and virtuously: "Whoever trusts in his own mind is a fool, but he who walks in wisdom will be delivered" (Prov. 28:26). The truly wise person recognizes what is good and right, then applies that simple truth to everyday life.

In other words, the wisdom in view here has nothing to do with intelligence quotients or academic degrees. It has everything to do with truth, honor, virtue, and the fruit of the Spirit. Indeed, "the fear of the Lord is the beginning of wisdom, and the knowledge of the Holy One is insight" (Prov. 9:10).

There's only one document in the entire world that can revive a spiritually dead soul and make him spiritually wise. No book penned by mere men could possibly do that, much less give us skill to live well in a world cursed by sin. There is no spiritual life, salvation, or sanctification apart from Scripture.

We all desperately need that transformation. It is not a change we can make for ourselves. All the glory on display in creation is not enough to accomplish it. *Only* Scripture has the life-giving, life-changing power needed to revive a spiritually dead soul and make the simple wise.

God's Word Is Right, Causing Joy

Psalm 19:8a gives a third statement about the perfect sufficiency of Scripture: "The precepts of the LORD are right, rejoicing the heart." The Hebrew noun translated as "precepts" ("statutes" in some versions) denotes principles for instruction. Close English synonyms would be *canons, tenets, axioms, principles,* and even *commands.* All those shades of meaning are inherent in the word. It includes the principles that govern our character and conduct, as well as the propositions that shape our convictions and our confession of faith. It covers every biblical precept, from the basic ordinances governing righteous behavior to the fundamental axioms of sound doctrine. All of these are truths to be believed.

That's because they are "right." David does not mean merely right as opposed to wrong (although that's obviously true). The Hebrew word means "straight" or "undeviating." It has the connotation of uprightness, alignment, and perfect order. The implication is that the precepts of Scripture keep a person going in the right direction, true to the target.

Notice that there is progress and motion in the language. The effect of God's Word is not static. It regenerates, restoring the soul to life. It enlightens, taking a person who lacks discretion and transforming him into one who is skilled in all manner of living. It then sanctifies—setting him on a right path and pointing him in a truer direction. "Your word is a lamp to my feet and a light to my path" (Ps. 119:105).

But Scripture is not only a lamp and a light; it is the living voice that tells us, "This is the way, walk in it" when we veer to the right or the left (Isa. 30:21). We desperately need that guidance. "There is a way that seems right to a man, but its end is the way to death" (Prov. 16:25). Scripture makes the true way straight and clear for us.

The result is joy: "The precepts of the LORD are right, rejoicing the heart" (Ps. 19:8a). If you are anxious, fearful, doubting, melancholy, or otherwise troubled in heart, learn and embrace God's precepts. The truth of God's Word not only will inform and sanctify you, but it also will bring joy and encouragement to your heart.

This is true *especially* in times of trouble. Worldly wisdom's typical answers to despondency and depression are all empty, useless, or worse. Every form of self-help, self-esteem, and self-indulgence promises joy, but in the end, such things bring only more despair. The truth of Scripture is a sure and time-tested anchor for troubled hearts. And the joy it brings is true and lasting.

The life-giving, life-changing power mentioned in verse 7 is the reason for the joy mentioned in verse 8. David, who wrote this psalm, knew that joy firsthand. So did the author of Psalm 119, who wrote, "This is my comfort in my affliction, that your promise gives me life" (v. 50); "When I think of your rules from of old, I take comfort, O LORD" (v. 52); "Your statutes have been my songs in the house of my sojournings" (v. 54). Clearly this is a major theme in Psalm 119, the longest of all the psalms: "I find my delight in your commandments, which I love" (v. 47).

Jeremiah is sometimes called "the weeping prophet" because so much of his message is full of sorrow and grieving. Most scholars believe he is also the prophet who wrote the biblical book of Lamentations. The people refused to listen to Jeremiah. Finally, they threw him in a pit to shut him up. But the prophet drew profound joy from the Word of God: "Your words became to me a joy and the delight of my heart, for I am called by your name, O LORD, God of hosts" (Jer. 15:16).

Christians are admonished to cultivate the joy that God's Word produces: "Let the word of Christ dwell in you richly, teaching and admonishing one another in all wisdom, singing psalms and hymns and spiritual songs, with thankfulness in your hearts to God" (Col. 3:16). The joyful heart depicted in verses like that is one of the key reasons Scripture is given to believers. As the apostle John greeted the recipients of his first inspired epistle, he said, "We are writing these things so that our joy may be complete" (1 John 1:4). On the night before his crucifixion, when Jesus's final instructions to his disciples were nearly complete, he told them, "These things I have spoken to you, that my joy may be in you, and that your joy may be full" (John 15:11).

God's Word Is Pure, Enlightening the Eyes

Psalm 19:8 continues: "The commandment of the LORD is pure, enlightening the eyes." This speaks of Scripture as a book of commands. The expression underscores the Bible's inherent authority. It is not a book of recommendations or suggestions. It is not a collection of thought-provoking proposals or helpful but optional advice. Its precepts are binding commandments from the sovereign King of the universe, whose authority extends to every minuscule detail of our lives.

Even the call to believe the gospel is a command: "This is his commandment, that we believe in the name of his Son Jesus Christ and love one another, just as he has commanded us" (1 John 3:23). The summons to repentance likewise comes as a command: "[God] commands all people everywhere to repent" (Acts 17:30b). The instructions given to us in Scripture are mandatory, because the Bible is the Word of God. Belief in, and obedience to, the Scriptures is not optional. So David simply refers to all of Scripture as "the commandment of the LORD."

And the commandment of the Lord is "pure." The Hebrew word means "clear." The Word of God is transparent or translucent; it is not murky or opaque. This is an affirmation of Scripture's *perspicuity*. In other words, the essential truth of the Bible is easily understood. God's Word expresses its meaning with sufficient clarity. There are indeed "some things . . . that are hard to understand, which the ignorant and unstable twist to their own destruction" (2 Pet. 3:16b). But the fundamental truths of Scripture are clear enough that "those who walk on the way; even if they are fools, they shall not go astray" (Isa. 35:8). You do not need to have advanced intelligence or superhuman skill to understand the basic truth of the Bible. As a rule, Scripture is simply not very hard to understand. Again, the author of Psalm 119 echoes and expands on this theme: "The unfolding of your words gives light; it imparts understanding to the simple" (v. 130).

Far from being inherently mysterious or cryptic, Scripture is divine *revelation*. It is an unveiling of truth that would be impossible to understand if God himself did not disclose it to us. It "is pure [clear, lucid], enlightening the eyes" (Ps. 19:8b). The Bible shines light into our darkness; gives knowledge that overthrows our ignorance; and brings understanding to clear away our confusion. This is how the apostle Paul said it in 2 Corinthians 3:16: "When one turns to the Lord, the veil is removed." Indeed, "'what no eye has seen, nor ear heard, nor the heart of man imagined, what God has prepared for those who love him'—these things God has revealed to us through the Spirit. For the Spirit searches everything, even the depths of God" (1 Cor. 2:9–10).

Of course, only genuine believers benefit from the enlightening effect of God's Word. Paul goes on to say, "The natural person does not accept the things of the Spirit of God, for they are folly to him, and he is not able to understand them because they are spiritually discerned" (v. 14). In the words of Jesus, God has deliberately "hidden these things from the wise and understanding and revealed them to little children" (Matt. 11:25b). Therefore, those who are wise in their own eyes gain little or nothing from the light of God's Word, while those with childlike faith receive it gladly and are thereby made *truly* wise. Jesus said, "Truly, I say to you, whoever does not receive the kingdom of God like a child shall not enter it" (Mark 10:15). The truth of Scripture is not an esoteric secret that a Gnostic guru must unlock for us. The faith required to accept it is simple, childlike trust.

Jesus taught and stressed those things against the backdrop of a very complex, confusing, allegorical, and mystical interpretation of the Old Testament that was perpetuated by many of the rabbis of his time. "And the common people heard him gladly" (Mark 12:37 NKJV).

God's commandments are clear. If they were not, they would be pointless. How could God hold us responsible to obey what we couldn't possibly understand? Therefore, to say the Bible isn't clear is to accuse God of deliberately confounding humanity. Scripture *is* clear—enlightening the eyes. Mark Twain was a hardened agnostic, and he is often quoted as saying: "It's not the things I don't understand in the Bible that bother me. It's the things I *do* understand."

That says it well. The problem for unbelievers is not that the Bible isn't clear enough. It's that God's Word is *absolutely* clear about the human problem—sin—and fallen people simply don't like what the Bible says. So in order to escape what is plain and easily apparent, they sometimes claim it's murky and indistinct. Believers know otherwise.

The Bible Is Clean, Enduring Forever

Psalm 19:9 adds a fifth couplet: "The fear of the LORD is clean, enduring forever." "The fear of the LORD" is a reference to the passion evoked in believers when their minds are awakened to the truth of Scripture. The subject hasn't changed. The poetic parallelism makes it clear that David is still talking about the Bible, and in this couplet he is referring to the sense of righteous trepidation a sinful soul feels before God when the Word of God does its work. This is not the craven fear of contempt and revulsion; it is the reverential awe that is the basis for true worship.

The Bible is a perfect handbook on worship. First, it moves us to worship by revealing the majesty and perfection of YHWH, the God of Abraham, Isaac, and Jacob (Ex. 3:6; Matt. 22:32)—the One who is the God and Father of our Lord Jesus Christ (Rom. 15:6; 2 Cor. 1:3; 11:31; Col. 1:3). He is the Creator, Sustainer, and Sovereign of the universe. He alone is holy, omniscient, omnipresent, omnipotent, immutable, and eternal.

Scripture not only tells us *who* is to be worshiped, but also *how* he is to be worshiped. He is a Spirit, and he is to be worshiped in spirit and in truth (John 4:23–24)—not through graven images, as if he were an idol or a manmade thing. Jesus said, "The Father is seeking . . . people to worship him" (v. 23).

As a manifesto and manual on worship, Scripture is "clean, enduring forever" (Ps. 19:9a). The Hebrew word translated as "clean" is used more than ninety times in the Old Testament to speak of ceremonial cleanness. It means there is no impurity, defilement, or imperfection of any kind in Scripture. Scripture is without any corruption at all; hence, it is without error.

Elsewhere, David makes this idea even more emphatic: "The words of the LORD are pure words, like silver refined in a furnace on the ground, purified seven times" (Ps. 12:6). Notice that the very words of Scripture are totally free from all imperfections. There is no dross, no blemish, no foreign element. It would be hard to devise a more emphatic statement of biblical inerrancy.

The proof of this absolute perfection is that the Word of God endures forever. It never changes. Any alteration to the text could only introduce imperfection. Scripture is eternally, unalterably perfect. Jesus said, "Heaven and earth will pass away, but my words will not pass away" (Matt. 24:35; Mark 13:31). He also said, "Truly, I say to you, until heaven and earth pass away, not an iota, not a dot, will pass from the Law until all is accomplished" (Matt. 5:18). Scripture is full of similar statements: "Forever, O LORD, your word is firmly fixed in the heavens" (Ps. 119:89); "The grass withers, the flower fades, but the word of our God will stand forever" (Isa. 40:8); "'The word of the Lord remains forever.' And this word is the good news that was preached to you" (1 Pet. 1:25).

The Bible Is True, Altogether Righteous

The closing phrase of Psalm 19:9 gives us the last of these six poetic statements about God's Word: "The rules of the LORD are true, and righteous altogether." "Rulings" might be a more precise translation than "rules." Both the King James Version and the New American Standard Bible translate the noun as "judgments." It is a Hebrew word that means "verdict."

It is courtroom terminology, and it can refer to a decision, an ordinance, a legal right, a statutory privilege, a judicial sentence, or a decree. The word envisions God as the Judge, the Lawgiver, and the One who grants all rights and privileges. All his judgments are true, and all his decrees are right.

And as the context makes clear, David still specifically has in mind the content of Scripture. All the Bible's statements are true, and its moral principles are "righteous altogether."

Scripture is the divine Magistrate's verdict on everything that pertains to life and godliness. When Scripture speaks, it is conclusive because it is God's own verdict. It is an immutable decree from the judgment seat of heaven. And "shall not the Judge of all the earth do what is just?" (Gen. 18:25b). God's judgments, by definition, are *true*.

This is a crucial statement, and it establishes the starting point and the foundation for a truly Christian worldview. In a world of lies and deception, Scripture alone is absolutely, unequivocally "true, and righteous altogether." There is no room in that expression for any view of Scripture that tries to allow for historical blunders, scientific errors, factual inaccuracies, or fallacies of any kind. David could not have made a more thorough or definitive statement about the inerrancy and sufficiency of Scripture. The same point is echoed in Psalm 119:160: "The sum of your word is truth, and every one of your righteous rules endures forever." Scripture is true in its entirety; and it is likewise true in the smallest particulars. To speak more precisely, it is *truth*. This is what Scripture consistently claims for itself. It is Jesus's own view of the Scriptures. He prayed, "Sanctify [my disciples] in the truth; your word is truth" (John 17:17).

Of course, most of the world rejects the Bible. It's not that the Bible is unbelievable (untold millions across the span of human history *have* believed Scripture, and their hearts and lives have been transformed by it). The reason obstinate unbelief is so widespread is that people simply don't want to believe Scripture, because it gives such a devastating analysis of the human condition and condemns those who love their sin. To unbelievers in Jesus's audience, he said:

> Why do you not understand what I say? It is because you cannot bear to hear my word. You are of your father the devil, and your will is to do your father's desires. He was a murderer from the beginning, and does not stand in the truth, because there is no truth in him. When he lies, he speaks out of his own character, for he is a liar and the father of lies. But because I tell the truth, you do not believe me. . . . Whoever is

of God hears the words of God. The reason why you do not hear them is that you are not of God. (John 8:43–47)

But don't miss the central point of Psalm 19. Scripture is not only true, inerrant, and authoritative; it is also *sufficient*. It gives us every truth that really matters. It shows us the way of salvation and then equips us for every good work (2 Tim. 3:15–17). It is "righteous altogether"—actually fostering righteousness in those who accept it.

Scripture is eternally true, always applicable, and perfectly sufficient to meet all our spiritual needs. Contrary to what many people today think, the Bible does not need to be supplemented with new revelations. It does not need to be reinterpreted to accommodate the latest scientific theories. It does not need to be corrected to harmonize with whatever psychotherapy is currently popular. It certainly does not need to be edited to make it conform with postmodern notions about morality and relativism. All those things will come and go, "but the word of the Lord remains forever" (1 Pet. 1:25)—as unchanged and unchanging as the God who gave it to us.

2

"Men Spoke from God"

2 PETER 1:16-21

Derek W. H. Thomas

What exactly is the Bible? On one level, it is a collection of approximately three-quarters of a million words in sixty-six books written in three distinct languages (Hebrew, Aramaic, and Greek) over a period of more than a thousand years by some forty disparate authors in a variety of forms, including history, prophecy, sermons, letters, formal covenant treaties, travel narratives, poetry, parables, proverbs, architectural blueprints, apocalypses, Gospels, laws (moral, civil, and ceremonial), inventories, and much more. To these various genres, distinctive rules of interpretation apply (history is to be read as history, parable as parable, apocalypse as apocalypse, and so on), ensuring that a "literal" interpretation is sensitive to the *literary* genre.

Every word of the Bible in its original Hebrew, Aramaic, or Greek is the product of divine "out-breathing" (*theopneustos*, "breathed out by God" [2 Tim. 3:16]). Strictly speaking, this attribution concerns the Old Testament, ensuring that every word of it is what God intended and therefore infallible and inerrant (totally true and entirely trustworthy).[1] Concerning

---

[1] Inerrancy is a corollary of inspiration. As Albert Mohler points out: "The inerrancy of the Bible is inextricably linked to a specific understanding of its inspiration. Inerrancy requires and defines verbal inspiration—the fact that God determines the very words of the Bible in the original text." R. Albert Mohler Jr.,

the New Testament, Peter adds a significant insight when he chastises "the ignorant and unstable" about twisting Paul's letters "to their own destruction, as they do *the other Scriptures*" (2 Pet. 3:16), thereby placing Paul's letters on a par with Holy Scripture. Thus, as Charles Hill comments, "a collection of at least some of Paul's letters was already known and regarded as Scripture and therefore enjoyed canonical endorsement."[2]

The Bible, then, is both "from men" and "from God"—something that Peter makes abundantly clear when he writes, "*Men* spoke from God as they were carried along by the Holy Spirit" (2 Pet. 1:21). The human authorship of Scripture (what theologians have termed its *organic* nature) ensures that we may legitimately say, "Moses wrote" or "John wrote," discerning stylistic features unique to individual authors (of which I will say more later in this chapter).

The Bible and Human Agency

Scripture is both human *and* divine: totally human and totally divine in its origin. Consider the following verses:

- "Then the LORD put out his hand and touched my mouth. And the LORD said to me, 'Behold, I have put my words in your mouth'" (Jer. 1:9).
- "[God,] through the mouth of our father David, your servant, said by the Holy Spirit, 'Why did the Gentiles rage, and the peoples plot in vain?'" (Acts 4:25).
- "Therefore, as the Holy Spirit says, 'Today, if you hear his voice . . .'" (Heb. 3:7, citing Ps. 95:7–11).
- "And the Holy Spirit also bears witness to us" (Heb. 10:15).
- "For the Scripture says to Pharaoh, 'For this very purpose I have raised you up, that I might show my power in you, and that my name might be proclaimed in all the earth'" (Rom. 9:17; note that it is God who spoke these words to Pharaoh [Ex. 9:16]; thus, Scripture says = God says).

Peter says "men spoke from God," so whatever the precise nature of the divine agency at work in and through these men, the Scriptures came into being through human agency. The human authors of the biblical books

---

"When the Bible Speaks, God Speaks: The Classic Doctrine of Biblical Inerrancy," in *Five Views on Biblical Inerrancy*, ed. J. Merrick and Stephen M. Garrett (Grand Rapids, MI: Zondervan, 2013), 37.

[2] Charles Hill, "The Canon of the New Testament," in *Understanding Scripture: An Overview of the Bible's Origin, Reliability, and Meaning*, ed. Wayne Grudem, C. John Collins, and Thomas R. Schreiner (Wheaton, IL: Crossway, 2012), 84.

included men of diverse educational and social backgrounds—think of Moses and his Egyptian upbringing, or Isaiah and Amos, who had urban and rural backgrounds respectfully—and diverse temperaments: sanguine, choleric, melancholic, and phlegmatic (one imagines Solomon, Paul, John, and Jeremiah in one or other of these categories). We need only think of the diversity of the four Gospel writers, who are depicted on the *Book of Kells*[3] by a winged man or angel (Matthew), a lion (Mark), an ox (Luke), and an eagle (John) to make the diversity of human authorship clear.

Human authorship gives rise to stylistic distinctions. Bible readers have noted, for example, that Isaiah has a tendency to employ the ascription "the Holy One of Israel" when speaking of God. Alec Motyer comments: "He uses, for example, the adjective 'holy' (*qādōš*) of the Lord more often than all the rest of the Old Testament taken together, and focuses it in a title which he could well have coined, characteristic of the Isaianic literature: The Holy One of Israel. The title is used throughout Isaiah twenty-five times as compared with seven in the rest of the Old Testament."[4]

Other examples include Jeremiah's tendency to introspection, giving way to subjective analyses of himself—one writer calls him "the most human prophet";[5] John's characteristic use of simple words in the prologue to his Gospel to express the profoundest of truths; and Paul's ability to employ lengthy sentence constructions (pleonasms) that "are extended by relative and causal clauses and participial constructions."[6]

Human authorship is also seen in the use of "ordinary" sources for information. Thus, the Chronicler refers to accessing material from "the Chronicles of Samuel the seer" (1 Chron. 29:29).[7] And in similar manner, Luke (almost pedantically) informs us of his research methodology:

> Inasmuch as many have undertaken to compile a narrative of the things that have been accomplished among us, just as those who from the beginning were eyewitnesses and ministers of the word have delivered them to us, it seemed good to me also, having followed all things closely for some time past, to write an orderly account for you, most excellent Theophilus, that you may have certainty concerning the things you have been taught. (1:1–4)

---

[3] The *Book of Kells* (or *Book of Columba*), an illuminated manuscript in Latin, containing the four Gospels of the New Testament, was created ca. 800 in a monastery in Britain or Ireland.

[4] Alec Motyer, *Isaiah*, Tyndale Old Testament Commentaries (Leicester, UK: Inter-Varsity, 1999), 26.

[5] John Skinner, *Prophecy and Religion* (London: Cambridge University Press, 1963), 350.

[6] Peter T. O'Brien, *The Letter to the Ephesians*, The Pillar New Testament Commentary (Grand Rapids, MI: Eerdmans; Leicester, UK: Apollos, 1999), 6.

[7] This may simply be a reference to the canonical books of Samuel and Kings.

The fact that this sounds like the way Thucydides introduced his *History of the Peloponnesian War* is not without significance:

> But as to the facts of the occurrences of the war, I have thought it my duty to give them, not as ascertained by any chance informant, nor as seemed to me probable, but only after investigating with the greatest possible accuracy each detail, in the case of both the events in which I myself participated and of those regarding which I got my information from others. And the endeavor to discover these facts was a laborious task.[8]

Like Thucydides, Luke did his homework.

Similarly, observations have been made of the biblical authors' use of similar stylistic features that reflect "secular" conventions. Much has been written, for example, on the influence of Ancient Near Eastern literature on the Bible,[9] especially the ANE canonical literature and treaty forms in the Old Testament.[10] On the other end of the historical scale, we should recall that the New Testament writers were Jewish, reared in Jewish cultures, all of which (more than likely) influenced how they thought, reasoned, and responded to various circumstances. And these influences were not as homogenous as was once thought. The rise of the so-called "new perspective on Paul" was, in large part, driven by what was claimed to be a fundamental misunderstanding of Second Temple Judaism—a view that essentially equated it with medieval Catholicism, thus aligning Martin Luther's sixteenth-century rhetoric with that of Paul. This is not the place to address this issue, but these claims have only intensified the study of first-century Judaism and the various contexts in which the New Testament apostles ministered.[11] Paul's analysis of his former self in Philippians 3:4–7, where he pinpoints his relationship to the law as "blameless" (v. 6), for example, has an enormous bearing on how we understand him. His

---

[8] Thucydides, *History of the Peloponnesian War*, trans. Rex Warner (Baltimore: Penguin, 1954), 24. Cited in Philip Graham Ryken, *Luke*, Reformed Expositional Commentary, 2 vols. (Phillipsburg, NJ: P&R, 2009), 1:8.

[9] For a recent conservative introduction, see John D. Currid, *Against the Gods: The Polemical Theology of the Old Testament* (Wheaton: IL: Crossway, 2013).

[10] See Meredith Kline, *The Structure of Biblical Authority* (Grand Rapids, MI: Eerdmans, 1971); George E. Mendenhall, *Law and Covenant in Israel and the Ancient Near East* (Pittsburgh: Biblical Colloquium, 1955). For a general introduction to this material, see Bill T. Arnold and Bryan E. Beyer, *Encountering the Old Testament: A Christian Survey* (Grand Rapids, MI: Baker, 1999), 148–50.

[11] For a comprehensive treatment, see *Justification and Variegated Nomism: The Complexities of Second Temple Judaism*, ed. D. A. Carson, Peter T. O'Brien, Mark A. Seifried (Grand Rapids, MI: Baker, 2001); Guy Prentiss Waters, *Justification and the New Perspective on Paul: A Review and Response* (Phillipsburg, NJ: P&R, 2004); Cornelis Venema, *The Gospel of Free Acceptance in Christ* (Edinburgh: Banner of Truth, 2006). For a general introduction, see Guy Waters, *Justification: Being Made Right with God* (Fearn, Ross-shire, UK: Christian Focus, 2010), 67–95.

antagonism toward the Judaizers has to be understood, from one point of view, as coming from the fact he *was* one himself. He understands them because he used to be one of them. My point here is simply to underscore the fact that human background and experience play a large part in shaping the contours of Paul's theology.

What have we said so far? We have seen that we can and do discern the input of individual authors (biblical writers) within the biblical canon—their personalities, backgrounds, and research methodologies, for example. And from this observation, another may be made: that individual authors contribute particular theological features, and grow and advance their own analyses and arguments. Isaiah, as we have seen, advances our understanding of holiness and thereby advances our understanding of the doctrine of God. Similarly, Hosea elaborates on the nature of covenant love. Ezekiel, from the vantage point of exile and the imminent destruction of Jerusalem and the temple, expands on the nature of God's glory. And in the New Testament, Paul—to limit ourselves to just one example—expands on the nature of justification and union with Christ. Indeed, the latter concept, as has often been pointed out, was surely derived from his own encounter with Jesus, when he heard, in effect, the charge that to the extent he had persecuted Stephen, he had in fact persecuted Jesus (Acts 9:4; 22:7; 26:14).

The point here is that revelation—the revelation of God to man—is not *flat* but *progressive* and *developmental*. God employed the authors of Scripture, with their unique personalities and backgrounds, to advance our understanding of his purpose and grace in the gospel. Furthermore, this advancement can be seen in the experience and understanding of the individual authors. Few would argue that there is a measurable difference between Paul's language in Galatians and 2 Timothy. After all, some twenty years separate them.

Some have been reticent to advance a robust doctrine of the human (organic) component of Scripture's origin ("men wrote," 2 Pet. 1:21) for fear that in doing so, Scripture might appear less "inspired." But this is a mistake. The fact is that Scripture is dual-authored. God wrote and men wrote. God wrote *through* human instruments. Obviously, this requires some explanation.

Dictation?

How did God write Scripture *through* men? It would be an error to assume that the *mode* of inspiration was always dictation—the idea that Bible writers were employed simply as old-fashioned secretaries taking down God's revelation word for word.

There were *occasions* when Bible writers took dictation! For example, the seven letters to churches in Asia Minor in Revelation 2–3 are all prefaced by a command from the Lord Jesus to the apostle John: "To the angel of the church in . . . *write*" (Rev. 2:1, 8, 12, 18; 3:1, 7, 14). Clearly, John took down exactly—word for word—what Jesus said to him. Similarly, the Ten Commandments are introduced with this formula: "And God spoke all these words, saying . . ." (Ex. 20:1; cf. Deut. 5:5: "He [the LORD] said . . .").

But this method is rare. For instance, as we have seen, Luke tells us his method was different: recording interviews with eyewitnesses, checking his facts, and engaging in meticulous historiographical research (Luke 1:1–4).

Occasionally, some allusions to the Old Testament Scriptures are made with surprising informality—"It has been testified somewhere . . ."—as though the author is relying on his "fallible" memory (Heb. 2:6). But we should not draw from such allusions the conclusion that these quotations are somehow *less* inspired. As J. I. Packer writes:

> The twin suppositions which liberal critics make—that, on the one hand, divine control of the writers would exclude the free exercise of their natural powers, while, on the other hand, divine accommodation to the free exercise of their natural powers would exclude complete control of what they wrote—are really two forms of the same mistake. They are two ways of denying that the Bible can be both a fully human and fully divine composition. And this denial rests (as all errors in theology ultimately do) on a false doctrine of God; here particularly, of His providence. For it assumes that God and man stand in such a relation to each other that they cannot both be free agents in the same action.[12]

In addition, there appear to have been occasions when Bible writers wrote *beyond their own comprehension*. Peter cites an example: "Concerning this salvation, the prophets who prophesied about the grace that was to be yours searched and inquired carefully, inquiring what person or time the Spirit of Christ in them was indicating when he predicted the sufferings of Christ and the subsequent glories" (1 Pet. 1:10–11). Clearly, the prophets wrote about things they didn't fully understand.

The relationship between the human and divine authors—"God's words

---

[12] J. I. Packer, *"Fundamentalism" and the Word of God* (Grand Rapids, MI: Eerdmans, 1972), 80.

in men's mouths"—is not easy to grasp. We should not, for example, attempt to parcel out "inspired bits" and "uninspired bits"—a trend all too common among evangelicals, past and present. Peter Enns, for example, in his discussions on the issue of whether or not there was a historical Adam, writes:

> Many Christian readers will conclude, correctly, that a doctrine of inspiration does not require "guarding" the biblical authors from saying things that reflect a faulty ancient cosmology. If we begin with assumptions about what inspiration "must mean," we are creating a false dilemma and will wind up needing to make tortuous arguments to line up Paul and other biblical writers with modes of thinking that would never have occurred to them. But when we allow the Bible to lead us in our thinking on inspiration, we are compelled to leave room for the ancient writers to reflect and even incorporate their ancient, mistaken cosmologies into their scriptural reflections.[13]

In shorthand, this statement suggests that Paul believed in a historical Adam *and was mistaken*. Inspiration, in this understanding of it, accommodates an erroneous view (in Genesis) of the origin of man, upon which Paul builds an entire theology (in Romans 5). On this view, certain parts of Scripture are less inspired than others, and this, according to Enns, is an example of the *incarnational* nature of revelation. But it is Enns who is mistaken, not the Bible. Moreover, the analogy with the incarnation, of course, is entirely misleading, since the human nature of Christ is sinless.[14]

Total, Absolute Sovereignty in Human Freedom

Peter writes: "No prophecy of Scripture comes from someone's own interpretation. For no prophecy was ever produced by the will of man, but men spoke from God as they were carried along by the Holy Spirit" (2 Pet. 1:20–21). Peter's choice of words here is fascinating (yes, Peter's choice as well as the Holy Spirit's choice: the Holy Spirit was superintending the human freedom of Peter in a compatibilist understanding of this relationship).

Several points need to be made:

First, what is the precise meaning of "prophecy" here? Is it referring simply to specific prophecies about the coming of Jesus (Peter has been alluding

---

[13] Peter Enns, *The Evolution of Adam: What the Bible Does and Doesn't Say about Human Origins* (Grand Rapids, MI: Brazos, 2012), 94–95.
[14] For more on this point, see chapter 17 in this volume, "The Holy Spirit and the Holy Scriptures: Inerrancy and Pneumatology" by Sinclair B. Ferguson.

to the coming and transfiguration of Jesus), or is it a more general reference to the Old Testament in its entirety? Even if we were to limit the term to, say, the writings of the prophets (rather than the entire body of Scripture), the point being made is substantially the same: the prophetic writings are "Scripture," and what is true about them is true *because* they are Scripture.

Second, the idea of inspiration is not applied to the writers. They were not breathed out by God or breathed into by God. Peter says that they were "carried along" by the Holy Spirit. Without lessening the human involvement—their "conscious" participation—the text is making the point that the prophets wrote what the Holy Spirit intended them to write; no more and no less.

Third, the verb in verse 21, "produced"[15]—"*no* prophecy was ever produced by the will of man"—is also employed in verse 17, where it refers to the voice of the heavenly Father that Jesus heard: "the voice was *borne* to him by the Majestic Glory." The English text hides the fact that Peter is completing a dual point in verses 20–21: "Our author is clearly negating one source of prophecy and affirming another, which is heavenly, just as the voice which came to Jesus was heavenly."[16]

Fourth, the positive verb, "carried along" (φέρω, *pherō*), is a very strong one. It is the verb employed by Luke to describe what happened to Paul and his captors when caught in the storm at sea. They lowered the mainsail to allow the ship to be "driven along" by the wind (Acts 27:15). The emphasis lies on total sovereignty. How is this secured? These men were carried along by the Holy Spirit. They were not simply prompted or led by him, but carried by him. When someone is carried, he is set down at the destination of the carrier. There is superintendence and restraint. In a magisterial analysis of this verse (along with its companion verse in 2 Tim. 3:16–17), Benjamin B. Warfield comments:

> The term used here is a very specific one. It is not to be confounded with guiding, or directing, or controlling, or even leading in the full sense of that word. It goes beyond all such terms, in assigning the effect produced specifically to the active agent. What is "borne" is taken up by the "bearer," and conveyed by the "bearer's" power, not its own,

---

[15] I am following the ESV text at this point, which renders the Greek word ἠνέχθη as "produced," suggesting that the issue at hand is a question about the *source* of the prophecy. Other translations suggest the issue is one of false *interpretation* of prophecy; cf. NRSV, "No prophecy of scripture is a matter of one's own interpretation." For a defense of the former view, see Gene L. Green, *Jude and 2 Peter*, Baker Exegetical Commentary on the New Testament (Grand Rapids, MI: Baker, 2008), 231.

[16] Peter H. Davids, *The Letters of 2 Peter and Jude*, The Pillar New Testament Commentary (Grand Rapids, MI: Eerdmans, 2006), 213.

to the "bearer's" goal, not its own. The men who spoke from God are here declared, therefore, to have been taken up by the Holy Spirit and brought by His power to the goal of His choosing. The things which they spoke under this operation of the Spirit were therefore His things, not theirs. And that is the reason which is assigned why "the prophetic word" is so sure. Though spoken through the instrumentality of men, it is, by virtue of the fact that these men spoke "as borne by the Holy Spirit," an immediately Divine word.[17]

And what is the result of this action by the Holy Spirit? No Scripture is the product of human initiative alone:

- Scripture does not come "from someone's own interpretation" (v. 20).
- Scripture is not "produced by the will of man" (v. 21).

We must take care not to contradict what we have already said about the human involvement and initiative in the production of Scripture. Men wrote. And their contributions are discernible. But the finished product is what God intends. The nuance is breathtaking: sovereignty and responsibility in compatibilist harmony.

Certainty

What, then, is Peter saying?

First, he is making a declaration regarding *the adequacy of human language to convey divine truth*. In the face of late modernity/postmodernity's skepticism about human language as a vehicle for objective truth, Scripture declares "God has spoken" by means of words—verbs, nouns, adjectives, and grammatical constructions that convey truth. To doubt this (as many do) is to doubt the incarnation of Jesus Christ, for when Jesus spoke, God spoke. The Bible, in no less a fashion, does the same thing. In the face of skepticism and doubt, holding the Bible in our hands and reading it is to hear the very voice of God—not *through* the words in some form of mystical encounter, but in the very words themselves.[18]

Second, Peter is making a statement that *Scripture can be trusted on all matters to which it speaks, however incidental they may seem*. Thus,

---

[17] Benjamin B. Warfield, "The Biblical Idea of Inspiration," in *The Inspiration and Authority of the Bible* (Philadelphia: Presbyterian and Reformed, 1970), 137.
[18] J. I. Packer's essay, "The Adequacy of Human Language," is vital reading on this topic. See his *Collected Shorter Writings*, 4 vols. (Carlisle, Cumbria, UK: Paternoster, 1999), 3:23–50.

even when Scripture alludes to relatively minor historical incidents, we can regard it as trustworthy. D. A. Carson writes:

> The Queen of the South visited Solomon (Matt. 12:42; Luke 11:31–32); David ate the consecrated bread (Mark 2:25–26); Moses lifted up the serpent in the desert (John 3:14); Abraham gave a tenth of the spoils to Melchizedek (Heb. 7:2); eight people were saved in the ark (1 Pet. 3:20); Balaam's ass spoke (2 Pet. 2:16)—to provide but a few examples. One of the most intriguing examples is found on the lips of Jesus (Matt. 22:41–46; Mark 12:35–37). Jesus cites Psalm 110, which, according to the superscription, is a psalm of David. The important thing to observe is that the validity of Jesus' argument here depends utterly on the assumption that the superscription is accurate. If the psalm were not written by David, then David did not speak of the Messiah as his Lord, while still referring to the "my Lord" to whom "the LORD" spoke. If, say, a courtier had composed the psalm, then "my Lord" could easily be understood to refer to David himself, or to one of the monarchs who succeeded him (as many modern critics suppose).[19]

The point here is this: the Bible can be trusted on matters of relative unimportance, and therefore in its *details* as well as its overall teaching. But the trend today is to suggest that we should not be too concerned about the details. A. T. B. McGowan writes:

> My argument is that Scripture, having been divinely spirated, is as God intended it to be. Having freely chosen to use human beings, God knew what he was doing. He did not give us an inerrant autographical text, because he did not intend to. He gave us a text that reflects the humanity of its authors but that, at the same time, clearly evidences its origin in the divine speaking. Through the instrumentality of the Holy Spirit, God is perfectly able to use these Scriptures to accomplish his purposes.[20]

The problem with such a view is that it is impossible to gauge where inspiration ends and human fallibility begins.

Peter's point in 2 Peter 1:19–21 is that *all* Scripture is "from God." Parceling out parts that are inspired and parts that are not is entirely illegitimate. Some insist that the *organic* nature of Scripture must involve

---

[19] D. A. Carson, *Collected Writings on Scripture* (Wheaton, IL: Crossway, 2010), 25–26.
[20] A. T. B. McGowan, *The Divine Authenticity of Scripture: Retrieving an Evangelical Heritage* (Downers Grove, IL: IVP Academic, 2007), 124.

error since "to err is human." But the reality is that, according to this line of argument, *all* Scripture is human and therefore subject to suspicion.

Third, the Scriptures are *more certain and therefore more trustworthy than our experience*. The English Standard Version renders 2 Peter 1:19 this way: "We have the prophetic word *more fully confirmed*." This suggests that the point is one of *comparison*. This was hardly controversial in Peter's day, when the Jewish view was that prophecy was always more reliable than any vision or voice from heaven. Peter, then, seems to be saying, "The prophetic Scriptures are surer than any experience I have to share, so I appeal to those Scriptures to confirm what I've told you."[21]

Ultimately, the point that Peter is making is that compared to even the incarnation ("the coming") and the transfiguration of Jesus (2 Pet. 1:16), plus the voice of the heavenly Father that accompanied the latter, the Scriptures—"the prophetic word"—are "more fully confirmed" (v. 19). The physical and tangible realities of the incarnation and transfiguration add a note of confirmation to the prophetic Scriptures. It is interesting, then, that Peter draws attention not to the incarnation and transfiguration, *but to the Scriptures themselves*. The ultimate source of certainty lies in the Scriptures because they are "from God" (2 Pet. 1:21).

And because the Scriptures are from God, we need to "pay attention" (2 Pet. 1:19) to what they say, not least because what Scripture says, God says. They are "a lamp shining in a dark place." The word for "dark place" occurs only here in the New Testament, but Peter may be thinking of Psalm 119:105: "Your word is a lamp to my feet and a light to my path." The "prophetic word" is the guidance we have "until the day dawns and the morning star rises in [our] hearts" (2 Pet. 1:19). The background to this imagery lies in Balaam's final oracle in Numbers 24:17:

> I see him, but not now;
>   I behold him, but not near:
> a star shall come out of Jacob,
>   and a scepter shall rise out of Israel.

Following the night ("dark place") comes the light of a new day—in this case, the second coming and the dawn of the new heavens and earth: "But according to his promise we are waiting for new heavens and a new earth in which righteousness dwells" (2 Pet. 3:13). When the morning star ap-

---

[21] J. I. Packer, *Truth and Power: The Place of Scripture in the Christian Life* (Wheaton, IL: Harold Shaw, 1996), 223.

pears, a new age will dawn—as Isaiah prophesied (Isa. 65:17; 66:22)—and there will be no further need of Scripture. The rising of Christ in our hearts will give us full knowledge: "As for prophecies, they will pass away; as for tongues, they will cease; as for knowledge, it will pass away. For we know in part and we prophesy in part, but when the perfect comes, the partial will pass away" (1 Cor. 13:8–10).[22]

The point, then, is that we do well to pay attention to Scripture as a lamp that shines in a dark place, anticipating the dawn and rising of the morning star in our hearts. The Scriptures (the Old Testament Scriptures in this case!) anticipated the coming of Christ in his fullness and glory—both his first and second comings. And as we traverse this interim between the "now" and the "not yet," we do well to counter unbelief and uncertainty by ensuring that the Scriptures occupy a central and foundational place in our minds and hearts. "Grow in the grace and knowledge of our Lord and Savior Jesus Christ," Peter says (2 Pet. 3:18). How are we to grow? What has been given to us to enable us to advance in our walk with Jesus Christ? *Scripture!* That is what we have and that is all we need. Scripture given. Scripture interpreted by the help of the Holy Spirit. Scripture hidden in our hearts and treasured. Scripture obeyed in all its warnings and exhortations. For when we read Scripture, it is the voice of God that we hear speaking in every word of it.

Pay attention to the written Word of God!

---

[22] The "perfect" in these verses may refer to the closing of the canon of the New Testament rather than the return of Christ. See Sinclair B. Ferguson, *The Holy Spirit* (Leicester, UK: Inter-Varsity, 1996), 226–28. For the view that it refers to the *parousia*, see Richard B. Gaffin, *Perspectives on Pentecost* (1979; repr., Phillipsburg, NJ: Presbyterian and Reformed, 1993).

3

How to Know God:
Meditate on His Word

PSALM 119

Mark Dever

I remember bumping into Stephen Hawking when I lived in England. Hawking is a best-selling author and celebrated theoretical physicist. At that time, he was the Lucasian Professor of Mathematics at Cambridge University, a position he held for thirty years. He and I met repeatedly during lunch in my years at Cambridge, maybe five or ten times. When I say "met," I mean we encountered each other as we were sitting down at the long tables in the Grad Pad, a postgraduate hall. I don't think I ever even introduced myself, though we must have exchanged "Excuse me's" multiple times. It was odd to have a close, common experience with such a celebrated person. It is strange to bump into a giant.

That may be something of what you experience as you read and explore Psalm 119. The Bible's longest chapter can hardly be charted and explored, or its depths fully plumbed, in this short chapter. But we can do a little more than just bump into the giant. We can ask some questions of the psalm:

What is God's law? What is God's law like? What does God's law do? And what should we do in response to God's law?

We don't know who wrote Psalm 119. It could have been David. It could have been someone after the exile, when the Torah, the Pentateuch, had become freshly valued by a people who no longer had the temple. Some have suggested that it could have been a faithful Hebrew, a man who kept a personal journal about the Word of God from the days of his youth to old age.

What we do know is that the psalm is composed of 1,064 words in Hebrew, arranged in 176 verses, which are compiled into twenty-two stanzas, one stanza for every letter of the Hebrew alphabet. There are eight verses in each stanza, and each of those verses begins with that stanza's signature letter. Each letter has its opportunity to lead us in praising God for his law and testimonies. The psalm uses all the letters to show that this praise is full and complete, but it also displays that the entire alphabet can be exhausted and gone through before we come to the end of the glories of God's testimonies.

We live in a culture of informality and spontaneity. We value that which is immediate and casual. This means we are just the kind of people—marked by love of ease and convenience—who can miss the beauty in art. After all, artfulness—deliberateness—shows thoughtfulness. In Psalm 119, we see a beauty of expression reflecting something of the beauty upon which the psalmist is reflecting. The psalm's conformity to a freely chosen form produces beauty, just as our conformity to God's precepts brings a beauty, a rightness, an appropriateness, a blessedness, and a happiness to our lives.

I pray that even as you read Psalm 119, you'll experience more than just bumping into a giant.[1]

> How blessed are those whose way is blameless,
>   Who walk in the law of the LORD.
> How blessed are those who observe His testimonies,
>   Who seek Him with all their heart.
> They also do no unrighteousness;
>   They walk in His ways.
> You have ordained Your precepts,
>   That we should keep them diligently.
> Oh that my ways may be established

---

[1] Scripture quotations in this chapter are from *The New American Standard Bible*®. Copyright © The Lockman Foundation 1960, 1962, 1963, 1968, 1971, 1972, 1973, 1975, 1977, 1995. Used by permission.

To keep Your statutes!
Then I shall not be ashamed
    When I look upon all Your commandments.
I shall give thanks to You with uprightness of heart,
    When I learn Your righteous judgments.
I shall keep Your statutes;
    Do not forsake me utterly!

How can a young man keep his way pure?
    By keeping it according to Your word.
With all my heart I have sought You;
    Do not let me wander from Your commandments.
Your word I have treasured in my heart,
    That I may not sin against You.
Blessed are You, O LORD;
    Teach me Your statutes.
With my lips I have told of
    All the ordinances of Your mouth.
I have rejoiced in the way of Your testimonies,
    As much as in all riches.
I will meditate on Your precepts
    And regard Your ways.
I shall delight in Your statutes;
    I shall not forget Your word.

Deal bountifully with Your servant,
    That I may live and keep Your word.
Open my eyes, that I may behold
    Wonderful things from Your law.
I am a stranger in the earth;
    Do not hide Your commandments from me.
My soul is crushed with longing
    After Your ordinances at all times.
You rebuke the arrogant, the cursed,
    Who wander from Your commandments.
Take away reproach and contempt from me,
    For I observe Your testimonies.
Even though princes sit and talk against me,
    Your servant meditates on Your statutes.
Your testimonies also are my delight;
    They are my counselors.

My soul cleaves to the dust;
>Revive me according to Your word.
I have told of my ways, and You have answered me;
>Teach me Your statutes.
Make me understand the way of Your precepts,
>So I will meditate on Your wonders.
My soul weeps because of grief;
>Strengthen me according to Your word.
Remove the false way from me,
>And graciously grant me Your law.
I have chosen the faithful way;
>I have placed Your ordinances before me.
I cling to Your testimonies;
>O LORD, do not put me to shame!
I shall run the way of Your commandments,
>For You will enlarge my heart.

Teach me, O LORD, the way of Your statutes,
>And I shall observe it to the end.
Give me understanding, that I may observe Your law
>And keep it with all my heart.
Make me walk in the path of Your commandments,
>For I delight in it.
Incline my heart to Your testimonies
>And not to dishonest gain.
Turn away my eyes from looking at vanity,
>And revive me in Your ways.
Establish Your word to Your servant,
>As that which produces reverence for You.
Turn away my reproach which I dread,
>For Your ordinances are good.
Behold, I long for Your precepts;
>Revive me through Your righteousness.

May Your lovingkindnesses also come to me, O LORD,
>Your salvation according to Your word;
So I will have an answer for him who reproaches me,
>For I trust in Your word.
And do not take the word of truth utterly out of my mouth,
>For I wait for Your ordinances.
So I will keep Your law continually,

Forever and ever.
And I will walk at liberty,
    For I seek Your precepts.
I will also speak of Your testimonies before kings
    And shall not be ashamed.
I shall delight in Your commandments,
    Which I love.
And I shall lift up my hands to Your commandments, which I love;
    And I will meditate on Your statutes.

Remember the word to Your servant,
    In which You have made me hope.
This is my comfort in my affliction,
    That Your word has revived me.
The arrogant utterly deride me,
    Yet I do not turn aside from Your law.
I have remembered Your ordinances from of old, O LORD,
    And comfort myself.
Burning indignation has seized me because of the wicked,
    Who forsake Your law.
Your statutes are my songs
    In the house of my pilgrimage.
O LORD, I remember Your name in the night,
    And keep Your law.
This has become mine,
    That I observe Your precepts.

The LORD is my portion;
    I have promised to keep Your words.
I sought Your favor with all my heart;
    Be gracious to me according to Your word.
I considered my ways
    And turned my feet to Your testimonies.
I hastened and did not delay
    To keep Your commandments.
The cords of the wicked have encircled me,
    But I have not forgotten Your law.
At midnight I shall rise to give thanks to You
    Because of Your righteous ordinances.
I am a companion of all those who fear You,
    And of those who keep Your precepts.

The earth is full of Your lovingkindness, O LORD;
  Teach me Your statutes.

You have dealt well with Your servant,
  O LORD, according to Your word.
Teach me good discernment and knowledge,
  For I believe in Your commandments.
Before I was afflicted I went astray,
  But now I keep Your word.
You are good and do good;
  Teach me Your statutes.
The arrogant have forged a lie against me;
  With all my heart I will observe Your precepts.
Their heart is covered with fat,
  But I delight in Your law.
It is good for me that I was afflicted,
  That I may learn Your statutes.
The law of Your mouth is better to me
  Than thousands of gold and silver pieces.

Your hands made me and fashioned me;
  Give me understanding, that I may learn Your commandments.
May those who fear You see me and be glad,
  Because I wait for Your word.
I know, O LORD, that Your judgments are righteous,
  And that in faithfulness You have afflicted me.
O may Your lovingkindness comfort me,
  According to Your word to Your servant.
May Your compassion come to me that I may live,
  For Your law is my delight.
May the arrogant be ashamed, for they subvert me with a lie;
  But I shall meditate on Your precepts.
May those who fear You turn to me,
  Even those who know Your testimonies.
May my heart be blameless in Your statutes,
  So that I will not be ashamed.

My soul languishes for Your salvation;
  I wait for Your word.
My eyes fail with longing for Your word,
  While I say, "When will You comfort me?"
Though I have become like a wineskin in the smoke,

I do not forget Your statutes.
How many are the days of Your servant?
    When will You execute judgment on those who persecute me?
The arrogant have dug pits for me,
    Men who are not in accord with Your law.
All Your commandments are faithful;
    They have persecuted me with a lie; help me!
They almost destroyed me on earth,
    But as for me, I did not forsake Your precepts.
Revive me according to Your lovingkindness,
    So that I may keep the testimony of Your mouth.

Forever, O LORD,
    Your word is settled in heaven.
Your faithfulness continues throughout all generations;
    You established the earth, and it stands.
They stand this day according to Your ordinances,
    For all things are Your servants.
If Your law had not been my delight,
    Then I would have perished in my affliction.
I will never forget Your precepts,
    For by them You have revived me.
I am Yours, save me;
    For I have sought Your precepts.
The wicked wait for me to destroy me;
    I shall diligently consider Your testimonies.
I have seen a limit to all perfection;
    Your commandment is exceedingly broad.

O how I love Your law!
    It is my meditation all the day.
Your commandments make me wiser than my enemies,
    For they are ever mine.
I have more insight than all my teachers,
    For Your testimonies are my meditation.
I understand more than the aged,
    Because I have observed Your precepts.
I have restrained my feet from every evil way,
    That I may keep Your word.
I have not turned aside from Your ordinances,
    For You Yourself have taught me.

How sweet are Your words to my taste!
  Yes, sweeter than honey to my mouth!
From Your precepts I get understanding;
  Therefore I hate every false way.

Your word is a lamp to my feet
  And a light to my path.
I have sworn and I will confirm it,
  That I will keep Your righteous ordinances.
I am exceedingly afflicted;
  Revive me, O LORD, according to Your word.
O accept the freewill offerings of my mouth, O LORD,
  And teach me Your ordinances.
My life is continually in my hand,
  Yet I do not forget Your law.
The wicked have laid a snare for me,
  Yet I have not gone astray from Your precepts.
I have inherited Your testimonies forever,
  For they are the joy of my heart.
I have inclined my heart to perform Your statutes
  Forever, even to the end.

I hate those who are double-minded,
  But I love Your law.
You are my hiding place and my shield;
  I wait for Your word.
Depart from me, evildoers,
  That I may observe the commandments of my God.
Sustain me according to Your word, that I may live;
  And do not let me be ashamed of my hope.
Uphold me that I may be safe,
  That I may have regard for Your statutes continually.
You have rejected all those who wander from Your statutes,
  For their deceitfulness is useless.
You have removed all the wicked of the earth like dross;
  Therefore I love Your testimonies.
My flesh trembles for fear of You,
  And I am afraid of Your judgments.

I have done justice and righteousness;
  Do not leave me to my oppressors.
Be surety for Your servant for good;

Do not let the arrogant oppress me.
My eyes fail with longing for Your salvation
    And for Your righteous word.
Deal with Your servant according to Your lovingkindness
    And teach me Your statutes.
I am Your servant; give me understanding,
    That I may know Your testimonies.
It is time for the LORD to act,
    For they have broken Your law.
Therefore I love Your commandments
    Above gold, yes, above fine gold.
Therefore I esteem right all Your precepts concerning everything,
    I hate every false way.

Your testimonies are wonderful;
    Therefore my soul observes them.
The unfolding of Your words gives light;
    It gives understanding to the simple.
I opened my mouth wide and panted,
    For I longed for Your commandments.
Turn to me and be gracious to me,
    After Your manner with those who love Your name.
Establish my footsteps in Your word,
    And do not let any iniquity have dominion over me.
Redeem me from the oppression of man,
    That I may keep Your precepts.
Make Your face shine upon Your servant,
    And teach me Your statutes.
My eyes shed streams of water,
    Because they do not keep Your law.

Righteous are You, O LORD,
    And upright are Your judgments.
You have commanded Your testimonies in righteousness
    And exceeding faithfulness.
My zeal has consumed me,
    Because my adversaries have forgotten Your words.
Your word is very pure,
    Therefore Your servant loves it.
I am small and despised,
    Yet I do not forget Your precepts.
Your righteousness is an everlasting righteousness,

And Your law is truth.
Trouble and anguish have come upon me,
    Yet Your commandments are my delight.
Your testimonies are righteous forever;
    Give me understanding that I may live.

I cried with all my heart; answer me, O Lord!
    I will observe Your statutes.
I cried to You; save me
    And I shall keep Your testimonies.
I rise before dawn and cry for help;
    I wait for Your words.
My eyes anticipate the night watches,
    That I may meditate on Your word.
Hear my voice according to Your lovingkindness;
    Revive me, O Lord, according to Your ordinances.
Those who follow after wickedness draw near;
    They are far from Your law.
You are near, O Lord,
    And all Your commandments are truth.
Of old I have known from Your testimonies
    That You have founded them forever.

Look upon my affliction and rescue me,
    For I do not forget Your law.
Plead my cause and redeem me;
    Revive me according to Your word.
Salvation is far from the wicked,
    For they do not seek Your statutes.
Great are Your mercies, O Lord;
    Revive me according to Your ordinances.
Many are my persecutors and my adversaries,
    Yet I do not turn aside from Your testimonies.
I behold the treacherous and loathe them,
    Because they do not keep Your word.
Consider how I love Your precepts;
    Revive me, O Lord, according to Your lovingkindness.
The sum of Your word is truth,
    And every one of Your righteous ordinances is everlasting.

Princes persecute me without cause,
    But my heart stands in awe of Your words.

I rejoice at Your word,
　　As one who finds great spoil.
I hate and despise falsehood,
　　But I love Your law.
Seven times a day I praise You,
　　Because of Your righteous ordinances.
Those who love Your law have great peace,
　　And nothing causes them to stumble.
I hope for Your salvation, O LORD,
　　And do Your commandments.
My soul keeps Your testimonies,
　　And I love them exceedingly.
I keep Your precepts and Your testimonies,
　　For all my ways are before You.

Let my cry come before You, O LORD;
　　Give me understanding according to Your word.
Let my supplication come before You;
　　Deliver me according to Your word.
Let my lips utter praise,
　　For You teach me Your statutes.
Let my tongue sing of Your word,
　　For all Your commandments are righteousness.
Let Your hand be ready to help me,
　　For I have chosen Your precepts.
I long for Your salvation, O LORD,
　　And Your law is my delight.
Let my soul live that it may praise You,
　　And let Your ordinances help me.
I have gone astray like a lost sheep; seek Your servant,
　　For I do not forget Your commandments.

Many Christians, such as William Wilberforce (1759–1833), have memorized this psalm and recited it regularly. Others have taken a single verse of it to meditate on every morning. I pray God will give us more than a rushed tour of these Alps. We will ask four questions that will help us understand and profit from this psalm.

1. What Is God's Law?

Law has both narrow and broad meanings in the Bible. It references both specific rules and a collection of rules. Consequently, the collection of rules that God gave to Moses must be part of what is being referred to in Psalm 119. So everything from Exodus 19 (the giving of the law at Mount Sinai) through Deuteronomy might be meant. However, given the fact that this psalm uses broader words, such as *word* and *promise*, it's clear that the psalmist has in mind not only the whole Torah, the first five books of the Bible, but also other portions of God's Word that he has access to. He seems to quote, or at least make allusions to, Isaiah, Jeremiah, Proverbs, and other portions of God's Word. The variety of words used for God's law throughout the psalm—*word, judgments, statutes, decree, law, commands, precepts, ways, promises*—evidences this broader understanding. To put it simply, Psalm 119 is not talking about just the Ten Commandments or the Pentateuch, but the totality of biblical revelation. This believing poet is reflecting on his relationship with God, and he sees that he is in that relationship only because God has revealed himself to his people in his commands, decrees, promises, and statutes.

God's Word had always been fundamental to the existence of his people. Of course, even the world itself and the first man and woman were made by God's Word. But even more specially, God's Word of promise came to the Gentile Abraham and made him the father of the faithful, the progenitor of God's special people. Again, God's Word came to Jacob, to Joseph, and to Moses. Through Moses, God's Word established the nation of Israel. Through the leaders who followed, from Joshua to David and beyond, God's Word led his people. Before the temple, it was the Torah that shaped God's people and made them his, but God continued to give new revelation to his people as the centuries passed.

Then, with his coming as the Messiah, Jesus fulfilled the Law and the Prophets (Matt. 5:17). A good picture of this is the way Jesus picked up the Passover meal, which was the meal of the Mosaic covenant, and revealed how it pointed to his own work and his own reign at the Last Supper (Luke 22:14–20). He fulfilled the Old Testament laws, whether they were civil, ceremonial, or moral. And after his ascension, he sent his Spirit to inspire and direct his apostles to reflect on the Old Testament and to instruct the Christians. Do you want to know how to apply the Old Testament today as a Christian? Read your New Testament. Christ summarized all of the law in Mark 12:28–31, when he said to love God and your neighbor (cf. Deut. 6:6; Lev. 19:18; Rom. 13:8–10; Gal. 5:14; 6:2). God's law in Psalm 119 is his Word.

2. What Is God's Word Like?

If God's Word is his revelation to us, then what is that revelation like? Psalm 119 becomes a solemnly joyful celebration as it reveals God's Word to be true, good, and everlasting. If we lose any one of these attributes, God's Word is greatly diminished, but with all three together, the future—which could otherwise be dark and foreboding—is flooded with light.

God's Word is *true*. In verse 29, the psalmist says God's ways are the opposite of false ways. In verse 142, he writes, "Your law is truth," and then, in verse 151, he says, "All Your commandments are truth." Verse 160 puts it like this: "The sum of Your word is truth." God has never spoken falsely, either to our first parents or to us. Our enemy, Satan, lies constantly, attaching his lies to half-truths. We can have our puny wits about us and still be deceived by sin. But God is nothing like that. He is always and only truthful. All of his law is true. The sum of his Word is truth. He never misleads us, never lies to us, never deceives us. Even things we do not know give us ground to look to him, to trust him, and to find out that what he speaks in his Word is always and only true!

God's Word is also *good*, which means that his truth is good. Again and again in this psalm, he says that his rules are righteous (vv. 62, 75, 106, 160). The promises God makes to us are righteous (v. 123). His testimonies are righteous (v. 144). There is nothing wrong or questionable about his promise to us that salvation is only by faith. God defines what is good. Goodness or righteousness is not an external standard that God effortlessly and perfectly conforms to; rather, goodness is a way of describing God and all his actions and commands. That which is "good" is not determined by the number of followers one has on Twitter, by what is currently fashionable, or by the Supreme Court. That court, just down the street from my church in Washington, DC, at one time or another has declared legal that two men can marry each other, that infants in the womb can be killed, and that people can own each other like property. The Supreme Court is hardly the final arbiter of goodness.

Well, if popularity, electability, or legality is not the final arbiter, then what is it that finally determines what is good? God! He has revealed it to us in his Word. Psalm 119:164 states, "Seven times a day I praise You, because of Your righteous ordinances." If you are ever confused about what is right or wrong, you can simply look to God's Word, because all his precepts are right (v. 128). I don't have to worry about which of his laws are good and which ones are not, for "all Your commandments are righteous"

(v. 172). We read in verse 39: "Your ordinances are good." It makes sense that what comes from God is good, because as the psalmist puts it so simply in verse 68, "You are good and do good."

But God's Word is not only true and good, it is *everlasting*. It will never change, expire, give out, or need updating with a patch sent down from the clouds of heaven. God's Word is from of old (v. 52). It is ancient; it is not a new thing. There is no sense of God's Word lasting any less than forever. Verse 152 reinforces that God's Word has been "founded . . . forever." Our actions and words change in the order of the day, but for God, "every one of Your righteous ordinances is everlasting" (v. 160). That's why the psalmist can rejoice in verse 86 that there is no uncertainty in God's Word: "All Your commandments are faithful." Or, again, in verse 89: "Forever, O LORD, Your word is settled in heaven."

Now it's true that when the psalmist wrote these words, God's special revelation of himself had not yet been concluded. Perhaps some of the Old Testament prophets were still to come. Certainly the Lord Jesus Christ and his apostles had not yet come and had not yet taught and written under the inspiration of the Holy Spirit. But none of these forthcoming events changed what God had already revealed. The walls of the New Testament were to be built squarely on the foundations of the Old. Apart from the New Testament, the Old would have been incomplete. And without the Old Testament, the New would make no sense. Isn't it wonderful to know that God's true and good Word is also eternal and unchanging? This is not the Word of a tentative, changing, or fickle being. This is the Word of the one and only God—the always true, ever good, everlasting, and unchanging God!

It is important to remember that God's Word is true, good, and everlasting because the One who wrote it is truthful, righteous, and eternal. Throughout Psalm 119, the Word of God is identified very closely with God himself. God's Word is his emissary, his ambassador, a revelation of himself, and a revelation of his will and character. The psalmist even parallels keeping the LORD's testimonies with seeking him (v. 2). In verse 137, we read, "Righteous are You, O LORD, and upright are Your judgments." Notice that God's judgments follow him; they are like him and reflect him. The Bible is not God, but apart from the Bible, we could not know him as we do. To attack the Word of God is to attack God, and to honor the Word of God is to honor God. Have you stopped to consider and appreciate what the Lord has given us in his Word? It is here for you to understand what is true, good, and everlasting. It is here for us to come to know God and his will.

There is so much more we could appreciate about what God's Word is like from this great psalm, but we must move on to our next question.

3. What Does God's Word Do?

Since the Bible is the Word of the all-powerful God, we shouldn't be surprised to learn that it is active and accomplishes much. Perhaps it is better to say that God does much with it and through it. Generally, what God's Word does is bless. We read in verses 1–2: "How blessed are those whose way is blameless, who walk in the law of the LORD. How blessed are those who observe His testimonies, who seek Him with all their heart." Also, note the kind of Aaronic benediction found in verse 135: "Make Your face shine upon Your servant." How does God do that? "Teach me Your statutes." God's Word blesses individuals in five specific ways:

FOR THOSE WHO BELIEVE THE BIBLE

God's Word inspires awe. We see in verse 161, "My heart stands in awe of Your words." And in the context of that verse, *Your* is emphasized. The psalmist is awed by God's words as opposed to those of a persecuting prince. Even when the psalmist could be preoccupied by other things—such as staying alive—he writes in verse 164, "Seven times a day I praise You, because of Your righteous ordinances." And verse 171 reads, "Let my lips utter praise, for You teach me Your statutes." God's Word inspires awe and causes us to pray and to praise him. It brings us into a relationship with him.

FOR THOSE WHO CARE ABOUT GOD AND OTHERS

God's Word causes us to grieve over sin. Verse 136 says, "My eyes shed streams of water, because they do not keep Your law." Verse 53 reads, "Burning indignation has seized me because of the wicked, who forsake Your law." Studying God's Word does not make us morally indifferent; instead, it educates our consciences, sharpens our minds, and causes us to see this world and the people in it more as God does.

FOR THOSE IN TEMPTATION

God's Word also helps us stay pure. Verse 9 is well known: "How can a young man keep his way pure? By keeping it according to Your Word."

We read in verse 11, "Your word I have treasured in my heart, that I may not sin against You." Do you have any doubt that God's Word encourages holiness? Look at verse 101: "I have restrained my feet from every evil way, that I may keep Your word." Remember how the Lord Jesus met temptation in the day of his flesh? He quoted the Bible to Satan. Why would you think that you stand in less need of knowing and using the Bible to help you with temptation than Jesus did? The Word of God is a storehouse of very practical helps for us as Christians.

FOR THOSE IN VARIOUS KINDS OF NEED

Through his Word, God gives hope to the hopeless. Again and again, the psalmist writes, "I hope in Your Word" (vv. 43, 49, 81, 114, 147). To the afflicted, the Lord gives comfort (vv. 50, 52, 76), and to those undergoing trials, he gives joy. I'm encouraged by verse 111: "I have inherited Your testimonies forever, for they are the joy of my heart." And verse 162: "I rejoice at Your Word, as one who finds great spoil." To those enduring trials, he gives peace through his Word: "Those who love Your law have great peace, and nothing causes them to stumble" (v. 165). To the young who read the Bible, he gives wisdom (v. 98) and understanding (vv. 99–100). We read in verse 104, "From Your precepts I get understanding."

This is why it makes sense to equate the Bible to a light: "Your word is a lamp to my feet and a light to my path" (v. 105). Also, "The unfolding of Your words gives light" (v. 130). This is what should be happening right now. As I'm unfolding God's Word in this chapter, as you're unfolding it by reading, and as God is unfolding it ultimately by giving it to us, light and understanding should be coming into your life.

God answers prayers you may have offered for better judgment: "Teach me good discernment and knowledge, for I believe in Your commandments" (v. 66). We need to pray this, because God's Word can be savingly understood only by God's gift. This kind of psalm should never be understood as anything like a call to save ourselves or to pull ourselves up by our own spiritual bootstraps. Do you remember when Jesus asked his disciples who the people said he was, and Peter answered, "You are the Christ" (Matt. 16:16)? Jesus said to Peter, "Congratulations, I always knew you were the smart one!" No, his response was, "Blessed are you, Simon Barjona, because flesh and blood did not reveal this to you, but My Father who is in heaven" (v. 17). We need the Father to reveal eternal truths to us, and Psalm 119 is full of prayers for him to teach us his Word (vv. 12, 26, cf. vv. 32, 125) and to open our eyes (v. 18). The psalmist prays in verse 27, "Make me understand the way of Your precepts." In verse 73, he says, "Give me understanding, that I may learn Your commandments." And in verse 29, "Graciously grant me Your law." In fact, the psalmist is aware that his own worldly profit might sometimes prejudice him against what God teaches in his law. Consequently, he prays, "Incline my heart to Your testimonies and not to dishonest gain" (v. 36). God's Word is to be learned only by God's gift. Have you prayed about your own study of Scripture, your own reliance on him? A crucial part of Bible study that too many Christians omit is simply asking God to reveal himself through his Word.

Friend, why would you not spend your life getting to know the Bible better than you do today? I love how the psalmist puts it in verse 24: "Your testimonies also are my delight; they are my counselors." Is the Bible your counselor in your decisions and questions in life? It's significant that throughout this psalm, the psalmist both trusts God and asks God to help him trust even more.

Would you listen to God if he spoke? He's speaking to us in his Word. In fact, the most amazing thing God gives us through his Word is life! "Your word has revived me" (v. 50). My Christian friend, how else could you have come to be interested in God's Word? It is only by God's grace! And his Word is the means he uses to give us spiritual life.

For Those in Trouble

God promises to delivers us. The psalmist knew what it meant to be in trouble. So if you're in trouble today, God's Word promises deliverance (v. 170) and gives help (v. 175), strength (v. 28), protection (v. 165), and even salvation (v. 41). The Lord shows us so much about himself through his Word. What we see in Psalm 119 is just some of what God's Word does.

4. How Should We Respond?

Given what God's Word is, what it is like, and what it does, there is a mandate for us to respond to it. Here are five basic responses we must have to God's Word.

Obey

First and most obvious, we must obey God's Word. The first stanza of the psalm contains declarations of intent to keep God's statutes (vv. 5, 8), and such declarations are repeated again and again throughout the psalm

(vv. 55–56, 87, 112, 117). Why would we think that God would give us life by his Word and not call us to obey him? No small part of God's reason for giving us new life is that, as we read in verse 115, we would "observe the commandments of [our] God." Thus, the psalmist writes in verse 145: "I cried with all my heart; answer me, O LORD! I will observe Your statutes." Our basic response to God's Word is to obey it. But as we will see in the following response, this obedience is not a simple commitment to an arbitrary set of rules or merely trying to please other people.

LOVE

Second, we are to love God's Word. The psalmist conveys this idea with the sheer length of the psalm and the intricacy of the acrostic. Also, we read in verse 14, "I have rejoiced in the way of Your testimonies, as much as in all riches" (cf. vv. 16, 24, 35, 70, 77, 92, 143, 174). In verse 129, the psalmist asserts, "Your testimonies are wonderful" (cf. v. 18). The psalmist even provides a comparison to food in verse 103: "How sweet are Your words to my taste! Yes, sweeter than honey to my mouth!" So he desires God's Word and longs for it (vv. 20, 40, 47, 82, 131). In verse 131, the psalmist uses a powerful image: "I opened my mouth wide and panted, for I longed for Your commandments." Clearly the psalmist values God's Word; he even values it more than "thousands of gold and silver pieces" (v. 72). Simply put, he loves God's Word, and so should we! As you read the following verses, ask yourself if this is your testimony as well: "I shall delight in Your commandments, which I love" (v. 47); "I love Your commandments above gold, yes, above fine gold" (v. 127); "My soul keeps Your testimonies, and I love them exceedingly" (v. 167). We must both obey *and* love God's Word.

MEDITATE

Third, we are to meditate on God's Word. The psalmist writes: "O how I love Your law! It is my meditation all the day" (v. 97). In verse 148, it appears that the psalmist even got up early in order to meditate on the Scriptures! He also sang God's Word: "Your statutes are my songs" (v. 54) and "Let my tongue sing of Your word" (v. 172). The hymns sung at my church, Capitol Hill Baptist, deliberately reflect the Psalms and are often thick with biblical content, allusions, quotations, and doctrine, because such hymns help us to encourage one another, to express ourselves to the Lord and to others, and to commit God's Word to memory. I can't tell you how many times I have been with saints near the end of their lives, and even though their memories were going, they could remember the hymns they had sung.

How many young Christians have memorized verse 11, "Your word I have treasured in my heart, that I may not sin against You" (cf. vv. 61, 83, 93, 109, 141, 153, 176)? One way to meditate on Scripture is to memorize it. But whatever your means, whether it is singing, memorizing, reading, praying, or pondering, you are called to meditate on God's Word.

Trust

Fourth, a proper response to God's Word is to trust it. The psalmist was wise to do just that: "For I trust in Your word" (v. 42). You cannot rely on some people's word, and so you shouldn't. But you can always trust God's Word, and therefore you always should! His Word is worthy of trust, because he is trustworthy! We can count on God's Word. It won't let us down. We can be confident, for his "faithfulness continues through all generations" (v. 90). Verse 140 is one of my favorite verses in this long chapter: "Your word is very pure, therefore Your servant loves it." Who knows all the trials the psalmist had been through? Physical challenges, being despised, having enemies, dealing with criminals and immoral people, oppression—he mentions these and many other things in this psalm. I'm sure God's promises were well-tried in this psalmist's hands! Have they been so tried in yours?

Fear

Fifth, we must fear the God whose Word it is. Look at verse 120: "My flesh trembles for fear of You, and I am afraid of Your judgments." God's Word brings us into contact with God himself. And this contact, by his grace, wakes us up spiritually and makes us realize how in God there is only what is good and right. That sense of the moral distance between us and the God who created us and who will judge us is profoundly disorienting to many. It confuses us until a new clarity comes in accepting it all. But even after we come to hear and believe the gospel, we are left with a true sense of the difference between God and us; something of his holiness and our unworthiness, which makes us regard him and his Word with the most profound respect and with a trembling gratitude as we marvel at his love and mercy toward us.

So, obey God's Word, love it, meditate on it, and trust it, and come to fear the God whose Word it is.

Conclusion

Psalm 119 is not just talking about the written Word of God. The way to glory, the ending of our exile, the completion of this true exodus, isn't fundamentally through obeying God's written Word, but through the Word made flesh perfectly obeying it in our place! It does no dishonor to God's written Word to say that it points to something greater than itself. "God, after He spoke long ago to the fathers in the prophets in many portions and in many ways, in these last days has spoken to us in His Son" (Heb. 1:1–2b). We read in John 1: "In the beginning was the Word, and the Word was with God, and the Word was God. . . . And the Word became flesh, and dwelt among us, and we saw His glory, glory as of the only begotten from the Father, full of grace and truth" (vv. 1, 14).

It is not that we don't obey God's Word. We do, genuinely, but imperfectly. And our lives, being genuinely but imperfectly circumscribed by the law of God, give evidence of our trust in the One whose life was perfectly circumscribed by the Word of God and whose perfect righteousness he gives to us as a gift. It is that gift that this psalm so wonderfully points to again and again—the perfect righteousness of Jesus Christ.

Look once more at the first two verses of this great psalm: "How blessed are those whose way is blameless, who walk in the law of the LORD. How blessed are those who observe His testimonies, who seek Him with all their heart" (Ps. 119:1–2). Whose way has been more blameless than that of the Son of God? Who has sought more wholeheartedly than the Son of God to do his Father's will here on earth? And who has done it more perfectly? Twice the Father said publicly to the disciples that he was "well pleased" with his Son! Surely no life was ever more blessed than that of the One who perfectly, blamelessly followed in the way of his heavenly Father and sought him with his whole heart!

And yet, God's Word says that his death by crucifixion shows that he was "cursed"! What an irony that the only One who perfectly kept the law was killed as if he was a lawbreaker. Jesus taught that his death was predicted and foreshadowed in the Old Testament. After he rose from the dead, he told his disciples, "All things which are written about Me in the Law of Moses and the Prophets *and the Psalms* must be fulfilled" (Luke 24:44).

What was written about the Word made flesh in Psalm 119? Notice these foreshadowings: Jesus called himself the servant of the Lord; the psalmist says, "You have dealt well with your servant" (v. 65). Even as a boy, Jesus said he must be about his Father's business; the psalmist writes: "I have more insight than all my teachers, for Your testimonies are my meditation. I understand more than the aged, because I have observed Your precepts" (vv. 99–100). Jesus wept over Jerusalem's rejection; the psalmist says, "My eyes shed streams of water, because they do not keep Your law" (v. 136). Do you hear echoes of Gethsemane in verse 143: "Trouble and anguish have come upon me, yet Your commandments are my delight"? Do you see a foreshadowing of suffering for righteousness' sake and of being smeared with lies in verse 69: "The arrogant have forged a lie against me; with all my heart I will observe Your precepts"? Is there a preview of the Savior being ensnared by the wicked in verse 61: "The cords of the wicked have encircled me, but I have not forgotten Your law"? Does verse 161 foreshadow Herod and Pontius Pilate joining together to persecute him: "Princes persecute me without cause"? Is verse 107 anticipating the kind of affliction Jesus experienced: "I am exceedingly afflicted; revive me, O LORD, according to Your word"? From where could verse 149 be prayed more truly than from the tomb of Christ: "Hear my voice according to Your lovingkindness; revive me, O LORD, according to Your ordinances"? Or verses 153–154: "Look upon my affliction and rescue me, for I do not forget Your law. Plead my cause and redeem me; revive me according to Your word"?

The LORD *did* give his life, and through the sacrifice and resurrection of the Word made flesh, Immanuel, he gave life to all who would come to trust in him. And so we are, as this psalm begins, *blessed*—for we are in Christ, who was both cursed and blessed for us in our place. Praise God for his Word.

4

Christ, Christians, and
the Word of God

MATTHEW 5:17-20

Kevin DeYoung

If you were to enter our house through the garage and turn into the first door on your left, you would step down into the small room we call our den. Against the far wall of our den, you would find a brown couch—a very special brown couch. It's special because I put it together all by myself with nothing more than a set of wordless instructions and a single Allen wrench. For this is an Ikea couch. Some of you are familiar with the fine household products made by our good Swedish friends at Ikea. This couch came in four huge boxes that filled our entire Suburban. The instructions contained dozens of pictures and not a single sentence in any language—nothing but drawings of little nuts and bolts and wooden dowels connecting stray pieces of furniture.

I foolishly began this project one night around ten, when everyone else in the house was asleep. There I was, staring at this mess, armed with nothing but Scandinavian pencil drawings and an L-shaped piece of metal with a hexagon on either end. Around one or two in the morning, I was faced with an existential decision: Would I deviate from the instructions? I had been stuck on one part of the assembly for forty-five minutes, which was about forty-five minutes more than I wanted to spend on the whole project. The picture just didn't make sense. The pieces couldn't possibly fit together the way Ikea wanted them to. I felt a little like the astronauts aboard *Apollo 13*, talking to mission control back in Houston: I was sleep-deprived, had not eaten in hours, was running low on oxygen, and was in desperate need of engineering assistance.

After trying to make sense of the instructions for what seemed like days, I finally came to a dramatic conclusion that would change my life: Ikea was wrong. The wordless, two-dimensional, black-and-white instructions had misled me. The picture showed a couch piece going to the right when the piece I needed to use was actually going to the left. Once I realized the manual was in error, I could breathe again. I felt the color returning to my face. I believed once more that if I really put my mind to it, I could assemble an Ikea couch before sunrise. Everything started to make sense again when I accepted that the well-meaning instructions were not entirely accurate.

Is the Bible ever like that Ikea instruction manual? Aren't there parts of the Old Testament that aren't really true anymore? Aren't there some miracles in the New Testament that seem a bit far-fetched? Aren't there some moral requirements in the Bible that no longer work in our world? Yes, the Bible is a wonderful book. Yes, the Bible is spot-on when it comes to the big-picture stuff. Yes, the Bible is basically reliable and is usually really helpful. But wouldn't it be better—in those rare instances when the biblical picture just doesn't fit anymore—to respectfully go in a different direction? Must we affirm that *every* word of *every* verse of *every* chapter in *every* book of the Bible is from God, inspired, authoritative, unbreakable, and without error?

Jesus's View

Before answering that question for ourselves, it might be helpful to hear what Jesus has to say:

> Do not think that I have come to abolish the Law or the Prophets; I have not come to abolish them but to fulfill them. For truly, I say to you, until heaven and earth pass away, not an iota, not a dot, will pass from the Law until all is accomplished. Therefore whoever relaxes one of the least of these commandments and teaches others to do the same

will be called least in the kingdom of heaven, but whoever does them and teaches them will be called great in the kingdom of heaven. For I tell you, unless your righteousness exceeds that of the scribes and Pharisees, you will never enter the kingdom of heaven. (Matt. 5:17–20)

The Sermon on the Mount is about discipleship. It answers questions like these: What does it look like to be a disciple of Jesus Christ? What do people look like when the kingdom comes in their lives? What sort of people are we when God reigns and rules in our hearts and minds? Jesus says that if you are a part of God's family—if you're on God's team, if you belong to God's kingdom—then you'll be meek, merciful, pure, and poor in spirit. He says you'll be like salt and light in the world, slowing decay and exposing the deeds of darkness.

In one sense, there is nothing particularly novel about what Jesus preaches. The Jewish disciples who gather around him will be challenged, to be sure, but they might nod in agreement at what Jesus says. The problem is what he doesn't say. He doesn't put the primary focus on the Law, the Torah. Any good Jew would expect a good rabbi to talk at length about the Law. Ordering your life around the Torah is not just what makes you a Jew, it is what makes you a good Jew. Yet, Jesus talks as if the focal point of their faith is to be Jesus himself: "Blessed are you when others revile you and persecute you and utter all kinds of evil against you falsely on *my* account" (v. 11). Oh, so this is all about *you*, Jesus?

Yes, it is. But Jesus takes pains to make clear that this didn't mean he is anti-Torah or anti-Scripture. His disciples cannot have a lackadaisical attitude toward the Word of God. That is why Jesus says what he says in verses 17–20.

I want to look at these verses under two simple headings: (1) Christ and the Bible and (2) the Christian and the Bible.

Christ and the Bible (5:17–18)

Jesus states emphatically that he has not come to abolish the tiniest little speck of Scripture. When he says "the Law or the Prophets" in verse 17, he is referring to all of the Hebrew Bible (what we know as the Old Testament). The word *Law* (*nomos* in the Greek or *Torah* in Hebrew) can refer to the commands of God, the Ten Commandments, the Mosaic covenant, or the first five books of the Bible. It can also refer to the entire Old Testament (John 10:34; 12:34; 15:25; 1 Cor. 14:21). In the New Testament, in addition to "the Law," the Hebrew Bible is sometimes called "Scripture" or "the Scriptures" (John 10:35); sometimes the Law and the Prophets (Matt. 5:17; 7:12; 11:13; 22:40; Luke 16:16; John 1:45; Acts 13:15; 28:23; Rom. 3:21); and sometimes the Law, the Prophets, and the Psalms (Luke 24:44). When Jesus talks about "the Law or the Prophets" in verse 17 and "the Law" in verse 18, he is talking about the same thing: the Hebrew Scriptures of the Old Testament. And since he's talking about his Bible, and since he understood his words and the future apostolic words about him to be as authoritative as the Hebrew Scriptures (Matt. 5:21–22, 27–28, 31–32, 33–34, 38–39, 43–44; 7:24, 26, 28–29; John 14:6; 16:12–15), we can rightly apply what Jesus says here to the Old and New Testaments of our Bibles.

And what Jesus says about the Bible is amazing.

First, he says plainly and dramatically that he has not come "to abolish the Law or the Prophets." The verb translated as "to abolish" is the Greek word *kataluo*. It's used three other times in Matthew:

- But he answered them, "You see all these, do you not? Truly, I say to you, there will not be left here one stone upon another that will not be *thrown down*" (24:2).
- "This man said, 'I am able to *destroy* the temple of God, and to rebuild it in three days'" (26:61).
- "You who would *destroy* the temple and rebuild it in three days, save yourself!" (27:40).

Jesus is saying: "If you think I've come to destroy the Scriptures, you are dead wrong. I have not come to abolish them, to pick them apart, to throw them down, to dismantle them, to annul them, to loosen them, or to set them aside in any way, shape, or form. That's not what I'm about. That's not what the kingdom is about. If you want a Messiah who plays fast and loose with the Bible, you've got the wrong guy."

At this point, you may be thinking: But what about all the stuff in the Old Testament we don't follow anymore? For instance:

- Mark 7:19 makes clear that Jesus declared all foods clean.
- Acts 10–11, 15 shows that a person does not have to become Jewish in order to become a Christian.
- Romans 14:14 relativizes the restrictions about foods and days.
- Hebrews 7:1–9:10 reveals that the whole temple-based priestly sacrificial system has become obsolete.

The answer to this seeming problem is found in my second point: Jesus says he has come to fulfill the Law and the Prophets. The word *fulfill* is the

English translation of the Greek word *pleroo*, and it is a very important word in Matthew, occurring sixteen times in the book (1:22; 2:15, 17, 23; 3:15; 4:14; 5:17; 8:17; 12:17; 13:35, 48; 21:4; 23:32; 26:54, 56; 27:9). Let's look at just a few of these passages to see how *fulfill* is used in Matthew's Gospel.

- Matthew 1:22: doing or saying what the Old Testament said
- Matthew 2:15: embodying
- Matthew 4:14: carrying out what is required
- Matthew 26:54: bringing to completion

Jesus fulfills Scripture in what he teaches, what he does, who he is, and how he dies, but the word *fulfill* does not simply refer to accomplishing specific prophecies. *Pleroo* means Jesus brings Scripture to completion. He brings it to its climax, to its intended goal, to its fruition. In Jesus's ministry, fulfillment is not just about doing and saying what the Old Testament predicted he would do and say. As Douglas Moo writes, "The word is used in the New Testament to indicate the broad redemptive-historical relationship of the new climactic revelation of God in Christ to the preparatory, incomplete revelation to and through Israel."[1]

The best way to grasp all that fulfillment means is to think of the word *fill* right in the middle. Jesus fills up and fills out all of Scripture. In Matthew 23:32, he says to the scribes and Pharisees, "Fill up, then, the measure of your fathers," meaning, "Go ahead and live out all the wickedness your fathers accomplished." That's the word *pleroo*. Jesus is saying in Matthew 5:17: "I have not come to set aside, put away, or belittle anything in the Bible. I have not come to fiddle with it. I have come to fill it up—to show what it's all about, to do what it says, to live out what it predicts, to put into color what is in black and white, to show you substance where you have been seeing only shadow. So, yes, you have to look at the Law and the Prophets in light of me, but don't think I'm trying to darken anything in this book."

And if that were not enough of a statement in support of the Scriptures, Jesus kicks it up another notch in verse 18. He says, "Truly, I say to you . . ." That's an oath formula. *Amen* is the word in the Greek. It's the Jewish way of saying: "Listen up! Let me tell you something. What I'm about to say to you is straight-up truth: you'll see heaven and earth pass away before you see a little iota or a tiny dot pass away from the Law."

---

[1] Douglas J. Moo, "The Problem of Sensus Plenior," in *Hermeneutics, Authority, and Canon*, ed. D. A. Carson and John D. Woodbridge (Grand Rapids, MI: Zondervan, 1986), 191.

Iota is a Greek letter, but Jesus is actually referring here to the Hebrew letter yodh. It's the smallest Hebrew letter. It looks like a little raised comma. One scholar has estimated there are sixty-six thousand yodhs in the Old Testament. Jesus says every single one of them matters. He doesn't want to take away even one instance of the tiniest letter in the Hebrew alphabet.

"Dot" likely refers to the small strokes (horns) that distinguish Hebrew letters (for instance, bet and kaf or dalet and resh). An example in English is the longer stroke that distinguishes an "h" from an "n." Not one of those little specks is going to pass away from one letter in one word in one verse in the whole Bible. Jesus could not state his affirmation of the Scriptures in any stronger language.

The Christian and the Bible (5:19–20)

Once we understand Christ's attitude toward the Bible, it's not difficult to understand what our attitude toward the Bible should be. The mature Christian disciple does not relax any of the commands of Scripture.

In John 10:35, Jesus declares, "Scripture cannot be broken." The Greek word translated as "broken" is *luo*, which can mean "break, loosen, or relax." It is related to *kataluo*, which is translated as "abolish" in Matthew 5:17. If Jesus did not come to abolish, break, loosen, or relax Scripture, neither should we. If we relax even one of the least of God's commandments and teach others to do so, Jesus says, we place ourselves among "the least" in the kingdom of heaven (v. 19).

You don't become relevant by messing around with Scripture. It's not hip to flirt with disobedience. It's not gospel-centered to celebrate all the ways you are violating the commandments of God. Jesus doesn't think you're cool; he thinks you're least in the kingdom of heaven.

What does it mean to be "kingdom minded"? It can mean many things, but not reading your Bible, thinking you know better than your Bible, and provoking people to ignore parts of the Bible is not kingdom living.

In verse 20, Jesus introduces a new category: someone who is not in the kingdom at all. He says that our righteousness must exceed that of the scribes and Pharisees or we will not be able to enter the kingdom. Jesus is not talking about the righteousness they need to receive from him. That's wonderful gospel truth, but it's not what Jesus is talking about here. He's talking about discipleship, about how we live, how we walk. Simply put, we must not walk as the scribes and Pharisees walked.

Jesus is going to explain in the rest of the Sermon on the Mount what kind of righteousness he is after. It's "law-upon-your-hearts" righteousness (Jer. 31:33). It's "I-will-put-my-Spirit-within-you-to-help-you-walk-in-my-statutes" righteousness (Ezek. 36:27).

Legalism is the attempt to earn salvation by keeping the law. We usually use the word *legalist* to mean "someone who is more serious about being obedient than I am." Jesus isn't against law-keeping. He's against hypocritical law-keeping. To be a follower of Jesus is to be someone who takes all the Bible and all the commands of the Bible seriously.

Conclusion

Let me finish with two points of application:

First, we must not ignore anything in the Bible because of Jesus. We must not make a false distinction between the Old Testament God and the New Testament God. We must not discount Old Testament miracles, chronologies, and genealogies. We must not doubt the power of God's Word. In his greatest spiritual battle prior to the cross, Christ stood his ground against the Devil by quoting three verses from Deuteronomy (Matt. 4:1–11).

Second, we must view the Bible in light of Jesus. Ask: "How does this point to Jesus? How does this prepare the way for Jesus? How did Jesus live this out? How will Jesus help me live this out?"

In one brilliant paragraph, Jesus established the one sure foundation we all need for Christian maturity: the authority of Scripture and his own authority as the Christ. They are not opposed. If you want to find Christ, you must run to the Bible. There are no shortcuts.

5

Jesus's Submission to Holy Scripture

JOHN 10:35-36

Ian Hamilton

When I was studying theology at the University of Edinburgh in the 1970s, my controversies in class were not with fellow evangelicals but with my professors, most of whom had swallowed what were called "the assured results of modern scholarship." They took pleasure in debunking the historic teaching of the church that the Bible is God's infallible Word. I remember one of my teachers saying that he thought people like me had died with Noah. He found it wryly amusing that I believed the Bible to be God's living, error-free Word.

Today, however, truths that once belonged to the essence and public identity of evangelicalism are being questioned and abandoned. Far from the Bible being seen as perspicuous and accessible to all, we are increasingly told that only experts on the Ancient Near East, literary forms, reader-response theory, or the sociology of cultures can meaningfully interpret the Bible and help us understand its "core truths" and "inherent significance." The conviction of the church throughout the ages that the Bible is not only accessible to all Christians but can be understood by all Christians is considered passé. Without the expertise of the academy, we are told, the "ordinary" Christian cannot hope to make sense of a document at least two millennia removed, culturally as well as historically, from the present day.

This view, however, fails to take account of one important fact: the Bible is no ordinary ancient text; it is the living Word of the living God. Benjamin B. Warfield, the great Princeton biblical theologian, well understood this. In answer to the question, "What is Christianity?" Warfield is reputed to have replied that it is "unembarrassed supernaturalism."[1] Warfield was stating the fundamental reality of the Christian faith. Christianity is not the product of the fertile thinking of mere men; it is the revelation in time and space of the triune God.

Just as no one can say that Jesus is Lord except by the Holy Spirit, so no one can truly understand the Bible and affirm its absolute truthfulness except by the Spirit. This conviction has been embedded in the life and doctrine of evangelical Christianity since the time of the sixteenth-century Reformation. The Westminster Confession of Faith beautifully and succinctly expresses this core gospel conviction:

> The authority of the Holy Scripture, for which it ought to be believed, and obeyed, depends not upon the testimony of any man, or Church; but wholly upon God (who is truth itself) the author thereof: and therefore it is to be received, because it is the Word of God.
>
> We may be moved and induced by the testimony of the Church to an high and reverent esteem of the Holy Scripture. And the heavenliness of the matter, the efficacy of the doctrine, the majesty of the style, the consent of all the parts, the scope of the whole (which is, to give all glory to God), the full discovery it makes of the only way of man's salvation, the many other incomparable excellencies, and the entire perfection thereof, are arguments whereby it does abundantly evidence itself to be the Word of God: *yet notwithstanding, our full persuasion and assurance of the infallible truth and divine authority thereof, is from the inward work of the Holy Spirit bearing witness by and with the Word in our hearts.*[2]

It would be a huge mistake to think that we have "done our job" once we have shown, incontrovertibly, that Jesus believed the absolute infallible

---

[1] In his inaugural address as professor of didactic and polemic theology in 1921, following Warfield's death, Casper Wistar Hodge said, "The old theology [meaning Princeton's theology] . . . is characterised by definiteness. . . . The distinctive mark of the old theology, then, is supernaturalism and the realisation of the infinitude and transcendence of God, in opposition to the paganism which finds God only in the world." *Princeton and the Work of the Christian Ministry*, ed. James M. Garretson (Edinburgh: Banner of Truth, 2012), 2:592–93.

[2] Westminster Confession of Faith (Edinburgh: Free Church of Scotland, 1955), 1.4, 5 (emphasis added).

authority of God's Word and lived under that authority. Without the *internum testimonium Spiritus Sancti* ("the inward witness of the Holy Spirit"), no one can be savingly or sanctifyingly affected by this truth.

How does anyone come to believe what Holy Scripture reveals about anything? It is only by the ministry of the Holy Spirit. The New Testament could not be clearer about this (1 Cor. 2:12–14). It was this conviction that led John Calvin to write, "As God alone is a fit witness of himself in his word, so also the word will not find acceptance in men's hearts before it is sealed by the inward testimony of the Spirit."[3] Calvin was concerned that we not subject God to our judgments: "God alone is a fit witness of himself in his word," he said. For Calvin, as for the New Testament writers before him, God's Word may "win reverence for itself by its own majesty," but "it seriously affects us only when it is sealed upon our hearts through the Spirit."[4]

This undeniable biblical truth must shape and influence how we go about seeking to persuade men and women regarding the infallibility of Holy Scripture. A blind man does not first need glasses to see through; he needs new eyes to see with. Only the regenerating ministry of the Holy Spirit can open our eyes to the inherent, native truthfulness and authority of God's written Word. Once our sin-blinded minds are renewed, we heartily embrace truths that once were either dark or mysterious (such as the Holy Trinity) or simply unbelievable (such as the infallibility of Holy Scripture). Thus, Calvin writes, "We seek no proofs, no marks of genuineness upon which our judgment may lean; but we subject our judgment and wit to it as to a thing far beyond any guesswork!"[5] For Calvin, believing and embracing the absolute, incontrovertible truthfulness and authority of God's Word is a matter of faith, which God gives to his elect.[6] As Calvin concludes his brief but deeply insightful focus on the *internum testimonium Spiritus Sancti*, he says: "Those who wish to prove to unbelievers that Scripture is the word of God are acting foolishly, for only by faith can this be known. Augustine therefore justly warns that godliness and peace of mind ought to come first if a man is to understand anything of such great matters."[7]

But how does this actually work? What does the Spirit do to persuade

---

[3] John Calvin, *Institutes of the Christian Religion*, ed. John T. McNeill, trans. Ford Lewis Battles, Library of Christian Classics, vols. 20–21 (Philadelphia: Westminster, 1960), 1.7.4.
[4] Ibid., 1.7.5.
[5] Ibid.
[6] Ibid.
[7] Ibid., 1.8.13.

us that Scripture truly is God's infallible word? The answer is not that the Spirit gives us revelation in addition to what is in Scripture, but that he awakens us, as from the dead, to see and taste the divine reality of God in Scripture, which authenticates it as God's own Word. Calvin says, "Our Heavenly Father, revealing his majesty [in Scripture], lifts reverence for Scripture beyond the realm of controversy."[8] This is the key for Calvin: the witness of God to Scripture is the immediate, unassailable, life-giving revelation to the mind of the majesty of God manifest in the Scriptures themselves.

Here's the way J. I. Packer puts it:

> The internal witness of the Spirit in John Calvin is a work of enlightenment whereby, through the medium of verbal testimony, the blind eyes of the spirit are opened, and divine realities come to be recognized and embraced for what they are. This recognition, Calvin says, is as immediate and unanalysable as the perceiving of a color, or a taste, by physical sense—an event about which no more can be said than that when appropriate stimuli were present it happened, and when it happened we knew it had happened.[9]

This "unembarrassed supernaturalism" was provocatively expressed by John Owen: "He that would utterly separate the Spirit from the word had as good burn his Bible. The bare letter of the New Testament will no more ingenerate faith and obedience in the souls of men . . . than the letter of the Old Testament doth so at this day among the Jews, 2 Cor. iii.6, 8."[10] Owen was saying no more than the apostle Paul said when he wrote, "The natural person does not accept the things of the Spirit of God, for they are folly to him, and he is not able to understand them because they are spiritually discerned" (1 Cor. 2:14). The blindness of the natural man and woman to spiritual truth—whether that truth be the incarnation of God's eternal Son, his virginal conception, his miraculous deeds, his sin-bearing and sin-atoning death, his bodily resurrection, his ascension into heaven, his personal and visible future return, or the infallible and perfectly authoritative character of God's Word—should never surprise us.

We are now in a position to consider Jesus's personal submission to the truthfulness and authority of God's Word.

---

[8] Ibid.

[9] J. I. Packer, "Calvin the Theologian," in *John Calvin*, ed. G. E. Duffield (Abingdon: Sutton Courtenay, 1966), 166.

[10] John Owen, *The Works of John Owen* (London: Banner of Truth, 1965), 3:192–93.

Jesus's View of Scripture

If any one truth dominated and shaped the earthly life of our Lord Jesus Christ, it was the absolute, inviolable, incontrovertible authority of Holy Scripture. For Jesus, it was enough simply to say, "It is written . . ." He understood Scripture to be nothing less than God's Word of self-revelation. Because it was breathed out by God, it is flawless, beyond all contradiction, and to be obeyed immediately, not hesitatingly; absolutely, not selectively.

Herman Bavinck helpfully sums up Jesus's attitude to the Old Testament Scriptures.[11] Jesus and his apostles never took a critical position toward the Old Testament, but accepted its teaching without any reservation or qualification—and not just its religious-ethical teaching! Jesus attributed Isaiah 6 to Isaiah (Matt. 13:14); Psalm 110 to David (Matt. 22:44); the prophecy cited in Matthew 24:15 to Daniel; and the law to Moses (John 5:46). He repeatedly cited and unconditionally believed the historical narratives of the Old Testament: the creation of human beings (Matt. 19:4–5), Abel's murder (Matt. 23:35), the flood (Matt. 24:37–39), the history of the Patriarchs (Matt. 22:32; John 8:56), the destruction of Sodom (Matt. 11:23; Luke 17:28–33), the burning bush (Luke 20:37), the serpent in the wilderness (John 3:14), the manna (John 6:32), the histories of Elijah and Naaman (Luke 4:25–27), and the story of Jonah (Matt. 12:39–41). To Jesus, the absolute authority of Scripture embraced every single word, including dots and iotas (Matt. 5:18; Luke 16:17; John 10:35; Gal. 3:16).

Of particular significance is Jesus's unequivocal statement, "Scripture cannot be broken" (John 10:34–35). In this passage, Jesus is quoting from Psalm 82. We do not need to make a final judgment as to whom these "gods" were; they may have been Israel's judges, angelic powers, or Israel at the time of the giving of the law.[12] What is abundantly clear is that the words "Scripture cannot be broken" mean, writes D. A. Carson, "that the Scripture cannot be annulled or set aside or proved false (cf. Mark 7:13). Conceptually, [this statement] complements 'your law': It is reprehensible [Carson is drawing out the substance of Jesus's teaching] to set aside the authority of Scripture, the Scripture whose authority you yourselves accept, just because the text I have cited seems inconvenient to you at the moment."[13]

That is, not only is the Bible's historical record accurate, but in prophecy, morality, theology, and every other teaching, the Scriptures cannot be

---

[11] Herman Bavinck, *Reformed Dogmatics*, 4 vols., ed. John Bolt, trans J. Vriend (Grand Rapids, MI: Baker Academic, 2003–2008), 1.395ff.
[12] See the extended discussion in D. A. Carson, *The Gospel According to John* (Leicester, UK: Inter-Varsity, and Grand Rapids, MI: Eerdmans, 1991), 397–99.
[13] Ibid., 399.

contradicted or confounded. In Luke 24:25–27, Jesus rebuked his disciples for not believing all that "the prophets" had spoken (which he equated with "all the Scriptures"). So, in Jesus's view, all Scripture is trustworthy and should be believed.

Jesus constantly quoted Scripture as a basis for his own teaching about how to live, such as church discipline (Matt. 18:16), marriage (Matt. 19:3–9), God's requirements for eternal life (Matt. 19:16–19), and the greatest commandment (Matt. 22:37–39).

Furthermore, he used the Old Testament to justify cleansing the temple (Matt. 21:12–17) and picking grain on the Sabbath (Luke 6:3–4). He relied on Scripture, the sword of the Spirit (Eph. 6:17), to resist the temptations of Satan (Matt. 4:1–11). He stated unambiguously that the Old Testament supersedes all man-made traditions and ideas. No standard is higher than Scripture for what we are to believe and obey (Matt. 15:1–9; Mark 7:5–13).

There is no evidence that Jesus picked and chose some parts of the Old Testament, such as the so-called theological, moral, or religious portions, and rejected others. For him, all the Scriptures were trustworthy and authoritative, down to the last letter (Matt. 5:18).

In this regard, we never find Jesus appealing to a higher authority to bring out some "hidden meaning" of Scripture. Jesus indicates that the Scriptures are essentially perspicuous (clear for the nonscholar to understand). Eleven times the Gospel writers record his saying, "Have you not read . . . ?" and thirty times he defends his teaching by saying, "It is written . . ." He rebukes his listeners for not understanding and believing what the text plainly says.

It has often been maintained that in his Sermon on the Mount, Jesus was criticizing the Old Testament and replacing it with his own authority. Nothing could be further from the truth. In Matthew 5:17–20, Jesus introduces his teaching with a categorical announcement that he has come not to abolish the law but to fulfill it. His language is unambiguous and his intent is plain to see. This is made unmistakably clear in what follows. The series of contrasts does not juxtapose Jesus's teaching with that of the Old Testament law, but Jesus's teaching with that of the Pharisees' twisted and corrupt teaching of God's law.[14]

From 5:21, Jesus illustrates his foundational and personal commitment

---

[14] See the excellent discussions in D. A. Carson, *The Sermon on the Mount* (Carlisle, Cumbria, UK: Paternoster, 1998); D. Martyn Lloyd-Jones, *The Sermon on the Mount* (London: Inter-Varsity, 1959); Herman Ridderbos, *Matthew*, Bible Student's Commentary (Grand Rapids, MI: Zondervan, 1987), 97–157; John Stott, *Christian Counter-Culture* (Leicester, UK: Inter-Varsity, 1978).

to God's law (cf. v. 17). Far from abolishing God's moral instruction, Jesus has come to recover it, restore it, and put his personal stamp of approval on it. Here is the "righteousness" that exceeds that of the scribes and Pharisees (v. 20). Here is God's law at its purest and most searching.

Isaiah 50:4

Jesus's submission to the Scriptures was complete, without hesitation, disputation, or compromise. He knew the Scriptures to be the Word of God, and because God cannot lie, his Word cannot be broken or annulled. There is, however, a question that is both generally interesting and theologically significant: How did Jesus come to embrace the absolute authority of God's Word and willingly allow it to shape and style his whole life? If his humanity was a true humanity and he truly "became flesh," we have to take seriously the ordinary mental and psychological processes by which any human being learns anything. We must guard against thinking that Jesus short-circuited the normal intellectual process of maturation. Luke tells us that Jesus "increased in wisdom" (2:52). The writer of Hebrews tells us that he "learned obedience" (Heb. 5:8).

It is with this background that we can begin to understand Isaiah 50:4: "The Lord God has given me the tongue of those who are taught, that I may know how to sustain with a word him who is weary. Morning by morning he awakens; he awakens my ear to hear as those who are taught." Jesus's understanding of the content of Scripture, and the inherent authority embedded in the content of Scripture, did not come to him all at once. His knowledge of God's Word was not supernaturally implanted in his DNA in the womb of the Virgin Mary. If it were, his humanity would not be our humanity.

In his outstanding commentary *The Prophecy of Isaiah*, Alec Motyer writes: "He (the Lord's Servant) was not endowed with an instant gift, *an instructed tongue*, but was subjected to the training procedures appropriate to all discipleship—concentration on the word of the Lord. . . . The sharpened sword and the polished arrow (49:2) did not happen automatically or all at once. They were the products of prolonged attention, defined here as the discipleship of the *morning by morning* appointment with God."[15] Our Lord Jesus's submission to the truthfulness and authority of Holy Scripture came in the context of personal discipleship. We need the ministry of the Holy Spirit to persuade us inwardly of the inerrancy of Scripture, but ordi-

---

[15] J. A. Motyer, *The Prophecy of Isaiah* (Leicester, UK: Inter-Varsity, 1993), 399.

narily he does this in the context of discipleship. As our ears are opened to "hear" the things of God, God is pleased to seal to our hearts and minds the divine truthfulness and infallible character of his Word.

Two facts stand out:

1. Our Lord's human nature was perfectly holy. He was untainted by Adam's sinful nature. Adam was not his head, and his nature was not morally twisted in any way. God's Word did not confront any semblance of fallenness in Jesus. As he first heard and then read God's Word, Jesus would have immediately sensed its inherent, native, Holy Spirit-inspired God-breathedness, and received it for what it was, the Word of God. When we hear and read God's Word, we are natively dull to its authority and truth. We all need God to open our eyes, unstop our ears, and enable us spiritually to discern the truthfulness and feel the authority of his Word. But Jesus was "holy, harmless, undefiled" (Heb. 7:26, KJV). It was natural for Jesus to receive God's Word and to embrace its unqualified authority.

2. Our Lord's human nature was nonetheless a true human nature.[16] It was a nature capable of maturation and growth. He "increased . . . in favor with God and man" (Luke 2:52). His knowledge of Scripture was therefore an acquired knowledge. It was a developed knowledge. Just as Jesus's holiness was an incremental holiness (not from the less holy to the more holy, but from the perfect holiness of a one-year-old to the perfect holiness of a thirty-year-old), so his knowledge of Scripture was an incremental knowledge. We surely know that "morning by morning," our Lord applied himself diligently, willingly hearing and receiving God's Word. He was an ever-ready student of the Scriptures. He had an unstained landing ground for Scripture in his mind and heart, unlike us. But he did not circumvent the ordinary intellectual process of learning as he continually submitted himself to the authority of God's Word.

These facts have much to say to us. The ministry of the Holy Spirit, convincing us of the absolute truthfulness and authority of Holy Scripture, does not take effect ordinarily in our lives apart from diligent and obedient mental application. God ordinarily uses means to bring to effect his saving and sanctifying purposes for our lives.

As the Son of Man, Jesus set us an example in his complete trust in Scripture's reliability and in his submission to its supreme authority. His promise that the Holy Spirit would lead his apostles into the truth (John

---

[16] In the self-emptying of his incarnation, God the Son voluntarily and temporarily laid aside the independent use of his divine attributes (cf. Phil. 2:7). Though he took on flesh (meaning, he became human), at no point did he ever cease to be God.

16:13) and the apostles' declaration that they wrote under divine inspiration (see 2 Pet. 3:16) show that Jesus's view of the Old Testament also applies to the New Testament. Are you following his example?

Theological Implications

First, "Dogmatically, to Jesus and the apostles the OT is the foundation of doctrine, the source of solutions, the end of all argument."[17] Jesus's oft-repeated statement, "It is written . . . ," was sufficient to support everything he said. The Old Testament was God's absolutely authoritative Word, the last word in any and every debate.

Second, this conviction was not novel to Jesus. The scribes and Pharisees believed in the inerrancy and absolute authority of Holy Scripture. They prided themselves on practicing the very letter of the law to its every jot and tittle. Where, then, did they differ from Jesus? It was principally in two areas. First, they were selective in their obedience to God's Word (Matt. 23:23–24). Second, their obedience was outward, not inward (vv. 25–28). It was this hypocrisy that Jesus so witheringly exposed in the Sermon on the Mount. In his sermon, as noted above, Jesus was not setting himself against the old covenant Scriptures. He was not enunciating a new law. He was recovering the true spirituality of God's law, pressing on his hearers the foundational truth of biblical religion that God looks on the heart. Where belief in the infallibility of Holy Scripture does not lead to a life of godliness and a desire for God's glory, the spirit of Pharisaism reigns.

Third, "Inspiration is a dogma, like the dogma of the Trinity, the incarnation, etc., which Christians accept, not because they understand the truth of it but because God so attests it. It is not a scientific pronouncement but a confession of faith. In the case of inspiration, as in the case of every other dogma, the question is not in the first place how much can I and may I confess without coming into conflict with science, but what is the witness of God and what, accordingly, is the pronouncement of the Christian faith?"[18] On this foundational presupposition, the Christian faith rests secure. Whereas science by its very nature is an evolutionary discipline, "the word of our God will stand forever" (Isa. 40:8).

Fourth, the battle for the Bible is first an ethical battle.[19] Just as the world is hostile to Jesus, who he is, and what he has done, so it is also hostile to Scripture (1 Cor. 2:12–14). People who engage in criticism of the

---

[17] Bavinck, *Reformed Dogmatics*, 1.395.
[18] Ibid., 1.436.
[19] Ibid., 1.429.

Bible assume that "simple believers" don't know or understand the objections of science (so called) to the inspiration of the Bible. This is nonsense. We know many of the objections. We cannot answer all of the objections; how could we? There are difficulties in the Bible we cannot and dare not ignore. But they are no barrier to faith in the wholly organic and inerrant character of God's written Word, any more than they are to faith in the Holy Trinity and the incarnation of the eternal Son of God!

For Jesus, "It is written . . ." signaled the divine, unimpeachable authority of Scripture.

Conclusion

There is one fundamental, foundational reason why Christians have a high view of Scripture. We hold to the absolute truthfulness of Scripture in all its human diversity because Jesus did. Christians are committed inerrantists first and foremost out of devotion to their Lord and Savior, Jesus Christ, the Son of God made flesh for us and for our salvation. Scripture testifies to its own inerrancy, and Jesus places his personal imprimatur on this self-testimony.

What Paul writes in 2 Timothy 3:16–17 exactly reflects the thinking and teaching of Jesus. It is because "all Scripture is breathed out by God" that it "cannot be broken" (John 10:35). How could it be otherwise? No matter how hard I try, my words reflect my nature. My nature is flawed. I am a forgiven sinner, but till the day I die, I am yet a sinner. But God's nature is absolutely pure, without flaw. He can no more speak a lie than I can climb to the sun on a rope of ice. Who God is guarantees that everything he speaks is incontrovertibly true. If all Scripture is God-breathed, as it declares itself to be, then it cannot but be all true. None of this means there will not be difficulties to unravel, or even internal conflicts that at present seem impossible to reconcile. How could it be otherwise?

Calvin captures the holy reverence with which Jesus treated God's written Word: "We owe to Scripture the same reverence as we owe to God, since it has its only source in Him and has nothing of human origin mixed with it."[20]

Paul's concluding doxology to his exposition of the "gospel of God" (Rom. 1:1) in Romans 11:33–36 expresses the testimony of all Christians as they reflect on God's revelation of himself and his way of salvation in

---

[20] John Calvin, *Calvin's Commentaries: The Second Epistle of Paul the Apostle to the Corinthians and the Epistles to Timothy, Titus and Philemon*, ed. D. W. and T. F. Torrance (Edinburgh: St. Andrew Press, 1964), 330 (2 Tim. 3:16).

the pages of Holy Scripture: "Oh, the depth of the riches and wisdom and knowledge of God! How unsearchable are his judgments and how inscrutable his ways! For who has known the mind of the Lord, or who has been his counselor? Or who has given a gift to him that he might be repaid? For from him and through him and to him are all things. To him be glory forever. Amen."

6

The Nature, Benefits, and Results of Scripture

2 TIMOTHY 3:16-17

J. Ligon Duncan III

It's my privilege to serve an institution, Reformed Theological Seminary, that is dedicated to preparing pastors, church planters, and missionaries for the work of the gospel for the rest of their lives. Every year we send people out, hundreds at a time, into the service of God's people in the work of evangelism and discipleship, and they have nothing with which to face this challenge but the Word of God. So it's my first responsibility as chancellor of this seminary to wake up in the morning and believe that the Bible *is* the Word of God, because the world is not going to help my students believe this when they're out pastoring, serving on the mission field, or doing evangelism, discipleship, or campus ministry. I and the faculty have to make sure that we pour everything we can into these brothers so that they stand fast on the Word of God.

Reformed Theological Seminary was actually started fifty years ago for this very purpose. The elders of First Presbyterian Church in Jackson,

Mississippi, offered to endow a chair of theology at a major Presbyterian seminary *if* the seminary would put a man in that chair who believed in inerrancy. The president of that institution scoffed at the elders and said that his institution would not be bought by a bunch of fundamentalists. They said: "That's fine, we'll put the money in the bank. If you change your mind, give us a call." Four years later, that money was used to start Reformed Theological Seminary, which was committed to the inerrancy of Scripture, the doctrines of grace, and the Great Commission. One of the pillars on which RTS was founded was biblical inerrancy.

The world, with its toxic unbelief, assaults your soul in a couple of ways. First, it causes you to lose confidence in the Word of God, and I've seen that happen to friends over the years. But it can also cause you to lose your delight in the God of the Word, and I think I've seen more brothers from conservative, Bible-believing backgrounds fall away from a belief in a high view of Scripture because of that latter assault than the former. You see, if you start believing that there's something out there that is better than the God of this Word and better than the promises that he makes to you, then you're just one step away from walking away from the Word.

Paul addresses this danger in 2 Timothy 3:14–17. He writes:

> But as for you, continue in what you have learned and have firmly believed, knowing from whom you learned it and how from childhood you have been acquainted with the sacred writings, which are able to make you wise for salvation through faith in Christ Jesus. All Scripture is breathed out by God and profitable for teaching, for reproof, for correction, and for training in righteousness, that the man of God may be complete, equipped for every good work.

I want to briefly outline this passage, then focus in on verses 16 and 17, taking in one little phrase from the end of verse 15 as well.

First, Paul says, "But as for you, continue in what you have learned" (v. 14a). Paul tells Timothy: "Keep on believing, Timothy. What you've been grounded in is true and right and good. Don't stop believing it."

Second, Paul adds, "knowing from whom you learned it" (v. 14b). In other words, he tells Timothy: "Remember who taught you the Scriptures. You learned them on your mother's and your grandmother's knees!" (cf. 2 Tim. 1:5). At the Together for the Gospel Conference in 2014, Mark Dever allowed me to have a panel on biblical inerrancy, and I asked John Piper, "John, why do you believe in biblical inerrancy?" Now this is a man with a doctoral degree from the University of Munich, a man who has studied the New Testament at the highest level. Yet John immediately answered, "Because my mama told me to!" That was a good answer, one that echoed Paul! Paul is saying to Timothy: "Remember, you learned this from your mama and your grandmama. Remember who taught you this." He's reminding him that people who cared about his soul taught him to believe the Word of God.

Third, the apostle says, "From childhood you have been acquainted with the sacred writings" (v. 15a). Paul is speaking here about Timothy's Hebrew Bible, the Old Testament. The New Testament didn't exist when Timothy was growing up. He is just getting the book of 2 Timothy! Paul says to Timothy, "You've known that Bible." By the way, at the end of that phrase, we have a wonderful two-word description of the Bible's view of itself: "sacred writings." That's a good biblical argument for the inerrancy of Scripture. That view is echoed in the words on the covers of most of our Bibles: "Holy Bible."

Fourth, Paul tells Timothy that the sacred writings "are able to make you wise for salvation through faith in Christ Jesus" (v. 15b). Paul is saying that Timothy's Hebrew Bible teaches him the way of salvation, which is through Jesus Christ. That is, Timothy's Hebrew Bible preaches salvation by grace alone through faith alone in Christ alone.

Fifth, Paul asserts, "All Scripture is breathed out by God" (v. 16a). Here, Paul is telling Timothy—and us—what Scripture is.

Sixth, the apostle says that Scripture is "profitable for teaching, for reproof, for correction, and for training in righteousness" (v. 16b). That's what Scripture is for.

Seventh, Paul says Scripture is useful to the end "that the man of God may be complete, equipped for every good work" (v. 17). That's what Scripture does.

So Paul reminds Timothy what the Bible is, what it's for, and what it does because he is exhorting him to live by the Book and minister by the Book. And just as the Psalms never tell us to praise God without telling us why we ought to do that, so Paul doesn't just say to Timothy, "Live by the Book and minister by the Book." He tells Timothy why: he learned it from his godly grandmother and mother, who cared for his soul; it is the God-breathed Word, all of it; it is for reproof, correction, training in righteousness, and teaching; and finally, the eyes of heaven are upon him. We see this if we peek into chapter 4, where Paul says, "I charge you in the presence of God and of Christ Jesus, who is to judge the living and the dead, and by his appearing and his kingdom" (v. 1). That's the crowd that is looking on, the audience that surrounds Timothy as he ministers the Word, and one day he will have to give an account. For all those reasons, Timothy needs to live by the Book and minister by the Book.

It's important to note that Paul is not telling Timothy something about the Bible that Timothy doesn't already know. Timothy believes what Paul is telling him about the Bible, as Alistair Begg makes clear in the next chapter. So why is Paul telling Timothy this? The answer is, I think, at least twofold. First, he is encouraging Timothy and reminding him of a truth that is absolutely vital for a minister to know if he is to go on expounding Scripture, Lord's Day after Lord's Day, year after year, faithfully trusting God to do his work through the Word. Timothy needs to be reminded of that. He's a young man starting out in his ministry. He is not where Paul is. Paul can see the finish line from where he's standing. Second, Timothy needs to understand how this truth applies to both his life and ministry, and so, in verses 14 and 15, Paul preapplies the truth about the Bible that he expounds in verses 16 and 17 to Timothy's life. Then, in 2 Timothy 4:1 and following, he applies it to his preaching.

I am confident that most of the shepherds of God's people who are reading these words are like Timothy—they know these things about the Bible. Why, then, am I writing about 2 Timothy 3:16–17? For the same reasons Paul wrote these things to Timothy. The world that you inhabit is not helping you believe the truth of 2 Timothy 3:16–17. The air that you breathe is toxic. Everywhere you turn, there are assaults on the integrity, authority, infallibility, and inerrancy of Scripture, both in its theology and in its ethics. This world is not helping you believe these things, and you need to be encouraged from God's Word about God's Word for your life and your ministry.

Even more devastating, we live in a world where, for more than two hundred years, the primary assault on the Word of God has come from people who call themselves Christians. Just a few years ago, the vice moderator of the Presbyterian Church in the United States of America announced that Scripture is only a reference point to the Word of God. It is not the Word of God with a capital "W." He went on to say, "*Sola Scriptura* is dead." Benjamin B. Warfield, speaking about 125 years ago, said:

> Wherever five advanced thinkers assemble, at least six theories as to inspiration are likely to be ventilated. They differ in every conceivable point or in every conceivable point save one. They agree that inspiration is less pervasive and less determinative than has heretofore been

thought, or than is still thought in less enlightened circles. They agree that there is less of the truth of God and more of the error of man in the Bible than Christians have been wont to believe. They agree accordingly that the teaching of the Bible may be, in this, that, or the other—here, there, or elsewhere—safely neglected or openly repudiated.[1]

This is why it's so important for us to hear what Paul says about the Bible in this passage. In the end, all of us have to decide whether we stand with Paul or with our contemporaries, with Moses or our contemporaries, and, ultimately, with Jesus or our contemporaries—because what Paul is saying here he has received from Jesus. He's not telling us anything that Jesus himself has not said. He's saying to Timothy what Jesus said about the Scriptures.

As we focus in on verses 16–17, I want to remind you of the three points Paul makes in these verses: what the Bible is, what the Bible is for, and what the Bible does. This is Paul's exhortation: "Timothy and faithful shepherds, live by the Book, because it comes right out of God's mouth, because it is the most practical Book in this world, and because it tells you how to live with God."

What the Bible Is

First, Paul speaks about the nature, qualities, and usefulness of Holy Scripture. Regarding the nature of Scripture, in three Greek words, he articulates the doctrine of plenary, verbal inspiration: *pasa graphe theopneustos*, or "All Scripture is breathed out by God." That itself is an argument for the inspiration of Scripture. Let's look at each of these words.

First, *pasa*, which can be translated as "all" or "every." If we take it as "all," it refers to the Bible as a whole (and *graphe* is used in that sense in the New Testament). If we take it as "every," then it refers to the totality of Scripture in its discrete parts. But either way, when Paul says "All Scripture is breathed out by God," he makes it clear that no theory of partial or selective inspiration can measure up to what he is asserting about the Word of God. There have always been people who have said, "Oh, I believe the Bible, but I don't believe Adam and Eve were specially created by God," or, "I believe the Bible, but I don't believe there was a talking snake; that's an etiological myth," or "I believe the Bible, but I don't believe Jonah was swallowed by a big fish." They affirm that they can learn scriptural truth from these stories, but they don't believe these particular stories.

---

[1] Benjamin B. Warfield, "The Inspiration of the Bible," in *The Bibliotheca Sacra*, vol. 51, ed. G. Frederick Wright and Z. Swift Holbrook (Oberlin, OH: E. J. Goodrich, 1894), 614.

There are all sorts of arguments against the Bible like this today: "Well, the Bible borrows from pagan cosmologies, and those cosmologies are wrong, so the Bible contains wrong cosmologies," or, "The Bible makes historical mistakes about geography and surrounding cultures," or, "The Bible shows evidence of different and competing theologies." Well, here's the apostle Paul saying: "No, let me explain something. All Scripture is God-breathed!" The genealogies in Genesis or Chronicles are God-breathed. Those mind-numbingly detailed laws in Leviticus are God-breathed. Those depressing stories in Judges are God-breathed. So inspiration is *plenary*; that means *all* Scripture is God-breathed, not just John 3:16.

Second, *graphe*, which means "inspired writings" or "Scripture." What is breathed out by God? Scripture! Paul isn't talking about the act of the Holy Spirit in carrying along the writers of Scripture; he is talking about the product. He is saying that Scripture is objectively inspired. In other words, Paul is not saying that the Bible is inspired because it inspires us; that's a subjective theory of inspiration. He is saying that the Bible is objectively inspired—the words themselves are the product of inspiration.

When I was a student at the University of Edinburgh, the Student Theological Society held a debate between Nigel Cameron, who was then at Rutherford House and who was a believer in biblical inerrancy, and Graeme Auld, who was a professor of Old Testament and who was not a believer in biblical inerrancy. During the debate, the moderator asked them to give their definitions of inspiration, and Auld said, "Well, I believe the Bible is inspired in that it inspires me."

When he heard that, Cameron blurted out, "Oh, you're a Coleridgean!"

Auld replied, "Pardon me?"

So Cameron said: "You're a Coleridgean! Samuel Taylor Coleridge articulated that discredited view of inspiration in the nineteenth century! Everyone's known it's wrong since then!"

The assertion that the Bible must be inspired because it inspires us constitutes a subjective view of inspiration. But Paul says that which is God-breathed is *graphe*, or Scripture. In the same way, he speaks in 2 Corinthians 3:14 about the reading of the old covenant. That covenant is something that can be read. So Paul isn't talking about the ideas; he is not articulating a dynamic view of inspiration. He is giving a *verbal* view of inspiration; the *words* are inspired.

Third, *theopneustos*, which means "breathed out by God" or "God-breathed." God is the Author and Source of Scripture. Behind this, I think, are the words of Jesus quoting Moses. Do you remember, when Jesus is in the wilderness and Satan tempts him, how Jesus replies with the words of Moses from Deuteronomy 8, saying, "Man shall not live by bread alone, but by every word that comes from the mouth of God" (Matt. 4:4)? With one word, *theopneustos*, Paul echoes that affirmation of Jesus. All Scripture is breathed out of the mouth of God. Paul is not giving a new theory of inspiration; he's articulating Jesus's view of the Bible. Just as in creation God spoke the world into being, so by his Word he spoke redemption and his redeemed people, his church, into being. By his Word he creates and redeems. It's God-breathed.

Why does Paul tell Timothy this? Because he's about to tell Timothy to base his life and his ministry on this Word, so Timothy must believe what this Word is. In the same way, when those of you who are ministers of the gospel stand up to preach the Word of God every Lord's Day, you are speaking a word above all earthly powers. If you preach it faithfully, if you expound it in accordance with its own meaning and significance, you have become the mouthpiece of the living God to facilitate an engagement between him and his people. The Word of God preaches a message through you about God, grace, and godliness to his people. Paul wants Timothy to have confidence in the Word of God, because sometimes it can seem so weak. It's certainly weak in the eyes of the world. The country is going crazy. The culture is spiraling down. The world is off its rocker. What are you going to do, preacher? "I don't know. I suppose I'll get up on Sunday morning and preach from John." Yes! That is the right answer, because the Bible is the Word of God, and it's living, active, powerful, and sharper than any two-edged sword (Heb. 4:12), and it's the very word from the mouth of God. That's what the Bible is.

By articulating plenary, verbal inspiration, Paul has just given us the reason why we believe in inerrancy. Understand this: we believe that the Bible is inerrant because we believe that the Bible is inspired, not the other way around. In other words, if you understand what the Bible is, you understand its quality of perfection. We affirm that its total truthfulness is entailed in what it is. It is from the mouth of God, who cannot lie, so it cannot lie! It is totally true. Because we believe it is inspired, because we believe it is God-breathed, we believe that it is inerrant.

As you look at the doctrine of Scripture, it is vital that you pay attention to what the Bible says about revelation and about inspiration; it is essential to pay attention to the claims of the Bible about itself. I have seen many, many evangelical scholars start out with a high view of Scripture, but then they study the so-called phenomena of Scripture and lose their confidence in the Word of God. When that happens, you can bet that they have tried to construct a doctrine of Scripture from their own provisional answers to the phenomena of Scripture and have not adequately taken into consideration what the Bible says about itself in regard to revelation and inspiration. You cannot learn what the Bible is, you cannot form a correct doctrine of Scripture, without paying attention to the claims of Scripture. So as you wrestle with the doctrine of Scripture, begin with its claims about revelation and inspiration, then deal with the phenomena of Scripture. Do not begin with the phenomena of Scripture and then try and read its claims and what it teaches about revelation and inspiration in light of your provisional answer to the phenomena. If you do, you will become a liberal.

What the Bible Is For

In 2 Timothy 3:16b, Paul tells us that the Bible is "profitable"—that is, "useful" or "beneficial"—"for teaching, for reproof, for correction, and for training in righteousness." Needless to say, Paul is making a huge claim about the Bible here. He is not merely saying that it is relevant. He is saying that it is profitable, and relevant and profitable are two very different claims. Saying that Scripture is relevant doesn't claim too much for the Bible; it doesn't claim enough. If you were to say to me, "You know, gasoline is relevant to the running of my automobile's engine," I am not going to think that you are brilliant! Of course gasoline is relevant to the running of your car's engine! It's not just relevant; it's essential!

In the same way, the Bible is not just relevant; it is much more. The Bible that we, as ministers of the gospel, pick up to preach from on Sunday morning is already more than relevant. It is profitable. And it is profitable, Paul says, for four things. First, it is profitable for teaching, that is, for imparting the truth of God. Second, it is profitable for reproof, that is, for giving warning against errors of belief and behavior. Third, it is profitable for correction, that is, for redirection. This is the positive side of warning. You don't want to only say to an erring brother, "That's wrong, don't do that." You want him to believe what's true and to live in the way that God calls him to live. You want to win your brother back. So correction is that redirection that goes on when you're challenging unbelief or faulty behavior.

Finally, the Word of God is profitable for training in righteousness, that is, for discipling and preparing the believer in godliness. In 1 Timothy 1:5, Paul describes the goal of his ministry: "The aim of our charge is love that issues from a pure heart and a good conscience and a sincere faith." In that context, he is criticizing false teachers. And what does he say that their teaching leads to? Endless speculations (v. 4). But what does true teaching lead to? Love from a pure heart, a good conscience, and a sincere faith. This is why we teach, and the Bible is profitable for this purpose! We want to see believers who live out the truth of the Word in love, and the Word is profitable to do that.

So the Bible is the most profitable, most useful, most beneficial Book in the world. That's why the psalmist in Psalm 119 keeps singing about why he loves it so much! "How I love your law, O Lord! It teaches me how to live and shows me who you are! It sends me on the way of life. I love your Word!" That's what Paul is saying to Timothy: "The Bible is inspired; it's God-breathed. The Bible is profitable; it's useful and beneficial."

What the Bible Does

Finally, Paul affirms that the Bible shows us the way of life and godliness, that is, it equips and prepares us for the Christian life. The apostle writes that "the sacred writings . . . are able to make you wise for salvation through faith in Christ Jesus" (2 Tim. 3:15b). That's justification. Then he goes on to say that the Scriptures are intended "that the man of God may be complete, equipped for every good work" (v. 17). That's sanctification. Between your conversion and the day God takes you home to glory (or when Jesus comes, whichever comes first), you are going to live in justification and sanctification. And the Bible is in the business of justification and sanctification. That's what it does. It sets out the way of salvation so that we trust not in ourselves but in Jesus; we put our faith in Christ as he is offered in the gospel, not in our own works. But though we are not saved by our works, Paul says in Ephesians 2:8–10 that we are saved *to* good works. So even as the Bible shows us the way of salvation apart from the works of the law by trust in Jesus, it also shows us the way of the Christian life, which is unto good works!

When Paul writes "that the man of God may be complete, equipped for every good work," he is making clear that the Bible is totally sufficient for the Christian life. It is able to equip us for faith, for life, for godliness, and for every good work. And Paul makes it clear that the job of the shepherd of God's people is not over until men and women have been conformed to Christ. That is the goal of scriptural learning and doctrine. We must not be content with people professing Christ, beginning to study their Bibles, or even embracing right doctrine. We must not rest until we see right doctrine, by God's grace and through the Spirit's power, working out in holy living and a life of love.

In 2 Timothy 3:17, Paul is echoing Jesus in the Great Commission. He said to his disciples: "Go therefore and make disciples of all nations, baptizing them in the name of the Father, and of the Son, and of the Holy Spirit, teaching them to observe all that I have commanded you" (Matt. 28:19–20a). Jesus tells the disciples to go to every nation and make disciples. How? By baptizing and teaching. Teaching what? *All* that he had commanded them. Paul knows that the minister's job isn't done until the Bible is lived, not simply believed. As the hymn writer says, "Trust and obey, for there's no other way, to be happy in Jesus, but to trust and obey."[2] We know that it is true that we won't obey what we don't believe. But it's also true that we won't believe what we don't obey.

Recently, I heard Mark Dever preach a powerful message in which he said, "Ungodliness leads to heresy." We all agree that heresy leads to ungodliness. We've seen it happen and we see it in Scripture. But we often don't remember that it also works the other way. Ungodliness leads to heresy. And it works that way with the doctrine of Scripture too. Look at many of the people in the evangelical world who are changing their view on Scripture in order to accommodate their immorality or the immorality that they want to permit in others. Ungodliness has led them to heresy. Ungodliness has led them to a low view of Scripture. And that's where the temptation can come for us personally. We may think, "I'll never stop believing in the inspiration, infallibility, inerrancy, and authority of Scripture," but if we let our hearts start loving something or someone more than the God of Scripture, start loving something more than the promises of the Word, we're only one step away from denying Scripture and walking away from the faith. Let us not simply hold to the Word in word, but let us hold to the Word in what we love and how we live, and so stand against the wiles of the Evil One.

---

[2] From the hymn "Trust and Obey" by John H. Sammis, 1887.

7

Let the Lion Out

2 TIMOTHY 4:1-5

Alistair Begg

My title for this chapter is borrowed from a well-known quote from a sermon by Charles H. Spurgeon:

> A great many learned men are defending the gospel; no doubt it is a very proper and right thing to do, yet I always notice that, when there are most books of that kind, it is because the gospel itself is not being preached. Suppose a number of persons were to take it into their heads that they had to defend a lion. There he is in the cage, and here come all the soldiers of the army to fight for him. Well, I should suggest to them, if they would not object, and feel that it was humbling to them, that they should kindly stand back, and open the door, and let the lion out! I believe that would be the best way of defending him, for he would take care of himself; and the best "apology" for the gospel is to let the gospel out. Never mind about defending Deuteronomy or the whole of the Pentateuch; preach Jesus Christ and him crucified. Let the Lion out, and see who will dare to approach him. The Lion of the tribe of Judah will soon drive away all his adversaries.[1]

---

[1] Charles H. Spurgeon, "Christ and His Co-Workers," in *The Metropolitan Tabernacle Pulpit* (London: Passmore, 1896), 42:256.

This, in essence, is what Paul is urging Timothy to do in the opening verses of 2 Timothy 4. The apostle here is identifying the necessity that is laid upon Timothy. The time for Paul's departure has come. He has fought the fight, finished the race, and kept the faith, and now it is absolutely crucial that Timothy, his young lieutenant, do likewise. Paul is urging upon him the absolute priority of the ministry of the Word of God, enjoining him to preach the Word, that is, to let the lion out. What Timothy believes about the Scriptures will become apparent in his preaching, and what is true of Timothy will be true for all contemporary Timothys.

In the concluding verses of chapter 3, Paul is not informing Timothy of truth that he doesn't know. Timothy would not have read verses 16 and 17 of that chapter and said, "Oh, wow, I didn't know that about the Bible." Timothy had grown up with an understanding of the Bible. He was familiar with the Old Testament phrase, "The word of the LORD came . . ." (to Solomon, to Samuel, and to all of the prophets). Timothy recognized that Paul was reminding him of a truth that he dare never forget. Essentially, my goal in this chapter is to do the same—to remind us of what we know, and hopefully to encourage us in the task of preaching the Word. The Scriptures are divinely inspired. They are completely reliable. They are totally sufficient, and as Paul has pointed out, they provide the key to the competence and usefulness of the man of God. Timothy knows that the apostle has faced a wholesale desertion in the context of Asia. "All . . . turned away from me" (2 Tim. 1:15). Now Timothy should be prepared for the fact that others will desert him too. From a human perspective, there is actually no guarantee that the fledging church will be sustained in the next generation. Therefore, it is crucial that Timothy continue in what he has learned and has become convinced of and firmly believed.

Timothy is actually ministering in an environment not too dissimilar to our own. He is to preach the Word of God in a time of wholesale confusion, particularly on two fronts: moral and doctrinal. It is a context in which people do not know how they are supposed to behave and what they are supposed to believe. So with the departure of the apostle, and the transition from the apostolic to the postapostolic church, it is time for Timothy to take up this charge. We will consider: (1) his charge (vv. 1–2), (2) his challenge (vv. 3–4), and (3) the opportunity to display his character (v. 5).

His Charge

Paul writes to Timothy: "I charge you in the presence of God and of Christ Jesus, who is to judge the living and the dead, and by his appearing and his kingdom; preach the word; be ready in season and out of season; reprove, rebuke, and exhort, with complete patience and teaching" (vv. 1–2). This charge is solemn, simple, and searching.

A Solemn Charge

When Paul writes, "I charge you in the presence of God and of Christ Jesus," there is nothing casual or inconsequential about this charge. Matthew Henry says aptly, "The best of men have need to be awed into the discharge of their duty."[2] Think of Moses, Isaiah, or Jeremiah, all of whom were initially reluctant to obey God's call to them. So Paul reminds his young friend that he exercises his ministry with the Father and the Son as his witnesses. He urges Timothy to live his life and fulfill his ministry in the very same way that Paul has—in the awareness of Christ's promised appearing, when he will come with power to judge the living and the dead. Paul has worked with his eye on the prize (Phil. 3:14), and Timothy needs to do the same.

The awesomeness of the responsibility comes across clearly in Hebrews 13:17, as the author reminds the people that they must pay attention to their leaders, because "they are keeping watch over your souls, as those who will have to give an account." The pastor is not accountable to the board of trustees, the elders, the deacons, or the congregation. Along with his fellow elders, he is responsible *for* the congregation. He will give an account to God, whom he serves.

Paul has lived his life in the "now" in light of the reality of the "then." When we read church history, we discover others who lived in this way, believers for whom the prospect of "then" so impinged upon the "now" that it made them different from what they would have been otherwise. The great Scottish Reformer John Knox, who lived with opposition, was said to have feared the face of God so much that he never actually feared the face of any man—or any woman, for that matter! Izaak Walton wrote of Richard Sibbes, "Of this blest man, let this just praise be given; heaven was in him, before he was in heaven."[3] Some of us are so concerned about living in the now that we've almost completely lost any thought of the then. Not so for Robert Murray McCheyne, who wrote: "When this passing world is done, and when hath sunk this glaring sun. / When we stand with Christ in glory, looking over life's finished story. / Then Lord, shall

---

[2] Matthew Henry, *Matthew Henry's Commentary on the Whole Bible* (McLean, VA: MacDonald Publishing, n.d.), 4:847.
[3] Izaak Walton, cited in Jessica Martin, *Walton's Lives* (New York: Oxford University Press, 2001), 279.

I fully know, not till then how much I owe."[4] We dare not miss this. To borrow from the words of the marriage ceremony, this ministry "is not to be entered upon lightly or carelessly, but thoughtfully, with reverence for God, with due consideration for the purpose for which it was established by God." Such is the call and the charge to the ministry of the Word of God. It is a solemn charge.

A SIMPLE CHARGE

Paul's charge to Timothy is simple, in the sense that it is straightforward. It is not hard to grasp. Timothy can get all of it immediately, and so may you and I. All that Paul has already written to Timothy in this letter concerning the pattern of sound words, the good deposit, the Word of truth, and the sacred writings (2 Tim. 1:13–14; 2:15; 3:15) underpins this directive. Timothy has been given a ministry of the Word. He is to exercise it in the awareness that the Word of God accomplishes the work of God by the Spirit of God, that powerful preaching of the Bible is not related to the histrionics of the preacher, but is directly related to a consciousness of God on the part of the preacher—as well as among the congregation. A consciousness of God has to do with a sense of God's presence, majesty, otherness, awesomeness, transcendence, and, at the same time, immanence. He is here; he is present. In sum, this charge is given and received in the presence of the Father and of the Son, and in light of the appearing and the kingdom of the Lord Jesus Christ.

That's why preaching, as Christopher Ash has helped me see, is culturally neutral. It doesn't matter where you go in the world, people understand how to sit and listen to someone speaking with authority. And it is there in Scripture from the very beginning. In Deuteronomy 4:10, God says, "Gather the people to me, that I may let them hear my words, so that they may learn to fear me all the days that they live on the earth, and that they may teach their children so." Moses later recounts: "The LORD spoke to you out of the midst of the fire. You heard the sound of words, but saw no form; there was only a voice" (v. 12). Only a voice! Preachers are often asked how they manage to "come up with something" each week. Sadly, too many pulpits are filled by inventive, well-meaning individuals who have lost confidence in the sufficiency of Scripture. The preacher's primary objective is not simply to increase the listener's knowledge of a passage and to provide a few practical pointers by way of application. That's all well and

---

[4] From the hymn "When This Passing World Is Done" by Robert Murray McCheyne. 1837.

good, but the primary objective of the ministry of the Word of God is that, as the Word is brought home by the Spirit of God, the hearer may have a life-shaping encounter with God himself. The end result is that the hearer is changed when God has accomplished his purposes.

The late J. Gresham Machen impressed this upon his students at West-minster Theological Seminary: "It is with the open Bible that the real Christian preacher comes before the congregation. He does not come to present his opinions. He does not come to present the results of his researches in the phenomena of religion, but he comes to set forward what is contained in the Word of God."[5] What God spoke to the apostles has been bequeathed to us in the New Testament so that we, like Timothy, are to preach the Word and nothing but the Word—nothing more, but also nothing less.

W. E. Sangster, the famous Methodist preacher from Methodist Central Hall in London, as he neared the end of his life in the 1950s, lamented: "Preaching is in the shadows. The world does not believe in it."[6] Now, in the second decade of the twenty-first century, is it unkind to suggest that the problem is greater? Preaching is in the shadows. The *church* does not believe in it. Is it fair to say that we are sorely in need of this solemn and simple charge? We must ask ourselves, "Am I convinced that the regular expository preaching and teaching of the Bible—owned by, clothed in, and sustained by the work of the Spirit of God—is the driving force that shapes authentic church life?"

A Searching Charge

This charge is searching insofar as it causes us to consider our commitment. Paul tells Timothy that he must be ready at all times. Some occasions will be more daunting and potentially discouraging than others, so it is important that he stands ready to press the message home on all occasions, convenient or inconvenient. There is no excuse for fearfulness or laziness. The Word is to be proclaimed when people are hostile or when they are receptive; when they are tuned in or when they are tuned out; when the prospect of a Sunday is delightful or when the thought of a Sunday is dreadful; when the crowd is growing or when the congregation is dwindling. Scripture will do what it does—it will reprove, rebuke, and exhort. Such work will not necessarily be comfortable, but it will always be profitable, as Paul has already pointed out (3:16).

---

[5] J. Gresham Machen, introduction to J. Marcellus Kik, *The Narrow and Broad Way* (Grand Rapids, MI: Zondervan, 1934), n.p.
[6] W. E. Sangster, *The Craft of the Sermon* (Harrisburg, PA: Epworth Press, 1954), 1.

Who is sufficient for this? When we think about the congregations we serve, how can we know everything and everyone? How will we know just exactly what to do, how to preach and make application to the listener? Our confidence in preaching the Word comes from the awareness that God opens blind eyes, softens hard hearts, and will accomplish his purposes. We ought not to expect overnight results. It demands "complete patience and teaching." J. B. Phillips paraphrases it this way: "using the utmost patience in your teaching" (PHILLIPS). The New International Version words it like this: "with great patience and careful instruction" (NIV). What daunting adjectives: *complete, utmost, great*. Why couldn't God have said "with *a wee bit* of patience"? Or "with *intermittent* patience"? But no, this charge requires *complete* patience!

This searches my heart. Years ago, on a summer evening in a park in Glasgow, I tried desperately to teach my son to ride a bike without any training wheels. I was so committed to him being able to ride a two-wheeler bike. I was passionately concerned that he would learn to do so. But the evening ended poorly, because I lost my patience with him. What should have been a wonderful memory was marred by my impatience. Far worse, however, have been the times when the benefit of the instruction of Scripture was inhibited by the impatience of the preacher. In his biography of D. Martyn Lloyd-Jones, Iain Murray quotes William M. Taylor as saying, "A young minister is prone to try to attain by one jump the height which others have reached 'by a long series of single steps in the labor of a quarter of a century.'"[7] James Montgomery Boice once warned me of the danger of overestimating what can be accomplished in one year and underestimating what may be accomplished in five.

Let's be clear. This charge is solemn. But it is also simple. The inerrant Word is to be preached when the wind is with us and when all occasions inform against us. It is to be preached patiently and carefully.

His Challenge

Paul now sets before Timothy his challenge: "For the time is coming when people will not endure sound teaching, but having itching ears they will accumulate for themselves teachers to suit their own passions, and will turn away from listening to the truth and wander off into myths" (vv. 3–4).

Paul has already made Timothy aware of those who have swerved from

---

[7] Cited in Iain Murray, *D. Martyn Lloyd-Jones: The Fight of Faith 1939–1981* (Edinburgh: Banner of Truth, 1990), 458.

the truth (2:17–18). Now Timothy must exercise his ministry in the absence of Paul and in the presence of people who are turning away from the truth and wandering into myth. Timothy must be prepared for the times when "people will not endure *sound* teaching" (or "put up with *sound* teaching"). He must continue to follow the "pattern of *sound* words" (1:13), including the "*sound* words of our Lord Jesus Christ" (1 Tim. 6:3). This word *sound* means "healthy," and it is important that we learn how important this is. Only when the congregation is taught sound doctrine will they be able to recognize the unhealthy and fraudulent.

As a boy growing up, I heard of those who apparently were sound and those who were not. I never really understood it until I came to realize that in certain cases, to declare someone's theology as "sound" was another way of saying, "He agrees with me"! Likewise, years ago, I was preaching in Northern Ireland, and my host was a retired bank manager named T. S. Mooney, who was held in high regard as a kind of unelected bishop of the Evangelical Presbyterian Church. He was a very kind man and quick-witted. Each evening before I spoke to the Young Peoples' Convention in Londonderry, he would come into the little room in the back of the Methodist church and we would have prayer together. He would pray very earnestly that God would help me as I preached, for which I was very grateful. He then would take his seat in the congregation. On the first evening, I had barely introduced my address before he was in the third stages of anesthesia. He was asleep. It happened on Monday night, on Tuesday, and on Wednesday. As we drove home to his apartment that evening, I broached the subject of his sleeping habits: "T. S., every night you have prayed with me before I spoke, but then you have fallen asleep." Looking at me somewhat curiously, he replied: "It's just like this, you see: I stay awake until I know you're sound and then I have a snooze!"

The issue Paul addresses here was not unique to Timothy's day. People have rejected sound doctrine since the fall. Instead of availing themselves of teachers and teaching that will make them godly, healthy, and useful, they go in search of the intriguing, the fascinating, the speculative, and the spicy. They are more interested in novelty than in orthodoxy. They look for teachers to tell them what they want to hear.

In Deuteronomy 4, we see Moses recounting how, speaking for God, he called the people of Israel to listen to God's voice, to pay attention to his Word. Despite their profession of obedience, they had been seduced by all the images and corruption of their neighbors. In contemporary terms, they felt it was much easier to invite their friends to the drama than to another "boring" sermon. As a result of refusing to bow before their Creator, they became creators themselves, fashioning their own manageable little gods who would accommodate them. Essentially, they exchanged the truth of God for a lie. As Martin Luther reportedly observed, "If a man will not have God, he must have his idols."

In Isaiah 30, we find God's people rejecting the instruction of the prophet, not because it wasn't clear, but because it was too clear: "They are a rebellious people, lying children, children unwilling to hear the instruction of the Lord; who say to the seers, 'Do not see,' and to the prophets, 'Do not prophesy to us what is right; speak to us smooth things, prophesy illusions, leave the way, turn aside from the path, let us hear no more about the Holy One of Israel'" (vv. 9–11). They didn't want Isaiah to stop preaching. They just wanted him to preach in a manner that suited their fancy; a manner that accommodated their passions.

The real challenge for most of us is not that we stop *believing* the Bible, but that we actually stop *using* the Bible, failing to submit to the authority of the Word of God in our own lives and in our proclamation. It is quite common to encounter those who are in search of and proponents of a spirituality that is actually disconnected from biblical truth. That surely is the environment in which most of us are operating now. People tell us all the time: "I am a very spiritual person. I just have no interest in the Bible." These individuals accumulate teachers along the lines of the weak women that Paul has already mentioned (2 Tim. 3:6). They were always learning and never able to arrive at a knowledge of the truth. They were always accumulating teachers the way some of us stack up heaps of golf instruction magazines. We are no better for them, as we constantly follow different ideas and strategies. They were trying to find new information all the time, but if you had asked them, "What do you know of the gospel of the Lord Jesus Christ?" they would have had no sensible answer. "An appalling and horrible thing has happened in the land; the prophets prophesy falsely, and the priests rule at their direction; and my people love to have it so" (Jer. 5:30–31).

I have the unfortunate distinction of living in Cleveland, Ohio, a city that has had more losing sports teams than most. But far more devastating is the fact that in Cleveland we have the headquarters of arguably the most liberal Protestant denomination in America, namely, the United Church of Christ. The UCC's current marketing slogan is "God is still speaking," (yes, it is followed by a comma, not a period). This came from a comment made by Gracie Allen, who was married for most of her life to the comedian George Burns: "Never place a period where God has placed a comma." It all sounds reasonable and accommodating. At a recent gathering in Cleveland, representatives of the denomination were arguing in favor of a gay-rights agenda. At the end of the evening, a friend of mine happened to be going down on the elevator with a man and his husband, who had been there representing the church in this discourse. My friend, taking his courage in his hands, said kindly to the man, "What do you make, sir, if I may ask, of Matthew 19, where Jesus said, 'Have you not read that he who created them from the beginning, made them male and female, and for this reason will a man leave his father and his mother and the two will become one flesh?'" The man looked at him quizzically for a moment and then said, "But of course we don't believe the Bible at all." According to the UCC, God is still speaking—but he is apparently contradicting all that he said in his Word. Those churches have people in them every single Sunday (not many, mercifully). This is the environment in which we are ministering.

His Character

In 2 Timothy 4:5, Paul shows how the charge and the challenge provide Timothy with an opportunity to display his character: "As for you, always be sober-minded, endure suffering, do the work of an evangelist, fulfill your ministry." This verse adds four imperatives to the five in verse 2. Timothy is given a tall order, a man-sized task. Here we have, as one commentator puts it, "a realistic statement of what Christian ministry is all about." Confronted by opposition, it would be all too easy for Timothy to throw in the towel, to quit the fight, to exit the race. But this is no time for self-pity. Here is an opportunity for him to stay steady, to face whatever suffering might come, to keep on preaching the gospel, and to complete the task.

Always Be Sober-Minded

Timothy is surrounded by some who have become intoxicated with all of their mythological notions. They have wandered away; they have drifted off. This is not a good time for Timothy to set his pastoral cruise control or automatic pilot. He doesn't dare to fall asleep—for his own sake and for the sake of those under his care. He must be vigilant. He must be prepared to endure. He must make sure that he's not susceptible to speculative notions and that he's not unduly influenced by the numbers of people who flock in the direction of false teachers. So Paul counsels him, "Always be sober-minded," or, "Keep your head in all situations" (NIV).

Endure Suffering

Paul began this letter by inviting Timothy to join him in "suffering for the gospel" (1:8). He has spoken about his suffering all the way through. He could never be accused of sugarcoating the troubles that Timothy will face. Timothy would not be able to recognize many of our approaches to gospel ministry because they are soft and self-focused. In Paul's case, the suffering was obviously physical, and it probably would be so for Timothy. Many of our brothers and sisters in the world face the same. For those of us in the West, at least for now, it may be more mental and emotional, but it is real nonetheless. However, as people grow to expect a more politically acceptable gospel, the cost involved in guarding the good deposit may grow. It is costly to declare publicly or privately the Bible's assessment of man as sinful, guilty, responsible, and lost. It's hard to proclaim that message over coffee and doughnuts. When the welcoming pastor explains, "We want you all to have a lovely time this morning and don't want anybody getting upset or unsettled!" it's hard to follow that by declaring: "It is appointed unto man once to die—and by the way, you're sinful, guilty, responsible, and lost! Don't spill your coffee." That's why superficial worship and silly introductions do not set the scene for decent biblical preaching. Man-centered gatherings that have only the vaguest approximation to biblical worship neither focus the mind nor stir the heart. Timothy is not called to create suffering, but to endure it. He (and contemporary Timothys) will be on the receiving end of the accusations and insinuations of the Evil One, who comes to deceive, discourage, and derail him if possible. No doubt Timothy often will have occasion to find rest in the encouragement from Paul: "Be strengthened by the grace that is in Christ Jesus" (2:1). This is how a believer can endure suffering.

Do the Work of an Evangelist

Paul does not want Timothy to get a new job. He is simply reinforcing Timothy's charge to preach the Word. As Phillips paraphrases verse 5, "Go on steadily preaching the Gospel" (PHILLIPS). Paul is saying: "Be a gospel man, Timothy. If you are going to be known for one thing, be known as a gospel man."

In *A Quest for Godliness*, J. I. Packer writes, "If one preaches the Bible biblically, one cannot help preaching the gospel all the time, and every sermon will be . . . at least by implication evangelistic."[8] The pastor is consistently saying, "We implore you on behalf of Christ, be reconciled to God" (2 Cor. 5:20). He issues a personal, passionate plea. He must preach, as the Puritan pastor Richard Baxter preached, as a dying man to dying men and women, declaring confidently and wooingly that God was in Christ reconciling the world to himself, not counting our sins against us, and that the only safe haven for the sinner is in the mercy of God himself. When this message begins to grip the preacher and dawn on the listeners, useful, effective, biblical evangelism is taking place. In my lifetime, I have watched sadly as a number of good, godly, effective gospel ministers turned from this message by exercising a ministry of denunciation, constantly cursing the darkness. They chose to point out the predicament but failed to point to the Savior. Others have embraced political agendas, ecology, or human rights. But when they changed their focus, what happened? The work of evangelism was neglected. At the turn of the nineteenth century, William Booth wrote, "I am of the opinion that the chief dangers which confront the coming century will be religion without the Holy Ghost, Christianity without Christ, forgiveness without repentance, salvation without regeneration, politics without God, and heaven without hell."[9]

Those entrusted with the gospel dare not neglect this work. We must declare that the Son of God came to die for us and that he offers to clothe us in his righteousness. We must make clear that all that God has done for us, as John Calvin said, "remains useless and of no value to us" as long as we remain outside of Christ.[10] The late John Murray observed, "The passion for evangelism is quenched when we lose sight of the grandeur of the gospel."[11] There is a new breed of young Reformed preachers who are in danger of going wrong at this point. Some have happily awakened to discover biblical theology, and for that we rejoice. However, in some cases, the incumbent problem that has come with this discovery is that somehow or another they are stymied when it comes to pressing upon people the claims of Christ and the free offer of the gospel. We must beware of this. Choose your mentors well and listen again to Murray: "It is on the crest of the wave

---

[8] J. I. Packer, *A Quest for Godliness: The Puritan Vision of the Christian Life* (Wheaton, IL: Crossway, 1990), 169.

[9] William Booth, cited in *The Homiletical Review: July–December 1902*, vol. 44 (New York: Funk and Wagnalls, 1902), 382.

[10] John Calvin, *Institutes of the Christian Religion*, ed. John T. McNeill, trans. Ford Lewis Battles, Library of Christian Classics, vols. 20–21 (Philadelphia: Westminster Press, 1960), 3.1.1.

[11] John Murray, *The Atonement and the Free Offer of the Gospel*, in *Collected Writings of John Murray* (Edinburgh: Banner of Truth, 1976), 1:59.

of divine sovereignty that the unrestricted summons of the gospel comes to the weary and the heavy laden. This is Jesus' own witness and it provides the direction in which our own thinking on this subject must proceed. Any inhibition or reserve in presenting the overtures of grace should no more characterize our proclamation than it characterizes the Lord's witness."[12]

FULFILL YOUR MINISTRY

Finally, Paul urges Timothy to keep going so as to finish the job. He must carry out to the full the commission that God has given him. In secular Greek, the verb sometimes denotes the fulfilling of a promise or the repaying of a debt. Timothy had promised in his ordination to follow Christ and to make him known, and we have done the same. Timothy is indebted to Paul, just as we are indebted to those who led us to Christ, who nurtured us, and who continue to encourage and inspire us. Jesus, in paying a debt he didn't owe, kept his promise to the Father. In turn, he received the promise of his Father, granting him the nations as his inheritance.

Forty years into pastoral ministry, I am not jaded or discouraged. Indeed, if I were given the opportunity to start again at the beginning, I would seize it in a moment. So we must work while it is day, for the night comes.

The *challenge* that we face is clear. The *character* that we forge is in process. The *charge* to preach the Word is straightforward. I say to you, open the door and let the lion out!

---

[12] John Murray, *The Sovereignty of God* (Grand Rapids, MI: Zondervan, 1940), 12.

Part 2

INERRANCY IN CHURCH HISTORY

Showing the Precedent

8

The Ground and Pillar of the Faith

THE WITNESS OF PRE-REFORMATION HISTORY TO THE DOCTRINE OF *SOLA SCRIPTURA*[1]

Nathan Busenitz

A high view of Scripture, both in terms of its inerrancy and authority, lay at the heart of the Protestant Reformation. For the Reformers, Scripture alone established the doctrines of the church, and any competing authority had to be rejected. In this regard, the Geneva Confession of 1536 is representative:

> We affirm that we desire to follow Scripture alone as [the] rule of faith and religion, without mixing with it any other thing which might be devised by the opinion of men apart from the Word of God, and without

---

[1] In preparing this material, I am particularly indebted to the work of three evangelical authors. The first is William Webster, *Holy Scripture: The Ground and Pillar of Our Faith*, vol. 2 (Battle Ground, WA: Christian Resources, 2001). It is perhaps the most extensive study on this important topic from an evangelical perspective. Those seeking a more thorough treatment of this subject would do well to engage with Webster's comprehensive survey. The second is James White, "*Sola Scriptura* and the Early Church," in *Sola Scriptura*, ed. Don Kistler (Lake Mary, FL: Reformation Trust, 2009), 17–37. This chapterlong survey is a helpful and concise treatment of this subject. The third is Gregg Allison's summary treatment in his *Historical Theology* (Grand Rapids, MI: Zondervan, 2011), which has been a useful resource on this topic just as it is on many other areas related to the history of Christian doctrine.

wishing to accept for our spiritual government any other doctrine than what is conveyed to us by the same Word without addition or diminution, according to the command of our Lord.[2]

Although the Reformers sought affirmation for their views from the writings of the church fathers (i.e., Christian leaders and theologians from the early centuries of church history), they looked to Scripture alone as the foundation and final authority for their theological claims. As Martin Luther explained in 1519 to Johann Eck:

> I have learned to ascribe the honor of infallibility only to those books that are accepted as canonical. I am profoundly convinced that none of these writers has erred. All other writers, however they may have distinguished themselves in holiness or in doctrine, I read in this way: I evaluate what they say, not on the basis that they themselves believe that a thing is true, but only insofar as they are able to convince me by the authority of the canonical books or by clear reason.[3]

For the Reformers, the doctrine of *sola Scriptura* encompassed both the purity and the authority of the Bible. They recognized that because Scripture consists of the perfect words of God, it not only reflects his holy character, it also comes with his absolute authority. In recognizing that *Christ alone* is the Head of his church, they further asserted that *his Word alone* is the supreme authority for determining the doctrines of the church. Consequently, they concluded that all other would-be authorities (including popes, councils, and church traditions) must be subjected to Christ and his Word.

But were the Reformers the first in church history to embrace such a view regarding the absolute authority of Scripture? Or can a distinct witness affirming this theological conviction be perceived in the writings of earlier Christian leaders? In order to answer those questions from a historical perspective, it is necessary to consider what the church fathers said in this regard.

Though not authoritative as only Scripture is, the witness of pre-Reformation church history provides valuable insight into the early church's perspective on the inerrancy and authority of the Bible. Believers today can benefit greatly from such a study, because it enables them to see how evan-

---

[2] Geneva Confession of 1536, 1, in *Reformed Confessions of the Sixteenth Century*, ed. Arthur C. Cochrane (Louisville: Westminster John Knox, 2003), 120.
[3] Martin Luther, *Contra malignum Iohannis Eccii iudicium super aliquot articulis a fratribus quibusdam ei suppositis Martini Lutheri defensio*, WA, 2.626, in *God's Inerrant Word*, ed. John W. Montgomery (Minneapolis: Bethany Fellowship, 1974), 84.

gelical convictions were articulated and defended by early generations of Christians. In this chapter, we will survey the writings of the church fathers under two headings: the inerrancy of Scripture and the authority of Scripture.

The Church Fathers and the Inerrancy of Scripture

Even a cursory reading of patristic literature demonstrates that early Christians considered the Scriptures to contain the very words of God. Because they understood that God is perfect, they recognized that his Word is also perfect. Because God cannot lie, his Word is necessarily without error or falsehood.

That commitment is expressed throughout patristic literature in several ways. First, the church fathers understood that because Scripture comes from the Holy Spirit, it cannot contain error.[4] For example, Clement of Rome (d. ca. 100) makes this connection when he tells the Corinthians, "You have searched the holy scriptures, which are true, which were given by the Holy Spirit; you know that nothing unrighteous or counterfeit is written in them."[5] Irenaeus (ca. 130–202) echoes that conclusion in his treatise *Against Heresies*: "The Scriptures are indeed perfect, since they were spoken by the Word of God and His Spirit."[6]

Second, because Scripture is without error, early church fathers (such as Justin Martyr [d. 165] and Irenaeus) affirmed that it does not contradict itself. Their belief that all Scripture is true led them to conclude that every portion of Scripture harmonizes perfectly with every other part. To cite Irenaeus again:

> All Scripture, which has been given to us by God, shall be found by us perfectly consistent: and the parables [i.e., the less-clear passages] shall harmonize with those passages which are perfectly plain; and those statements the meaning of which is clear, shall serve to explain the parables.[7]

To those who might claim there are contradictions in Scripture, Justin offers this reply: "Since I am entirely convinced that no Scripture contradicts another, I shall admit rather that I do not understand what is recorded, and shall strive to persuade those who imagine that the Scriptures

---

[4] For additional examples from patristic literature on this point, see chapter 9 in this volume, "The Power of the Word in the Present: Inerrancy and the Reformation" by Carl R. Trueman.

[5] Clement, *First Clement*, 45.2–3, in *The Apostolic Fathers*, 3rd ed., ed. and trans. Michael Holmes (Grand Rapids, MI: Baker, 2007), 105.

[6] Irenaeus, *Against Heresies*, 2.28.2, in *Ante-Nicene Fathers*, ed. Alexander Roberts and James Donaldson (repr., Peabody, MA: Hendrickson, 2012), 1:399. Hereafter, *ANF*.

[7] Ibid., 2.28.3, in *ANF*, 1:400.

are contradictory, to be rather of the same opinion as myself."[8] Athanasius (296–373) similarly asserts: "It is the opinion of some, that the Scriptures do not agree together, or that God, who gave the commandment, is false. But there is no disagreement whatever, far from it, neither can the Father, who is truth, lie; 'for it is impossible that God should lie.'"[9]

Early Christian leaders were resolute in their conviction that God's Word is absolutely true. Tertullian (ca. 160–220) states, "The statements of holy Scripture will never be discordant with truth."[10] Athanasius offers a similar assertion: "The sacred and inspired Scriptures are sufficient to declare the truth."[11] In his exposition of John 17:17, John Chrysostom (ca. 347–407) explains, "'Your word is truth,' that is, 'there is no falsehood in it, and all that is said in it must happen.'"[12] Augustine (354–430) is especially clear in this regard, as evidenced by the following excerpts:

> I have learned to yield this respect and honor only to the canonical books of Scripture: of these alone do I most firmly believe that the authors were completely free from error. And if in these writings I am perplexed by anything which appears to me opposed to truth, I do not hesitate to suppose that either the manuscript is faulty, or the translator has not caught the meaning of what was said, or I myself have failed to understand it. . . . Concerning which it would be wrong to doubt that they are free from error.[13]

> The Scriptures are holy, they are truthful, they are blameless. . . . So we have no grounds at all for blaming Scripture if we happen to deviate in any way, because we haven't understood it. When we do understand it, we are right. But when we are wrong because we haven't understood it, we leave it in the right. We have gone wrong, we don't make our Scripture to be wrong, but it continues to stand up straight and right, so that we may return to it for correction.[14]

> It seems to me that most disastrous consequences must follow upon our believing that anything false is found in the sacred books: that is

---

[8] Justin Martyr, *Dialogue with Trypho*, 65, in *ANF*, 1:230.
[9] Athanasius, *Easter Letter*, 19.3, in *Nicene and Post-Nicene Fathers*, Second Series, ed. Philip Schaff and Henry Wace (repr., Peabody, MA: Hendrickson, 2012), 4:546. Hereafter, *NPNF²*.
[10] Tertullian, *A Treatise on the Soul*, 21, in *ANF*, 3:202.
[11] Athanasius, *Against the Heathen*, 1.3, in *NPNF²*, 4:4.
[12] John Chrysostom, *Homily on John 17:17*, in *John 11–21*, Ancient Christian Commentary on Scripture, ed. Joel C. Elowsky (Downers Grove, IL: InterVarsity Press, 2007), 252.
[13] Augustine, *Letters*, 82.3, in *Nicene and Post-Nicene Fathers*, First Series, ed. Philip Schaff (repr., Peabody, MA: Hendrickson, 1994), 1:350. Hereafter, *NPNF¹*.
[14] Augustine, *Sermons*, 23.3, in *Colossians, 1–2 Thessalonians, 1–2 Timothy, Titus, Philemon*, Ancient Christian Commentary on Scripture, ed. Peter Gorday (Downers Grove, IL: InterVarsity Press, 2000), 269.

to say, that the men by whom the Scripture has been given to us, and committed to writing, did put down in these books anything false. . . . For if you once admit into such a high sanctuary of authority one false statement as made in the way of duty, there will not be left a single sentence of those books which, if appearing to anyone difficult in practice or hard to believe, may not by the same fatal rule be explained away, as a statement in which . . . the author declared what was not true.[15]

Seven centuries later, Anselm of Canterbury (ca. 1033–1109) expresses the same conviction with these words: "For I am sure that if I say anything which is undoubtedly contradictory to holy Scripture, it is wrong; and if I become aware of such a contradiction, I do not wish to hold that opinion."[16]

Because these church fathers recognized God's Word to be wholly true, they took seriously the warnings in Scripture directed at anyone who would subtract from it or add to it. Athanasius illustrates this principle in his *Thirty-Ninth Festal Letter*. After listing the canonical books of Scripture, he explains: "These are fountains of salvation, that they who thirst may be satisfied with the living words they contain. In these alone is proclaimed the doctrine of godliness. Let no man add to these, neither let him take ought from these."[17]

Basil of Caesarea (330–379) likewise asserts, "To delete anything that is written down or to interpolate anything not written amounts to open defection from the faith and makes the offender liable to a charge of contempt."[18] In a similar vein, Augustine emphasizes the fact that, because God's Word is perfect, it must not be altered in any way. He writes:

If anyone preaches either concerning Christ or concerning His church or concerning any other matter which pertains to our faith and life; I will not say, if we, but what Paul adds, if an angel from heaven should preach to you anything besides what you have received in the Scriptures of the Law and of the Gospels, let him be anathema.[19]

As this brief survey demonstrates, evidence from prominent church fathers shows that they regarded Scripture as the very revelation of God given through the Holy Spirit, such that it reflects his perfect character.

---

[15] Augustine, *Letters*, 28.3, in *NPNF*[1], 1:251–52.
[16] Anselm, *Why God Became Man*, 1.18, in Allison, *Historical Theology*, 83.
[17] Athanasius, *Easter Letter*, 39.6, in *NPNF*[2], 4:550.
[18] Basil of Caesarea, "Concerning Faith," in *Saint Basil: Ascetical Works*, Fathers of the Church, vol. 9, trans. M. Monica Wagner (Washington DC: The Catholic University of America Press, 1962), 59.
[19] Augustine, *Against Petilian, the Donatist*, 3.6, in White, "*Sola Scriptura* and the Early Church," 25. Cf. *NPNF*[1], 4:599.

They taught that it contains no error, that it is absolutely true, and that anyone who adds to it or subtracts from it will be judged accordingly by God. In this way, they clearly affirmed their belief in the inerrancy of Scripture.

The Church Fathers and the Authority of Scripture

Just as these early Christian leaders recognized that Scripture reflects the perfect character of God, they also recognized that Scripture comes with God's own authority. As Justin Martyr explains:

> [Scripture ought to] be believed for its own nobility, and for the confidence due to Him who sends it. Now the word of truth is sent from God. . . . For being sent with authority, it is not necessary that it should be required to produce proof of what is said; since neither is there any proof beyond itself, which is God.[20]

Because there is no higher authority than God, there can be no higher authority than the Word that he has revealed.

Augustine connects inerrancy with authority by explaining that when someone attacks the truthfulness of God's Word, he simultaneously attempts to undermine God's authority. Augustine writes: "For, truly, when he [i.e., a false teacher] pronounces anything [in Scripture] to be untrue, he demands that he be believed in preference, and endeavors to shake our confidence in the authority of the divine Scriptures."[21] Elsewhere, Augustine reiterates the truth that Scripture has the highest authority because it is God's Word:

> This Mediator, having spoken what He judged sufficient first by the prophets, then by His own lips, and afterwards by the apostles, has besides produced the Scripture which is called canonical, *which has paramount authority*, and to which we yield assent in all matters of which we ought not to be ignorant.[22]

The commitment of early Christians to the paramount authority of Scripture is evidenced in at least three ways: in their reverence for Scripture within the church, in their reliance on Scripture to expose false teaching, and in their regard for Scripture over every other alleged source of authority.

---

[20] Justin Martyr, *Fragments of the Lost Work of Justin on the Resurrection*, 1, in *ANF*, 1.294 (English rendered clearer).
[21] Augustine, *Letters*, 28.4, in *NPNF²*, 1:252.
[22] Augustine: *The City of God*, 11.3, in *NPNF¹*, 2.206 (emphasis added).

The Patristic Reverence for Scripture in the Church

The high regard that early Christians had for the authority of God's Word is evidenced first in the fact that the Scriptures occupied a central and authoritative place in the life of the early church. In his *First Apology*, written around 150, Justin provides one of the earliest extrabiblical descriptions of a church service. He writes:

> And on the day called Sunday, all who live in cities or in the country gather together to one place, and the memoirs of the apostles or the writings of the prophets are read, as long as time permits; then, when the reader has ceased, the president [the pastor] verbally instructs, and exhorts to the imitation of these good things.[23]

As Justin's description demonstrates, the early church regarded Old Testament texts ("the writings of the prophets") and New Testament texts ("the memoirs of the apostles") as authoritative, such that they were read and preached during the corporate gathering. Believers attending the weekly worship service were admonished and urged to obey the good things revealed in Scripture.

This attitude toward God's Word is made explicit by Irenaeus. Speaking of the apostles, he writes:

> We have learned from none others the plan of our salvation, than from those through whom the Gospel has come down to us, which they did at one time proclaim in public, and, at a later period, by the will of God, handed down to us in the Scriptures, to be the ground and pillar of our faith.[24]

In response to the heretical teachings of the Gnostics, Irenaeus appealed to Scripture as his final authority—as the "ground and pillar" of the faith of the church.[25] Commenting on Irenaeus's view of Scripture, William Webster observes:

> It is clear that Irenaeus taught that Scripture is the pillar and ground of the faith. . . . To Irenaeus, then, Scripture is the full and final revelation given by God to man through the apostles. It is inspired and authoritative and a source of proof for discerning truth and error. It is Scripture that has final

---

[23] Justin Martyr, *First Apology*, 67, in *ANF*, 1:186.
[24] Irenaeus, *Against Heresies*, 3.1.1, in *ANF*, 1:414.
[25] Webster points out: "The phrase 'handed down' is the verb form of the word 'tradition.' . . . The Bible is the means by which the *traditio* (tradition), or teaching of the apostles is transmitted from generation to generation and by which true apostolic teaching can be verified and error refuted." *Holy Scripture*, 2.24–25.

and sufficient authority and is the ground and pillar of the Church's faith. The Scriptures are both materially and formally sufficient.[26]

As Irenaeus's words illustrate, the Scriptures occupied a central place in the weekly worship of the early church because they provided the authoritative basis for what Christians believed and what the church taught.

The Patristic Reliance on Scripture in Condemning Heresy

An early Christian commitment to the authority of Scripture is seen, second, in the fathers' repeated appeal to Scripture in defense of sound doctrine, especially in the face of heretical attack. Historian J. N. D. Kelly sums up this characteristic of patristic theology with these words:

> The clearest token of the prestige enjoyed by [Scripture] is the fact that almost the entire theological effort of the fathers, whether their aims were polemical or constructive, was expended upon what amounted to the exposition of the Bible. Further, it was everywhere taken for granted that, for any doctrine to win acceptance, it had first to establish its Scriptural basis.[27]

Numerous examples could be produced to demonstrate the veracity of that statement. For example, Irenaeus condemned his Gnostic opponents by appealing to Scripture. He wrote: "Such, then, is their system, which neither the prophets announced, nor the Lord taught, nor the apostles delivered, but of which they boast that beyond all others they have a perfect knowledge. They gather their views from other sources than the Scriptures."[28] For Irenaeus, the fact that the Gnostics based their teachings on something other than God's Word was sufficient evidence, in and of itself, to prove that their system was false.

Tertullian makes a similar point in his treatise on the resurrection. He writes, "Take away, indeed, from the heretics the wisdom which they share with the heathen, and let them support their inquiries from the Scriptures alone: they will then be unable to keep their ground."[29] Tertullian did not hesitate to label the false teachers as heretics because they could not support their teachings from God's Word.

Like Tertullian, Hippolytus (ca. 170–236) responds to heretics by comparing their teachings with Scripture:

---

[26] Ibid., 2.24, 26.
[27] J. N. D. Kelly, *Early Christian Doctrines* (repr., New York: Continuum, 2006), 46.
[28] Irenaeus, *Against Heresies*, 1.8.1, in ANF, 1:326.
[29] Tertullian, *On the Resurrection of the Flesh*, 3, in ANF, 3:547.

Let us turn to the exhibition of the truth itself, that we may establish the truth, against which all these mighty heresies have arisen without being able to state anything to the purpose. There is, brethren, one God, the knowledge of whom we gain from the Holy Scriptures, and from no other source. . . . All of us who wish to practice piety will be unable to learn its practice from any other quarter than the oracles of God. Whatever things, then, the Holy Scriptures declare, at these let us look; and whatsoever things they teach, these let us learn.[30]

In confronting the falsehood of Arianism, Athanasius writes:

Which of the two theologies sets forth our Lord Jesus Christ as God and Son of the Father, this which you vomited forth [i.e., Arianism], or that which we have spoken and maintain from the Scriptures [i.e., Trinitarianism]? . . . Nor does Scripture afford them [the Arian heretics] any pretext; for it has been often shown, and it shall be shown now, that their doctrine is alien to the divine oracles.[31]

Likewise, in his controversy with the Donatists, Augustine appeals to Scripture as the only adequate standard for discerning truth from error:

Let us not bring in deceitful balances, to which we may hang what weights we will and how we will, saying to suit ourselves, "This is heavy and this is light;" but let us bring forward the sacred balance out of holy Scripture, as out of the Lord's treasure-house, and let us weigh them by it, to see which is the heavier; or rather, let us not weigh them for ourselves, but read the weights as declared by the Lord.[32]

Such examples demonstrate a standard patristic approach: sound doctrine was defended and false teaching denounced on the basis of biblical authority. These early Christian leaders rested their case in the Scriptures, because there was no higher authority to which they could appeal.

THE PATRISTIC REGARD FOR SCRIPTURE ABOVE EVERY OTHER AUTHORITY

A commitment to biblical authority in the early church is seen, third, in the fathers' elevation of Scripture above other potential sources of authority. From a survey of patristic literature, a compelling case can be made that the

---

[30] Hippolytus, *Against the Heresy of Noetus*, 8–9, in *ANF*, 5:227.
[31] Athanasius, *Four Discourses against the Arians*, 1.3.10, in *NPNF²*, 4:311–12.
[32] Augustine, *On Baptism, Against the Donatists*, 2.6 (9), in *NPNF¹*, 4:429.

early church viewed Scripture as its highest authority in the determination of sound doctrine. This commitment to the ultimate authority of God's Word (what the Protestant Reformers would later call *sola Scriptura*) can be demonstrated along the following lines.

First, patristic theologians such as Origen and Augustine insisted that noncanonical books—though they might be edifying and beneficial for believers—do not have an authority equal to Scripture. As Origen (ca. 182–254) explains: "No man ought, for the confirmation of doctrines, to use books which are not canonized Scriptures."[33] Elsewhere, he expands on this conviction:

> In the two testaments every word that pertains to God may be required and discussed, and all knowledge of things may be understood out of them. But if anything yet remains which the Holy Scripture does not determine, no other third Scripture ought to be received for authorizing any knowledge or doctrine.[34]

Augustine makes a similar comment about any book written after the closing of the New Testament canon. He writes:

> There is a distinct boundary line separating all productions subsequent to apostolic times from the authoritative canonical books of the Old and New Testaments. The authority of these books has come down to us from the apostles . . . and, from a position of lofty supremacy, claims the submission of every faithful and pious mind. . . . In the innumerable books that have been written afterwards we may sometimes find the same truth as in Scripture, but there is not the same authority. Scripture has a sacredness peculiar to itself.[35]

Elsewhere, Augustine reiterates this principle:

> Let those things be removed from our midst which we quote against each other not from divine canonical books but from elsewhere. Someone may perhaps ask: Why do you want to remove these things from the midst? Because I do not want the holy church proved by human documents but by divine oracles.[36]

---

[33] Origen, *Tractates in Matthew*, 26, in Charles Elliott, *Delineation of Roman Catholicism* (New York: George Lane, 1841), 1:120.
[34] Origen, *Homily on Leviticus*, 5, in ibid., 1:119 (English rendered clearer).
[35] Augustine, *Reply to Faustus*, 11.5, in NPNF[1], 4:180. In this same context, Augustine further asserts, "In consequence of the distinctive peculiarity of the sacred writings, we are bound to receive as true whatever the canon shows to have been said by even one prophet, or apostle, or evangelist."
[36] Augustine, *The Unity of the Church*, 3, in White, "*Sola Scriptura* and the Early Church," 25.

Second, Christian leaders such as Ambrose (ca. 337–397) regarded Scripture (in which the wisdom of God is revealed) as more authoritative than any form of human wisdom. Ambrose expressed that principle with these words:

> Do not follow the traditions of philosophy or those who gather the semblance of truth in the "vain deceit" of the arts of persuasion. Rather, accept, in accordance with the rule of truth, what is set forth in the inspired words of God and is poured into the hearts of the faithful by the contemplation of such sublimity.[37]

In his treatise *The Unity of the Church*, Augustine similarly writes: "Let us not hear: This I say, this you say; but thus says the Lord. Surely it is the books of the Lord on whose authority we both agree and which we both believe. There let us seek the church, there let us discuss our case."[38] The context of that statement is notable, because Augustine is appealing to Scripture as his ultimate authority even in matters pertaining to the church.

Third, a number of church fathers expressly state that they regarded the Scriptures as more authoritative than their own opinions and teachings. Rather than elevating their interpretations to a level of equal authority with Scripture, they elevated Scripture above their own perspectives. Consider the following examples:

> **Dionysius of Alexandria (ca. 265):** We did not evade objections, but we endeavored as far as possible to hold to and confirm the things which lay before us, and if the reason given satisfied us, we were not ashamed to change our opinions and agree with others; but on the contrary, conscientiously and sincerely, and with hearts laid open before God, we accepted whatever was established by the proofs and teachings of the Holy Scriptures.[39]

> **Cyril of Jerusalem (ca. 315–386):** For concerning the divine and holy mysteries of the faith, not even a casual statement must be delivered without the Holy Scriptures; nor must we be drawn aside by mere plausibility and artifices of speech. Even to me, who tell you these things, do not give absolute credence, unless you receive the proof of the things which I announce from the divine Scriptures. For this salvation which

---

[37] Ambrose, *Six Days of Creation*, 2.1.3, in *Psalms 51–150*, Ancient Christian Commentary on Scripture, ed. Quentin F. Wesselschmidt (Downers Grove, IL: InterVarsity Press, 2007), 318.

[38] Augustine, *The Unity of the Church*, 3, in White, "*Sola Scriptura* and the Early Church," 25.

[39] Dionysius of Alexandria, cited from Eusebius, *Church History*, 7.24.7–9, in NPNF², 1:309 (English rendered clearer).

we believe depends not on ingenious reasoning, but on demonstration from the Holy Scriptures.[40]

Basil of Caesarea: Those hearers who are instructed in the Scriptures should examine what is said by the teachers, receiving what is in conformity with the Scriptures and rejecting what is opposed to them; and that those who persist in teaching such doctrines should be strictly avoided.[41]

John Chrysostom, noting that all arguments must be supported from Scripture: These then are the reasons; but it is necessary to establish them all from the Scriptures, and to show with exactness that all that has been said on this subject is not an invention of human reasoning, but the very sentence of the Scriptures. For thus will what we say be at once more deserving of credit, and sink the deeper into your minds.[42]

Augustine: For the reasonings of any men whatsoever, even though they be [true Christians], and of high reputation, are not to be treated by us in the same way as the canonical Scriptures are treated. We are at liberty, without doing any violence to the respect which these men deserve, to condemn and reject anything in their writings, if perchance we shall find that they have entertained opinions differing from that which others or we ourselves have, by the divine help, discovered to be the truth. I deal thus with the writings of others, and I wish my intelligent readers to deal thus with mine.[43]

As Augustine suggests, intelligent readers are those who evaluate patristic writings against the standard of biblical truth, not vice versa.

Along those same lines, Augustine elsewhere asserts that Scripture is more authoritative than the writings of earlier church fathers. He writes:

Who can fail to be aware that the sacred canon of Scripture, both of the Old and New Testament, is confined within its own limits, and that it stands so absolutely in a superior position to all later letters of the bishops, that about it we can hold no manner of doubt or disputation whether what is confessedly contained in it is right and true; but that all the letters of bishops which have been written, or are being written, since the closing of the canon, are liable to be refuted if there be anything contained in them which strays from the truth.[44]

---

[40] Cyril of Jerusalem, *Catechetical Lectures*, 4.17, in NPNF[2], 7.23 (English rendered clearer).
[41] Basil of Caesarea, *The Morals*, Rule 72, in *Saint Basil: Ascetical Works*, 185–86.
[42] John Chrysostom, *Concerning the Statutes*, Homily 1.14, in NPNF[1], 9:336–37.
[43] Augustine, *Letters*, 148.4.15, in NPNF[1], 1:502.
[44] Augustine, *On Baptism, Against the Donatists*, 2.2–3, in NPNF[1], 4:427.

When Augustine (writing in the fifth century) disagreed with Cyprian (a third-century father), he did not hesitate to assert that Cyprian's writings must be evaluated in light of Scripture. Thus, Augustine explains:

> We do no injustice to Cyprian when we make a distinction between his epistles and the canonical Scriptures; we may freely pass judgment on the writings of believers and unbelievers alike. . . . For that reason Cyprian's epistles, which have no canonical authority, must be judged according to their agreement with the authority of the divine writings. Thus we can accept from Cyprian only what agrees, and safely reject what does not agree, with Scripture.[45]

As Augustine's example illustrates, it is no slight to early generations of Christians (including those who lived in the second and third centuries) to subject their writings to the authoritative guide of biblical truth.

Fourth, there is evidence that early Christians also viewed Scripture as more authoritative than church councils. Even after the Council of Nicaea took place in 325, Athanasius, the renowned defender of Trinitarian orthodoxy, still regarded the authority of Scripture as superior to it. The council was authoritative only insofar as it accurately reflected the teachings of God's Word. Speaking of Arian theologians, Athanasius wrote:

> Vainly then do they run about with the pretext that they have demanded Councils for the faith's sake; for divine Scripture is sufficient above all things; but if a Council be needed on the point, there are the proceedings of the Fathers, for the Nicene Bishops did not neglect this matter, but stated the doctrine so exactly, that persons reading their words honestly, cannot but be reminded by them of the religion towards Christ announced in divine Scripture.[46]

Notice that Athanasius argues that "Scripture is sufficient above all things," including councils. Furthermore, he defends the orthodoxy of the Council of Nicaea on the grounds that its determinations reflected the truth "announced in divine Scripture." Arianism was not in error because it violated the findings of a council, but rather because it distorted and rejected the clear teaching of God's Word.

Augustine similarly notes that the councils of the church are not the Christian's ultimate authority. In debating an Arian heretic named

---

[45] Augustine, *Contra Cresconium*, 2.39–40, in A. D. R. Polman, *The Word of God according to St. Augustine* (Grand Rapids, MI: Eerdmans, 1961), 65. Cf. Webster, *Holy Scripture*, 2:76.
[46] Athanasius, *De Synodis: Councils of Ariminum and Seleucia*, 1.6, in NPNF[2], 4.453.

Maximinus, Augustine openly states: "I must not press the authority of Nicea against you, nor you that of Ariminum against me; I do not acknowledge the one, as you do not the other; but let us come to ground that is common to both, the testimony of the Holy Scriptures."[47] In other words, where the authority of councils fails, the authority of God's Word continues to reign supreme.

Fifth, in doctrinal matters, evidence from the fathers demonstrates that they generally regarded Scripture as more authoritative than church tradition. Though some of the fathers occasionally cite oral tradition to support certain ecclesiastical practices, on the whole, they look to Scripture as the final authority in matters of doctrine.[48] Basil provides an example in this regard. In places, he references unwritten customs such as triple immersion in baptism and facing east to pray.[49] But in the determination of sound doctrine, he looks solely to Scripture as his authoritative guide.[50]

Consider, for example, how Basil responds to the proponents of Arianism:

> Their complaint is that their custom [i.e., tradition] does not accept this and that Scripture does not agree. What is my reply? I do not consider it fair that the custom which obtains among them should be regarded as a law and rule of orthodoxy. If custom is to be taken in proof of what is right, then it is certainly competent for me to put forward on my side the custom which obtains here. If they reject this, we are clearly not bound to follow them. *Therefore let God-inspired Scripture decide between us*; and on whichever side be found doctrines in harmony with the word of God, in favor of that side will be cast the vote of truth.[51]

In denouncing the errors of Arian theology, Basil's ultimate appeal was not to tradition or to church councils, but to the Word of God. From his perspective, the definitive reason Arianism was wrong was not that it violated Trinitarian custom, but that it departed from biblical truth.

Elsewhere, Basil reiterates this point:

> What our fathers said, the same say we, that the glory of the Father and of the Son is common; wherefore we offer the doxology to the Father

---

[47] Augustine, *Against Maximinus the Arian*, 2.14, in George Salmon, *The Infallibility of the Church* (London: John Murray, 1888), 288.
[48] For a thorough examination, from an evangelical perspective, of the church fathers' use of tradition, see Webster, *Holy Scripture*, 2:22–238.
[49] Basil of Caesarea, *On the Holy Spirit*, 27.66, in NPNF², 8:40–42.
[50] Cf. Webster, *Holy Scripture*, 2:73.
[51] Basil of Caesarea, *Letters*, 189.3, in NPNF², 8.229 (emphasis added).

with the Son. But we do not rest only on the fact that such is the tradition of the Fathers; for they too followed the sense of Scripture, and started from the evidence which, a few sentences back, I deduced from Scripture and laid before you.[52]

As Basil's statement demonstrates, his case for the deity of Christ did not ultimately rest on the teachings of earlier Christian leaders, but on an even greater authority: the Word of God.

In summary, abundant examples from early Christian writings can be produced to show that, in matters of doctrine, the early church elevated the Scriptures above (1) noncanonical writings, (2) human wisdom, (3) their own teaching (and the teaching of earlier church fathers), (4) the findings of church councils, and (5) the traditions of the church. On this basis, then, a strong case can be made to show that a chorus of patristic voices anticipated the Reformation doctrine of *sola Scriptura*, that Scripture is perfectly true and that it stands alone as the ultimate authority for determining what the church is to believe and to teach.

A Note about Tradition

But what about those places where the church fathers do speak of "tradition"? How should such references be understood in light of the fathers' clear affirmation of the inerrancy and authority of Scripture?

The Roman Catholic Church insists that certain Christian doctrines were preserved not only through the *writings of inspired Scripture*, but also through *the transmission of extrabiblical oral tradition*. Such oral tradition supposedly explains the origination of distinctly Catholic doctrines such as the infallibility of the pope and the immaculate conception and assumption of Mary.

In responding to such claims, it is helpful to recognize that the church fathers used the term *tradition* in a variety of ways, none of which ultimately substantiates modern Catholic claims. For example, Irenaeus defines tradition not in terms of extrabiblical doctrines, but in terms of the essentials of the Christian faith, all of which are expressly taught in Scripture. Irenaeus explains that the "ancient tradition" of the apostles consists of the following:

> Believing in one God, the Creator of heaven and earth, and all things therein, by means of Christ Jesus, the Son of God; who, because of His

---

[52] Basil of Caesarea, *On the Holy Spirit*, 7.16, in *NPNF*[2], 8:10.

surpassing love towards His creation, condescended to be born of the virgin, He Himself uniting man through Himself to God, and having suffered under Pontius Pilate, and rising again, and having been received up in splendor, shall come in glory, the Savior of those who are saved, and the Judge of those who are judged, and sending into eternal fire those who transform the truth, and despise His Father and His advent.[53]

For Irenaeus, "tradition" includes (1) belief in one God, (2) belief that he created all things through Christ, (3) belief in the incarnation, (4) belief in the deity and humanity of Christ, (5) belief in Christ's passion, (6) belief in his resurrection, (7) belief in the ascension, and (8) belief in the second coming. That list articulates the fundamentals of the Christian faith and corresponds to doctrinal truths that are clearly taught in Scripture.[54]

Importantly, Irenaeus was using the term *tradition* as a direct refutation of Gnostic heretics who claimed that they possessed a secret tradition that had been orally passed down from the apostles but was different from Scripture. In response, Irenaeus explains that the traditions of the apostles are contained in the teachings of Scripture. Thus, the Gnostics were wrong because they elevated unbiblical, secret tradition above Scripture, whereas true believers had no other authoritative tradition besides God's Word.

To be sure, the church fathers sometimes appealed to prior generations of Christian leaders to show that, unlike the heretics, their teachings were not novelties. However, this appeal to earlier church history was never regarded as being an authority above or equal to Scripture. As Gregg Allison explains:

> This practice of appealing to church authority, especially to the writings of [earlier] church fathers, was never intended to deprive Scripture of its rightful place of authority. In battles against heresy, the point of appeal was to provide support for true doctrines because they were the doctrines the church had always embraced; they were not the novel ideas of the false teachers. And of course, whatever the church believed had to be traced back to Scripture itself, because that was the ultimate authority in all matters.[55]

Admittedly, there were also times when some church fathers (such as Basil of Caesarea) used the word *tradition* to speak about church practices

---

[53] Irenaeus, *Against Heresies*, 3.4.2, in *ANF*, 1:417.

[54] Cf. White's discussion of this quotation in "*Sola Scriptura* and the Early Church," 20–22.

[55] Allison, *Historical Theology*, 81.

of secondary importance, such as triple immersion in baptism and facing east to pray.[56] Importantly, modern Catholic doctrines such as the infallibility of the pope and the assumption of Mary are not included in the traditions of which Basil speaks. Furthermore, in the early church, even secondary practices were subject to evaluation on the basis of Scripture. Thus, Basil himself can explain that "every word and deed should be ratified by the testimony of the Holy Scripture to confirm the good and cause shame to the wicked."[57]

A century before Basil, Cyprian (ca. 200–258) provides a helpful example of this kind of biblical evaluation of tradition. Cyprian was addressing the question of whether or not heretical Novatianists who returned to the orthodox church should be rebaptized. Our goal in this chapter is not to address that particular issue, but instead to look at the authority to which Cyprian appealed in order to answer the question he posed. Significantly, he wished to follow a traditional practice only if it came from the Bible. Thus, he writes:

> Where is that tradition from? Does it come from the authority of the Lord and of the Gospel, or does it come from the commands and the epistles of the apostles? For God bears witness to the fact that those things which are written must be done. . . . If, therefore, it is either prescribed in the Gospel, or contained in the epistles or Acts of the Apostles, . . . [then] let this divine and holy tradition be observed."[58]

In sum, when the church fathers spoke of tradition in a doctrinal sense, or in the sense of the "rule of faith," they were generally referring to truths that are expressly taught in Scripture, as the example from Irenaeus demonstrates. At the same time, some patristic writers (such as Basil in the fourth century) occasionally spoke of unwritten, extrabiblical "traditions" that pertained to certain ecclesiastical practices and customs. Even so, the evidence suggests that most of the church fathers would have gladly agreed with the principle that everything—whether doctrinal or practical—is ultimately subject to the Word of God. Consequently, their use of the word *tradition* does not contradict their commitment to the final authority of Scripture.

---

[56] Cf. Webster, *Holy Scripture*, 2:142–48. It should be noted that many of the secondary practices mentioned by Basil are not practiced by the Roman Catholic Church today.
[57] Basil of Caesarea: *The Morals*, Rule 26, in *Saint Basil: Ascetical Works*, 106.
[58] Cyprian, *Letters*, 73.2, in *ANF* 5:386–87 (English rendered clearer).

Conclusion

Based on evidence from the writings of the church fathers, a strong case can be made to demonstrate that the early church affirmed the doctrine of *sola Scriptura*—namely, the conviction that Scripture is without error and that it alone is the highest authority and the final court of appeal for the establishment of sound doctrine. It is the rule by which all things must be measured.

Scripture is God's Word. Therefore, it reflects his perfect character and comes with his absolute authority. The early church understood that to submit to Scripture is to submit to the lordship of its divine Author. Thus, in the writings of the church fathers, we find statements such as the following:

> We make the Holy Scriptures the rule and the measure of every tenet; we necessarily fix our eyes upon that, and approve that alone which may be made to harmonize with the intention of those writings.[59]

> For among the things that are plainly laid down in Scripture are to be found all matters that concern faith and the manner of life.[60]

> What more shall I teach you than what we read in the apostle? For holy Scripture fixes the rule of our doctrine, lest we be wiser than we ought. . . . Therefore, I should not teach you anything else except to expound to you the words of the Teacher.[61]

In light of such evidence, contemporary evangelicals can have great confidence that their commitment to the inerrancy and authority of Scripture has a rich history that spans the last two millennia. The doctrine of *sola Scriptura* was not a sixteenth-century invention. Though it may not always have been articulated as clearly or directly in the pre-Reformation period as it was during the sixteenth century, it has nonetheless been the cherished conviction of believers throughout the entire history of the church.

Along those lines, Webster writes:

> The opinion of the fathers and theologians throughout the history of the Church and up to the Reformation was overwhelmingly in favor

---

[59] Gregory of Nyssa, *On the Soul and the Resurrection*, citing his sister Macrina, in *NPNF²*, 5:439.
[60] Augustine, *On Christian Doctrine*, 2.9, in *NPNF¹*, 2:539.
[61] Augustine: *On the Good of Widowhood*, 2, in White, "*Sola Scriptura* and the Early Church," 24–25. Cf. *NPNF¹*, 3.442.

of the Reformation principle of *sola Scriptura* and antithetical to the position of the Council of Trent. Contrary to claims by Roman Catholic apologists, the principle of *sola Scriptura* is not only biblical, it is historical.[62]

Armed with the confidence that this doctrine is established in Scripture and affirmed in church history, believers can go forth boldly in the knowledge that there is no higher authority than the Word of God, because there is no authority greater than God himself.

---

[62] Webster, *Holy Scripture*, 2:92.

9

The Power of the Word in the Present

INERRANCY AND THE REFORMATION

Carl R. Trueman

In addressing the issue of inerrancy and the Reformation, I have a relatively modest intention. Inerrancy as a doctrine has been attacked as a result of the infusing of Enlightenment epistemology into Christian faith. Central to this thesis is the idea that Scottish Common Sense Realism profoundly shaped the way in which the theologians of Old Princeton, specifically Charles and A. A. Hodge and Benjamin B. Warfield, approached the biblical text. Elsewhere, there have been those who claimed the doctrine to be an American innovation, arising out of the distinctively American Fundamentalist-Modernist controversy of the late nineteenth and twentieth centuries. In response, I wish to argue simply that a number of the basic elements that made up the later inerrancy doctrine were present in the church from a very early period and that the doctrine is quite compatible with the teaching of key Reformers. While issues of continuity and discontinuity in theological development are often more complicated than we might imagine, I would suggest that the later formulations of inerrancy are founded on notions of inspiration and textual integrity consistent with the positions of earlier generations.

The Protestant Reformation is often regarded as placing Scripture at the center of the church's life and practice. It was, after all, the era of great Bible translations—the Luther Bible, the Geneva Bible, the Authorized Version. Theologically and indeed culturally, Scripture was a major preoccupation of the time. That church architecture also shifted at this point, placing the pulpit in a central position, is indicative of a move from sacrament-centered to Word-centered worship and, by implication, a Word-centered understanding of the whole of the Christian life.

There is thus no dispute regarding the importance of Scripture for the Reformation. Certain questions on Scripture were matters of contentious debate; obvious examples include the extent of the canon and the correct principles of interpretation, especially with regard to the Lord's Supper. On both of these matters, there were significant differences even among Protestants who affirmed the Scripture principle. Still, on that Scripture principle, the magisterial Reformers were all agreed.

As Protestants today, we should be self-conscious in the way in which we appropriate our heritage and seek to remain faithful to its confessions. Yet we need to remember that there is always a problem when Christians in one era demand answers to their questions from texts written in another. This is not to say that earlier texts cannot speak to later times. Obviously, the Christian faith is predicated on precisely that principle: every Sunday, pastors preach from an ancient text in order to provide their people with answers to their situations today. But questions of a technical theological nature often arise in specific circumstances and against the background of specific prior dogmatic formulations. That makes the move from question to answer more complicated than we might like.

Thus it is with inerrancy. If scholars are agreed on the centrality of Scripture to the Protestant Reformation, they have found the issue of inerrancy in the Reformation far more contentious. This is largely for the very simple reason that the questions that later formulations of the doctrine of inerrancy sought to answer were not posed in quite the same form in the sixteenth and seventeenth centuries.

In addressing the issue of inerrancy in the Reformation, we must remember that the articulation of the idea that we find in Charles Hodge and Warfield was developed in a specific polemical context. The precise details of this context, primarily the higher criticism of the nineteenth century and the development of trajectories of post-Kantian theology stemming from Friedrich Schleiermacher, did not apply in the sixteenth and seventeenth centuries. Thus, the specific concerns and many of the particular arguments we find in the nineteenth and twentieth centuries do not have direct counterparts in earlier history.

The Reformers were wrestling with a different set of issues. In a predominantly illiterate society, they focused on the Word read and especially the Word proclaimed. Preaching was thus the primary context for thinking about the authority of the Word of God. Thus, their immediate concern when reflecting on the nature of biblical authority was typically the power of the Word in the present, not the origins of the Word in the past. Further, the kind of questions that Hodge and Warfield faced arose out of the elaborate development of the world the Reformers helped to initiate but with which they did not have to wrestle extensively. For example, the higher criticism that lies in the background of the Princetonians' work was, of course, the result of the serious linguistic and textual engagement with Scripture that the Reformers' convictions helped create. But these developments really started in the mid-seventeenth century. They were largely unknown to Martin Luther, John Calvin, and company.

Before coming to the matter of doctrine proper, it is worth sketching the context in which the Reformation Scripture principle emerged. The church had engaged in the exposition of Scripture since its inception. Why, then, did Scripture become such a focus in the sixteenth century? The answer is the confluence of an increasing focus in the late Middle Ages on what we would term special revelation and the collapse of traditional structures of authority.

Several factors influenced this development. First, an increasing lack of confidence in human reason emerged in Europe in the late thirteenth and fourteenth centuries. Intellectually, this was represented by the so-called voluntarists, who accented the sovereignty of God's will in all his actions and thus the need to base any theological claims upon his particular revelation of himself. This revelation was not typically identified with Scripture but with church tradition. Nevertheless, the principial issue—that theology was based on God's revelation—was an important step toward the Reformation position.

Second, material conditions, most notably the Black Plague in the late Middle Ages, also served to undermine human confidence and certainty. In an uncertain world, people turn to that which appears constant and reliable. As human reason and abilities seemed futile in the face of dramatic and unpredictable acts of God, minds increasingly focused on the notion of revelation—what we would call special revelation—as the primary and normative means of knowing God.

Third, there was a breakdown of the church's authority structures, cul-minating in the disastrous claims of three rival popes in the late fourteenth and early fifteenth centuries and the necessity of an imperial council at Constance to solve the problem. One hundred years later, at the Leipzig Disputation, John Eck would press Luther on the issue of authority. It was at that moment that Luther realized the significance both of his own theological development and of the Council of Constance: if the papacy had failed and the council had erred, what was left? It was Scripture alone.

Still, the Reformers themselves did not spend significant time develop-ing a doctrine of Scripture. This could be interpreted as them not being particularly interested in such a doctrine. However, that would be a histori-cally inept conclusion. It seems far more reasonable to see the comparative confessional silence on the issue as indicative of the fact that, in terms of matters such as divine inspiration and authority understood in the narrow-est sense, the Reformers did not see themselves as deviating fundamentally from the received tradition. Thus, it will be helpful to broaden our discus-sion to connect to views of Scripture prior to the Reformation.

The Mode of Inspiration

It is clear from very early in the postapostolic church's history that inspi-ration in terms of inscripturation was seen as intimately connected to the Holy Spirit. Thus, 1 Clement states, "Look carefully into the Scriptures, which are the true utterances of the Holy Spirit."[1] No specifics are given here about the way in which the text of Scripture is the utterance of the Holy Spirit; there is simply a confident statement that such is the case. In-deed, a few paragraphs later we read: "Beloved, you understand the holy Scriptures very well. You have looked deeply into the prophecies of God."[2] Again, the words of Scripture and the speech of God are identified.

Neither is this unique to Clement. Theodoret of Cyr (fifth century) speaks in similar terms: "Some have said that not all the psalms come from David, but that some are the work of others. I have no opinion either way. What difference does it make to me whether they are all David's or whether some are the compositions of others, when it is clear that they are all the fruit of the Holy Spirit's inspiration?"[3] And in the sixth century, Gregory the Great dismissed questions about the authorship of anonymous books

---

[1] 1 Clement 1:45, cited in Gerald L. Bray, *Ancient Christian Doctrine I: We Believe in One God* (Downers Grove, IL: InterVarsity Press, 2009), 13.
[2] 1 Clement 1:53, cited in Bray, *Ancient Christian Doctrine I*, 13.
[3] Theodoret of Cyr, *Preface to the Psalms*, cited in Bray, *Ancient Christian Doctrine I*, 23.

with reference to inspiration: "It is pointless to ask who wrote the book of Job, since the Holy Spirit is rightly believed to have been its author. In other words, the one who wrote it is the one who dictated what is to be written."[4]

This is also evidence that ancient church writers could on occasion use language that indicates a dictation approach to the inscripturation process. Thus, the Greek apologist Athenagoras uses the analogy of musical instruments in order to ground the authority of Scripture in the mode of inspiration:

> We have the prophets as witnesses of the things we understand and believe. Men like Moses, Isaiah, Jeremiah and other prophets declared things about God and the things of God. It would be irrational of us to disbelieve God's Spirit and accept mere human opinions instead, for God moved the mouths of the prophets as if they were musical instruments.[5]

This would also appear to be the concept that underlies a statement in the Muratorian Fragment: "Although different things are taught in the different Gospels, there is no difference with respect to the faith of believers, because all of them were inspired by the same controlling Spirit."[6]

Of course, in quoting these sources, I am not claiming that the writer of the Fragment, Athenagoras, or Gregory had a fully adequate understanding of inspiration and inscripturation. I am merely pointing out that a very high view of the scriptural text as inspired revelation was explicitly present in some of the earliest postapostolic literature. That is the only inference that can be drawn from dictation-style language.

As with so much else in theology, the Middle Ages provide key conceptual developments relative to Scripture and inspiration that lie in the background of the Reformation. One obvious problem with dictation language is that, if it is understood too univocally, it becomes impossible to give an adequate account of the varying styles and even the variety of genres in Scripture. And, as is so often the case, it is Thomas Aquinas who makes the necessary conceptual distinctions that pave the way for a more elaborate and adequate understanding of inspiration.

Aquinas makes a basic distinction between revelation and inspiration. The former is the miraculous provision of new information. The latter is the exaltation of the human faculties. In this way, Aquinas allows the church to

---

[4] Gregory the Great, *Morals on the Book of Job*, Preface 1.2, cited in Bray, *Ancient Christian Doctrine I*, 23.
[5] Athenagoras, *A Plea Regarding Christians*, 9, cited in Bray, *Ancient Christian Doctrine I*, 13.
[6] The Muratorian Fragment, cited in Bray, *Ancient Christian Doctrine I*, 14.

avoid the pitfalls of too blunt or univocal an emphasis upon dictation. He was well aware that in some cases, the Bible itself describes a form of dictation, as when the Lord instructs his prophets to write his words down. But he also knew that there were times when revelation came through a vision. More importantly, there were times when the mind was simply guided by the Holy Spirit to write down that which the Lord providentially wished to be inscripturated. This allowed for explanation of both the varied writing styles of the biblical authors, and also for the explicit methodological claims of someone like Luke, who specifically stated his historical approach to gathering information and constructing a narrative.

When we come to the Reformation, we should remember what we noted earlier: that the kind of higher-critical questions that began to emerge in the mid-seventeenth century and reached their apex in the nineteenth century were not of great concern. The issues at the time of the Reformation were canon and perspicuity, and these pushed Scripture's self-authentication and issues of interpretation to the forefront, neither of which made the origin of Scripture a primary focus of attention.

Nevertheless, in the writings of the Reformers, we find language on the Holy Spirit, inspiration, and dictation similar to that which we noted in the early church. While I cannot address each and every Reformer, it is worth noting that Luther, of all the Reformers, tended to favor the prophetic mode of inspiration that often implied a form of dictation. Reflecting in the preface to his *Dictata super Psalterium* (1513–15) on 2 Samuel 23:1–4, he declares:

> Other prophets used the expression "The word of the Lord came to me." This one, however, does not say, "The word of the Lord came to me," but he says, in a new manner of speaking, "His word was spoken by me." With this expression he indicates some extremely intimate and friendly kind of inspiration.[7]

Luther articulates a similar idea, with a more general application, when, speaking of Simeon in Luke 2, he writes: "Luke says of Simeon that he is a personification of all prophets filled with the Holy Ghost. They spoke and wrote as they were inspired by the Holy Ghost."[8]

Thus, for Luther, the origin of Scripture lies in the speaking of God to inspired speakers and writers. This is why he frequently cites Scripture in

---

[7] Martin Luther, *Luther's Works*, ed. Jaroslav Pelikan and Helmut Lehmann (St. Louis: Concordia, 1955–), 10.10. Hereafter *LW*.
[8] Ibid., 52.105.

terms of "the Holy Spirit says" or "the Holy Spirit points out." Indeed, the present tense here is important, underlining the practical importance of the inspiration of Scripture in its origin for the application and power of Scripture in the present. Basic to Luther's pastoral advice is the notion of quoting Scripture to reassure your conscience or the conscience of a troubled friend. Thus, when the Devil comes to tempt you, you are to present him with Scripture verses. Those verses constitute the Spirit's statement in the present because they were inspired by the Spirit in the past.[9] This connection is one that lies at the heart of Reformation pastoral practice and preaching.

Calvin is similar in his high view of the original inspiration of Scripture and is even prepared at times to use the language of dictation. Thus, in commenting on 1 Peter 1:11, he says:

> At the same time, a high praise is given to their doctrine, for it was the testimony of the Holy Spirit; the preachers and ministers were men, but he was the teacher. Nor does he declare without reason that the Spirit of Christ then ruled; and he makes the Spirit, sent from heaven, to preside over the teachers of the Gospel, for he shews that the Gospel comes from God, and that the ancient prophecies were dictated by Christ.[10]

Some caution is appropriate, however. We need to remember that the language of dictation can itself be used metaphorically, as a means of underlining the authority of the content rather than as a specific account of the mode of delivery. Thus, Calvin's comment on 1 Peter 1:11 needs to be set alongside his comment on 2 Peter 1:21:

> He says that they were *moved*—not that they were bereaved of mind, (as the Gentiles imagined their prophets to have been,) but because they dared not to announce anything of their own, and obediently followed the Spirit as their guide, who ruled in their mouth as in his own sanctuary. Understand by *prophecy of Scripture* that which is contained in the holy Scriptures.[11]

Here Calvin shows a degree of caution about prophetic inspiration. It involves the prophets being *moved* by the Holy Spirit, but not in such a way that they are *bereaved of mind*. We might summarize this view by saying that Calvin is precise about the content of Scripture—it is divinely

---

[9] Ibid., 3.308.
[10] John Calvin, *Commentaries on the Catholic Epistles*, trans. John Owen (Bellingham, WA: Logos Bible Software), 39–40.
[11] Ibid., 391.

inspired and exactly what God intends—while being modest, if not some-what vague, about the means of inspiration.

This is very similar to the position of Heinrich Bullinger:

> Furthermore, the doctrine and writings of the prophets have always been of great authority among all wise men throughout the whole world. For it is well perceived by many arguments, that they took not their beginning of the prophets themselves, as chief authors; but were inspired from God out of heaven by the Holy Spirit of God: for it is God, which, dwelling by his Spirit in the minds of the prophets, spea-keth to us by their mouths. And for that cause have they a most large testimony at the hands of Christ, and his elect apostles. What say ye to this moreover, that God by their ministry hath wrought miracles and wonders to be marvelled at, and those not a few; that at the least by mighty signs we might learn that it is God, by whose inspiration the prophets do teach and write whatsoever they left for us to remember?[12]

Again, we should note that Bullinger is vague on the mechanics of in-spiration, but certain about the outcome: a thoroughly truthful, reliable, and powerful text. Of course, this doctrine is not being worked out in order to address variant manuscript readings, although it does put in place a conceptual framework that will be useful for such.

Errors in the Bible?

This brings us at last to the issue of the Reformers and their beliefs about the possibility that the Bible contained errors. Some have argued that the Reformers either were not perturbed by the possibility of errors in the Bible or happily accepted it. Such claims are often built on the notion that concern for errors and contradictions is the result of asking modernist or Enlightenment questions of a premodern text. Such questions were alleg-edly of no interest to the premodern, and perhaps even the early modern, mind. Here, it is helpful to be aware that we find the issue being raised in a basic form as far back as Augustine in the fifth century. He writes:

> Of all the books of the world, I believe that only the authors of holy Scripture were totally free from error, and if I am puzzled by anything in them that seems to go against the truth, I do not hesitate to suppose

[12] Heinrich Bullinger, *The Decades of Henry Bullinger: The First and Second Decades*, trans. T. Harding (Cambridge: Cambridge University Press, 1849), I.1, 50.

that either the manuscript is faulty or the translator has not caught the sense of what was said, or I have failed to understand it for myself.[13]

Here Augustine offers three reasons as to why there might appear to be errors in Scripture: a faulty manuscript, a wrong translation, or a failure in his own understanding. At no point does he offer the possibility of an actual error in the original text as a reason for the problem. Again, this seems clear evidence that concern for errors in the Bible is not a modern phenomenon, rooted in Enlightenment epistemologies and preoccupations.

One quote from Augustine is admittedly not enough to demonstrate a widespread consensus on the issue in the ancient church.[14] What the reference proves, however, is that the kind of concerns expressed and arguments offered by later inerrantists in the Hodge-Warfield tradition is not unprecedented in earlier texts. As far back as the fifth century, theologians were aware of the problem posed by apparent or potential errors.

While the problems of higher criticism were more or less unknown in the sixteenth century, the area where the possibility of error did press in on the Reformers was that of biblical chronology. In this context, it is interesting to look at Luther's work. He is interesting because it is arguable that the overwhelming scholarly consensus dismisses any notion of him, or all the Reformers, holding to inerrancy as so ridiculous as to need no justification.

Sometimes such dismissal is supported with reference to Luther's attitude toward the book of James. We might respond to that, however, by pointing out that Luther's issues with James are not that it is a piece of Scripture that contains theological errors so much as it is a book that should simply not be part of the Bible. Inspiration and canonicity, not inspiration and error, is the issue.

More problematic for the precise issue of errancy is Luther's approach to the nature of biblical chronology, which he declares to be highly confusing and somewhat chaotic. Nevertheless, a couple of examples provide some opportunity for instructive reflection. First, perhaps the most taxing chronological issue for Luther is the conflict between Moses and Stephen over God's call to Abram. Moses places the call in Haran (Gen. 11:31), while Stephen sets it in Mesopotamia (Acts 7:2).

Luther's way of addressing the problem is interesting and instructive. First, he refers to the approach of some other unnamed exegetes:

---

[13] Augustine, Letter 82, to Jerome, cited in Bray, *Ancient Christian Doctrine I*, 22.

[14] For a fuller treatment of this issue in the patristic period, see chapter 8 in this volume, "The Ground and Pillar of the Faith: The Witness of Pre-Reformation History to the Doctrine of *Sola Scriptura*" by Nathan Busenitz.

The customary answer is that Abraham was called twice, once in Ur of the Chaldeans, perhaps by the patriarch Shem, and later on in Haran, but that Moses is satisfied with relating the later call in Haran. Thus these witnesses do not disagree; for Moses relates the later, Stephen the earlier call.[15]

Luther rejects this approach on the grounds that such a reading would imply that Moses was not the source of Stephen's knowledge of the incident, which he clearly was. Instead, Luther sees the answer as lying in authorial intent and genre:

> Nevertheless, it seems to me that the accurate account of what happened is given by Moses and not by Stephen, who certainly derived his knowledge of this story from Moses alone. But when we relate something incidentally, it often happens that we do not pay such close attention to all details as do those who are engaged in leaving behind a written account of an event for their descendants. And so Moses is the historian, but Stephen is little concerned about the details; for the account appears in Moses, and Stephen merely aims at having his hearers realize that the father of this people had neither Law nor temple and yet was acceptable to God and pleased Him. The chief point of the matter is this: Stephen emphasizes that God does not disclose Himself on account of the temple or circumcision or the Law; but He justifies, remits sins, and bestows eternal life solely on account of the promised Seed, whom the synagogue had previously slain.[16]

I use this example not to argue that Luther's approach is necessarily the correct one, but to point out two things. First, he was aware of conflicts between different passages of Scripture and indeed of traditions of proposed solutions to such conflicts. Second, he was concerned to offer a rationale for the conflict that did not simply say: "Scripture contains errors. Please do not worry about it." He appears to have been most reluctant to countenance error as error; rather, he used what we might describe as a sensitivity to literary genre and authorial intention in order to avoid having to declare Scripture as erroneous. We may disagree with his approach, but it is clear that he was most concerned to argue for the trustworthiness of scriptural statements. Underlying his thinking was the basic assumption that God is trustworthy and so Scripture therefore must be.

The passage lends itself to comparison with the approach of Calvin. In

---

[15] *LW*, 2.277–78.
[16] Ibid., 2.278.

his Genesis commentary, Calvin makes no allusion to the problem Genesis 11:31 poses for Stephen's speech in Acts, but draws on the ancient geographical convention of describing Haran as being part of Mesopotamia:

> Moreover, the town which by the Hebrews is called Charran, is declared by all writers, with one consent, to be Charran, situated in Mesopotamia; although Lucan, poetically rather than truly, places it in Assyria. The place was celebrated for the destruction of Crassus, and the overthrow of the Roman army.[17]

This is also the assumption of his comments on Acts 7:2.[18]

Elsewhere, Luther refers to the problems of producing a harmony of the royal chronologies in the books of Kings and indeed of harmonizing the accounts of Christ as presented in the Gospels. Yet even here we need to be careful about drawing too sharp a conclusion based on his acknowledgment of difficulties and carelessness in chronological construction among the evangelists. He himself attempted to produce harmonies of the classic places in the Gospels where this is an issue: the temptations in the wilderness, the cleansing of the temple, and the denials of Peter. If, as has been claimed, Luther was only interested in the existential encounter between Christ and the individual in the present that the Word of God mediated, he would hardly have been concerned to harmonize such passages. The same surely applies to Calvin and others who attempted similar feats.

Inerrancy in a Theological Context

I have thus far argued that the general silence of the Reformers on the issue of Scripture's inspiration allows us to infer that, by and large, they were happy with the tradition that they inherited. This tradition had a high view of the Holy Spirit's inspiration of the original authors and thus of the text of Scripture. This tradition had developed distinctions in the Middle Ages that allowed theologians to think beyond the category of dictation when it came to inspiration. And this tradition was well aware of the difficulties posed by apparent contradictions in Scripture. Luther is a great example of evidence that this is the case.

Nevertheless, amid all of the contemporary debate about inerrancy, focused as it is on the text as originally given, I want to conclude by mak-

---

[17] John Calvin. *Commentary on the First Book of Moses Called Genesis*, vol. 1, trans. J. King (Bellingham, WA: Logos Bible Software, 2010), 339.
[18] John Calvin, *Commentary upon the Acts of the Apostles*, vol. 1, trans. H. Beveridge (Bellingham, WA: Logos Bible Software, 2010), 250–51.

ing a plea for two things. I want to use the Reformers as a means of setting inerrancy itself into some kind of theological context.

First, while the contemporary evangelical imagination is gripped by a narrative that places assaults on the veracity of the scriptural text at its heart, the historical narrative of the decline of the church is more complicated. Reformed theology did not collapse simply because the scriptural text came under attack; it collapsed because the doctrine of God came under attack. My own work on the seventeenth century convinced me that certain strands of Socinianism, the progenitor of Unitarianism, were in many ways a biblicist movement that took Scripture as absolutely authoritative.

If we keep in mind that the central element of the Reformers' approach was the trustworthiness of God (the point upon which justification by grace through faith depends), then we will not lose sight of the connection between the doctrine of God and the doctrine of Scripture. The evangelical world is adept at selective outrage, but on this issue, selectivity could prove lethal. The doctrine of Scripture and the doctrine of God need to be closely correlated, lest the one undermine the other.

Indeed, when the doctrine of Scripture became a separate theological locus in the era of post-Reformation orthodoxy, it is surely significant that many of the attributes of Scripture were the same as those of God. Scripture was considered authoritative, perfect, effective, powerful, holy, and necessary. The same things could be said of God. In short, Scripture was regarded as a reflection of the being of God himself because it was God's speech.

Second, and consequent upon this point, let us not be so mesmerized by inerrancy or by the alliances it can build that we miss the bigger dogmatic picture and leave other doctrines unguarded. Inerrancy must be coordinated with other aspects of Scripture (such as sufficiency and perspicuity) and, above all, it must stand in positive relation to the doctrine of God. Given the general repudiation of much of classical theism within evangelical circles, at least classical theism as envisaged by the men who formulated the Protestant doctrine of Scripture, this should give us all cause for thought and, indeed, for concern.

Finally, we should remember why the trustworthiness of God's speech in Scripture was so important to the Reformers: it was the foundation of their understanding of the trustworthiness of preaching. The Word correctly preached was the speech of God addressed to congregations in the present, as is made so clear by the very first chapter of the Second Helvetic

Confession, Bullinger's great statement of confessional faith for the Zurich of his day:

> The preaching of the Word of God is the Word of God. Wherefore when this Word of God is now preached in the church by preachers lawfully called, we believe that the very Word of God is proclaimed, and received by the faithful; and that neither any other Word of God is to be invented nor is to be expected from heaven: and that now the Word itself which is preached is to be regarded, not the minister that preaches; for even if he be evil and a sinner, nevertheless the Word of God remains still true and good.

10

How Scotland Lost Her
Hold on the Bible

A CASE STUDY OF INERRANCY
COMPROMISE

Iain H. Murray

There are times when books come into the hands of Christians just when they need them. It was so with me one February day in 1954, when I was a student at Durham University. A secondhand book came into my hands entitled *A Critical History of Free Thought in Reference to the Christian Religion* by Adam S. Farrar. The volume originated in Farrar's talks in the Bampton Lectures series at Oxford in 1862. The date is significant. It was before the authority of Scripture was discounted in British universities, and Farrar, an evangelical, spent nearly seven hundred pages reviewing attacks on the Word of God across the centuries.[1] I was having my first personal experience of opposition to the trustworthiness of Scripture, and this book

---

[1] A. S. Farrar, *A Critical History of Free Thought in Reference to the Christian Religion* (London: John Murray, 1862). Dr. Farrar became professor of divinity at Durham, dying June 11, 1905. He is not to be confused with Dean Farrar of Westminster Abbey.

showed me that the experience was no new thing. Attacks on the Word of God are as old as the history of fallen man. I needed to learn a key to an understanding of history.

Here is the explanation for the hostility of the heathen nations to Israel in the Old Testament. What made the people of Israel uniquely different from others was the revelation they received from heaven. God gave them prophets who could say, "The Spirit of the LORD speaks by me; his word is on my tongue" (2 Sam. 23:2). This is why the psalmist wrote: "He declares his word to Jacob, his statutes and rules to Israel. He has not dealt thus with any other nation" (Ps. 147:19–20a). And the apostle Paul affirmed: "Then what advantage has the Jew? . . . To begin with, the Jews were entrusted with the oracles of God" (Rom. 3:1–2). At its heart, the assault on Israel was a war on the Word of God.

Move on to the New Testament and the early church era. Why the three hundred years of persecution of Christians? John on Patmos tells us it was "on account of the word of God" (Rev. 1:9). Sufferers are described by Christ as those who "have kept my word" (3:8), and those put to death are said to be "slain for the word of God and for the witness they had borne" (6:9).

The same thing is repeated at the Reformation. Why was William Tyndale burned to death in 1536? It was because he had attached himself to the Word of God and translated it into English. Twenty years later, John Rogers, his friend and helper, was on trial for his life in London. Bishop Gardiner, Rogers's Roman Catholic judge, challenged him to specify one doctrine that the pope taught against the Word of God. Rogers at once pointed to the papal enforcement of all services in the Latin tongue contrary to 1 Corinthians 14:19. When he offered to explain the passage, Gardiner exclaimed: "No, no, thou canst prove nothing by the Scripture: the Scripture is dead and must have a lively exposition." Rogers replied, "No, no, the Scripture is alive." But as he offered to say more, he was interrupted: "Nay, nay, all heretics have alleged the Scriptures for them, and therefore must we have a living exposition for them."[2] In other words, the church must determine the truth, explain Scripture, and say what is to be believed.

A few days later, Rogers wrote a final testimony. He declared that the message recovered by the Reformation was that Parliament must "give

---

[2] This was a crucial difference between Protestants and Roman Catholics. The latter argued that our faith comes to us on the authority of the church; Protestants asserted that Scripture alone is the rule of faith. See, for example, William Whitaker, *A Disputation on Holy Scripture: Against the Papists* (1610; repr., Cambridge: Parker Soc., 1849).

place to the Word of the ever living God, and not God to the act of Parliament: of God's Word there shall not one tittle perish, but it shall be all fulfilled and performed that is therein contained, and unto it must all men, king and queen, Emperor, Parliaments and general councils obey—and the Word obeyeth no man—it cannot be changed nor altered, neither may we add or put anything thereto, nor take nothing therefrom." For this faith, Rogers was also burned to death in London on February 4, 1555.

Move on again to the Puritan period. In the 1620s, under Puritan preaching in Ulster, in northern Ireland, there was a remarkable revival, with many hundreds coming to faith in Christ. Twenty years later, there was a Catholic uprising in the same place, supported by priests, and thousands of Protestants were put to death. A report from the time tells us that "the Bible, in a particular manner was an object on which the Romanists vented their detestation of the truth. 'They have torn it in pieces, they have kicked it up and down, treading it under foot, leaping and trampling thereupon; saying, "a plague on it, this book has bred all the quarrel," hoping within three weeks that all the Bibles in Ireland should be so used, and wishing they had all the Bibles in Christendom, that they might use them so.'"[3] In the Reformation and Puritan periods, attacks on the Bible commonly took the form of physical persecution, and they came from false religion.

In the eighteenth century, the attacks came from the world and in the form of philosophy. Many of the attackers claimed to believe in God, but not the God of the Bible. They rejected revelation given from heaven. It was said of Voltaire, a leader in the period that was falsely called the "Enlightenment," that "the sole object of all his efforts was to destroy belief in the plenary inspiration of the Scriptures, and the divine origin of revelation which is attested by them. There is hardly a book in Scripture that he did not attack . . . he tried to show absurdities and contradictions in them all."[4]

The popularizer of Voltaire and the philosophers was Tom Paine, whose books *The Rights of Man* and *The Age of Reason* had enormous sales on both sides of the Atlantic. Paine boasted: "I have gone through the Bible as a man would go through a wood with an ax and felled trees. Here they lie and the priest may replant them, but they will never grow."[5]

The attack I want to consider most particularly is one that has had a more devastating effect on our contemporary world than anything written by Voltaire or Paine. It came from a different source—not from the Roman

[3] Quoted in J. S. Reid, *History of the Presbyterian Church in Ireland* (Belfast: Mullan, 1867), 1:330.
[4] Cited in Farrar, *Critical History*, 246.
[5] Cited in Arthur B. Strickland, *The Great American Revival* (Cincinnati: Standard, 1934), 36.

Church and not from the philosophy of the world, but from within the Protestant churches. Further, it was a great deal more subtle, because it did not present itself as an attack at all. It came with the claim that it was for the Bible and for Christianity.

The nineteenth century saw great progress in many areas of knowledge, for which we should be thankful. However, instead of attributing this progress to the providence of God, there were those who explained it in terms of the supposed evolutionary march of mankind. They claimed that geology proved the Genesis account of the beginning of the world to be impossible. They denied the authenticity of the Pentateuch. They doubted whether primitive man even knew how to write in the time of Moses.

When Christians were first confronted with such ideas, they recognized them as the products of unbelief. The Protestant churches all believed the authority of the Word of God. But by the 1880s, a different response had arisen. Prominent teachers came forward in the churches who argued that there was no need to defend every part of Scripture. Some concessions could be made to modern scholarship. Christianity could be better defended by holding only to what is essential and fundamental. Here was a new movement setting out, it said, not to destroy faith, but to put it on a firmer basis, leaving aside only the less important and incidental matters, and concentrating on the preservation of what is most vital. This teaching took the name "the New Apologetic," an apologetic not for unbelief but for Christianity.

For a closer look at this development, I want to concentrate on Scotland, and particularly on the Free Church of Scotland, the denomination that became the powerhouse for ideas that would reach all parts of the English-speaking world.

Beginnings

The Free Church of Scotland was formed in 1843 by some five hundred ministers who separated from the Church of Scotland on account of the state's interference in the church. It was a movement born out of a revival of evangelical faith, and it was marked by prayerfulness, outreach, and missionary zeal, both at home and abroad. Its leaders were revered across the Protestant world. Some spoke of it as the most apostolic church in the world.

But forty years later, it was from this church that the New Apologetic entered the scene.

William Robertson Smith, a pupil of A. B. Davidson and Julius Well-hausen (who was to call him "the cleverest man in Britain"), was the first in the Free Church to make public a program to put an understanding of Scripture on a new basis. From the start, his career was extraordinary; gifted in speech, knowledge, and languages, he was already a phenomenon when, from theological college, he moved straight to a position as professor of Hebrew at Aberdeen at the age of twenty-three. But in the next seven years, his published writings raised an increasing concern. He so disregarded admonitions to be more circumspect that in 1881 he was removed from his post. Robert Rainy, principal of New College, Edinburgh, who would increasingly shelter the new school of teachers, sought to prevent that decision, giving as one of his reasons that such action against Professor Smith could promote the same action against others. Rainy lost his defense of Smith by one vote, but he was right in warning that the matter did not concern one man alone. Others were already in the wing.

Marcus Dods (1834–1909) was one of the first to come forward. In a sermon, "Revelation and Inspiration" (1877), he presented the view that an acceptance of inaccuracies in the Old Testament need not affect the substance of the faith. The next decade was to show how quickly the position of the church was changing. In 1889, despite opposition, Dods succeeded George Smeaton as professor of New Testament exegesis at New College. But in his inaugural lecture, Dods described belief in the plenary inspiration of the Bible as "a theory of inspiration which has made the Bible an offence to many honest men, which is dishonouring to God, and which has turned inquirers into sceptics by the thousand,—a theory which should be branded as heretical in every Christian Church."[6] The next year, when an attempt was made to try him for heresy at the General Assembly, the case against him was dismissed. It was proof that caution in supporting the New Apologetic was no long necessary.

In close support of Dods was George Adam Smith (1856–1942), born in India of evangelical and missionary-minded parents. For a while, he had followed the deposed Robertson Smith at Aberdeen, for he also was a pupil of Davidson and German theologians. But how far he would go was not yet anticipated. In 1882–92, he built a reputation as a dynamic preacher in Aberdeen, and was then appointed professor of Old Testament at the Free Church College, Glasgow. Opposing what he called "dogmas of verbal inspiration," George Adam Smith professed to handle the Old

---

[6] Marcus Dods, cited in H. F. Henderson, *The Religious Controversies of Scotland* (Edinburgh: Clark, 1905), 238.

Testament in a way "revolutionary in respect of methods of interpreting Scripture hitherto accepted among us." This was made clear when he gave the Yale Lectures on Preaching in 1899 under the title "Modern Criticism and the Preaching of the Old Testament." The Old Testament, he believed, demonstrated man's evolutionary advance upward from primitive religion. The early chapters of Genesis were not historical, but had been composed "from the raw material of Babylonian myth and legend." He added, "The god of early Israel was a tribal god." The existence of Abraham was questionable. When an attempt was made to call the professor to account for his teaching at the General Assembly of 1902, Rainy was again the defender of the accused, and this time his motion of no action was carried by 534 votes to 263, indicative of the changed times since the deposition of Robertson Smith twenty years earlier.[7]

These men, and others who supported them, were to change the whole direction of the church. On the question of how they gained such influence and popularity, there are several things to be said:

1. *All the leading spokesmen for the New Apologetic, or "believing criticism," as it was called, presented themselves as definite evangelicals.* When the young Robertson Smith was appointed, there were sure "guarantees of his orthodoxy." He was said to be a humble man and loyal to the church. He "proved," W. R. Nicoll believed, "that an advanced critic might be a convinced and fervent evangelical."[8]

Because Nicoll was editor of the widely ready *British Weekly*, his opinion carried weight. He had described Dods as "the most Christlike man I have ever known," while Dods himself referred to his calling as that of an "evangelist." Henry Henderson said of Dods, "His aim was high and worthy, to restore to men faith and joy in the truths of the Divine Word."[9]

George Adam Smith claimed that he and his colleagues were all evangelicals and that they were providing a basis for "faith more stable than ever the old was imagined to be—richer mines of Christian experience, better vantage grounds for preaching the Gospel of Christ . . . infinitely wider prospects of the power of God."[10]

2. *The abandoning of what George Adam Smith called "the older orthodoxy" seemed to promise great spiritual success.* The young were for the new. They knew how to speak effectively to "the modern mind," some

[7] Patrick C. Simpson, *Life of Principal Rainy* (London: Hodder & Stoughton, 1909), 2:273.
[8] W. R. Nicoll, "Henry Drummond," in *The Eclectic Magazine*, 66:129.
[9] Henderson, *Controversies of Scotland*, 247–48.
[10] G. A. Smith, *Life of Henry Drummond* (London: Hodder & Stoughton, 1910), 243–44.

of their publications had wide circulation, and the future seemed to lie with them. They were impervious to the criticism, "The young bloods in the ministry let go the Faith of their fathers."[11] Such words, from the defenders of "the doctrine of verbal inspiration," came only from yesterday's men, "traditionalists," who were doing much damage, for they led "many earnest and pure spirits to give up Christianity because they have ignorantly thought that it is identified with everything in both the Testaments."[12] They represented an evangelicalism "beset by narrowness, inaccuracy and the fear to acknowledge some of the healthiest and divinest movements of our time."[13]

3. *The new teaching, it was claimed, was bringing a closer attachment to Christ.* Certainly, it was said, the Bible helps, "as sign posts help a traveler on the road," and it could be praised as "an exceptional, a divine book." But it could not be the last word, because Christians have something greater and better than signposts—they have Christ as a living Guide! However much help may be found in the Bible, faith rests on personal experience of Christ, not in the text of a book. Gospel faith and the New Apologetic could go forward together!

So a reduced view of Scripture was to be seen not as a loss but as a spiritual gain. Thus, R. W. Dale sought to encourage preachers with the thought that "there is now no authority to come between *us*—to come between the *congregations* to which you and I have to minister—and Him who is the very truth of God."[14]

For such reasons, spelled out by attractive and able speakers, the new teaching had a mighty and persuasive influence. Those of us who never felt the spell may wonder how the large numbers it won included well-known evangelicals such as Alexander Whyte and W. Y. Fullerton, biographer of Charles H. Spurgeon, yet such was the case. Whyte spoke in support of Robertson Smith in the General Assembly. When T. R. Glover was made president of the Baptist Union in 1925, Fullerton acclaimed him as "a prophet whom God has sent us." But Glover was the man who said, "Verbal inspiration is a monstrous belief."[15]

---

[11] John Macleod, *Scottish Theology, In Relation to Church History* (Edinburgh: Banner of Truth, 1974), 314.
[12] Ibid., 371. Smith agreed with Drummond in saying that the old belief in all Scripture "wrecked" Christian faith.
[13] Ibid., 92.
[14] R. W. Dale, *The Evangelical Revival: And Other Sermons* (London: Hodder & Stoughton, 1880), 267.
[15] On Glover, see Benjamin B. Warfield, *Critical Reviews* (New York: OUP, 1932), 388. "This Jesus is to Mr Glover no more than a good man, who was not a 'mediator between God and man, making atonement' in His blood."

Error can be made to look exceedingly attractive, so attractive that we are already deceived if we think we can preserve ourselves from it on our own: "By the Holy Spirit who dwells within us, guard the good deposit entrusted to you" (2 Tim. 1:14).

The Fatal Mistake

Disbelief in Scripture leads inevitably to disbelief in Christ himself. The foundation principle of the New Apologetic was that the substance of Scripture can be maintained and promoted without defending it in every part. Scripture is infallible, these teachers said, but not *everywhere* infallible. But this thinking contains a flawed assumption: that it is possible to identify which parts of Scripture *are* the word of God. Previously, the fundamental question for Christians was, "What does the Word of God say?" The new question had to be, "How much of the Bible *is* the Word of God?"

At first, the answer that was offered looked simple: such things as Noah's flood, Jonah in the belly of a great fish, and the authorship of the book of Daniel could be set to one side as not involving the substance of the faith. Christian belief, it was said, did not depend on such matters. But it did not take long for people to see that those particulars were all treated by the Lord Jesus Christ as authentic history. So the new scholarship began to assert, for instance, that the Pentateuch did not come from Moses, but Christ believed that it did (Mark 7:10; 12:26; Luke 24:27).

This raised another question: How much that Christ said is to be believed? He believed that "Scripture cannot be broken" (John 10:35). He believed that marriage originated as declared by God in Genesis 2 (Matt. 19:5). He taught that not one "iota" or "dot" of the law would fail (Matt. 5:18). He said that his life and death had been according to "all that the prophets have spoken" (Luke 24:25), for "Scripture must be fulfilled" (Luke 22:37).

The only escape from such texts was to accept that not all that Jesus taught is trustworthy. He said, "Heaven and earth will pass away, but my words will not pass way" (Matt. 24:35), but this had to be corrected to say that only "some" of his words would not pass away. Which ones depended on the ability of scholars to find "the historical Jesus." This was the quest that German theology had attempted, and it had not been successful. David Strauss, one of the originators of that quest, concluded, "It may be doubted indeed, whether a real knowledge of the historical Jesus be now possible."[16]

---

[16] Cited in Henderson, *Controversies of Scotland*, 258.

Other German theologians were more optimistic, but their supposed findings led to the advancement of a succession of different "Christs." In a review of one of Dods's books, Benjamin B. Warfield writes that Dods was willing to give up the inspiration of Scripture so long as Christ was preserved. But which Christ? he asked. Was it to be Dods's Christ? "What about the Christ that Wernle gives us? or Wrede? or Oscar Holtzmann? or Auguste Sabatier? or Réveille? or Brandt? or Harnack? Which Christ of the fallible Scriptures shall we be ultimately forced to put up with?"[17]

In the end, Dods had no answer. The confidence of his youth had gone. In 1907, two years after that Warfield review, in a private letter, he opened his heart to a friend with a chilling forecast of how he saw the future of the church in Scotland: "The churches won't know themselves fifty years hence. It is to be hoped some little rag of faith may be left when all's done."[18]

The New Apologetic not only was a failure, it was a failure at a tremendous cost. One of the old men who had protested against the new teaching a quarter century earlier was Moody Stuart, who had been Robert Murray McCheyne's pastor in earlier years. He wrote:

> The Word of the Lord is pure, and out of this trial it will come forth in all its brightness as silver out of the furnace. But, meanwhile, an unutterable calamity may overtake us, for our children may lose the one treasure we were bound to bequeath them; and for long years they may wander "through dry places seeking rest, and finding none," before they recover their hold of the Word of life, and regain their footing on the rock of eternal truth.[19]

I shall always have in my mind's eye the church in which I grew up. It is an outstanding building of red sandstone, with an auditorium to seat at least a thousand, a spacious hall, and many additional rooms. It was opened in 1900, and the preacher invited for such an important occasion was Professor George Adam Smith, full of confidence for the new church and the new century. What happened? Today that fine building stands deserted and closed. Preachers and hearers are all gone, but they were not the first to go. First the Word of God was lost, the light was lost, until only an

---

[17] Warfield, *Critical Reviews*, 125.

[18] Marcus Dods, *Later Letters of Marcus Dods* (London: Hodder & Stoughton, 1911), 67.

[19] A. Moody Stuart, *Our Old Bible: Moses on the Plains of Moab* (Edinburgh: Maclaren, 1880), 70–71. Horatius Bonar spoke of the same danger in 1883: "The extent of the mischief no one can calculate. A soul without faith, a church without faith, a nation without faith, a world without faith—what is to be their future? What is their present? When faith goes, all good things go. When unbelief comes in, all evil things follow." *Our Ministry: How It Touches the Questions of the Age* (Edinburgh: MacNiven & Wallace, 1883), 4.

empty monument remained. That is the history of not one but thousands of church buildings in Britain today.

Recently, a large volume on Nonconformity in England was published. *Nonconformity* is another word for what are also called, south of the border, the "Free Churches," the name covering all the historic mainline denominations outside the Church of England. It includes a quotation from a 1962 book by Christopher Driver, *A Future for the Free Churches?* The emphatic question mark at the end of the title is significant. Describing the contemporary scene, Driver writes:

> Over large tracts of the country . . . behind the peeling facades and the plaintive wayside pulpits there is nothing left but a faithful, ingrown remnant, whiling away its Pleasant Sunday Afternoons and its Women's Bright Hours in dingy rooms from which whole generations and classes have long since fled.[20]

What language is more applicable than the words of Jeremiah: "Behold, they have rejected the word of the LORD, so what wisdom is in them? . . . Oh that my head were waters, and my eyes a fountain of tears, that I might weep day and night for the slain of the daughter of my people" (Jer. 8:9; 9:1).

Worldwide Disaster

While the effects of this abandonment of Scripture have been tragic in British history, there is something worse. Horatius Bonar was moderator of the Free Church of Scotland in 1883 when the New Apologetic was taking hold of his denomination. He pleaded that the General Assembly should stop and think about what the world outside was hearing from them:

> Brethren in far India and farther Australia are listening to us. Brethren in America, in Africa, in Europe, and in the distant islands of the far south, are watching us. . . . A hundred newspapers going out into all parts, not only of the land, but of the globe, will print your words.[21]

The church did not listen to Bonar. Instead of disciplining erroneous teachers, it honored them. Backed by the evangelical reputation of the Free

---

[20] Cited in R. Pope, ed., *T&T Clark Companion to Nonconformity* (London: Bloomsbury, 2013), 24. The same volume reports that Leslie D. Weatherhead, one of the most popular leaders of Nonconformity, who denied the resurrection of Christ, became an advocate of reincarnation and frequently attended séances, at which he claimed to have met John Wesley (699).

[21] Bonar, *Our Ministry*, n.p.

Church, the message went out to all the mission fields of the world that it is not necessary to believe *all* of Scripture in order to be an evangelical. Slowly the great missionary expansion of the nineteenth century came to a stop; unbelief was destroying its roots. In the 1920s and the 1930s, attempts were made to require leading missionary agencies to employ and send out only such missionaries as believed in all Scripture. For instance, in 1922, an appeal was made to the Church Missionary Society of England to examine where its candidates stood on Scripture. Its board refused any such test.

In 1933, through the Presbytery of New Brunswick, J. Gresham Machen appealed to the General Assembly of the Presbyterian Church of the USA that its Foreign Missions Board should appoint only men who held to "the full trustworthiness of Scripture." To support the appeal, Machen produced a publication of 110 pages that gave evidence of the extent to which unbelief was being tolerated and promoted on the mission field. He showed that the "inclusivist policy," which was being allowed in the churches at home, was proving a disaster in China, where some church leaders had come to deny the bodily resurrection of Christ. He cited the literature of liberals then being published in Chinese. In one of these books, the author spoke of how a mother was reading to her child part of the Old Testament where the destruction of the Amalekites is recorded. The mother sought to explain the judgment to her daughter by saying that "revelation was progressive, and now in Jesus we were told to love our enemies and to do good to them that despitefully use us. The little girl thought for a moment and then her face lighted up and she said, 'Now I understand . . . this back here was before God was a Christian.'"[22]

Despite all that Machen wrote and said, the General Assembly gave the personnel of the Foreign Missions Board "whole-hearted" support. The inclusivist policy was upheld. When Machen and others then formed an Independent Mission Board, the General Assembly ordered it to be disbanded and forbade any of its church members to serve on it. When Machen did not obey the direction, he was tried, not allowed to question the legitimacy of the Assembly's order, found guilty, and suspended from the ministry.

The so-called inclusivist policy was in reality an anti-biblical policy. Machen had quoted teachers in China who expressed the hope that modernists and not fundamentalists would come to that mission field. The likes of Machen would not be welcome, and now he was not to be welcome in the church where he had served all his life.

---

[22] J. Gresham Machen, *Modernism and the Board of Foreign Missions of the Presbyterian Church in the USA* (Philadelphia: Allen, Lane and Scott, 1933), 74–75.

What Is the Controversy over Scripture Really About?

It is common for those who oppose evangelicals to present this controversy as a battle over what they call the "traditionalist view" of the Bible. But that representation ignores the real issue. The fundamental objection is not so much what the Bible teaches about its inspiration; it is about what it teaches about God, man, and the way of salvation. It teaches that since the fall of man, the human mind is at enmity toward God: "It does not submit to God's law; indeed, it cannot" (Rom. 8:7). This is why Jesus said: "Why do you not understand what I say? It is because you cannot bear to hear my word" (John 8:43). Paul adds, "The natural person does not accept the things of the Spirit of God, for they are folly to him, and he is not able to understand them because they are spiritually discerned" (1 Cor. 2:14). To receive spiritual truth, a man first has to be born of the Spirit. Only then does he have "the Spirit of truth, whom the world cannot receive, because it neither sees him nor knows him" (John 14:17).

What the Bible reveals about God and us is the last thing that the non-Christian wants to believe. Do I want to be told not only that I do wrong, but that I am wrong at the very center of my being? That my heart is deceitful and desperately wicked? That there is none righteous, no, not one? That to live for self, and not my holy Creator, deserves his righteous anger and condemnation? That I cannot save myself, and that if God does not deliver me, I am lost in hell forever? That Christ alone must save, and that only by repentance and faith in him will any reach heaven? No! We are all offended. We have no heart for it. It contradicts my good opinion of myself. The natural man does not want Christ: "We do not want this man to reign over us" (Luke 19:14).

So the answer to the question of what must be done to make the Bible acceptable to men and women is not the answer that the New Apologetic proposed. Much more than one doctrine (biblical inerrancy) needs to be laid aside. We must leave out all that humbles man, take out the supernatural, and suppress God's Word on what sin deserves. If we do this, the church and the world can live in peace. Such was the end result of the New Apologetic and its approach to the Bible. It set out with the professed aim of retaining the substance, leaving aside only the incidental. But in the end, left among the debris were many false Christs and a message often the opposite of the truth. It was no longer about God being reconciled by the death of his Son, but about how *we* are to make ourselves and the world better "with his help." It was not a message of grace, but of works. "The

Christian ethic," and Christ as the example for us, became the gospel; not the offense of what Christ has done to deliver sinners from the wrath to come, but the congenial message of what we can decide for ourselves.

This is no misrepresentation. Wherever the rule of Scripture is set aside, this is the way human nature goes.[23] It has been true in every country, whatever the date.[24]

But there is another question: Was this consequence *intended* by those who undermined the trustworthiness of Scripture in the nineteenth century? Is the present state of the churches and the country what they *planned*?

I know no reason to believe that it is. The teachers of the New Apologetic were the unconscious instrument in a great deception, and the author of that deception was one whose existence they did not seem to recognize. The scholars who undermined Scripture excluded a vital part of Scripture from their thinking: they had nothing to say about angels or demons; about Satan's revolt against God; or about Christ's words, "Then the devil comes and takes away the word from their hearts, so that they may not believe and be saved" (Luke 8:12), or Paul's, "The spirit that is now at work in the sons of disobedience" (Eph. 2:2).[25]

This omission changed the mind-set of Protestantism, and it continues to the present day. D. Martyn Lloyd-Jones said, "I am certain that one of the main causes of the ill state of the Church today is the fact that the devil is being forgotten."[26] Ignorance of history plays a part in this forgetfulness. The attacks on the Bible, although taking different forms, have had similar characteristics throughout the ages because they originate from the same source. Certainly there are variations at the human level, yet even at that level, there are characteristics of the demonic that ought to be discerned. Satan's fingerprints are on the page. Consider two of those characteristics in the period we have been discussing:

1. *Satan ever prompts and supports the idolizing of men.* How can he

---

[23] What Farrar listed as the "three great truths . . . the very foundation of the Christian religion" are the very truths most absent wherever the authority of Scripture is set aside: "(1) the doctrine of the reality of the vicarious atonement of Christ provided by the passion of our blessed Lord; (2) the supernatural and miraculous character of the religious revelation in the book of God; and (3) the direct operation of the Holy Ghost in converting and communing with the human soul. Lacking the first of these, Christianity appears . . . to be a religion without a system of redemption; lacking the second, a doctrine without authority; lacking the third, a system of ethics without spiritual power." *Critical History*, xv.

[24] Biblical truth is not time-bound. Paul explains the persecution of Christians by Jews by pointing to what was true in the time of Abraham: "But just as at that time he who was born according to the flesh persecuted him who was born according to the Spirit, so also it is now" (Gal. 4:29).

[25] Robertson Smith confessed to believing in neither angels or demons. Even James Denney did not believe in the demonic.

[26] D. Martyn Lloyd-Jones, *The Christian Warfare* (Edinburgh: Banner of Truth, 1976), 292.

best achieve his objective of the overthrow of Christian belief? By elevating men, acclaiming their brilliance, and admiring their amazing scholarship. The last thing he wants is men of contrite spirit who see the need to "tremble" at God's Word (Isa. 66:5). Rather, he still tempts with the promise, "You shall be like God" (Gen. 3:5), and appeals to the pride that belongs to our fallen nature. John Owen, in his book *The Nature and Causes of Apostasy*, puts pride first in the list of causes.

The Free Church of Scotland came to see itself at the forefront of the evangelical world; it led in preaching and in foreign missions, and it wanted to lead in theological scholarship. The best way to do that seemed to be to send its bright students to Germany, where prestige for theological learning was second to none. But the apostolic warnings were forgotten: "You stand fast through faith. So do not become proud, but fear" (Rom. 11:20); "Test the spirits to see whether they are from God, for many false prophets have gone out into the world" (1 John 4:10). So great was the ability of the German teachers that the Free Church saw no need of any warnings. The German scholars were praised and applauded, and their disciples brought back to Scotland the habit of congratulating one another as they took up positions in theological colleges. They, too, were heralded and flattered; if they had asked for endorsements for their books, they would have had them in abundance. Certainly they were gifted men, and the idolizing of men commonly comes from a blind admiration of gifts. Yet Satan has intellectual gifts far above any to be found in men. Where pride is evident, we can be sure he has found entrance. It is the Devil who wants men idolized and regarded as celebrities.

Speaking of the Free Church of Scotland, John Macleod has written: "It was so much of the irony of history that a Church which had prided itself on the place that it gave to the Reformed Faith so soon became the home of that revolutionary movement in Theology which has transformed the whole aspect of the religious life of Scotland. The other churches, too, were feeling the changed spirit of the age. But it was reserved for the younger ministers of the Free Church to take the lead in the abandonment of the Faith of their fathers."[27]

2. *Satan works by the underhanded, the subtle, the evasive, and the devious.* His chief weapon is what Scripture calls the "deceitfulness of sin" (Heb. 3:13). It is a way of working that is the opposite of the openness and straightforwardness of Christianity. Paul said of the gospel's history, "This

---

[27] Macleod, *Scottish Theology*, 309.

has not been done in a corner" (Acts 26:26). The truth has nothing to hide, but error is like a serpent that prefers the dark.

This element was to be found in the years when the Free Church was embracing the new teaching. The undermining of Scripture at first went on slowly; it was introduced quietly in the theological colleges before it was ever read or heard in the church at large. I do not mean that its teachers were intentional deceivers, but from the outset, the caution to be expected of Christians was often lacking. For example, Dods was not alone in expressing the fear that in fifty years only "some little rag of faith may be left." There is record of a conversation between Robert Rainy, the leader of the Free Church, and Professor D. S. Cairns in the Aberdeen home of the latter in 1892. Cairns asked whether "to hold one's mind open on the infallibility of Scripture" (as Rainy professed to be doing) would not lead to doubt over the whole system of doctrine that had been built on that foundation. Rainy replied that the effect of the removing of the old basis would produce a species of "land-slide" in many minds regarding characteristic evangelical doctrines. No such admissions were ever made in public. Rainy's biographer disclosed this conversation only in 1910, adding that Rainy believed that, from the landslide, the evangelical doctrines "would re-emerge."[28] How that would happen, without the foundation on which those truths stood, was not explained. That the modern criticism of Scripture would lead to progress was still believed in 1910 and for many years after.

The most fundamental prevarication had to do with the underhanded way in which the doctrine of Scripture came to be revised. This is directly related to the present serious controversy in the Church of Scotland, which has seen a number of the strongest evangelical congregations compelled by conscience to leave the denomination. For the background to this controversy, mention has to be made of the two major unions of Scottish denominations that have taken place since the late nineteenth century. The first was the union of the Free Church of Scotland with the United Presbyterian Church in 1900, which saw them reconstituted under the name the United Free Church.[29] The second was the joining in 1929 of the United Free Church and the national Church of Scotland—the body its congregations had left at earlier dates.

These mergers were brought about by a relaxation of the articles of faith that ministers were required to affirm. Before 1900, Free Church ministers

---

[28] Simpson, *Principal Rainy*, 2:116.
[29] Both unions saw small minorities continuing separately.

vowed that they believed "the *whole doctrine of the Confession of Faith*, approved by the General Assemblies of this Church, to be the truths of God." After 1900, the wording became, "*the doctrine of this Church* set forth in the Confession of Faith." The significance of the words I have italicized will be clearer below. After this revision on the part of the United Free Church, the Church of Scotland made preparation for a union with her by revising its own constitutional articles in 1921. This paved the way for the union of 1929, when the revised articles of 1921 became authoritative for the enlarged Church of Scotland. Article 1 declared in part:

> The Church of Scotland adheres to the Scottish Reformation; receives the Word of God which is contained in the Scriptures of the Old and New Testaments as its supreme rule of faith and life; and avows the fundamental doctrines of the Christian faith founded thereupon and contained in its own Confession.

These words remain part of the constitution of the Church of Scotland today. How, then, has its doctrinal purity descended to the level of permitting and upholding ministers who are practicing homosexuals? How can the General Assembly now allow what the Word of God plainly condemns?

The answer is that the articles of 1900 and 1921 were framed so as to permit compromise. True, at those dates, no one considered the possibility of homosexual pastors, but a door was opened that would make even that possible. It had to do with the seemingly innocent use of the word *contained*. The faith to be upheld, said the article, is in "the Word of God which is *contained* in the Scriptures." But *contained* can mean two things. When you are carrying home a bag of groceries, you may tell me that it "contains" potatoes. You may mean that you are only carrying potatoes, but you may also mean that the bag contains potatoes along with some other items. The promoters of the New Apologetic deliberately made use of this ambiguity.

It may sound uncharitable to suggest that an evasion was deliberately allowed by Article 1 of the Church of Scotland in 1929, but the evidence appears incontrovertible. The use of *contained* in the broad sense was in wide use well before that date. In the 1890s, J. C. Ryle protested against the introduction of this ambiguous word, saying, "I hold that the Scripture not only *contains* the Word of God, but is the Word of God."[30] In that same period, a Free Church promoter of the New Apologetic spoke in the

---

[30] J. C. Ryle, *Old Paths*, 4th ed. (London: Thynne, 1898), 20.

language to which Ryle objected when he said, "The Bible contains the Word of God; it records a revelation which came from him; its inspiration is the highest of all literature."[31] This sounds like praise of the Bible, but the writer was by no means asserting the trustworthiness of *all* Scripture. His words were an evasion.

As this sense of *contained* was common knowledge before 1929, is it believable that the Church of Scotland would have chosen to speak of "the Word of God which is contained in the Scriptures" if it did not mean to allow the legitimacy of the broad usage?

But the evidence goes beyond supposition. Article 1 *had to be drawn up* in language permitting the ambiguous usage of *contained* because numbers of the leaders and teachers in the United Free Church, with which the Church of Scotland wanted to unite, openly rejected the old belief. Both in the Free Church (after 1881) and then in the United Free Church, no one was silenced for denying the inerrancy of Scripture. When, as already mentioned, a charge was brought against George Adam Smith on those grounds in 1902, he was exonerated, and it was those who brought the charge who were criticized. In the words of one of the United Free Church's most popular professors, James Denney, "When an unlearned piety, swears by verbal, even by literal, inspiration . . . , [it] takes up an attitude to mere documents which in principle is fatal to Christianity."[32] After 1902, there were no further attempts in the United Free Church to uphold the confession's position on Scripture.

The plain fact is that the union of 1929 could not have been effected without wording that permitted compromise over the authority of Scripture. So if anyone had asked how, in 2009, the Church of Scotland could sanction the appointment of a homosexual minister in the light of Article 1, there was a ready answer: "The Bible contains error as well as the Word of God! The Church never undertook to uphold *all* Scripture as the Word of God."

It may be objected that this response cannot be justified from the

---

[31] Cited in Benjamin B. Warfield, "Evading the Supernatural," in *Selected Shorter Writings of Benjamin B. Warfield* (Nutley, NJ: Presbyterian and Reformed, 1973), 2:681.

[32] James Denney, *The Second Epistle to the Corinthians*, 5th ed. (London: Hodder & Stoughton, n.d.), 126. He held not the infallibility of Scripture but of Christian experience. It is to his credit that when a confession of faith committee on which he served wanted to present what looked like the old and untenable (he believed) view of the Bible, he called its motion "two-faced" and "equivocal." James M. Gordon, *James Denney (1856–1917)* (Milton Keynes, UK: Paternoster, 2006), 136. Denney's decline from historic Christianity did not stop at his doctrine of Scripture. His editor and friend, William Nicoll, wrote of his concern that Denney was apparently ready to allow Arians and Unitarians into the ministry of the church in 1908. Nicoll commented, "I know quite well what the end of such a Church would be, for all history points it out." T. H. Darlow, *William Robertson Nicoll, Life and Letters* (London: Hodder & Stoughton, 1925), 364. Nicoll added, "Religion died under their teaching." Ibid., 362.

wording of Article 1, because that article, partially quoted above, also "avows the fundamental doctrines of the Christian faith . . . contained in its own Confession," and surely the inspiration of Scripture is a fundamental doctrine of the Westminster Confession. Therefore, it has to be part of the faith that the church is committed to uphold.

To this there have been two answers. First, the advocates of the New Apologetic did not accept that the Westminster divines professed belief in the inerrancy of Scripture. It strains charity to believe that this was a sincere understanding of the confession, for the confession clearly teaches that Scripture is God-given truth *written*: "It pleased the Lord for the better propagating of the truth . . . to commit the same wholly unto writing, which maketh the holy scripture to be most necessary" (1.1). Again, in the Westminster Shorter Catechism, question 3 reads: "*What is the Word of God?* The holy scriptures of the Old and New Testament are the word of God, the only rule of faith and obedience." Patrick Simpson, in his book *Life of Principal Rainy*, admits that "the verbal inspiration of the Bible had remained unchallenged in the Scottish Church since the Reformation," yet he denies that the belief is in the confession.[33]

Even so, supposing that the confession does teach the trustworthiness of all Scripture, it does not follow that it is one of the "fundamental doctrines." The framers of the revised articles had a built-in escape from any such conclusion. This had come down from the pre-1900 Free Church, where Rainy popularized the principle that the church has the power to determine its own faith and to decide what are "fundamental doctrines" and what are not.[34] This principle was implicit in the changed wording, already noted, of 1900, committing ministers no longer to "the whole doctrine of the Confession of Faith," but to "the doctrine of this Church set forth in the Confession of Faith." The significance of this was expanded

[33] Simpson, *Principal Rainy*, 1:311. For a detailed examination of this subject, see Benjamin B. Warfield, "The Westminster Doctrine of Holy Scripture," in *The Westminster Assembly and Its Work* (New York: Oxford, 1931). Simpson, a disciple of Marcus Dods, claimed that the confession did not teach the inerrancy of Scripture; rather, it "carefully avoids committing itself to any theory of the mode or degree of inspiration." *Principal Rainy*, 2:114. But this was a subterfuge. Scripture's own claim to infallibility does not rest on questions of mode, just as our believing that Christ spoke "the words which the Father gave him" does not depend on our knowing the manner of that giving. There was real prevarication on Scripture in the Free Church of the 1890s. A deliverance of the General Assembly affirmed "their full and steadfast adherence to the doctrine laid down in the Confession as to the great truths of the inspiration, infallible truth, and Divine authority of Holy Scripture," yet James Denney was applauded when he said, "For verbal inspiration he cared not a straw," and the assembly refused an amendment stating that the Bible "as originally given, contained no error or mis-statement, either of fact or doctrine, in any part of it." See M. Macaskill, *The New Theology in the Free Church* (Edinburgh: R. W. Hunter, 1892). It would have been more honest to argue, as was later done, that the Westminster divines' understanding of Scripture was due to their lack of "modern scholarship." But such an admission would have put the advocates of change in opposition to the confession they had vowed to maintain.
[34] See Simpson, *Principal Rainy*, 2:123, 130.

in the articles of 1921, carried into the union of 1929. These left it free for the church to decide how the confession should be interpreted and what was "fundamental." Article 5 reads: "This Church has the inherent right to declare the sense in which it understands its Confession of Faith, to modify the forms of expression therein, or to formulate other doctrinal statements . . . but always in agreement with the Word of God, and the fundamental doctrines of the Christian Faith contained in the said Confession, of which agreement the Church shall be sole judge." Article 8 claims the same right for the church to "modify or add to" its articles, "but always consistently with the provisions of the first Article." Given the ambiguity present in Article 1, the proviso contains no safeguard at all. The upshot of the matter is that the church may determine that plenary inspiration is not fundamental, or even that it is not part of "the Word of God." Here the door was left open enough to permit the church to uphold homosexuality.

In brief, I have sought to show that a change in the creedal basis of the churches of Scotland was introduced in language that was by no means straightforward. Yet the change was momentous. Orthodoxy would no longer mean believing the Bible, but believing whatever the church told its people to believe. The claim of Article 1 of the Church of Scotland adhering to the Scottish Reformation was false. It had been a primary object of the Reformation to overthrow the belief that the church is the rule of faith. The whole Reformation conflict had to do with the reassertion of Scripture against human authority in the spiritual realm. Yet in justification of the church's right to revise her own faith, the example of the Reformers was pleaded. The Scots Confession of 1560 worked on a contrary principle, with the church stating its readiness to accept any revision, not by its own decision, but if anyone were to note anything "repugnant to Scripture." Scripture *alone* was authoritative in determining faith. In the words of the confession that Article 1 professed to follow:

> The supreme Judge, by which all controversies of religion are to be determined . . . can be no other but the Holy Spirit speaking in the Scripture. (1:10)

> All synods or councils, since the Apostolic times, whether general or particular, may err; and many have erred. Therefore they are not to be made the rule of faith or practice; but to be used as a help in both. (31:4)

The outcome of the changed basis of faith was an inclusivist church with a radically different ministry. Within a hundred years, the Scottish

Church was permitting the opposite of what once had been seen as fundamental.[35] With reference to the mid-nineteenth century, W. Robertson Nicoll wrote, "Any Free Church minister who asserted the existence of errors in the Bible would have been summarily deposed."[36] Yet before the end of the following century, it could be asserted by a Church of Scotland minister, Dr. Peter Cameron, that "very few of them believe in the literal truth and inerrancy of the Bible." Appointed principal of St Andrew's College, Sydney, in 1991—where the principal had to be a member of the Presbyterian Church—Cameron believed himself free to assert that Paul was "wrong," and that the words attributed to Christ in Matthew 23 were not his words at all, but rather "a masterpiece of vituperation." He was astonished when the Presbyterian Church of Australia made his rejection of inerrancy grounds for a heresy charge, and wanted to know, "If the Westminster Confession of Faith does require a Fundamentalist interpretation of the Bible, how is it that so many Presbyterian Churches outside Australia manage *both* to have a majority of non-Fundamentalist ministers *and* to subscribe to the Westminster Confession of Faith?"[37]

I hope I have provided an answer to that question above.

As an example of how ambivalent language on Scripture was used on the mission field, I would point to what happened on the island of Tangoa, part of the New Hebrides (now Vanuatu) in the South Pacific on July 1, 1948. That date saw the Presbyterian Church of the New Hebrides gain independence from the oversight of the Presbyterian Church of New Zealand. For a century, the islands of the New Hebrides had been evangelized by faithful, Bible-believing missionaries (Scots Presbyterians), aided by the Presbyterian Church of New Zealand. But with the passing of years, the New Zealand Church (under direct influence from Scotland) turned liberal, while the native Christians of the New Hebrides held to the Bible. This led to an incident that threatened the granting of independence by the New Zealand body. A condition was laid down that the New Hebrides church

---

[35] There were those who continued in the remnant of the Free Church who saw the danger. Alexander Stewart and J. Kennedy Cameron wrote of the United Free Church's revised articles: "In seasons of spiritual quickening, when the edge of loyalty is keen, and the investigation of truth is regulated by the spirit of reverence, 'the living faith of the Church' may doubtless be accepted as a reliable guide with regard to questions of creed. But in times of critical unsettlement and spiritual decadence the consequences are likely to be disastrous." *The Free Church of Scotland, A Vindication* (Edinburgh: Hodge, 1910), 123.

[36] W. Robertson Nicoll, "Henry Drummond," in *The Contemporary Review* (London: A. Strahan, 1897), 71:502.

[37] Peter Cameron, *Heretic* (Sydney: Doubleday, 1994), 117. When the case against Cameron was carried in his presbytery and by the General Assembly of New South Wales, he appealed to the General Assembly of Australia, but then chose to resign before it met. He had entered the ministry "to explore the possibilities of a god." Now he believed it was "not the purpose of either the Bible or of Christianity to offer certainties," but he was certain that "the God of Fundamentalism does not exist" (200–201).

would be granted independence only if it included in its constitution the words "the Scriptures which contain the Word of God."

The native Christians did not understand the ambiguity that the phrase allowed, and when one missionary, J. Graham Miller, himself a New Zealander, protested that the wording ought to be "the Scriptures . . . which are the Word of God," he was overruled. Miller was a strong, athletic man, but that day, for the first and last time in his life, he broke down under the stress of the emotion. However, he was a Christian greatly revered by the local Christians, and the next year, when he was the first moderator of the Presbyterian Church of the New Hebrides, he moved in the General Assembly that the church change its statement of faith to remove the words "contained in." He was not commonly a man to use visual aids on such occasions, but at this crucial moment, he did. The native Christians had to understand what the difference meant. So he brought with him a disused and worn-out Bible. As he stated his case, he held this Bible up before the assembly and proceeded slowly and solemnly to tear out a page here and a page there, explaining as he did so that this was what "contained in" meant. The native Christians saw something they were not to forget, and in 1949 their young church was brought back to the historic Christian belief in all Scripture as the Word of God.[38]

Our Response

Evangelicals make a serious mistake when we do not draw a definite line between those who uphold the authority of all Scripture and those who do not. In Britain in the last century, a faithful stand by the Inter-Varsity Fellowship kept this line drawn firmly in the student world, despite much opposition. But when evangelical students went into denominations where the inerrancy of Scripture was dismissed and treated as a closed question, they found themselves pressured to leave it aside. A hearing might be given on other subjects, but not on this.

Dr. J. I. Packer makes an insightful comment on the failure in Britain on this point. He writes that in the ongoing North American debate between evangelicals and liberals, many evangelicals "took the name 'fundamentalists' as a badge of honour, signifying their stand for Christian fundamentals, [so that] biblical inerrancy was from the first made the touchstone more directly and explicitly than was ever the case in parallel debates in Britain.

---

[38] J. Graham Miller, *A Day's March Nearer Home: Autobiography of J. Graham Miller*, ed. Iain H. Murray (Edinburgh: Banner of Truth, 2010), 96–100.

This, I now think (I did not always think so), argues for clear sightedness in the New World, for without inerrancy the structure of biblical authority as evangelicals conceive it collapses."[39]

It seems to me that this recognition brought Packer close to the principle that Lloyd-Jones expressed: "There is a call today to separation. It is the only distinction in the Church which I recognize at all. Those who submit to the Word of God, and its revelation, and its teaching, and those who do not."[40]

The evidence is that when debate on church issues does not begin with a common recognition of the rule of Scripture, much time is lost and nothing gained. Furthermore:

1. *This history provides us with a very humbling view of human nature.* How weak we are! How fallible the opinions of the ablest of men! Yet how easily trust is put in men, and Christ's warning to "beware of men" (Matt. 10:17) neglected. Whole generations have been led astray by the persuasive, attractive personalities of men, and sometimes women, who promised great things and yet led many away from godliness and truth. "Let anyone who thinks that he stands take heed lest he fall" (1 Cor. 10:12).

2. *The demonic dimension should make it clear that we need the supernatural to fight against the supernatural.* Of necessity, "The kingdom of God does not consist in talk but in power" (1 Cor. 4:20). Only superior spiritual power can effectively attain success in a warfare that is not "against flesh and blood, but against the rulers, against the authorities, against the cosmic powers over this present darkness, against the spiritual forces of evil in the heavenly places" (Eph. 6:12). Hence the nature of the weapons: "In all circumstances take up the shield of faith, with which you can extinguish all the flaming darts of the evil one; and take the helmet of salvation, and the sword of the Spirit, which is the word of God" (vv. 16–17). It is not with opinions, words, or even with doctrines that we can resist the Devil. The fate of the Jews in Ephesus is a salutary lesson for all times. Luke says they "undertook to invoke the name of the Lord Jesus over those who had evil spirits, saying, 'I adjure you by the Jesus whom Paul proclaims.' . . . But the evil spirit answered them, 'Jesus I know, and Paul I recognize, but who are you?' And the man in whom was the evil spirit leaped on them, mastered all of them and overpowered them" (Acts 19:13–16).

It is surprising today, when paganism increases and interest in magic is

---

[39] J. I. Packer, *Truth & Power: The Place of the Bible in Christian Life* (Guildford, Surrey, UK: Eagle, 1996).
[40] D. Martyn Lloyd-Jones, *Revival* (Westchester, IL: Crossway, 1988), 152.

fashionable, that not many seem interested in thinking about how the early church survived and overcame through three centuries of persecution. Certainly there were apologists who spoke for Christianity, but the main battle was not on the intellectual level. The victory came through the moral power of the gospel transforming lives and shedding light in darkness. Today we have much for which to be thankful. There has been some recovery of preaching and of biblical truth. But these alone are not enough. Our greatest want may be our lack of a deeper sense of need, a clearer recognition of "Thine is the kingdom, the power, and the glory."

We need more prayer, more humility, and more devotion to Scripture. God has promised, "This is the one to whom I will look: he who is humble and contrite in spirit and trembles at my word" (Isa. 66:2). This is where every spiritual advance begins. The turning points of history have been times when Christians so loved the Word of God and the souls of men that they were ready to lay down their lives for Christ.

I urge young men to guard your time well. It will be all too short. Let nothing distract you from that apostolic resolution, "We will devote ourselves to prayer and to the ministry of the word" (Acts 6:4). I commend to you the resolution of John Wesley:

> I am a creature of a day, passing through life as an arrow through the air. I want to know one thing: the way to heaven; how to land safe on that happy shore. God himself has condescended to teach that way; for this very end he came down from heaven. He has written it down in a book! O give me that book! At any price, Give me the Book of God! I have it: here is knowledge enough for me. Let me be, "a man of one book."[41]

---

[41] John Wesley, preface to *Sermons on Several Occasions* (London: Kershaw, 1825), vii.

11

How Did It Come to This?

MODERNISM'S CHALLENGES TO INERRANCY

Stephen J. Nichols

Herman Bavinck was appointed rector of theology at the Free University of Amsterdam in 1911. To mark the occasion, he delivered an address entitled *"Modernisme en Orthodoxie."* Bavinck extolled the virtues of the modern world, a world that he referred to as "altogether different from that of our ancestors." He spoke of the great achievements and advances of the modern world. And he marveled at what was to come. "God is busy doing great things these days," he told the audience gathered for this austere academic occasion.[1]

But what Charles Dickens said of his day was also true of Bavinck's. Not only was it the best of times, it was also the worst of times. The very next year, 1912, Bavinck addressed the Convention of Modernist Theologians—that was the actual name. In this address, he recalled his theological training at Leiden. This was not in the pietist strain with which Bavinck was more familiar; this was not the "Kampen School" in the Dutch theological

---

[1] Herman Bavinck, "Modernism and Orthodoxy," cited in John Bolt, "Grand Rapids between Kampen and Amsterdam: Herman Bavinck's Reception and Influence in North America," *Calvin Theological Journal* (38) 2003: 267.

and ecclesiastical tradition. The professors at Leiden drank deeply at the well of modernity and prided themselves in their academic respectability. And all of that had a deleterious impact on their view of the Bible. As Bavinck reminisced about his time at Leiden, he could remember receiving only stones when he was seeking after bread. Mirroring developments in Germany, the professors at Leiden applied the method of modernity, the scientific method, to the specimen, that is, the Bible. In the end, they determined the Bible to be little more than a clanging cymbal. As Bavinck was caught up in his reminiscences, he looked at the audience of modernist theologians in front of him and thundered his response to their view of Scripture:

> They [the realities of the Christian faith] remain realities. Were I to give them up, I would lose myself. And then I said: That cannot be true. These realities are worth more, they are more real as facts in nature and Scripture. I am, therefore, not bound by any tradition but rather by that which is for me personally, in the depth of my soul, the life of my life, the very salvation of my soul.[2]

And so we have the challenge of modernity. The challenge is simply this: Is the Word of God, the Bible, authoritative and over us? Or is it passé, an ancient book that simply does not pass the test of credulity in the modern world? Is it a clanging cymbal? Or is it the truth?

What was true of Bavinck's context in the Netherlands was also true in Germany, in the United Kingdom, and in America. About the time Bavinck was grappling with modernists in his Dutch context, J. Gresham Machen was wrestling with modernism in his American context. Though his views surfaced in many writings, Machen's short article "Skyscrapers and Cathedrals" in (of all places) *McCall's* magazine in 1931 is a salient representation. Like Bavinck, Machen celebrates the achievements of the modern world; "I am no medievalist," he writes. But Machen raises some significant questions about modernity. Modernity crowds out God and God's ancient Word. So while consenting that modernity can do much for the body, Machen asks: What can modernity do for the soul? Then he concludes:

> Even today, amid all the noise and shouting and power of machinery, there are hearts hungry for bread that is bread indeed, hearts thirsting for the living water. The things in which the world is interested are the

---

[2] Ibid., 269.

things that are seen; but the things that are seen are temporal, and the things that are not seen are eternal.[3]

About the time Machen was wrestling with modernity in America, D. Martyn Lloyd-Jones was contending with modernity's impact on the church in the UK. In fact, prior to "the Doctor," as Lloyd-Jones was fondly known, Charles Haddon Spurgeon fired back at modernity's salvos during the Downgrade Controversy. The issues of the controversy orbited orthodox doctrines, including the verbal, plenary inspiration of Scripture and inerrancy. In 1892, months after Spurgeon's death, those wishing to stem the tide of modernism sweeping through the church in Great Britain formed the Bible League in a galvanization of Spurgeon's stand on the full-throttled authority of Scripture and on inerrancy.[4] It was in *The Bible League Quarterly* in 1930 that these words appeared:

> Critic and fundamentalist are poles apart. The gulf between them is not between knowledge and ignorance, intellectual superiority and mental incapacity, unfettered liberalism and diehard conservatism. It is something wider and deeper. It is the gulf between two fundamentally different conceptions of God, His Word, and His Christ.[5]

Thomas Houghton, editor of *Gospel Magazine*, a sister publication to *The Bible League Quarterly*, would add this pinpoint analysis: "Once admit that the Bible is to no longer be regarded as an inspired, infallible, inerrant, authoritative Divine revelation, from which there can be no appeal, and the whole fabric of Christian doctrine is in danger of crumbling to dust."[6]

The original challenge to God and his Word stretches all the way back to the beginning. In the garden of Eden, Satan tempted Eve by sowing seeds of doubt and by twisting God's actual words. And so we see a challenge to the Word of God in the temptation that plunged humanity into the sinful state. Every age since has had its unique opposition to the Word of God.

---

[3] J. Gresham Machen, "Skyscrapers and Cathedrals," *McCall's* 59 (October 1931). See *J. Gresham Machen's The Gospel in the Modern World and Other Shorter Writings*, ed. Stephen J. Nichols (Phillipsburg, NJ: P&R, 2005), 44–46.

[4] See Andrew Atherstone and John Maiden, *Evangelicalism and the Church of England in the Twentieth Century: Reform, Resistance, and Renewal* (Woodbridge, UK: The Boydell Press, 2014); Iain H. Murray, *The Forgotten Spurgeon* (Edinburgh: Banner of Truth, 2010).

[5] Cited in Andrew Atherstone, "The Inter-War Church of England," in *Evangelicalism and Fundamentalism in the United Kingdom During the Twentieth Century*, ed. David Bebbington and David Ceri Jones (Oxford: Oxford University Press, 2013), 61.

[6] Thomas Houghton, "Ominous Signs," *Gospel Magazine* (January 1922), 12. See Atherstone, "The Inter-War Church of England," for more on Houghton and others engaged in this battle.

And so we come to our age, our moment, and our challenge in the early decades of the twenty-first century.

The challenge to God's Word in our time comes with all the trappings and predilections of modernity. The scientific method is seen as the unbiased way of arriving at truth and knowledge, justice and morality. Ultimately, science and technology lead to human betterment and flourishing. So the promise of modernity goes. In the wake of the Enlightenment, the scientific method was applied to the social sciences, politics, economics, history, and religion. Religious texts were viewed as reflecting the worldview of their writers and their original hearers or readers. The mythological world of the prescientific age was not only the backdrop for the Bible, it necessarily hemmed in the Bible. The word here is *historicism*, which is the idea that texts or ideas are always bound to the particular context, the place in space and time, in which they arise. There are no universal or abiding ideas. There are no ideas free from a context; no "view from nowhere," as it were. Instead, all views are from somewhere, and all views reflect their moment.

Applying historicism to the Bible means that the Bible can be brought forward in time only if it is taken more relatively and less absolutely. To be more blunt, the Bible must submit to our cultural sensibilities, not vice versa. Miracles do not clear the bar of scientific inquiry, so they are re-thought. What the Bible might have to say about human nature does not concur with the findings of contemporary social science research. For that matter, the Bible's thoughts on gender, sexuality, and marriage also do not resonate with social science data. Or so the argument goes.

This is liberalism. Liberalism is a desire to have Christianity, but to have it on our own terms, or on the terms of our own day. Rather than our submitting to the text, the text submits to us. In America, this movement reached a cultural zenith in 1925 at the "Scopes Monkey Trial." It was *The State of Tennessee v. John Thomas Scopes*, a high school science teacher who had violated Tennessee's Butler Act, which prohibited the teaching of the theory of evolution. It became much more. It became a case of God versus modernity, a case of the Bible versus the modernist worldview.

But, again, every age and every generation seems to have its battles for the Bible. And so we have our own battle in these early decades of the twenty-first century.

This essay raises this question: How did it come to this? But first we need to answer a simpler question: What is the meaning of *this* at the end of the first question? The *this* refers to the point in (mostly) North American evangelicalism where the long-held view of the verbal, plenary inspiration, infallibility, and inerrancy of Scripture is being challenged, rethought, and rejected by those who claim to be evangelicals. We could put the question this way: How did it come about that evangelicals have grown past the doctrine of inerrancy?

Three Periods of Development

This question is especially startling when we consider the previous century or so. We can see three distinct periods of development leading up to our time:

1880s–1930s: the Fundamentalist-Modernist controversy
1940s–1970s: the rise of evangelicalism
1970s–2000s: the generation of the Chicago Statement on Biblical
    Inerrancy

Looking back over these moments, we see that in each one a full commitment to inerrancy was a nonnegotiable boundary marker for theological conservatives. Inerrancy was the line in the sand. This was certainly true of the 1880s–1930s. The representatives cited above, including Bavinck, Machen, and the Bible League members, all attested to the necessity and centrality of inerrancy. The liberals and the modernists stood against inerrancy. The theological conservatives stood for it.

This was also true of the next generation, the one that spanned from the 1940s through the 1970s. Again, the liberals stood against inerrancy, but the conservatives stood for it. In 1949, when a group of theologians from a variety of seminaries joined together to form a scholarly society, they needed only one sentence for their doctrinal statement. So the doctrinal statement for the Evangelical Theological Society was: "The Bible alone, and the Bible in its entirety, is the Word of God written and is therefore inerrant in the autographs."[7] That was enough.

But as that generation was expanding its wings, especially in the halls of the academy, fissures and cracks began to appear in the doctrine of Scripture. The stage was being set for the Chicago Statement on Biblical Inerrancy.

R. C. Sproul sensed this acutely. Like Bavinck, he had received stones when he desired bread. He had but one lifeline at his theologically liberal college, Thomas Gregory, and he had but one lifeline at his very liberal theo-

---

[7] In 1990, a statement regarding the Trinity was added to the ETS doctrinal statement. See www.etsjets
.org/about/constitution#A3

logical seminary, John Gerstner. When Sproul went to the Free University of Amsterdam for his doctoral studies, he sat under G. C. Berkouwer, who was, in many ways, Bavinck's successor. Sproul watched, however, as Berkouwer, who began his career critical of Karl Barth, inched continuously toward Barth's view of the Bible. Barth was not interested in the verbal, plenary view of inspiration, advocating instead a more dynamic view. This view began to gain traction. Berkouwer was caught in its gaze.

Barth also had a profound impact across the Atlantic. To be of scholarly respectability in those post-World War II decades meant to be a Barthian or a Bultmannian, a follower of Rudolf Bultmann. Sproul had already seen this as a student, and when he returned to America to take his place behind the lectern, he saw it even more. When he founded Ligonier Ministries, he was quick to publish The Ligonier Statement on Scripture in 1973. This statement affirmed inspiration, infallibility, and inerrancy as crucial to the Christian faith, all while declaring full confidence in God's Word.[8]

In 1976, Harold Lindsell published *The Battle for the Bible*. Sproul wrote Lindsell suggesting that Lindsell use his post as editor at *Christianity Today* to convene a gathering of scholars to draft a statement on inerrancy. Lindsell declined, but suggested that Sproul take the lead in convening such a group and drafting such a statement. That eventually happened.

The International Council on Biblical Inerrancy met in Chicago October 25–28, 1978. More than three hundred scholars and pastors heard papers by various members of the council and then pored over the five main points and the additional nineteen articles of affirmation and denial that would constitute the Chicago Statement on Biblical Inerrancy.[9] Imagine trying to convene such a large and diverse group of evangelical theologians today and have them agree on such a detailed and thorough statement. It would be difficult, to say the least. The fact that such a thing happened in Chicago in 1978 testifies to both the urgency of the issue and the widespread consensus among theological conservatives on inerrancy.

Once again, the line in the sand was clear. Evangelicals stood on the side of inerrancy.

One institution that stood on the other side of the line from the Chicago Statement was Fuller Theological Seminary in Pasadena, California. One young Fuller student found himself rather disillusioned by the faculty and

---

[8] See R. C. Sproul, *Scripture Alone: The Evangelical Doctrine* (Phillipsburg, NJ: P&R, 2005), 175.
[9] See ibid. See also Appendix: The Chicago Statement on Biblical Inerrancy. See also Stephen J. Nichols, "For Such a Time as Then: The Chicago Statement on Biblical Inerrancy," *Expositor* (1) Sept./Oct. 2014, 32–35.

the teaching he received there. On March 25, 1971, he offered a "One Minute Speech to the Faculty and Trustees of Fuller Seminary." In this short speech, Wayne Grudem had this to say: "Not one of my courses here has strengthened my confidence in the Bible. Even more distressing is an intellectual narrow-mindedness; I have not had one professor who teaches Biblical inerrancy as a possible option."[10]

George Marsden chronicled the story of Fuller in his *Reforming Fundamentalism: Fuller Seminary and the New Evangelicalism.*[11] This book, like the book's subject, has an interesting history. In the preface to the paperback edition, Marsden notes how the book came to be a cautionary tale of declension, especially the declension of academic institutions. Marsden never intended that aim for his book. Despite his intentions, however, Marsden offers a front-row view of a rapid and precipitous decline. Fuller represented the decline and the movement away from its founding generation and commitment to inerrancy. By contrast, the Chicago Statement represented a firm stand.

The Chicago Statement steeled a generation as they battled for the Bible in their institutions, churches, and denominations. It became both a boundary marker and a rallying point. As a result, not all institutions suffered decline. Southern Baptist conservatives "took back" the denomination and eventually took back the seminaries as the Barthians retired or left and were replaced by a new generation of scholars committed to inerrancy.[12] The Chicago Statement offered a place to stand—and those standing with it could take assurance in the fact that they were not standing alone.

New Arguments

But in these early decades of the twenty-first century, whole new arguments are being made against the Chicago Statement and against inerrancy within evangelicalism itself. In an interview with Dan Reid of InterVarsity Press, the authors of *The Lost World of Scripture*, John Walton and Brent Sandy, address the issue of how Scripture functions and how we should rethink the issue of Scripture's authority. Both Walton and Sandy reflect on how these issues are coming to them from their students, and their students'

[10] Wayne Grudem, "One Minute Speech to the Faculty and Trustees of Fuller Seminary," March 25, 1971, Papers of Harold Lindsell Collection, Billy Graham Center Archives, Wheaton College. The typed speech comes with a handwritten note mentioning that Wayne Grudem was invited to give the speech by Dr. Hubbard, and that "this is a verbatim transcript of my speech."

[11] George M. Marsden, *Reforming Fundamentalism: Fuller Seminary and the New Evangelicalism* (Grand Rapids, MI, Eerdmans, 1987; paperback edition, 1995).

[12] See L. Russ Bush and Tom J. Nettles, *Baptists and the Bible* (Nashville: B&H, 1999).

uneasiness with inerrancy. At one point, Walton says: "Many who ask such questions have not lost their commitment to the truth and authority of the Bible. They have just found the term *inerrancy* ill-suited to an all-encompassing way to express their convictions and wonder why some still retain it so militantly."[13] Peter Enns also speaks of the problems of a "culture of inerrancy" in his book *The Bible Tells Me So: Why Defending Scripture Has Made Us Unable to Read It.* Only a few pages into the book, Enns speaks of "stories that are hard to take at face value and read more like a script for a fairy tale."[14] There are ethical issues, as well. All of the "messiness" of Scripture leads Enns to counsel readers to rethink the Bible and to leave behind positions resembling inerrancy.

These recent claims against inerrancy seem to come in three categories: the exegetical, the philosophical, and the cultural. In fact, these three categories of complaint and objection have been used since the 1880s and the modernist challenge to the Bible, if not in eras long before.

The exegetical concerns include harmonization issues between accounts in the Old Testament historical books and the narratives in the Gospels. They also include the use of Old Testament citations in the New.[15]

The philosophical concerns represent the ideas of some of the twentieth-century schools of thought, especially the analytical philosophers and logical positivists. These schools contend that our language is local and contextual, although we naively think it is objective. The logical positivist tells us that we think our words accurately represent objective realities and absolute truths and ethics. But in reality, they don't. These schools were simply precursors to postmodernism and an emphasis on our "situatedness." All language is contextual and never transcends the "group" or the context of the group. That was true of the biblical authors themselves. They were hopelessly and necessarily situated in their context. Their words do not transcend their times.

These philosophical views give ballast to the cultural objections. The Bible is misogynistic, representative of bygone eras. The Bible is imperialistic and colonial, not suited to our postcolonial times. The Bible is anti-homosexual. The Bible is exclusive and intolerant, not being well-suited to an inclusive and tolerant society. In short, the cultural objections are

---

[13] "Where Bible Scholars Fear to Tread," IVP Academic *Academic Alert* (22:3), Winter 2014, 1.
[14] Peter Enns, *The Bible Tells Me So: Why Defending Scripture Has Made Us Unable to Read It* (New York: HarperOne, 2014), 4.
[15] See G. K. Beale, *The Erosion of Inerrancy in Evangelicalism: Responding to New Challenges to Biblical Authority* (Wheaton, IL: Crossway, 2008).

saying, in effect, that we now know more—and know better—than the biblical authors.

We can see a common thread running through these three lines of objection: the failure to submit. They all lack humility, the necessary and essential ingredient as one stands before God and looks to his Word.

We can gain some perspective here by looking back to a moment in church history. Jerome, the figure associated with leading the task of translating the Bible into Latin and giving the church the Vulgate, had a curious interaction with Augustine over the authority and truthfulness of Scripture. The dispute arose over Jerome's handling of Galatians 2:11–14 and the actions of Peter in first associating with and then withdrawing from the Gentile Christians out of fear of the Judaizers. Jerome advocated the view of Origen, who held that Paul made up the entire episode to serve his purpose of roundly condemning the Judaizers. In other words, the event never happened.

Augustine immediately connected the dots of the implications of this particular view for the authority of Scripture and sent off a rather long letter to Jerome.[16] Augustine intones, "It seems to be very disastrous to believe that there can be any falsehood in the sacred books—I mean that those men who wrote and transmitted to us the Scripture, in any way lied in what they wrote."[17] He adds:

> Admit even a single well-meant falsehood into such an exalted authority, and there will not be left a single section of those books which, if appearing to anyone to present difficulties from the point of view of practice or to be hard to believe from the point of view of doctrine, will escape, by the same very baneful principle, from being classified as the deliberate act of an author who was lying.[18]

Augustine then refers to writings of the Bible as "the authority of unadulterated truth." He concludes:

> An effort must be made to bring to the knowledge of the sacred Scripture a man who will have such a reverent and truthful opinion of the holy books that he would refuse to find delight in a well-meant falsehood anywhere in them, and would rather pass over what he does not

---

[16] As an aside, and to illustrate the challenges of communication in the fifth century, the letter took nine years to reach Jerome.
[17] Augustine to Jerome, "Epistle 28," in *Augustine: Select Letters*, The Loeb Classical Library, vol. 239, trans. James Houston Baxter (Cambridge: Harvard University Press, 1998), 61.
[18] Ibid., 63.

understand than prefer his own intelligence to their truth. For indeed when he expresses such a preference, he demands credence for himself and attempts to destroy our confidence in the authority of the holy Scriptures.[19]

Three things are worth noting from Augustine's response to Jerome. First, Augustine ascribes nothing less than complete and utter truthfulness to the Bible. Admittedly the word *inerrancy* does not appear in this letter, but the concept clearly does. When he speaks of Scripture's unadulterated truth, he is affirming the inerrancy position. Second, Augustine readily admits that there are both theological and interpretative difficulties in the text. Critics of inerrancy like to point out, wrongly, that they alone are engaging difficulties in the text and that inerrantists are naively ignorant of any such difficulties. But Augustine acknowledges difficulties; the crucial question is how he responds to them. That leads to the third (and rather significant) thing to note from Augustine's exchange with Jerome. Augustine demands that we submit to the text, not that the text submit to us. It was unfathomable to him that one would assert his or her own credence over the credence of Scripture. Instead, we are to approach Scripture humbly, recognizing it as from God and therefore truthful. And we are to recognize that our only posture toward it is to be one of reverence, never a posture of questioning, suspicion, or rejection.

Before the face of God, we have but one option—to fall to the ground and confess our sinfulness and unworthiness, as the prophet Isaiah did (Isaiah 6). Before the pages of God's Word, we should assume the same posture of humility and reverence.

Augustine's approach accords with that of the Reformer Peter Martyr Vermigli. As Vermigli engaged Rome and made his own contribution to the Reformation doctrine of the authority of Scripture, he continually circled back to two Latin words: *Dominus dixit*, or, "Thus says the Lord." In the preface to his commentary on 1 Corinthians, Vermigli writes, "The first principle by which all true theological truths are determined should be considered this: *Dominus dixit*."[20] The authority of the Scriptures alone establishes the dogma of the church. This is because popes and councils, the traditions behind the dogma of Rome, err. Vermigli then takes the time to catalog some of the more salient errors from councils past. He concludes,

---

[19] Ibid., 65.
[20] Peter Martyr Vermigli, *"Praefatio,"* cited in Douglas H. Shantz, "Vermigli on Tradition and the Fathers," in *Peter Martyr Vermigli and the European Reformation: Semper Reformanda*, ed. Frank L. James III (Leiden: Brill, 2004), 128.

"For as the Word of God is trustworthy and abides forever, so the beliefs of men are uncertain and are always untrustworthy."[21]

Many more moments in church history could be cited that would further establish this point.[22] But if we consider the period from the 1880s until the present, we must look to the Princetonians, namely, Hodge—both Charles and A. A.—Benjamin B. Warfield, and Machen. What becomes clear regarding the Princetonian contribution to the doctrine of Scripture is the clarity, not to mention the forcefulness, with which they stated the doctrine of inerrancy. Warfield's argument for inerrancy was rather straightforward. If you assert that Scripture is divine revelation, then you are led to verbal, plenary inspiration, given the character and nature of God. If you assert verbal, plenary inspiration, then you are led to inerrancy. The Princetonian contribution was one of clarity and conviction, not one of innovation or invention.

One could make the same argument regarding the Chicago Statement on Biblical Inerrancy. As the challenges to inerrancy grew and changed over the centuries of the church, the response needed to reflect the particulars of those challenges. So it was with the Princetonians and so it was at Chicago in 1978.

New Challenges

New challenges have emerged since that time, so we return again to the exegetical, philosophical, and cultural areas of objection and challenge.

The exegetical issues are still the same. Peter Enns's argument regarding the Pentateuch is not all that different in the main from Charles Augustus Briggs. Enns's insistence that we must acknowledge more of the humanness of Scripture, lest we risk a "docetic" view of inspiration, is not at all different from Barth's view of inspiration.

By the end of Enns's book *Inspiration and Incarnation*, the current philosophical emphases are also clearly reflected. The "linguistic" turn in philosophy in the twentieth century brought a new emphasis to context, and Enns sees us as hopelessly contextual, never able to escape our own context interpretively or theologically. But then Enns goes one step further and sees the Bible itself as contextual: "The Bible has a dynamic quality to it, for God himself is dynamic, active, and alive in our lives and in the

---

[21] Ibid., 129–30.
[22] For more evidence, see chapter 8 in this volume, "The Ground and Pillar of the Faith: The Witness of Pre-Reformation History to the Doctrine of *Sola Scriptura*" by Nathan Busenitz, and chapter 9, "The Power of the Word in the Present: Inerrancy and the Reformation" by Carl R. Trueman.

life of his church," he writes. Then he adds, "The Bible sets trajectories, not rules."[23] Earlier in his book, Enns not only speaks of the "situational dimension" of the Old Testament Wisdom Literature and Historical Books, but also of the Law.[24]

Here, again, we see the influence of Barth. In fact, it is interesting to note that the increasing uneasiness of evangelicals with inerrancy is in direct proportion to the increasing favor with which Barth is viewed. Andrew McGowan's *The Divine Spiration of Scripture* is a case in point.[25] This change in Barth's reception among evangelicals today is a marked difference from the Chicago Statement era. Even Carl F. H. Henry, who opted not to sign the Chicago Statement, took a critical posture toward Barth.

In his autobiography, Henry recalled the time he engaged Barth during a news conference. Henry writes:

> Identifying myself as "Carl Henry, editor of *Christianity Today*," I continued: "The question, Dr. Barth, concerns the historical factuality of the resurrection of Jesus." I pointed to the press table and noted the presence of leading religion editors or reporters representing United Press, Religious News Service, *Washington Post*, *Washington Star* and other media. If these journalists had their present duties in the time of Jesus, I asked, was the resurrection of such a nature that covering some aspect of it would have fallen into their area of responsibility? "Was it news," I asked, "in the sense that the man in the street understands news?"
>
> Barth became angry. Pointing at me, and recalling my identification, he asked: "Did you say *Christianity Today* or *Christianity Yesterday*?" The audience—largely nonevangelical professors and clergy—roared with delight. When countered unexpectedly in this way, one often reaches for a Scripture verse. So I replied, assuredly out of biblical context, "Yesterday, today and forever."[26]

There is much at stake in the implications of Barth's doctrine of Scripture for the other doctrines of systematic theology; the gospel quickly comes into view. The ways in which Barth currently is being appropriated

---

[23] Peter Enns, *Inspiration and Incarnation: Evangelicals and the Problem of the Old Testament* (Grand Rapids, MI: Baker, 2005), 170.
[24] Ibid., 88.
[25] A. T. B. McGowan, *The Divine Spiration of Scripture: Challenging Evangelical Perspectives* (Nottingham, UK: Apollos, 2007). See also Kevin J. Vanhoozer, "A Person of the Book? Barth on Biblical Authority and Interpretation," in *Karl Barth and Evangelical Theology*, ed. Sung Wook Chung (Grand Rapids, MI: Baker Academic, 2006), 26–59.
[26] Carl F. H. Henry, *Confessions of a Theologian: An Autobiography* (Waco, TX: Word, 1986), 211.

by evangelicals will not be without consequences in all areas of systematic theology and orthodox understanding.

The cultural objections clearly reflect the predilections of the day. This can be poignantly seen in the brazen comments by Rob Bell. He told Oprah Winfrey: "The church will continue to be even more irrelevant when it quotes letters from 2,000 years ago as their best defense when you have in front of you flesh-and-blood people who are your brothers and sisters and aunts and uncles and co-workers and neighbors, and they love each other and they just want to go through life with someone."[27] Bell is rejecting what the Bible teaches about homosexuality in favor of his own observations. This is, using the expression from Augustine, Rob Bell demanding credence for himself over credence for God and his Word.

In 1 Thessalonians 2:13 Paul writes, "And we also thank God constantly for this, that when you received the word of God, which you heard from us, you accepted it not as the word of men but as what it really is, the word of God, which is at work in you believers." The Bible is God's revelation to us. It is perfect and pure, holy, and true. We must humbly receive it as such. The Word alone is what we must preach, what we must welcome into our lives, and what alone is at work in us.

Yet, there have always been challenges to it. Our new challenge is our old challenge, and not at all unlike the first challenge, the challenge that came along in the very beginning. The Serpent wryly asked Eve, "Did God actually say . . . ?" Our answer must be, "Yes, he did."

---

[27] Rob Bell, on "Super Soul Sunday," February 15, 2015, OWN.

Part 3

INERRANCY IN
THEOLOGICAL
PERSPECTIVE

Answering the Critics

12

Foundations of Biblical Inerrancy

DEFINITION AND PROLEGOMENA

John M. Frame

It has always been difficult for Christians to defend biblical inerrancy. Cultural opinion makers, including scientists, philosophers, journalists, and even theologians of a certain kind, are quite ready to dismiss biblical inerrancy as a superstition even when they are willing to give some attention to the claims of Christ. Some have asked whether it would not be advantageous to proclaim Christ without Scripture. We are saved, after all, by Christ, not by a book. Why, then, do we need an inerrant Bible? Many people have heard of Christ not by the Bible, but by oral preaching or witness. God is able to communicate his will to us by many means: nature and preaching, as well as written words. So it seems at least possible that he himself has chosen to communicate with us in these ways, not through an inerrant Bible. For these reasons, it can appear that inerrancy is dispensable or that it is a fairly minor doctrine, one that can be ignored without much consequence.

But in theology, connections are everything, and context is all-important. And the doctrine of inerrancy has a context, a system of theological

186 Inerrancy in Theological Perspective

connections, that makes it impossible for us to dispense with it and makes it a doctrine of major consequence.

First, let us define *inerrancy*, along with some other important terms in its doctrinal context:

Inspiration: An act by which God creates an identity between some human word and his own word. The term is used more loosely by some writers. But the only place in Scripture where English translations make use of the term is 2 Timothy 3:16, and the Greek word used there, *theopneustos*, means, as in the English Standard Version, "breathed out by God," that is, "spoken by God." So to say that Scripture is inspired is to say that the words of Scripture, by the hand of human writers, are God's own words.

Authority: The right to rule. God has supreme authority, so he has the right to tell us what to do and to receive obedience in return. Given that Scripture is his inspired Word, Scripture has the same right. What Scripture says, God says.[1]

Infallibility: Impossibility of error. To say that God is infallible is not only to say that he *does not* err, but that he *cannot* err. If Scripture is his Word, the same may be said of Scripture. Some writers use the term in a looser sense, to indicate general reliability in religious matters. But the word *infallibility* itself does not suggest any such limitation. It is a *stronger* term than *inerrancy* (see below), not a weaker term.

Inerrancy: The quality of being without error, whether caused by ignorance or deceit. Since God cannot deceive or be ignorant, God is inerrant in what he thinks and what he says. Given that Scripture is his Word, Scripture, too, is inerrant.

Notice that from the top to the bottom of this list, there runs a chain of reasoning. If Scripture is the *inspired* Word of God, then it shares in God's *authority*. God's *authority* extends over all of life, including our beliefs. So his Word has the right to tell us what to believe. That means that we may not criticize Scripture. Since we may not criticize it, we must regard it as *inerrant*, and, even more, as *infallible*. So our list of definitions presents an important biblical context for the doctrine of inerrancy.

In general, we may describe that context as the doctrine of God. Scrip-

---

[1] See Benjamin B. Warfield, "'It Says:' 'Scripture Says:' 'God says,'" *Presbyterian and Reformed Review* 10 (1899), 472–510. Available at http://www.monergism.com/thethreshold/sdg/warfield/warfield _itsays.html#fn01

ture is inerrant because God is inerrant. Because God is inerrant and has chosen to speak to us in written words, those written words are inerrant as well.

In the rest of this chapter, I will trace this pattern in more detail. We shall begin by looking at God as a speaking God, and conclude with Scripture as one important instance of his divine speech, and therefore inerrant.[2]

God Is a Speaking God

God is a being whose very nature is communicative. He speaks, not only to creatures, but within his Trinitarian existence, Father to Son, Son to Father, both to the Spirit, and the Spirit to both of them.[3] He is communicative because he is personal rather than impersonal—tripersonal, in fact. God is not a physical substance or an abstract principle. Rather, he knows, plans, loves, and makes. He does the things that persons do. This is why he speaks. Speaking is the way in which persons communicate with one another. So just as God is eternal, omniscient, omnipotent, loving, just, and good, so he is a *speaking* God. Speaking is one of his eternal attributes. A God who cannot speak is not the God of the Bible.

And speaking is not something God merely *happens* to do. As with all the attributes mentioned above, speaking is a *necessary* attribute of God, an attribute without which he would not be God. Compare the Bible's teaching about God's love. God's love is not merely something he has; it is something he *is* (1 John 4:8, 16). So the Bible says that God's speaking is identical with God himself: "In the beginning was the Word, and the Word was with God, and the Word was God" (John 1:1).

So the "Word of God" is something wonderful, bearing the highest dignity. It is (1) God himself and (2) all of God's communications, both among the members of the Trinity and with creatures.

When God speaks to creatures, he speaks as Lord. Over seven thousand times, Scripture uses this title for God, and often for Jesus Christ. God's lordship refers to his power, authority, and presence. These are what I

---

[2] I will be developing this context from the teaching of Scripture itself. Some may think this is reasoning in a circle: determining the inerrancy of Scripture from Scripture's own testimony. Much can be said about that. I have dealt with this question in *The Doctrine of the Knowledge of God* (Phillipsburg, NJ: P&R, 1987) and elsewhere. For now, it will suffice to recognize that the inerrancy of Scripture, like the resurrection of Jesus, is a biblical doctrine, and if we are to understand it at all, we must first try to understand it in its biblical context. At the very least, the biblical context tells us what it *means* to say that Scripture is inerrant.

[3] Much of the following discussion comes from my *The Doctrine of the Word of God* (Phillipsburg, NJ: P&R, 2010), chapters 7, 8, 11, and 42. See also my *The Doctrine of God* (Phillipsburg: P&R, 2002), 470–75.

have sometimes described as God's "attributes of lordship."[4] So when God speaks, that spoken word has the same qualities. He always speaks as the Lord. Let us look more closely at these lordship attributes:

First, God's spoken word is his controlling *power*. It is not only a communication of linguistic content to our minds, though it is certainly that. It is also a great power that makes things happen. When God says, "Let there be light" (Gen. 1:3), light comes into existence. Even before it exists, light obeys this word of God. Such is the power that "calls into existence the things that do not exist" (Rom. 4:17). So Scripture often extols the power of God's word. Summarizing Genesis 1, Psalm 33 says: "By the word of the LORD the heavens were made, and by the breath of his mouth all their host. . . . For he spoke, and it came to be; he commanded, and it stood firm" (vv. 6, 9; cf. Ps. 148:5; John 1:3, 10; Heb. 1:2; 11:3; 2 Pet. 3:5–7).

Since God made the world, he has continued to govern it by the word of his power. Note what is ascribed to "the voice of the Lord" in Psalm 29 and to the words and commands of God in Psalms 147:15–18 and 148:7–8. God's word governs providence as well as creation (cf. Gen. 1:9, 11, 22; Job 37:12; Ps. 18:15; 33:11; 119:89–91; Matt. 8:27; Heb. 1:3; 2 Peter 3).

When God speaks to rational creatures, the word continues to be powerful. God's word brings judgment upon sinful people, and often the power of that judgment-word is palpable (Ps. 46:6; Isa. 30:30–31; 66:6; Hos. 6:5; Joel 2:11; Amos 1:2). In 2 Peter 3:5–7, the apostle compares the judgment of Noah's flood with the original creation by the word of God. Just as God's word was powerful enough to bring the world into being, so it will destroy all the works of wickedness. God's word is like a fire (Job 41:19–21), a sword (Isa. 49:2), and a hammer (Jer. 23:29).

But God's word is also powerful to save, powerful in grace. In Genesis 18:14, after God has promised a miraculous child to Abraham and Sarah in their old age, he ascribes the miracle to his word. He asks, "Is anything too hard for the LORD?"—literally, "no word [*rhema*] will be impossible for God." When a centurion asks Jesus to heal his servant, he tells Jesus not to come personally to his home, but only to "say the word" (Luke 7:7). Jesus commends the centurion's faith, for the centurion believes in the omnipotence of the word of Jesus.

So when the apostles bring the gospel of Christ to the world, they rejoice that it is not only a body of content, but also a power (Rom. 1:16; 1 Thess. 1:5; 2:13). The word itself changes hearts and strengthens believers

[4] See my *The Doctrine of God*, chapters 1–7.

(Rom. 16:25). It is the "word of life" (Phil. 2:16; see 1 John 1:1), the gospel that brings life and immortality to light (2 Tim. 1:10).

How powerful is the word? No less than God's own omnipotence:

> So shall my word be that goes out from my mouth;
>> it shall not return to me empty,
> but it shall accomplish that which I purpose,
>> and shall succeed in the thing for which I sent it. (Isa. 55:11)

What God says with his mouth he fulfills with his hand (2 Chron. 6:15; cf. Ezek. 1:3; 3:22).

Second, God's word is his divine *authority*. We have seen that God's *authority* is his right to rule. By his power, he makes things happen. By his authority, he imposes obligations. So when he speaks to us, we are obligated to do as he says. When his word states facts, we have an obligation to believe those facts just as he has stated them. When he commands us, we have a duty to heed him.

The story of the Bible is that God speaks to human beings, who respond in obedience or disobedience, whereupon God sends consequences: blessings for obedience and curses for disobedience. In Genesis 1:28, the first experience of our first parents is listening to God speak. God's word describes their fundamental task on the earth: to fill and subdue it. But in Genesis 2:16–17, he adds a negative command, forbidding Adam to eat from the tree of the knowledge of good and evil.

Then, in Genesis 3, there is a rival word, the word of a talking snake, representing Satan. The contest is between two words that claim supreme authority: God's and the Devil's. Satan's attack is precisely on the word that God has spoken. He questions whether God has uttered such a word (v. 1), and then, assuming that God has spoken it, Satan contradicts it (vv. 4–5). Adam and Eve have no third authority to arbitrate the dispute. They have no way to test which word is true, apart from the words themselves and the speakers of those words. In the end, they make their decision by their own autonomous reasoning—by following their own word rather than God's.

That is the nature of sin, to trust one's own reason against God's word. Adam and Eve should have accepted the naked word of God—without verification from any other source—even though it was contradicted by another source claiming expertise.

There are consequences for the disobedience of our first parents. God declares punishment. But amazingly, he also proclaims grace, saying that he will one day send a deliverer to crush the head of the Serpent, and that deliverer will be a descendant of Adam and Eve (v. 15). This good news also comes from the sheer word of God. Again, Adam and Eve have no way to test God's word by some higher authority, certainly not by their own autonomous reason. But this time, they believe.

The Bible repeats that pattern over and over again. Noah is not a master of meteorological science; he knows a flood is coming only by the word of God, and he obeys (Gen. 6:22; 7:5, 9). Hebrews 11:7 commends Noah's faith as a model of Christian trust in God: he responds to God "in reverent fear." Indeed, he not only obeys God's word, but also proclaims it to others (2 Pet. 2:5). Abraham, too, receives a word from God, in his case an announcement of a biological miracle, that in their old age he and his wife, Sarah, will have a son. As with Noah, his faith in the word of God is a model for Christians:

> No unbelief made him waver concerning the promise of God, but he grew strong in his faith as he gave glory to God, fully convinced that God was able to do what he had promised. That is why his faith was "counted to him as righteousness." But the words "it was counted to him" were not written for his sake alone, but for ours also. It will be counted to us who believe in him who raised from the dead Jesus our Lord, who was delivered up for our trespasses and raised for our justification. (Rom. 4:20–25)

The same pattern continues through the Old Testament stories of Moses, David, and the prophets. It culminates in Jesus, who is the Word of God *par excellence* (John 1:1, 14). Jesus's words, too, are words of utmost authority. He teaches that calling him Lord is meaningless unless we do the will of the Father (Matt. 7:21–23). When he returns in glory, he will be ashamed of those who are ashamed of him—notably, those who have been ashamed of his words (Mark 8:38; Luke 9:26). His mother and brothers are those who "hear the word of God and do it" (Luke 8:21). In the Gospel of John, he makes this principle even more explicit:

> If anyone hears my words and does not keep them, I do not judge him; for I did not come to judge the world but to save the world. The one who rejects me and does not receive my words has a judge; the word that I have spoken will judge him on the last day. For I have not spoken on my own authority, but the Father who sent me has himself given me a commandment—what to say and what to speak. And I know that his

commandment is eternal life. What I say, therefore, I say as the Father has told me. (John 12:47–50)

Third, God's word is his personal *presence*. This is also a quality of the Bible, for Scripture is a place where God personally dwells with his people. In the Old Testament, God's dwelling with Israel is focused in the nearness of his word (Deut. 4:7–8; 30:11–14). As we have seen, God performs his powerful works through speech. So in that speech, he is present to judge and to save. The speech of God, in fact, has divine attributes: righteousness (Ps. 119:7), faithfulness (119:86), wonderfulness (119:129), eternality (119:89, 160), omnipotence (Gen. 18:14; Isa. 55:11; Luke 1:37), omniscience (Heb. 4:12–13), and perfection (Ps. 19:7ff). No mere creature has such attributes. The fact that the word of God has them implies that it is divine, that it is nothing less than God himself speaking. So the word of God is an object of worship (Ps. 56:4, 10; cf. Ps. 119:48, 161). Such worship may be given only to God; giving it to anything else is idolatry. Therefore, the word of God is either an idol or it is God himself. Scripture clearly says that it is the latter.

So John 1:1–14 not only says that Jesus is God, but also that the word of God is God. There is a three-way identification: God=the word=Jesus. What that means for us is that God is always present in his word. You can't have God apart from his word, or his word apart from God. God is a speaking God, and the word is God's speech.

Clearly, God's speech is authoritative, infallible, and inerrant, as in my earlier definitions. Errors come from two sources: mistakes and deceit. God does not make mistakes, because he knows everything (Heb. 4:13). And he does not tell lies (Titus 1:2).

How God Speaks to Us

We must now ask how this marvelous speech of God comes into our experience. How does it reach our ears, our minds, and our hearts?

Scripture speaks about God revealing himself through nature (Ps. 19:1; Rom. 1:19–21), and that is important. But God's natural revelation is not expressed in words and sentences, though it is certainly an expression of the word of God. In this chapter, I am focusing on God's revelation in human language, the revelation that leads directly to the publication of Scripture. This happens in three stages: the divine voice, prophets and apostles, and the written Word.

First, the *divine voice*. In this form of revelation, God speaks to human beings without any human mediator. The paradigm of this revelation can be found in Exodus 20, the only occasion when all Israel is gathered in one place (camped around Mount Sinai) to hear words from God's own lips. He speaks to them the Ten Commandments (Ex. 20:3–17). The people are terrified, and they ask Moses to speak to God on their behalf. He accepts this task.

From that point, this kind of direct revelation is rare. Moses speaks "mouth to mouth" with God (Num. 12:8) as he "beholds the form of the LORD." Other prophets also hear directly from God, as we shall see. And at special moments, God the Father speaks from heaven to people on earth, as at Jesus's baptism: "This is my beloved Son, with whom I am well pleased" (Matt. 3:17). Further, we should not forget that during his earthly ministry, Jesus himself was the divine voice. He says that on the last day, his word will judge those who reject him (John 12:48).

But this is not the common means of divine revelation, even during the times described in the Bible. Normally, God speaks to his people by mediators.

Second, *prophets and apostles*. These are the mediators by whom God has normally spoken to his people. Deuteronomy 18:18–19 defines the nature of a prophet:

> I will raise up for them a prophet like you from among their brothers. And I will put my words in his mouth, and he shall speak to them all that I command him. And whoever will not listen to my words that he shall speak in my name, I myself will require it of him.

A prophet is someone who has God's words in his mouth. These words, God says, are "my" words. Those who don't obey must answer to God. That is to say, there is no difference between the word of the prophet and the divine voice in terms of power, authority, and divine presence. We usually understand that God's word, spoken directly as the divine voice, is absolute, but we persist in the idea that this absoluteness disappears when the word passes from God's lips to human lips. But Scripture rebukes that notion. The words Moses speaks are "my" words, says God. He says the same of the words of David, Isaiah, Jeremiah, and the rest. Jeremiah says:

> Then the LORD put out his hand and touched my mouth. And the LORD said to me, "Behold, I have put my words in your mouth. See, I have set you this day over nations and over kingdoms, to pluck up and to break down, to destroy and to overthrow, to build and to plant." And

the word of the LORD came to me, saying, "Jeremiah, what do you see?" And I said, "I see an almond branch." Then the LORD said to me, "You have seen well, for I am watching over my word to perform it."[5] (1:9–12)

This passage emphasizes the *power* of the prophetic word, that it is able to *do* all the things that God's word does.

There are prophets in the New Testament as well (Acts 2:17–18; 11:27–28; 21:9–14), but we hear more often about the *apostles* as vessels of the word of God. Jesus appoints apostles, men closest to him, to speak the word of God (Matt. 10:19–20). He says that the Holy Spirit will enable them to remember all that Jesus said (John 14:26). The Spirit will also reveal to them "all the truth," and will declare to them "the things that are to come" (John 16:13). So the revelation to the apostles concerns the past (what Jesus said), the present (all the truth), and the future (things that are to come).

Again, we are tempted to ask whether the apostles' words have the same power, authority, and divine presence as the words of the divine voice. But Jesus says that when the Spirit gives words to the apostles, "he will not speak on his own authority, but whatever he hears he will speak" (John 16:13). The Spirit speaks nothing other than "what he hears" from someone else. And that someone else is no one other than the Father.

The apostles themselves report that this extraordinary speaking of the Spirit took place. Paul writes to the Galatians:

For I would have you know, brothers, that the gospel that was preached by me is not man's gospel. For I did not receive it from any man, nor was I taught it, but I received it through a revelation of Jesus Christ. (1:11–12)

The consequence is that Paul's gospel is not only Paul's. It is the gospel of Jesus Christ. Therefore, it has absolute authority: everyone who hears is obligated to believe it.

That gospel also carries with it the *power* of God:

For I am not ashamed of the gospel, for it is the power of God for salvation to everyone who believes, to the Jew first and also to the Greek. (Rom. 1:16)

---

[5] "Almond" and "watch" are similar in Hebrew.

So God's word bears his lordship attributes, even on the lips of human beings whom God has appointed to speak his word.

Third, the *written Word* of God, that is, Scripture. We know that the prophets and apostles sometimes committed the words God gave them to writing. Do those written words have the same power, authority, and divine presence as the words delivered orally? Well, why not? Imagine that you hear a stimulating lecture by an expert on Renaissance art, and then you buy a book written by the lecturer. Would you expect that the book would be less authoritative than the lecture, that the professor would be less expert in writing than in speaking? No. We assume that a person's writing usually has the same quality as his oral communications.

The same is true about the biblical view of the Word of God. God's written Word bears God's power, authority, and presence, just as certainly as his divine voice, his prophets, and his apostles. The written Word, in fact, plays a central role in God's communication with his people. The important thing about writing is that it gives *permanence* to communication. Although some modern theologians have said otherwise, God's revelation is not to be a momentary thing that exists and then disappears. It is, rather, something solid, a communication that we can pass down from one generation to another. The Old Testament saints erected stone pillars so that their descendants would remember God's words (Gen. 12:7; 13:18; 28:18; 35:14). In the New Testament, the word of the Spirit becomes a *tradition* (*paradosis*), something "passed down" (Matt. 11:27; 1 Cor. 15:3; 2 Thess. 2:15; 3:6; 1 Tim. 6:20; Jude 3).

So although Israel in Exodus 19–20 heard the divine voice from heaven, and although they heard the word from the prophet Moses at their own request, the definitive revelation from God was a written document. That document begins with the Ten Commandments, written on "two tablets of the testimony" (Ex. 31:18), stone tablets "written by the finger of God." This document is not only God's word; it bears his own penmanship! The document is a "covenant document," a "suzerainty treaty" between the Great King Yahweh and his vassal people, Israel.[6] This treaty is the governing document of Israel, just as the written Constitution is the fundamental law of the United States of America.

The document is placed in the sanctuary of the Lord (indicating its holiness), and it is read to the people on a regular basis. Throughout the

---

[6] See Meredith G. Kline, *The Structure of Biblical Authority* (Grand Rapids, MI: Eerdmans, 1972).

Pentateuch, God urges Israel to obey all the statutes, testimonies, commandments, laws, and ordinances (for example, Deut. 4:1–8; 6:1–9, 24–25; 7:11; 8:11). After Moses dies and Joshua prepares to lead Israel into the Promised Land, God says:

> Only be strong and very courageous, being careful to do according to all the law that Moses my servant commanded you. Do not turn from it to the right hand or to the left, that you may have good success wherever you go. This Book of the Law shall not depart from your mouth, but you shall meditate on it day and night, so that you may be careful to do according to all that is written in it. For then you will make your way prosperous, and then you will have good success. (Josh. 1:7–8)

The covenant document takes on many additional texts, written by Joshua (Josh. 24:25–28) and other prophets (Isa. 30:8–11; Jer. 25:13). Throughout the Bible, God continues to urge his people to obey his written covenant, and the Jews accept it as sacred Scripture. Jesus never criticizes Scripture, but rather, criticizes the Jews for failing to obey it (John 5:45–47). He says "Scripture cannot be broken" (John 10:35). Paul, toward the end of his life, calls Timothy to a source of God's truth that will survive the apostle:

> All Scripture is breathed out by God and profitable for teaching, for reproof, for correction, and for training in righteousness, that the man of God may be complete, equipped for every good work. (2 Tim. 3:16–17)

"Breathed out by God" means simply that the text contains God's spoken words.

The apostles' written words also transmitted their prophetic authority. Paul says this about his letter to the Corinthians:

> If anyone thinks that he is a prophet, or spiritual, he should acknowledge that the things I am writing to you are a command of the Lord. If anyone does not recognize this, he is not recognized. (1 Cor. 14:37–38)

Here Paul's written word is the criterion that determines whether a person really is a prophet or not. So that written word, rather than the oral words of the prophets, serves as the highest authority in the church.

The written text of the Old Testament covenant document and the New Testament words of the apostles are what we call today "the Bible." That Bible is God's written revelation to us.

Conclusion

As we have seen, the foundation of biblical inerrancy is the nature of God himself. God is not an impersonal principle, but a personal being who speaks—both within the Trinity and with his creatures. But he always speaks as Lord, in power, authority, and presence. Any word that is truly of God will bear his lordship: we can trust it as we can trust God's direct divine voice.

He has chosen to speak to human beings in that direct divine voice, but also through human prophets and apostles. These human speakers have God's very word on their lips. They also have that word in their hands, as they write it on stone, parchment, or papyrus. So we can trust that written text as if God were speaking directly to us.

There is much more to be said, of course. Questions arise about how to interpret that text, how to be sure which text is the right one, precisely which books belong in the Bible, and so on. Other essays in this book take up such questions. But our "foundations" are relevant to those questions, too, for we have a God who has answers to those questions. Although such problems may seem formidably difficult for us, they are not difficult for God. If he desires to speak to human beings, it really is not difficult for him to do so. And he *does* want to speak to us. That is why he sent the Word, his beloved Son, both to witness to the truth (John 18:37) and to die for sin.

At the beginning of this chapter, I posed this question: Why do we need an inerrant Bible when we have Christ? The answer, I think, is found in the context that I have sketched. Salvation is not a mechanical process, but a relationship between God and us. That relationship is fully personal, and therefore it includes a conversation. God wants to *speak* to us, not just to transform us. When God speaks, he speaks infallibly and therefore inerrantly. For us to receive his Word is an act of worship. We receive it humbly, not critically, because his Word is precious to us. His Word, ultimately, is our Savior, Jesus Christ. As we worship, we ascribe to him all "power and wealth and wisdom and might and honor and glory and blessing!" (Rev. 5:12). We do not for a moment think that there could be defect in his character or work. Neither can there be any untruth in his Word, his gospel. We praise his Word as we praise him (Ps. 56:4, 10). In that context, as we bow down in worship, we understand why the Bible can be nothing other than inerrant.

13

Rightly Dividing the Word of Truth

INERRANCY AND HERMENEUTICS

R. Albert Mohler Jr.

To be human is to be a hermeneutical creature—a creature who interprets. We engage in a process of interpretation from the moment we leave the womb. We are constantly observing and learning, and at every point, we act as interpreters of all we sense, observe, and experience.

To be a Christian is to accept the gift of divine revelation and to come to a saving knowledge of Jesus Christ. Salvation comes to those who hear the Word of Christ and believe, who repent of their sins and follow Christ in obedience to the pattern of sound words revealed within the Holy Scriptures.

Thus, the faithful Christian seeks to be a faithful interpreter of the Bible, knowing that the Bible is nothing less than the Word of God, inerrant, infallible, and inspired. There is no escaping the hermeneutical task, but the Christian comes to that task armed with a knowledge of what the Bible is in order faithfully to understand what it says.

Inerrancy and the Evangelical Moment

The inerrancy of the Bible has been a crucial issue of evangelical debate for the past half century and more. From the beginnings of the evangelical movement, an affirmation of the divine inspiration and authority of the Bible has stood at the center of evangelical faith and identity. In making this central affirmation, evangelicals have sought to maintain a conscious convictional continuity with the faithful theological trajectory of classic Christianity, and especially with the central theological affirmations of the Reformation. The Reformers' affirmation of *sola Scriptura* is echoed in our contemporary affirmation of the Bible's inerrancy, trustworthiness, and total truthfulness.

The basic impulse behind the affirmation of biblical inerrancy is straightforward. We mean to say what the faithful church has always said about the Bible: "When the Bible speaks, God speaks."

Benjamin B. Warfield explained this evangelical affirmation with singular clarity when he insisted that what he rightly called the "church doctrine of inspiration" had always sought to affirm the simple truth that the Bible is God's Word—an *oracular* Word, the Word God himself has spoken. In speaking of the "church doctrine of inspiration," Warfield made clear that this is what the faithful church has always and everywhere affirmed about the Bible. Plenary verbal inspiration and the inerrancy of the Bible have been characteristic avowals of God's people through millennia, even as these truths are revealed and affirmed within the Bible itself.

In defending the inerrancy of the Bible, Warfield stated simply that "in every way possible, the church has borne her testimony from the beginning, and still to our day, to her faith in the divine trustworthiness of her Scriptures, in all their affirmations of whatever kind."[1]

In 1978, American evangelicals were seeking to affirm this very understanding of the nature and authority of the Bible when the Chicago Statement on Biblical Inerrancy (CSBI) was adopted (see Appendix). As the framers of the statement indicated, they simply were attempting to affirm what the faithful church had always affirmed—the plenary inerrancy of the Bible. Furthermore, they were seeking to do so as the ground was shifting in the larger theological world, and even as some who claimed to be evangelical openly denied the Bible's inerrancy.

In its essence, the Chicago Statement on Biblical Inerrancy is a declaration and definition of the Bible's total truthfulness and trustworthiness. "Being wholly and verbally God-given," it states, "Scripture is without error or fault in all its teaching, no less in what it states about God's acts in creation, about the events of world history, and about its own literary

---

[1] Benjamin B. Warfield, *The Inspiration and Authority of the Bible* (Philadelphia: Presbyterian and Reformed, 1948), 112.

origins under God, than in its witness to God's saving grace in individual lives" (A Short Statement, point 4).

In a CSBI preface, the framers warned: "To stray from Scripture in faith or conduct is disloyalty to our Master. Recognition of the total truth and trustworthiness of Holy Scripture is essential to a full grasp and adequate confession of its authority." They then declared that the CSBI "affirms this inerrancy of Scripture afresh, making clear our understanding of it and warning against its denial."

The section known as "A Short Statement" sets forth the main thrust of the CSBI:

1. God, who is Himself Truth and speaks truth only, has inspired Holy Scripture in order thereby to reveal Himself to lost mankind through Jesus Christ as Creator and Lord, Redeemer and Judge. Holy Scripture is God's witness to Himself.

2. Holy Scripture, being God's own Word, written by men prepared and superintended by His Spirit, is of infallible divine authority in all matters upon which it touches: it is to be believed, as God's instruction, in all that it affirms; obeyed, as God's command, in all that it requires; embraced, as God's pledge, in all that it promises.

3. The Holy Spirit, Scripture's divine Author, both authenticates it to us by His inward witness and opens our minds to understand its meaning.

4. Being wholly and verbally God-given, Scripture is without error or fault in all its teaching, no less in what it states about God's acts in creation, about the events of world history, and about its own literary origins under God, than in its witness to God's saving grace in individual lives.

5. The authority of Scripture is inescapably impaired if this total divine inerrancy is in any way limited or disregarded, or made relative to a view of truth contrary to the Bible's own; and such lapses bring serious loss to both the individual and the Church.

I believe that any loss of confidence in the inerrancy of the Scriptures and any attempt to marginalize or subvert the affirmation of inerrancy will spell disaster for the evangelical movement. I believe that the affirmation of the Bible's inerrancy has never been more essential to evangelicalism as a movement and as a living theological and spiritual tradition. Furthermore, I believe that the inerrancy of Scripture is absolutely crucial to the project of perpetuating a distinctively evangelical witness into the future. Without inerrancy, the evangelical movement will inevitably become dissolute and indistinct in its faith and doctrines, and increasingly confused about the very nature and authority of its message.

I will make my position plain once again. I do not believe that evangelicalism can survive without the explicit and complete affirmation of biblical inerrancy. Given the pressures of late modernity, an epoch growing ever more hostile to theological truth claims, there is little basis for any hope that evangelicals will remain distinctively evangelical without a principled and explicit commitment to the inerrancy of the Bible.

Beyond this, inerrancy must be understood as necessary and integral to the life of the church, the authority of preaching, and the integrity of the Christian life. Without a total commitment to the trustworthiness and truthfulness of the Bible, the church will be left without its defining authority, lacking confidence in its ability to hear God's voice. Preachers will lack confidence in the authority and truthfulness of the very Word they are commissioned to preach and teach. This is not an issue of homiletical theory, but a life-and-death question of whether the preacher has a distinctive and authoritative Word to preach to people desperately in need of direction and guidance. Individual Christians will be left without either the confidence to trust the Bible or the ability to understand the Bible.

In our current evangelical moment, the affirmation of biblical inerrancy is linked to the necessary affirmation of the total Christian truth claim in a context of open cultural hostility and ideological subversion. Furthermore, the doctrine of divine revelation points to the only way out of the current hermeneutical context of nihilism, subjectivism, and relativism presented to us in our current intellectual climate.

That raises a crucial question: Does inerrancy entail a hermeneutic?

A State of Continuous Hermeneutical Crisis

Ever since the Enlightenment dawned, a sense of hermeneutical crisis has haunted the Western mind. Immanuel Kant recognized this and sought to move religion and spiritual concerns from inquiry by empirical observation, as would befit the material world (the *phenomenal* world), into a realm of more speculative investigation (the *noumenal* world). Kant's skepticism about the very possibility of divine revelation denied him the only means of finding any epistemological grounding for Christian belief.

A line can be drawn from Kant to Friedrich Schleiermacher, who was both the founding father of modern liberal theology and the inventor, in a very true sense, of the modern science of hermeneutics. Schleiermacher saw the hermeneutical task not as a precise science but as essentially a form of art—seeking to re-create and re-enter the thoughts and feelings of an author. A romanticist to the end, Schleiermacher understood well the hermeneutical crisis presented by the Enlightenment's "turn to the subject." But he understood something even more far-reaching. Schleiermacher believed that hermeneutics is essentially the problem of human understanding, *as such*. His conception of hermeneutics sets the stage for asking whether human beings can actually know anything at all.

In more modern eras, the church has been confronted by a virtual avalanche of successive hermeneutical shifts and a never-ending cavalcade of hermeneutical proposals. The great intellectual crisis of the West has produced a culture of continuous hermeneutical crisis grounded in a deep epistemological skepticism. A pervasive antisupernaturalism produced a collapse of intellectual authority. The church and the Scriptures were displaced by the authority of sovereign human reason and the empirical approach to all knowledge.

The antisupernaturalism of modern secular culture led to the proposal that the Bible should be both read and investigated as any other literary artifact. Modern "higher criticism" of the Bible emerged directly from this proposal, and it quickly gained dominance in liberal Protestantism and Roman Catholic modernism. By the early twentieth century, liberal churchmen such as Harry Emerson Fosdick were openly describing the Bible as a "problem." To these liberal preachers and theologians, the Bible was a problem to be solved rather than the solution to the problem of knowledge.

In crystalline prose, author John Updike describes a fictional Presbyterian preacher to a sophisticated New York congregation losing his faith in this era. In his novel *In the Beauty of the Lilies*, Updike tells of the Rev. Clarence Arthur Wilmot, who loses his faith and comes to the conclusion— while studying for a sermon, no less—that there is no God. The Rev. Wilmot traces his loss of faith to the historical-critical approach to the Bible he had been taught at seminary, where, "hungry for knowledge and fearless in his youthful sense of God's protection close at hand," he "had plunged into the chilly Baltic sea of Higher Criticism."[2] The higher critics, Updike explains, took their salaries from the Christian faithful, but they "undermined Christianity's ancient supporting walls and beams" with their biblical criticism.[3]

The twentieth century saw hermeneutical proposals come from Martin

---

[2] John Updike, *In the Beauty of the Lilies* (New York: Knopf, 1996), 15.
[3] Ibid.

Heidegger and Ludwig Wittgenstein, but Heidegger's existentialism and Wittgenstein's language games produced no way out of the hermeneutical crisis. Heidegger influenced Rudolf Bultmann, whose proposal to "demythologize" the New Testament led to the outright denial of the supernatural within the Bible. Karl Barth's attempt to relocate revelation from the text to a divine-human encounter allowed for a short-term recovery of confidence in the Bible, but his own Kantian epistemology undermined that very confidence and left him personally befuddled when he saw the resurgent theological liberalism that came in his wake.

In the middle years of the twentieth century, attention turned in the larger academic world to the hermeneutical proposals put forth by philosophers such as Hans-Georg Gadamer, who sought to redefine the hermeneutical challenge in terms of a "fusion of horizons" between the horizon of the text and the horizon of the interpreter. This embrace of interpretive indeterminacy, which offered brilliant insights into the process of human understanding, quickly gave way to a profusion of liberationist and revisionist schools of criticism, subjecting every text and authority to constant critique from liberationists, feminists, and a host of others.

In the theological world, the "New Hermeneutic" emerged in an attempt to rescue the Bible from total subjectivism, but its inability to bridge the chasm between the text and the modern world doomed it to failure. All too soon, the intellectual situation changed yet again, with the emergence of what would become known as "postmodernism," with its radical relativism and the proposal that all truth claims and texts are merely artifacts of social construction. The "death of the metanarrative" went hand in hand with Jacques Derrida's famed "death of the author," and the reader, rather than the text or its author, became the agent of the determination of meaning.

As the twenty-first century dawned, postmodernism quickly fell in on itself, but its legacy of relativism and radical subjectivity remained. The hermeneutic of submission to the biblical text that had guided the reading and understanding of the Bible for centuries had given way, in large sectors of the church, to a hermeneutic of suspicion, in which the biblical text was to be interrogated and subjected to constant critique rather than read, received, and obeyed.

Inerrancy and Interpretation

When we ask whether inerrancy entails a hermeneutic, Kevin Vanhoozer answers straightforwardly: "It is one thing to posit the Bible's truthfulness in all that it affirms, quite another to say what the truth of the Bible *is.* Inerrancy alone, then, is not yet a full-fledged hermeneutic."[4]

Vanhoozer is certainly right to insist that inerrancy, taken alone, is not a "full-fledged hermeneutic." Nevertheless, I would argue that inerrancy, taken alone, establishes certain boundaries, ground rules, principles, and habits for the faithful interpretation of the Bible.

Some of these were already visible in the interpretive methods taught and demonstrated by early defenders of inerrancy in the American context, such as Warfield and J. Gresham Machen, and similar defenders of the Bible on British soil, such as J. I. Packer and D. Martyn Lloyd-Jones. Though separated by both geography and time, these figures are representative of a unified hermeneutical approach that was explicitly based on biblical inerrancy and the approach to the Bible that was characteristic of the Reformers and their heirs.

That approach aimed to understand the Bible as the oracular book Warfield described, the Word that God *spoke.* Scripture was to be interpreted by means of a historical-grammatical method that sought to affirm the most literal meaning of the text, using the best tools available to the interpreter (especially a knowledge of the biblical languages), understanding the different forms of biblical language and literature, and affirming the total truthfulness of everything claimed by the text, in every respect.

That is the hermeneutical approach that is addressed in the CSBI. That statement clearly affirms that divine inspiration extends to the very words of Scripture, and denies that "human language is so limited by our creatureliness that it is rendered inadequate as a vehicle for divine revelation" (Art. IV). Inspiration is affirmed for "the whole of Scripture and all its parts" (Art. VI), thus extending from the entire canon to the individual words of the original text. The CSBI affirms that God intended to deploy the individual human authors of Scripture with their "distinctive personalities and literary styles" (Art. VIII), thus honoring authorial intent and the varieties of literary forms. The statement explicitly affirms "the unity and internal consistency of Scripture," and denies that any legitimate reading of the Bible can allow for genuine contradictions or discrepancies (Art. XIV).

Furthermore, on one very important set of propositions, the statement expresses a succinct but clear hermeneutic:

---

[4] Kevin J. Vanhoozer, "Lost in Interpretation? Truth, Scripture, and Hermeneutics," *Journal of the Evangelical Theological Society*, 48/1 (March 2005): 97.

We affirm that the text of Scripture is to be interpreted by grammatical-historical exegesis, taking account of its literary forms and devices, and that Scripture is to interpret Scripture. We deny the legitimacy of any treatment of the text or quest for sources lying behind it that leads to relativizing, dehistoricizing, or discounting its teaching, or rejecting its claims to authorship. (Art. XVIII)

While those points and principles do not constitute a "full-fledged hermeneutic," they do establish clear boundary markers and criteria for the development of any hermeneutical approach that would be consistent with the affirmation of inerrancy.

The International Council on Biblical Inerrancy followed the CSBI, with the Chicago Statement on Biblical Hermeneutics (CSBH), released in 1982. In that statement, the signatories affirmed that every text of the Bible has a meaning that is "single, definite and fixed" (Art. VII),[5] which offers a variety of applications. They affirmed that "the Bible expresses God's truth in propositional statements," and they denied that error in Scripture should be defined only as an intent to mislead (Art. VI).

Responding to Gadamer and his followers, they denied that "the 'horizons' of the biblical writer and the interpreter may rightly 'fuse' in such a way that what the text communicates to the interpreter is not ultimately controlled by the expressed meaning of the Scripture" (Art. IX).

In another crucial section, the statement affirms an awareness of different literary styles and the necessity of paying due attention to literary forms. It denies, however, any effort to use literary genre to "negate historicity" (Art. XIII). That would set the stage for a decisive debate at the Evangelical Theological Society's meeting in 1983, when this very issue became a test case for the affirmation of inerrancy.

The Chicago Statement on Biblical Hermeneutics has never gained the status enjoyed by the Chicago Statement on Biblical Inerrancy, partly because the hermeneutical issues accumulate so quickly in this era of constant hermeneutical crisis. At the same time, building upon the foundation set by the CSBI, the CSBH added yet more detail to the hermeneutic the signers believed was entailed by the affirmation of inerrancy.

In an essay intended as a consensus summary of the summit that produced the statement on hermeneutics, Packer reduced the issues to three

---

[5] For the full text of the Chicago Statement on Biblical Hermeneutics, see http://library.dts.edu/Pages/TL/Special/ICBI_2.pdf

convictions that framed "basic perspectives on the hermeneutical task." He wrote:

> First, Scripture, being God's own instruction to us, is abidingly true and utterly trustworthy. Second, hermeneutics is crucial to the battle for biblical authority in the contemporary church. Third, as knowledge of the inerrancy of Scripture must control interpretation, forbidding us to discount anything that Scripture proves to affirm, so interpretation must clarify the scope and significance of that inerrancy by determining what affirmations Scripture actually makes.[6]

Packer affirmed all that is found within the statement on hermeneutics itself, and then affirmed as well a christological norm for an evangelical hermeneutic that never sets an antithesis between Christ and any biblical text, but affirms Christ as the fulfillment of the entire Bible and all of its parts. A truly evangelical hermeneutic will focus on Jesus Christ at the center and the gospel as its theme.

In a final word, Packer pointed to the issues at stake:

> The twentieth century has seen many attempts to assert the instrumentality of Scripture in bringing to us God's Word while yet denying that the Word has been set forth for all time in the words of the biblical text. These views regard the text as the fallible human witness by means of which God fashions and prompts those insights which he gives us through preaching and Bible study. But for the most part these views include a denial that the Word of God is cognitive communication, and thus they lapse inescapably into impressionistic mysticism. Also, their denial that Scripture is the objectively given Word of God makes the relation of that Word to the text indefinable and hence permanently problematical. This is true of all current forms of neo-orthodox and existentialist theology, including the so-called "new hermeneutic," which is an extreme and incoherent version of the approach described.[7]

Building upon the explicit statements found in the Chicago Statement on Biblical Inerrancy and the Chicago Statement on Biblical Hermeneutics, we can see that inerrancy would also entail the rejection of: (1) more contemporary efforts to evade the question of historicity by illegitimate use of genre criticism; (2) the effort to relativize the text of the Bible by means of

---

[6] J. I. Packer, "Exposition on Biblical Hermeneutics," in *Hermeneutics, Inerrancy, and the Bible*, ed. Earl D. Radmacher and Robert D. Preus (Grand Rapids, MI: Zondervan, 1984), 905–6.
[7] Ibid., 913.

postmodern forms of thought; (3) the effort to deny the authority of the human authors of Scripture in terms of meaning; and, ultimately, (4) any effort to deny the final and ultimate authority of God as the Author of the entire text of the Bible, right down to the very words.

There is no room for a hermeneutic of suspicion within the affirmation of inerrancy. Though the proper interpretation of some texts may require considerable study, research, and hard work, the text is to be affirmed as totally true in all that it claims and in every respect, throughout the entire interpretive process. Though we can gain legitimate insights on the importance of social location and social context, on the importance of an interpretive community, and on the challenges of cross-cultural communication, we cannot surrender to a hermeneutical method that places final authority or interpretive control on any of these concerns.

The Current Hermeneutical Landscape: Where Go the Evangelicals?

Shortly after the release of the Chicago Statement on Biblical Hermeneutics, controversy erupted within evangelical circles when Professor Robert H. Gundry of Westmont College in California published a major commentary on Matthew. In that commentary, Gundry claimed that Matthew had reworked material in order to serve the needs of his intended readers. Gundry employed redaction criticism to argue that much of the infancy narrative in Matthew's Gospel came in the form of midrash, and was not to be taken historically or, at the very least, was to be taken as partially nonhistorical. For example, he claimed that Matthew took the shepherds found in the infancy narrative of Luke's Gospel and turned them into magi from the East. The wise men, he suggested, never visited Jesus.

In 1983, Gundry was asked to resign from the Evangelical Theological Society, which, at the time, had a one-sentence doctrinal statement that all members were required to sign annually: "The Bible alone, and the Bible in its entirety, is the Word of God written and is therefore inerrant in the autographs."[8]

The ETS vote in 1983 was not unanimous, but it was overwhelming, and the central issue was exactly that raised by this chapter: Does inerrancy entail a hermeneutic? More specifically, as it applied to the Gundry case: Can one affirm inerrancy and then deploy redaction criticism (as Gundry had done in his commentary)? Can one affirm inerrancy and then argue

---

[8] See www.etsjets.org/about/constitution#A3

that the author of Matthew freely invented details, reconstructed events, and then presented his Gospel as a historical account? The vote to ask for Gundry's resignation indicated clearly that the ETS did not believe that the affirmation of inerrancy could allow for such a hermeneutic.

Since then, a host of new hermeneutical issues has arrived on the scene. In 2005, Peter Enns, then associate professor of Old Testament at Westminster Theological Seminary in Philadelphia, released *Inspiration and Incarnation: Evangelicals and the Problem of the Old Testament*, in which he argued that evangelicals should continue to see the Bible as "ultimately from God," but that for many people, "the Bible has already become a serious theological problem," echoing the words used by Fosdick almost a century earlier.[9]

Enns argued that the way out of "the problem" is to see the Bible as both divinely inspired (in some sense) and fully human: "*as Christ is both God and human, so is the Bible.*"[10] But when Enns argued for a link between inspiration and incarnation, he posited the existence of what most evangelicals would quickly recognize as genuine error in the Bible. He argued that the Old Testament, in particular, is shaped by the inherent cultural and intellectual limitations of the ancient humans who wrote, collected, edited, and assembled it. He also stated: "In other words, understanding the Old Testament in its ancient Near Eastern setting will raise the question of how normative certain portions of the Old Testament are: if the Old Testament is a cultural phenomenon, how binding is it upon us whose cultural landscape is quite different?"[11]

That book was quite sufficient to raise a serious question about Enns's ability to sign the Westminster Theological Seminary statement of faith. He eventually left the faculty at Westminster, and he currently teaches at Eastern University in Pennsylvania.

In 2014, he released *The Bible Tells Me So: Why Defending the Bible Has Made Us Unable to Read It.*[12] In this book, Enns openly suggests that problematic passages such as the Old Testament's account of the conquest of Canaan should be understood to reflect the limited theological and moral worldview of the ancient Israelites. Put bluntly, Enns does not believe that the conquest of Canaan happened, at least not remotely like the Old

---

[9] Peter Enns, *Inspiration and Incarnation: Evangelicals and the Problem of the Old Testament* (Grand Rapids, MI: Baker, 2005), 14–15.
[10] Ibid., 17 (emphasis original).
[11] Ibid., 67.
[12] Peter Enns, *The Bible Tells Me So: Why Defending Scripture Has Made Us Unable to Read It* (New York: HarperOne, 2014).

Testament narrative claims. He also does not believe that the exodus from
Egypt happened, at least not in keeping with the details found in the book
of Exodus. He freely rejects the divine sanction of the conquest of Canaan
and finds archaeological evidence for the biblical account of the exodus to
be lacking.

With reference to the conquest of Canaan, Enns proposes: "The ancient Israelites were an ancient tribal people. They saw the world and their
God in tribal ways. They told stories of their tribal past, led into battle
by a tribal warrior God who valued the same things they did—like killing
enemies and taking their land. This is how they connected with God—in
their time, in their way."[13]

Even more bluntly, Enns describes the Bible as "the story of God told
from the limited point of view of real people living at a certain time and
place."[14] Of course, this raises the question of what any sense of divine
inspiration might mean in his scheme. But it also raises another point—this
hermeneutic is certainly not compatible with an affirmation of inerrancy.

To his credit, Enns understands that. I recently served as a contributor to a book on the inerrancy of the Bible, and Enns also was a major
contributor. In a very real sense, Enns and I represented the bookends of
the project. I defended the classical view of biblical inerrancy, while Enns
rejected inerrancy altogether. "Simply put," he wrote, "inerrancy, however
defined and nuanced, has great difficulty in addressing adequately and convincingly Scripture as a historical phenomenon."[15] That is the way he sees
it. I fundamentally disagree, but I do respect the fact that he knows and
acknowledges that his hermeneutic is not consistent with the affirmation
of inerrancy.

Enns thus provides, in his own way, evidence for the fact that, even
if inerrancy does not represent a "full-fledged hermeneutic," it certainly
excludes at least some, indeed most, of the hermeneutical innovations currently popular in the secular academy and represented to at least some
degree in Christian institutions.

The greater frustration is caused by someone from within evangelical
circles trying to offer what Enns describes as a "nuanced" definition of the
Bible's inerrancy, then using that revised definition to defend the use of a
hermeneutic that inerrancy actually rules out of bounds.

---

[13] Ibid., 61.
[14] Ibid., 62.
[15] Peter Enns, "Inerrancy, However Defined, Does Not Describe What the Bible Does," in *Five Views on Biblical Inerrancy*, ed. J. Merrick and Stephen M. Garrett (Grand Rapids, MI: Zondervan, 2013), 113.

This kind of approach was used recently in a book titled *Evangelical Faith and the Challenge of Historical Criticism*, written by a team of scholars who attempted to argue that evangelicals must make a peace of sorts with historical critics of the Bible and learn to live with and to employ some form of historical criticism ourselves.[16]

The editors claim to "set aside the subject of inerrancy" and to propose a positive evangelical disposition toward historical criticism.[17] In the main, the contributors to this project do not answer most of the questions they raise, but they provide ample evidence of the fact that the editors "set aside" inerrancy for good reason. The book includes suggestions that Adam's fall may not have been a historical event. One contributor/editor states, "It is true that the fantastic elements within the exodus account and the lack of direct evidence for an Israelite escape from Egypt pose challenges to the historicity of the biblical narrative."[18] Nevertheless, he assures us, this may leave room for "some sort" of "(proto-)Israelite departure from Egypt."[19]

This kind of proposal is not limited to this volume and its contributors. Similar hermeneutical proposals are found in other writings coming from professors within evangelical institutions and from other scholars in the evangelical academy.

To be human is to be a hermeneutical creature. To be a Christian is to be a hermeneutical disciple. To be an evangelical, in the fullest and most urgent sense, is to hold to a believing hermeneutic that affirms that the Bible, in whole and in its parts, is the Word of God.

The evangelical affirmation of Scripture remains: "When the Scriptures speak, God speaks." This affirmation defines inerrancy. In turn, inerrancy entails a hermeneutic. It may not be a "full-fledged" hermeneutic, but inerrancy does set the basic rules for the faithful interpretation of God's Word. It excludes any effort to deny, to evade, or to minimize the truth status of any text of the Bible. It excludes any hermeneutic that would approach the biblical text as a text to be considered and studied like any other historical text. It rejects out of hand any "hermeneutic of suspicion" and calls for the reverent and obedient study of God's Word.

Yes, inerrancy *does* entail a hermeneutic. Now, it is the job of faithful evangelical scholars in every generation to work—with fear and trembling and joy—toward an understanding of all that such a hermeneutic entails.

---

[16] Christopher M. Hays and Christopher B. Ansbury, eds., *Evangelical Faith and the Challenge of Historical Criticism* (Grand Rapids, MI: Baker Academic, 2013).
[17] Ibid., 4.
[18] Christopher Ansbury, "The Exodus: Fact, Fiction, or Both," in *Evangelical Faith*, 69.
[19] Ibid.

14

The Use of Hosea 11:1 in Matthew 2:15

INERRANCY AND GENRE

G. K. Beale

Matthew's use of Hosea 11:1 is a notoriously difficult and debated text: Joseph "was there [Egypt] until the death of Herod in order that what had been spoken by the Lord through the prophet should be fulfilled, '*Out of Egypt I called my son*'" (AT).[1] There are three problems with the way in which Matthew uses the Old Testament passage from Hosea. The first is that the verse in Hosea is a mere historical reflection, but Matthew clearly understands it as a direct prophecy that is fulfilled in Christ. The second problem is that what Hosea attributes to the nation Israel, Matthew attributes to the individual Jesus. Third, the Hosea 11:1 reference to Israel coming out of Egypt first introduces the holy family with Jesus entering into Egypt, and it is only later in Matthew 2:21 that Jesus and his parents come out of Egypt.

In view of these problems, there have been a variety of responses. One commentator has said that this passage is "a parade example of the manner in which the NT uses the OT," especially in not being "interested in

---

[1] It is clear that Matthew has quoted the Hebrew of Hos. 11:1 (which reads "my son") and not the Greek Old Testament (which reads "his children"), on which, e.g., see D. A. Carson, *Matthew: Chapters 1–12*, The Expositor's Bible Commentary (Grand Rapids, MI: Zondervan, 1995), 91. Unless otherwise indicated, Scripture quotations in this chapter are from *The New American Standard Bible®*. Copyright © The Lockman Foundation 1960, 1962, 1963, 1968, 1971, 1972, 1973, 1975, 1977, 1995. Used by permission.

reproducing the meaning" of the Old Testament texts but in reading into the Old Testament foreign Christological presuppositions.[2] Another commentator has said that this is "the most troubling case" of "NT exegesis of the OT" for many people.[3] Others have viewed the use of Hosea 11 as a mere mistaken interpretation by Matthew, somehow viewing Hosea 11:1 as a prophecy when it was only a historical reflection on the original exodus.[4] For example, M. Eugene Boring has said that "Matthew's use of Scripture" in Matthew 1 and 2, including the Hosea 11 quotation, is "in contrast with their obvious original meaning," and "the changes he makes in the text itself . . . make him subject to the charge of manipulating the evidence in a way that would be unconvincing to outsiders."[5] Others have attributed to Matthew a Qumran-like special revelatory insight into the "full meaning" (*sensus plenior*) of Hosea 11:1, a revelatory stance no longer available to subsequent church interpreters.[6] Still others have understood Matthew to be employing a faulty hermeneutic used elsewhere in Judaism, which Christian interpreters should not emulate, but that nevertheless the interpretative conclusion is purportedly inspired by God.[7] Somewhat similarly, but with a new wrinkle, others have concluded that Matthew's interpretation of Hosea 11:1 is not to be considered correct according to our modern standards of interpretation, but was part of an acceptable Jewish hermeneutic in the first-century world, which modern scholars have no right to judge as wrong.[8]

[2] Peter Enns, "Biblical Interpretation, Jewish," in *Dictionary of New Testament Background*, ed. C. A. Evans and S. E. Porter (Downers Grove, IL: InterVarsity Press, 2000), 164. For the Enns reference, I am thankful to James W. Scott, "The Inspiration and Interpretation of God's Word with Special Reference to Peter Enns, Part II: The Interpretation of Representative Passages," *Westminster Theological Journal* 71 (2009): 264.
[3] Martin Pickup, "New Testament Interpretation of the Old Testament: The Theological Rationale of Midrashic Exegesis," *Journal of the Evangelical Theological Society* 51 (2008): 371, who says, "It is futile to try to defend Matthew's messianic interpretation of Hos 11:1 on grammatical-historical grounds" (372; so also see 373) and "to put it bluntly Matthew appears to be reading Hos 11:1 out of context" (374).
[4] E.g., D. M. Beegle, *Scripture, Tradition, and Infallibility* (Grand Rapids, MI: Eerdmans, 1973) 236–38. See also David L. Turner, *Matthew*, Baker Exegetical Commentary on the New Testament (Grand Rapids, MI: Baker, 2008), 90, who, while not in agreement, gives a sampling of scholars holding this view. Cf. G. E. Ladd, "Historic Premillennialism," in *The Meaning of the Millennium*, ed. R. G. Clouse (Downers Grove, IL: InterVarsity Press, 1977), 20–21, who says that Matthew's interpretation of Hos. 11:1 as a prophecy was not intended by Hosea as a prophecy, but only a description of a past event (Israel's exodus out of Egypt).
[5] Eugene Boring, *The Gospel of Matthew*, The New Interpreter's Bible 8 (Nashville: Abingdon, 1995), 153. Similarly, S. V. McCasland, "Matthew Twists the Scriptures," *Journal of Biblical Literature* 80 (1961): 144–46, says that Matthew "misunderstood Hosea 11:1" and "found a meaning entirely foreign to the original" of that in the Hosea passage. So also William Barclay, *The Gospel of Matthew* (Philadelphia: Westminster, 1956), 35–36; and Theodore H. Robinson, *The Gospel of Matthew* (London: Hodder & Stoughton, 1928), 9.
[6] See, e.g., G. D. Fee and D. Stuart, *How to Read the Bible for All It's Worth* (Grand Rapids, MI: Zondervan, 1981) 166–67; see again Turner, *Matthew*, 90, for examples for this among other commentators.
[7] See, e.g., Richard N. Longenecker, *Biblical Exegesis in the Apostolic Period*, 2nd ed. (Grand Rapids, MI: Eerdmans, 1999), 124–25, especially when seen together with Longenecker's general hermeneutical approach to the Old in the New in "'Who Is the Prophet Talking About?' Some Reflections on the New Testament's Use of the Old," *Them* 13 (1987): 4–8; and "Can We Reproduce the Exegesis of the New Testament?," *TynBul* 21 (1970): 3–38. Beegle's view also comes close to this perspective.
[8] This is the general approach to the Old in the New by Peter Enns, *Inspiration and Incarnation: Evangelicals and the Problem of the Old Testament* (Grand Rapids, MI: Baker, 2005), 113–63, who includes the use of Hos. 11:1 in Matt. 2:15 among his examples (134); Enns wants to classify this as an "odd use," on which see

According to this view, the interpretative procedure, while strange, is to be seen as Spirit-inspired and even to be seen as a pattern for the contemporary church to follow. From another perspective, some see the interpretative procedure not to be wrong but so unique that Christians today should not dare practice the same procedure in approaching similar Old Testament passages that merely narrate a historical event.

Usually such conclusions are made because Matthew (and other New Testament writers) is being judged by what is often called a "grammatical-historical" interpretative method and by a particular understanding of that method.

Finally, there are scholars who understand Matthew to be viewing Israel's past exodus out of Egypt in Hosea 11:1 as generally typological of Jesus coming out of Egypt in the light of the broader Old Testament canonical context.[9] Typology can be defined as the study of analogical correspondences between persons, events, institutions, and other things within the historical framework of God's special revelation, which, from a retrospective view, are of a prophetic nature. According to this definition, the essential characteristics of a type are: (1) analogical correspondence; (2) historicity; (3) forward-pointing; (4) escalation; (5) retrospection (though this last element will be qualified below).[10]

The notion that Old Testament history could be a foreshadowing of events in the New Testament has a longstanding history among interpreters, stretching back to the apostolic fathers. The hermeneutical legitimacy of such typological interpretation rests on the presuppositional legitimacy of what is considered to be a biblical philosophy of history, in which God is seen to be designing patterns of earlier history to foreshadow later patterns of history.[11] Scholars, of course, vary on their acceptance of this presupposition and thus differ about the hermeneutical legitimacy of the typological approach by the New Testament writers. Some have criticized the typological approach as being virtually identical to the *sensus plenior* view, since New Testament authors' typological insight has often been viewed as

---

further his subsequent article "Response to Professor Beale," *Them* 32 (2007): 9–11; and Dan McCartney and Peter Enns, "Matthew and Hosea: A Response to John Sailhamer," *Westminster Theological Journal* 63 (2001): 97–105. Nevertheless, Enns's actual explanation is what I would consider to be a biblical-theological one that is not contrary to the standards of doing biblical theology today and that biblical theologians would accept and understand (see my further analysis in my *The Erosion of Inerrancy in Evangelicalism: Responding to New Challenges to Biblical Authority* [Wheaton, IL: Crossway, 2008], 88–89).

[9] Among many, see R. T. France, *Matthew*, Tyndale New Testament Commentaries (Grand Rapids, MI: Eerdmans, 1985), 40, 86; Carson, *Matthew: Chapters 1–12*, 91–93; and Turner, *Matthew*, 90–91.

[10] For discussion of this definition of typology, see G. K. Beale, *Handbook on the New Testament Use of the Old Testament: Exegesis and Interpretation* (Grand Rapids, MI: Baker, 2012), chapters 1 and 4.

[11] Among many sources that could be cited on typology in the New Testament, see the classic work in the field by Leonard Goppelt, *Typos* (Grand Rapids, MI: Eerdmans, 1982).

insight that could only have come through the work of the Spirit retrospectively, after the death and resurrection of Christ.[12] Accordingly, Old Testament authors would not have been privy to such typological interpretation of their writings.

My approach in this chapter is to broadly agree that Matthew employed a typological approach but to attempt to show that Matthew's typological perspective was not something unique to his own charismatic revelatory perspective. Therefore, Matthew's interpretation was not purely something that he would have viewed to have been accessible only retrospectively through the Spirit's revelatory work, after the coming of Christ. Rather, what Matthew sees was already something seen to some degree by Hosea himself. Another way to put this is that Matthew's typological interpretation of Hosea 11:1 was stimulated by Hosea's own typological understanding of that verse, much of which can even be discerned by a broad grammatical-historical exegesis of that entire chapter in Hosea.

Discussion in this introductory section could review recent discussions of so-called "intertextuality" or, my preference, "inner-biblical exegesis," but I do not think it will substantially affect my following interpretation of the use of Hosea 11:1 in Matthew 2:15.[13]

Besides a "strict" grammatical-historical method, there are other approaches to interpreting Scripture that have hermeneutical viability and integrity. For instance, could it be that Matthew is intentionally not only employing a balanced "grammatical-historical" approach, but is also employing a kind of biblical-theological approach, and the two approaches are complementary?[14]

---

[12] There are some who do not view typology as deriving exclusively from a retrospective vantage point, but believe it has seeds in the Old Testament that are developed in the New (e.g., see Carson, *Matthew: Chapters 1–12*, 91–93).

[13] For further discussion of this subject, see Beale, *Handbook on the New Testament Use of the Old Testament*, chapter 3, and some representative sources cited therein. The remainder of this chapter is based on a paper delivered at the Affinity Theological Studies Conference in Hoddesdon, Hertfordshire, England (Feb. 2–4, 2011) and again at the Southern Baptist Theological Seminary for the Gheens Lectures (March 15–16, 2011), which was summarized briefly in Beale, *A New Testament Biblical Theology: The Unfolding of the Old Testament in the New* (Grand Rapids, MI: Baker, 2011), 406–12.

[14] The usual "strict" understanding of a grammatical-historical approach is too limited in its scope, since it studies a passage primarily from only two angles: (1) investigation of only the human author's viewpoint through a study of the historical, linguistic, grammatical, genre contexts, etc., of a passage; and (2) the divine Author can theoretically be left out of consideration until the grammatical-historical study is complete, since the meaning sought for is only that of the human author. For example, even an interpreter who does not believe in divine inspiration must study a prophet like Isaiah from the viewpoint that Isaiah himself believed that he was inspired in what he wrote, and, therefore, that intention must be projected onto the process of interpreting Isaiah. How much more should this be the case for the believing exegete? Accordingly, this is only one example showing that considering divine intention should be part of a grammatical-historical approach. Thus, grammatical-historical exegesis and typology are two aspects of the same thing: hearing God speak in Scripture. (I am grateful for a personal communication from Vern Poythress for this observation; see further his "The Presence of God Qualifying Our Notions of Grammatical-Historical Interpretation: Genesis 3:15 as a Test Case," *Journal of the Evangelical Theological Society* 50 [2007]: 87–103.)

The argument of this chapter is that Matthew is interpreting Hosea 11:1 in light of its relation to the entire chapter in which it is found and in light of the entire book, and that his approach does, indeed, verge upon a grammatical-historical approach combined with a biblical-theological methodology. In Hosea 11, after alluding to Israel's exodus out of Egypt (v. 1), the history of the nation in her land is narrated briefly. The people did not respond faithfully to God's deliverance of them from Egypt and to his prophetic messengers exhorting them to be loyal to God, but they worshiped idols, despite the grace that God had shown to them (vv. 2–5). Consequently, God will judge them for their lack of repentance (vv. 6–7). Nevertheless, the judgment will not be absolute because of God's compassion on the nation (vv. 8–9). God's compassion is said to express itself through future restoration of his people, who "will walk after the LORD" and "come trembling from the west. And they will come trembling like birds from Egypt, and like doves from the land of Assyria," so that God "will settle them in their houses" in their land (vv. 10–11).

The Focus in Hosea on Israel's Future Eschatological Return from Egypt

In the end time, according to Hosea 11:10–11, there will be a restoration of Israel from several lands, including "Egypt."[15]

1. *The significance of the use of Numbers 23 and 24 in Hosea 11:10–11.* Even the lion imagery in Hosea 11:10–11 in direct connection to Israel coming "out of Egypt" is an allusion to her first exodus in Numbers 23 and 24, where God is said to lead her "out of Egypt' and the people and the king are compared to a "lion":[16]

---

[15] There are some commentators who say that "Egypt" is metaphorical for Assyria, but the "west" is also mentioned here, which would seem to point to a restoration from a number of lands. Such a restoration from multiple lands appears to be supported also by other Old Testament prophecies (e.g., Isa. 11:11 says, "The Lord will again recover the second time . . . the remnant of his people . . . from Assyria, Egypt, Pathros, Cush, Elam, Shinar, Hamath, and from the islands of the sea"; Isa. 11:15–16 likewise foresees Israel's future return from both Egypt and Assyria; cf. Isa. 49:12; 60:4–9). On this issue of whether or not "Egypt" is literal or metaphorical, see Appendix 2 of this chapter.

[16] See Duane Garrett, *Hosea*, New American Commentary (Nashville: Broadman and Holman, 1997), 229, who also argues that Num. 24:8–9 is an allusion in Hos. 11:10–11. Intriguingly, the twenty-seventh edition of the Nestle-Aland Greek text cites as an allusion in Matt. 2:15 not only Hosea 11:1, but also Num. 23:22 and 24:8. See John H. Sailhamer, "Hosea 11:1 and Matthew 2:15," *Westminster Theological Journal* 63 (2001): 87–96, in support of Nestle-Aland's proposal; so also W. D. Davies and Dale C. Allison, *The Gospel According to Saint Matthew*, International Critical Commentary (Edinburgh: T&T Clark, 1988), 1:262; Donald A. Hagner, *Matthew 1–13*, Word Biblical Commentary, vol. 33A (Dallas: Word, 1993), 37 (for a list of others in support, see Carson, *Matthew: Chapters 1–12*, 93). It is unlikely the Numbers texts are allusions in Hos. 11:1, but perhaps they stand as echoes behind Hos. 11:1 that anticipate the clearer allusions to Num. 23:22, 24 and 24:9 in Hos. 11:10.

NUMBERS	HOSEA
23:22a: "God brings them *out of Egypt*, He is for them like the horns of the wild ox."	
23:24: "Behold, a people rises *like a lioness*, And *as a lion* it lifts itself; It will not lie down until it devours the prey, And drinks the blood of the slain."	11:10–11: "He will roar *like a lion*; Indeed He will roar And His sons will come trembling. . . . Like birds *from Egypt* . . .'"
24:8: "God brings him *out of Egypt*, He is for him like the horns of the wild ox . . ."	
24:9a: "He crouches, he lies down *as a lion*, And *as a lion*, who dares rouse him?"	

The two Numbers passages together with Hosea 11:11 are the only places in the Old Testament where there is the combined mention of (1) God bringing Israel "out of Egypt" and (2) of either the deliverer or the delivered being compared to a lion. In Numbers 23, the people who came "out of Egypt" in the past are compared to a lion, and in Numbers 24, Israel's king is said to have come "out of Egypt" and is also compared to a lion (though it is possible that this describes God).[17] It is possible that the Numbers 24 portrayal is of a future exodus, but more likely the past exodus is in view in both Numbers passages, and then Israel's future victories come into view in the following contexts, which likely include an eschatological perspective (Num. 23:24; 24:8b, 9b, 17–19). A possible problem with Numbers 24:7–8a being a reference to a past exodus is that there was no "king" who came out of Egypt at that time, unless one identifies such a leader with Moses, which would appear to be the case

---

[17]That the individual king of Israel is referred to is evident from Num. 24:7, the pronouns "him" in 24:8, and the blessing and cursing in 24:9 that refer to the king. In addition, Num. 24:8–9a is an allusion itself to the prophecy of the eschatological king from Judah in Gen. 49:9: "Judah is a lion's whelp. . . . He couches, he lies down as a lion, and as a lion who dares rouse him up?" I think that it is likely that Num. 24:7–8a, 9a portrays the past exodus, but it is possible that it describes a future coming out of Egypt in light of the Gen. 49:9 allusion and in view of the clear eschatological prophecy of the end-time king in Num. 24:17–19, which appears to continue the description of the king in 24:7–9. This future kingly identity is underscored by the LXX, which translates the Hebrew of Num. 24:7 ("Water shall flow from his buckets, and his seed will be by many waters") by "there shall come a man out of his seed, and he shall rule over many nations." The fact that allusion to the end-time king of Gen. 49:9 occurs in both Num. 23:24 and 24:9 complicates the temporal scope of Numbers 23 and 24, though the Numbers texts may indicate a beginning fulfillment of Gen. 49:9.

(see Ex. 2:14, where Moses is called a "prince" [MT] or a "ruler" [LXX; so also Acts 7:35]).

The exact identification of the "lion" in Hosea 11:10 is thorny. It is possible that the lion in Hosea 11 is the king coming "out of Egypt" from Numbers 24:7–9, but it appears to continue a description of God himself.[18] Nevertheless, in both Numbers 23 and 24 God is said to be *"for them* [or him] like the horns of the wild ox," so that the directly following lion description in Numbers may likewise be applied to the people and the king because they are identified with their God, who is the One giving ultimate power for deliverance. This ambivalence may be reflected also in Hosea 11:10. Nevertheless, in the light of Israel and her king being likened to a "lion" in Numbers 23 and 24, God may well be the one compared to a "lion" in Hosea 11 because of the corporate identification between Israel and her God and because God is the one who brings Israel "out of Egypt" in both Numbers texts. On the other hand, as we will see below, the parallel between Hosea 1:11 and 11:11 could suggest further that the "lion" of 11:10 may be the eschatological kingly leader of Israel's return. This might be pointed to further by Hosea 3:5, where Israel's return from captivity is also led by an eschatological Davidic king. That an Israelite leader could be compared to a "lion" in 11:10 is also pointed to by Numbers 23 and 24, where the lion represents Israel and her human leader.

Thus, the precise identification of the "lion" figure in Hosea 11:10 is somewhat difficult, and there may be an intentional ambiguity, though on the surface the reference seems to point to God being "like a lion,"[19] which is my own final assessment. In this respect, the reference to "he" (Hos. 11:10b, "he will roar like a lion") likely has its antecedent in "the LORD" (11:10a, "They will walk after the LORD)."

Though there are some difficult interpretative issues in the Numbers 23 and 24 references and their use in Hosea 11:10–11, in the latter passage it would appear likely that Hosea sees that these Numbers allusions about the past coming "out of Egypt" together with the "lion" image will

---

[18] See Sailhamer, "Hosea 11:1 and Matthew 2:15," for discussion of these allusions in Hosea 11.

[19] Could it be that Matthew was aware of the possible echo to Num. 23:22 and 24:7–9 (v. 8, "God brings him [the king] out of Egypt") in Hos. 11:1 and the later allusion to Num. 23:22, 24, and 24:8–9 in Hos. 11:10? (See R. T. France, *The Gospel of Matthew*, New International Commentary on the New Testament [Grand Rapids, MI: Eerdmans, 2007], 80, who sees that Hos. 11:1 reflects the above Numbers 23 and 24 texts.) This is pointed to from the fact that many commentators view the background of the "King of the Jews" and "his star" in Matt. 2:2 to be a clear allusion to Num. 24:17! If these connections are plausible, could this have fueled Matthew all the more to have applied Hos. 11:1 to Jesus *the Messiah* as representative of *Israel*, doing what she had failed to do (as argued, e.g., by Davies and Allison, *Matthew*, 1.262; cf. similarly David Hill, *The Gospel of Matthew* [Greenwood, SC: Attic, 1972], 85)? As we have seen earlier, some commentators even see Matt. 2:15 as an allusion to these Numbers texts together with Hos. 11:1. Cf. similarly Robert H. Gundry, *Matthew* (Grand Rapids, MI: Eerdmans, 1982), 34.

be recapitulated again in the eschatological future. Accordingly, the past exodus is seen to foreshadow a later end-time exodus, which is a typological understanding. And, if Numbers 24:8–9 is not a narration of the first exodus but a prediction of an end-time exodus, then Hosea 11:10–11 may even be the reiteration of that prophecy, though Numbers 23 would still be included, likely in a typological sense.

Thus, the main point or goal of Hosea 11:1–11 is the accomplishment of Israel's future restoration from the nations, including "Egypt."[20] The overall meaning of chapter 11 is to indicate that God's deliverance of Israel from Egypt, which led to their ungrateful unbelief, is not the final word about God's deliverance of them; though they will be judged, God will deliver them again, even from "Egypt." The chapter both begins and ends with the exodus out of Egypt, but the former refers to the past event and the latter to a yet future event. The pattern of the first exodus at the beginning of Israel's history (Hos. 11:1) will be repeated at the end of Israel's history in the end time. It is unlikely that Hosea saw these two exoduses to be accidentally, coincidentally, or unconnected similar events. Hosea appears to understand that Israel's first exodus (Hos. 11:1) was to be recapitulated at the time of the nation's latter-day exodus. This understanding of 11:1 *in its context* is fueled further by recalling that Hosea has already seen the first exodus in Numbers 23 and 24 to be recapitulated in a latter-day exodus.

2. *The significance of repeated references throughout Hosea of Israel's first exodus from Egypt and of Israel's end-time exodus from Egypt.* Mention of a first exodus from Egypt outside of 11:1 occurs elsewhere in Hosea, and a future return from Egypt would appear to be implied by repeated prophecies of Israel returning to Egypt in the future, though Hosea 1:10–11 (see chart on p. 218) and 11:11 are the only texts explicitly affirming a future return from Egypt (though, as we have seen above, there are several texts in Isaiah that are also explicit about this).

If one were to have asked Hosea if he believed that God was sovereign over history and that God had designed the first exodus from Egypt as a historical pattern that foreshadowed a second exodus from Egypt, would he not likely have answered yes? At least, this appears to be the way Matthew understood Hosea, especially using the language of the first exodus from Hosea 11:1 in the light of the broader and particularly the immediate context, especially of Hosea 11,[21] where a "return to Egypt" is predicted

---

[20] Hos. 11:12, concerning Israel's deception and rebellion, is actually the beginning of the next literary segment, which is a negative narrative continued throughout chapter 12.
[21] And in light of the hopes of the first exodus and implied second exodus elsewhere in the book.

FIRST EXODUS FROM EGYPT	FUTURE RETURN TO EGYPT (IMPLYING A FUTURE RETURN FROM EGYPT)
Hosea 2:15b: "And she will sing there as in the days of her youth, As in the day when she came up from the land of Egypt" [though this passage compares the first exodus with a future exodus].	Hosea 7:11: "So Ephraim has become like a silly dove, without sense; They call to Egypt, they go to Assyria."
Hosea 12:13: "But by a prophet the LORD brought Israel from Egypt, And by a prophet he was kept."	Hosea 7:16b: "Their princes will fall by the sword Because of the insolence of their tongue. This will be their derision in the land of Egypt."
Cf. Hosea 12:9a: "But I have been the LORD your God since the land of Egypt."	Hosea 8:13b: "Now he will remember their iniquity, And punish them for their sins; They will return to Egypt."
Cf. Hosea 13:4: "Yet I have been the LORD your God since the land of Egypt; And you were not to know any god except Me, For there is no savior besides Me."	Hosea 9:3: "They will not remain in the LORD's land, But Ephraim will return to Egypt, And in Assyria they will eat unclean food."
	Hosea 9:6: "For behold, they will go because of destruction; Egypt will gather them up, Memphis will bury them. Weeds will take over their treasures of silver; Thorns will be in their tents."
	See also Hosea 1:11b: "And they [Israel] will go up from the land [of Egypt]."
	Hosea 11:5: "He [Israel] assuredly will return to the land of Egypt" (AT).
	Note the implication of a future exodus from Egypt in Hosea 2:15 above.

(v. 5), and where the main point and goal is the end-time exodus from Egypt (v. 11). What better language to use for Hosea's prophecy of the second exodus and the beginning of its fulfillment in Jesus than the language already at hand describing the first exodus? This is a short step away from saying that the first exodus was seen by Hosea and, more clearly, by Matthew as a historical pattern pointing to the reoccurrence of the same pattern later in Israel's history. In this respect, Matthew's use of Hosea 11:1 may also be called "typological" in that he understood, in light of the entire chapter 11 of Hosea, that the first exodus mentioned in verse 1 initiated a historical process of sin and judgment to be culminated in another final exodus (vv. 10–11). After writing the above, I found that Duane Garrett has said:

> We need look no further than Hosea 11 to understand that Hosea, too, believed that God followed patterns in working with his people. Here the slavery in Egypt is the pattern for a second period of enslavement in an alien land (v. 5), and the exodus from Egypt is the type for a new exodus (vv. 10–11). Thus the application of typological principles to Hos 11:1 [by Matthew] is in keeping with the nature of prophecy itself and with Hosea's own method.[22]

Many commentators have observed that the placement of the quotation of Hosea 11:1 in Matthew 2:15 appears to be out of order, since the quotation is appended directly only to the report of Joseph, Mary, and Jesus going to Egypt and not coming out of Egypt. Rather, they are said to come out of Egypt only later in 2:21. Accordingly, a number of commentators have noted that the quotation would seem to have been better placed directly after Matthew 2:21, where it says that the holy family returned

---

[22] *Hosea*, 222. See also the recent article by Richard B. Gaffin, "The Redemptive-Historical View," in *Biblical Hermeneutics: Five Views*, ed. S. E. Porter and B. M. Stovell (Downers Grove, IL: InterVarsity Press, 2012), 106–8, who has also briefly noticed the typological significance of the past and future references to an exodus throughout Hosea and within chapter 11 of Hosea itself, and that Matthew follows Hosea's method in Matt. 2:15, thus exhibiting a grammatical-historical exegesis of Hos. 11:1 in its context. He sees Jesus summing up Israel in himself, which actually also reflects a biblical-theological approach. I have also found subsequently that apparently the only other commentator who sees significance in the relation of Hos. 11:1 to 11:10–11 is T. L. Howard in his very brief discussion in "The Use of Hosea in Matthew 2:15: An Alternative Solution," *Bibliotheca Sacra* 143 (1986), 321–22, 324, who argues that since Matthew would have viewed that Jesus would be the one to restore Israel into her yet future, final millennial kingdom, purportedly implied by Hos. 11:10–11, this would have sparked Matthew's analogical identification of Jesus with Hos. 11:1. Strangely, Howard does not see Matthew using Hos. 11:1 typologically but only analogically, seeing no foreshadowing element in Hos. 11:1, so that Matt. 2:15 does not represent any kind of beginning prophetic fulfillment of Hos. 11:1. This dilutes Matthew's "fulfillment" formula. See also the recent article by Robert W. Wall, "The Canonical View," in *Biblical Hermeneutics: Five Views*, 127, who implies that the repeated past references to the exodus in Hosea (11:1; 12:9, 13; 13:4) have a forward-pointing significance that is recognized by Matthew, and who reminded me about the more muted references to a past exodus in Hos. 12:9 and 13:4.

from Egypt and "came into the land of Israel." Those who acknowledge the odd placement in 2:15 explain it to be an anticipation of the return from Egypt narrated in the following context.[23] That this, in fact, is partly the case is evident from noticing that the beginning of 2:15 mentions that the holy family "was there until the death of Herod." This clearly anticipates verses 20–21, which narrate the return of Joseph and his family in inextricable connection to the death of Herod. Others contend that the quotation could not have been put after verse 21 because it would have distracted from the geographical focus at the end of verse 21 and in verses 22–23 on the destination of Israel and particularly Nazareth. Hence, the chapter's overriding concern with *geographical* locations led Matthew to put the quotation at verse 15, even though logically, the quotation appears to be out of place.[24] The geographical view would still see verse 15 as an anticipation of verses 20–21.[25]

In this connection, the repeated Old Testament pattern of Israel or Israelites reentering Egypt and then coming back out of Egypt may stand in the background of Matthew's reference to Hosea 11:1 and have bearing on the apparent odd placement of the quotation. The passages typically adduced by several commentators to compose this pattern are 1 Kings 11:40; Jeremiah 26:21–23; 44:12–15; 2 Kings 25:26; and Jeremiah 41:16–18; 43:1–7.[26] All of these passages portray Egypt as an apparent place of refuge from danger in Israel,[27] though in each case, it is disobedient Israelites seeking the refuge, and, except for 1 Kings 11:40, Egypt becomes a place of

---

[23] For a view that is compatible with this perspective, see M. J. J. Menken, "Out of Egypt I Have Called My Son: Some Observations on the Quotation from Hosea 11.1," in *The Wisdom of Egypt: Jewish, Early Christian, and Gnostic Essays in Honour of Gerard P. Luttikhuizen*, ed. A. Hilhorst, Geurt Hendrik Van Kooten, and Gerard P. Luttikhuizen (Leiden: Brill, 2005), 143–52, who sees that Matthew's editorial intentions caused the apparent displacement "to emphasize that the command of the angel of the Lord and the word spoken by the prophet are of equal authority and are fulfilled at the same time" (150).

[24] For a summary of these views, see Joel Kennedy, *The Recapitulation of Israel*, Wissenschaftliche Untersuchungen zum Neuen Testament 2/257 (Tübingen: Mohr Siebeck, 2008), 128–31, who finds these explanations unsatisfying and solves the problem by identifying "Egypt" in Matt. 2:15 metaphorically in contrast to the literal geographical references to "Egypt" in 2:13, 14, and 19. His main argument is that Israel has become like Egypt, with Herod as another persecuting Pharaoh, so that when the holy family leaves Israel for Egypt, they are really departing from metaphorical Egypt to go to literal Egypt (see ibid., 313–14). Kennedy's argument is creative, interesting, and attractive but still not as persuasive as the views that he criticizes, especially as these views are enhanced by the following discussion here about the context of Hosea. His view entails viewing "Egypt" in verse 15 to be metaphorical, while the directly preceding and following references are literal, which is a hard inconsistency to overcome, even given his creative proposals.

[25] E.g., see France, *Matthew*, 79–80.

[26] Only going into Egypt is mentioned in the last three references, perhaps with the implication of returning back to Israel. See Kennedy, *Recapitulation of Israel*, 134, as among those commentators who cite these references as relevant for Matt. 2:14–15. Cf. 1 Kings 11:14–22.

[27] Cf. Josephus, *Jewish Antiquities* 12.387–88; 14.21; 15.45–47; 2 Maccabees 5:8–9, though a return to Israel is not mentioned in these passages; see, however, Josephus, *Jewish War* 7.409–10, 16, which mentions both entering into Egypt and return from Egypt. See France, *Matthew*, 79, who sees all of the preceding passages viewing Egypt as a place of asylum to be relevant to Matt. 2:13–15.

danger. Craig Blomberg sees the possibility that 1 Kings 11:40 in particular may stand behind Matthew 2:14–15:[28] "Solomon sought therefore to put Jeroboam to death; but Jeroboam arose and fled to Egypt to Shishak king of Egypt, and he was in Egypt until the death of Solomon" (Matt. 2:14–15 reads, "So Joseph got up and took the Child and His mother while it was still night, and left[29] for Egypt. He remained there until the death of Herod"). This pattern of entering and then returning from Egypt is a recapitulation of Israel's original entering into Egypt and their exodus (Gen. 46:4; Ps. 105:23; 37–38). Egypt also became a place of suffering and sin (e.g., see Ezek. 20:7–8; 23:3, 8, 19, 27), as it was in the case of the Israelites who later sojourned into Egypt.[30]

This broader Old Testament pattern of entering and then returning from Egypt is highlighted particularly by Hosea, a pattern (that we have discussed earlier) found throughout his prophecy. The broader Old Testament pattern, especially as it is found in Hosea, may have some bearing on the purported odd placement of Hosea 11:1 in Matthew 2:15. We have observed that Hosea's broader context indicates Israel's future reentering into Egypt and a future subsequent coming out of Egypt again. The reference to Hosea 11:1, we have argued, is to be seen within the context of repeated references throughout the book to a past exodus *and* Israel's future *reentering and subsequent return out of Egypt*. In particular, this pattern is fully found within chapter 11 of Hosea itself: Hosea 11:5, only four verses after Hosea 11:1, says that "he [Israel] indeed will return to the land of Egypt," and this is followed by the main narrative point of the entire chapter, that "his sons . . . will come trembling like birds from Egypt" (11:11). Thus, the eleventh chapter of Hosea begins with Israel's past exodus from Egypt (v. 1), is punctuated in the middle with reference to Israel reentering Egypt, and concludes with a promise of their future return from Egypt (v. 11). James Limburg has summarized the storyline of Hosea 11 in the following manner: "Thus the story comes to its end [in verse 11]: out of Egypt, back into 'Egypt' because of rebellion; then out of 'Egypt,' back home again because of the Lord's compassion."[31] And all of these references in verses 1, 5, and 11 are logically and narratively linked to one another.

In this light, if Matthew is aware of the broader and especially the im-

---

[28] See Craig Blomberg, "Matthew," in *A Commentary on the New Testament's Use of the Old Testament*, ed. G. K. Beale and D. A. Carson (Grand Rapids, MI: Baker, 2007), 7. Cf. John Nolland, *The Gospel of Matthew* (Grand Rapids, MI/Cambridge: Eerdmans and Bletchley, UK: Paternoster, 2005), 122.

[29] Note the use of "flee" in the angel's command in Matt. 2:13, bringing verses 14–15 even closer to 1 Kings 11:40 (though the Greek words rendering "flee" in both passages are different).

[30] For Jeroboam, it was only a place of refuge.

[31] James Limburg, *Hosea-Micah* (Atlanta: John Knox, 1988), 40.

mediate context of his Hosea 11:1 quotation, then would he not have in mind both reentering into Egypt as well as return out of Egypt? Therefore, if the broader context of Hosea, especially Hosea 11, is in mind in Matthew 2:15, as we have argued, then the quotation in Matthew 2:15 is not oddly placed. In this regard, the holy family's return to Egypt is a very crucial part of the packed typological Hosea 11:1 reference.[32] The narration of the family going to Egypt is viewed as an inauguration of the contextualized Hosea 11:1 reference that included in its wider purview Israel's future reentering into Egypt,[33] and then Matthew 2:21 records a later stage of the fulfillment by recording the return back from Egypt to the land of Israel. This borders on Matthew having a "grammatical-historical" exegetical perspective of Hosea 11:1 in the context of 11:2–11! Matthew is unpacking what is already exegetically latent in Hosea 11. This explanation adds further evidence to support the view of many commentators that the quotation in Matthew 2:15 anticipates 2:21. However, this explanation also importantly shows that 2:15 is not completely anticipatory, but indicates that 2:14 is an actual beginning fulfillment of Hosea 11:1, *understood in the immediate context* of Hosea, especially chapter 11. As we have seen, the more specific "reentering into and returning from Egypt" pattern found in Hosea is corroborated elsewhere in the Old Testament and may enhance the force of the Hosea pattern.[34]

The One King Who Represents Israel in the Future Return from Egypt

Some have seen it to be problematic that what was spoken of the nation in Hosea 11:1 is applied by Matthew, not to the nation, but to an individual messianic figure. Accordingly, Matthew is seen by some as distorting the original corporate meaning of Hosea 11:1.

However, the application of what was applied to the nation in 11:1 to the one person, Jesus, also may have been sparked by the narrative about

[32] Others have concluded that Matthew understood Hos. 11:1 to be generally typological of Jesus in light of the broader Old Testament canonical context (and not the narrower Hosea context): e.g., see France, *Matthew*, 40, 86; and Turner, *Matthew*, 90–91.

[33] William Hendrickson, *New Testament Commentary: Exposition of the Gospel according to Matthew* (Grand Rapids, MI: Baker, 1973), 178, is the only commentator who even remotely suggests that the Hosea 11:1 quotation pertains to the holy family's entering into Egypt, since he sees that the broader Old Testament typology of the exodus in relation to Jesus includes God's initial protection of Israel in bringing them into Egypt.

[34] References only to a future reentering into Egypt occur in Deut. 28:68; Isa. 30:2–3; 31:1; Jer. 2:18; 42:14–18; 44:8, 12, 14; cf. Jews living in Egypt in the future in Isa. 20:3–4; Jer. 24:8; 44:1, 13, 15, 26–27. References only to a final eschatological return from Egypt, which assumes that Israelites would reenter Egypt in the future, are found in Isa. 11:11, 15–16; 27:13; Zech. 10:10.

the king of Israel coming out of Egypt in Numbers 24, which appears to be partly alluded to in Hosea 11:10–11. In fact, Numbers itself applies the very same lion imagery to the people (23:24) as to the king (24:9). The potential to apply corporate language to the individual is also suggested by Hosea 1:10–11, where it is said that the Israelites will be called "sons of the living God" at the time of their future restoration, which will be led by "one leader." In fact, even the statement at the end of 1:11, "and they will go up from the land," is a reference to going up from the "land" of Egypt,[35] especially since it is an allusion to Exodus 1:10 and Isaiah 11:16.[36] After all, what sense does it make that this refers to the land of Israel, since at the end time, Israel was to be restored *to her land*, and to describe this as Israel "going up from her own land" would be exceedingly odd?

If this is a reference to Israel's future return from Egypt, it fits admirably with the hope expressed in Hosea 11:10–11 (and other such implied references noted above), and it would specifically affirm that such a future exodus would be led by an individual leader (literally the Hebrew reads "one head"). Such an individual leader appears to be further described in 3:5 as a latter-day Davidic king: "Afterward the sons of Israel will return and seek the LORD their God and David their king, and they will come trembling to the LORD . . . in the last days." This image of "trembling" in Hosea 3:5 to describe the manner in which Israel approaches God when they are restored is parallel to the description of the manner of their restoration in 11:10–11,

---

[35] The Hebrew word "land" (*'eres*) refers in Hosea to Israel (seven times), Egypt (five times), earth (two times), Assyria (one time), and the wilderness of Israel's sojourn (one time). However, the idea of "going up from the land" occurs only in 1:11 (= 2:2, MT) and 2:15 (= 2:17, MT): the former text has "they will go up from the land" (*wĕ ālû min-hā'āres*) and the latter has "she [Israel] went up from the land [*'ălōtâh mē'eres*] of Egypt," the latter referring to Israel's first exodus. This identifies the two passages, suggesting that 1:11 is a reference to Israel "going up from the land" of Egypt at the time of her future restoration.

[36] What confirms that the expression in Hos. 1:11 refers to "coming up from the land" of Egypt is the observation that it is an allusion to either Ex. 1:10 or Isa. 11:16, which have *'ālâ + min + 'eres* in the expression "they [or "he" = Israel] went up from the land [of Egypt]" (though Judg. 11:13 and especially 19:30 are nearly identical to Isa. 11:16; almost identical to Isa. 11:16 is Zech. 10:10, though it uses the verb "return" followed by "from the land," and both Egypt and Assyria are referred to as in Isa. 11:16). Fifteen other times in the Old Testament, the same Hebrew wording is used, but refers to God causing Israel to "go up from the land" of Egypt (Ex. 3:8; 32:4, 8; Lev. 11:45; 1 Kings 12:28; 2 Kings 17:7, 36; Jer. 2:6; 7:22; Amos 2:10; 3:1; 9:7; Mic. 6:4; Ps. 81:10 [11]; cf. Deut. 20:1), and five times the expression is used with reference to Moses doing the same thing (Ex. 32:1, 7, 23; 33:1; Num. 16:13). It is possible that the expression in Hos. 1:11 (= 2:2, MT) is a collective allusion to all of these references, which would only enforce a reference to "going up from the land" of Egypt in the Hosea passage. See Derek Drummond Bass, "Hosea's Use of Scripture: An Analysis of His Hermeneutic" (PhD diss., The Southern Baptist Theological Seminary, 2008), 128–29, who has proposed that Ex. 1:10 is the allusion in Hos. 1:11 (= 2:2, MT). Isa. 11:16 may be uppermost in mind, since it is the only other reference using this wording that refers to Israel's future restoration and uses it in conjunction with restoration from "Assyria," which Hos. 11:11 also does together with restoration from Egypt (note the similar combination of Egypt and Assyria in Hos. 7:11; 9:3; 12:1). Or Isaiah (written ca. 739–690 BC) could be dependent on Hosea (written ca. 755–725 BC), since their ministries overlapped by about fifteen years. If so, then a plausible inner-biblical trajectory would be Ex. 1:10 > Hos. 1:11 > Isa. 11:11. Or both Hosea and Isaiah could be alluding to Ex. 1:10 independently and understanding it typologically of the future.

where also "they will come trembling from Egypt" ("trembling" is repeated twice in 11:10–11, though a different Hebrew verb is used than in 3:5). This may point further to Hosea's biblical-theological understanding that when Israel would come out of Egypt in the future (according to 1:11 *and* 11:10–11), they would, indeed, be led by an individual king, which enhances further why Matthew could apply the corporate national language of Hosea 11:1 to an individual king, Jesus. Could Matthew not have had such a biblical-theological reading of Hosea? We could even say that Matthew may be interpreting Hosea 11:1 and 11:10–11 by Hosea 1:10–11.

Interestingly, the reference to the restoration of "the sons of the living God" in Hosea 1:10 has its closest parallel in all of the Bible to Matthew 16:16, where Peter professes that Jesus is "the Messiah, the Son of the living God." This may well be an allusion to Hosea 1:10,[37] by which Jesus is seen as the individual kingly son leading the sons of Israel, whom he represents.[38] Such an identification of this individual son with the corporate sons is likely the reason that Matthew 2:15 applies the corporate "son" reference of Hosea 11:1 to the individual Jesus.

There is one last rationale for understanding how Matthew can take what applied to the nation in Hosea 11:1 and apply it to the individual Messiah. Garrett has analyzed the use of Genesis in Hosea and has found that repeatedly the prophet alludes to descriptions in Genesis of the individual patriarchs and to other significant individuals in Israel's history. Sometimes these are good portrayals and sometimes bad. The prophet applies these descriptions to the nation of his day. For example, the iniquity of Israel in the present involves her following the same pattern of disobedience as that of Adam (Gen. 6:7) or Jacob (Gen. 12:2–5), and the promise made to the individual Jacob to "make your seed as the sand of the sea, which cannot be numbered because of multitude" (Gen. 32:12; cf. 15:5 and 22:17, addressed to Abraham) is now reapplied and addressed directly to the nation Israel: "yet the number of the sons of Israel will be like the sand of the sea, which cannot be measured or numbered" (Hos. 1:10). Similarly, the Valley of Achor, where Achan and his family were taken to be executed for his sin (Josh. 7:24–26), is taken by Hosea and reversed to indicate that God would reverse Israel's judgment of defeat and exile, and Israel would not be exterminated for her sin but would have a hope of redemption (Hos.

---

[37] See Mark J. Goodwin, "Hosea and 'the Son of the Living God' in Matthew 16:16b," *Catholic Biblical Quarterly* 67 (2005): 265–83, who has proposed such an allusion.

[38] The only other occurrence of "sons" together with "living God" occurs in early Jewish literature, though not as close to the wording of Hosea 1 and Matthew 16: Est. 16:16 ("sons of the most high, the most mighty living God") and 3 Maccabees 6:28 ("sons of the almighty and living God of heaven").

2:15). Instead of going from the one to the many, Matthew goes from the many (Israel) to the one (Jesus), but utilizes the same kind of "one and many" corporate hermeneutical approach to interpreting and applying prior Scripture as did Hosea.[39]

Conclusion

Therefore, Matthew contrasts Jesus as the "son" (2:15) with Hosea's "son" (11:1). The latter, who came out of Egypt, was not obedient, and was judged but would be restored (11:2–11), while the former did what Israel should have done: Jesus came out of Egypt, was perfectly obedient, and did not deserve judgment, but he suffered it anyway for guilty Israel and the world in order to restore them to God. Matthew portrays Jesus to be recapitulating the history of Israel because he sums up Israel in himself. Since Israel disobeyed, Jesus has come to do what they should have done, so he must retrace Israel's steps up to the point they failed, then continue to obey and succeed in the mission Israel should have carried out. The attempt to kill the Israelite infants, and the journey of Jesus and his family into Egypt and back to the Promised Land again, is the same basic pattern of Israel of old. Hence, Jesus did what Israel should have done but did not do.[40] This use of Hosea 11:1 also is an example of how important exodus patterns were to Matthew and the other New Testament writers in understanding the mission of Jesus. His journey out of Egypt is identified as an eschatological exodus out of Egypt, to which Israel's first exodus out of Egypt pointed.

This chapter also attempts to show, contrary to a number of scholars, that Matthew's quotation of Hosea 11:1 shows exegetical and grammatical-historical sensitivity to the immediate context of Hosea 11:2–11, together with the broader context of the entire book, the latter of which involves a biblical-theological perspective on how the various parts of Hosea relate to one another.[41] It is from the quarry of the book of Hosea

---

[39] See Duane Garrett, "The Ways of God: Reenactment and Reversal in Hosea" (unpublished inaugural address for Duane Garrett's installation as professor of Old Testament at Gordon-Conwell Theological Seminary, South Hamilton, MA, fall 1998). See also Bass, "Hosea's Use of Scripture," which was written under Garrett's supervision.

[40] Following here Enns, *Inspiration and Incarnation*, 134, though we understand Matthew's hermeneutical approach differently.

[41] *Pace* France, *Matthew*, 81, who says, "Matthew's Christological interpretation consists not of exegesis of what the text [of Hos. 11:1] quoted meant in its original context, but of a far-reaching theological argument which takes the Old Testament text and locates it within an overarching scheme of fulfillment which finds in Jesus the end point of numerous prophetic trajectories." France's point about Matthew viewing Hos. 11:1 within a broader theological argument and fulfillment scheme from several Old Testament trajectories concerning Israel is correct, but is not exclusive of Matthew paying close attention to the immediate context of Hosea 11 within its context in the entire book of Hosea. In fact, this latter notion is more probably the primary focus, which Matthew likely then understood secondarily in a biblical-theological sense in light of the broader Old Testament canonical context and trajectories.

itself (and possibly even from Hosea 11 itself) and its reverberations of Numbers 23–24, that Matthew gleans everything he has expressed in the Hosea 11 quotation. Thus, we can push back the question "Is Matthew's typological exegesis of Hosea 11:1 legitimate hermeneutically and exegetically?" to "Is Hosea's typological exegesis, which Matthew follows, legitimate hermeneutically and exegetically?" There is no room here to answer this adequately, except to say that typological exegesis in Hosea can be discerned by a grammatical-historical exegesis of Hosea itself. Is typology legitimate hermeneutically for Old Testament writers? I think so, at least on a biblical-theological level, but I cannot argue this here, though I have attempted to do so elsewhere.[42]

In light of this, can it be mere coincidence that the last two verses of Hosea 10, directly preceding Hosea 11, conclude by referring to a "tumult that will arise," "when mothers were dashed in pieces with their children" and "the king of Israel will be completely cut off" (vv. 14–15)? Then the next verse, Hosea 11:1, says, "Out of Egypt I called My son." This is uncannily like Matthew 2:13–21, where "all the male children in Bethlehem" were "slain" (v. 16) and there was "weeping and great mourning" by the mothers for their children (v. 18), followed by "Herod the king's" (vv. 1, 3) death (vv. 15, 20), mention of which both precedes and follows the Hosea 11:1 quotation, "Out of Egypt I called My son."[43]

This study on Hosea 11 in Matthew 2 has attempted to give an in-depth illustration and confirmation of R. T. France's assessment over thirty years ago of the rich contextual background of the Old Testament behind the quotations in Matthew 2:

> Matthew . . . was deliberately composing a chapter rich in potential exegetical bonuses, so that the more fully a reader shared the religious traditions and scriptural erudition of the author [i.e., the Old Testament context], the more he was likely to derive from his reading, while at the same time there was a surface meaning sufficiently uncomplicated for even the most naïve reader to follow it. . . . The bonus meanings convey an increasingly rich and positive understanding of the person and role of the Messiah, not integrated into a tidy theological scheme, but diverse and suggestive for those with eyes to see.[44]

---

[42] See Beale, *Handbook on the New Testament Use of the Old Testament*, chapters 1 and 4.

[43] The possible significance of Hos. 10:14–15 was brought to my attention by an attendee at a conference at which I was speaking.

[44] R. T. France, "The Formula-Quotations of Matthew 2 and the Problem of Communication," *New Testament Studies* 27 (1981): 233–51 (my brackets).

Appendix 1: The Translation Problem of Hosea 11:5a

English translations render Hosea 11:5a as "they [or literally "he" = Israel] will not [*lō'*] return to the land of Egypt" (NASB, KJV, ASV, Douay, HCSB, Targum). Several English translations, however, have "they shall return to the land of Egypt" (or "they will *surely* return to the land of Egypt"), apparently and implicitly construing *lō'* to have a positive asseverate force[45] (RSV, NRSV, JB, NLT, NEB[46]; likewise JPS and NETB[47]);[48] others take *lō'* to be a negative, but render verse 5a as a question, "Will they *not* return to the land of Egypt?" (NIV).[49] Accordingly, the rhetorical question expects a positive answer, so that this rendering has the same positive sense as the ones directly preceding. Commentators likewise are split in their view of the verse, some taking it as an explicit negative reference[50] and others taking it positively.[51] Thus, both translations and commentators are fairly evenly split on whether or not verse 5a refers to a return to Egypt or denies a return to Egypt.

---

[45] For *lō'* with such a positive force, see *The Dictionary of Classical Hebrew*, vol. 4, ed. David J. A. Clines (Sheffield: Sheffield Academic Press, 1998), 495, where also alternate vocalizations of the particle are discussed. An explicit rendering would be expressed as "they surely will return to Egypt," on which see below the ESV and the preference of some commentators.

[46] "Back they shall go to Egypt."

[47] On which see further below.

[48] The ESV reads, "They shall not return to Egypt," but it has a marginal note saying the verse could be rendered "they shall surely return to Egypt."

[49] See Francis Brown, S. R. Driver, and Charles A. Briggs, *A Hebrew and English Lexicon of the Old Testament* (Oxford: Clarendon, 1907), 519, who also see the negative particle *lō'* possibly to have an interrogative force here.

[50] John Calvin, *The Commentaries of John Calvin on the Prophet Hosea* (Grand Rapids, MI: Baker, 1984), 394–95; Ebenezer Henderson, *The Twelve Minor Prophets* (1858; repr., Grand Rapids, MI: Baker, 1980), 66; Francis Landy, *Hosea* (Sheffield: Sheffield Academic Press, 1995), 139; A. A. Macintosh, *A Critical and Exegetical Commentary on Hosea* (Edinburgh: T&T Clark, 1997), 450–51; Thomas Edward McComiskey, "Hosea," in *The Minor Prophets: An Exegetical and Expository Commentary*, vol. 1, ed. Thomas Edward McComiskey (Grand Rapids, MI: Baker, 1992), 188. See Garrett, *Hosea*, 225, who views verse 5a to be a negative reference, though he allows for the possibility that verse 5a affirms that a few would go to Egypt voluntarily and many would go to Assyria by force. See also J. Andrew Dearman, *Hosea* (Grand Rapids, MI: Eerdmans, 2010), 276, 285, who also prefers to read verse 5a negatively but allows for the plausibility of several options generally in line with a positive reading, including the notion that verse 5a is a rhetorical question expecting a positive answer. Marvin A. Sweeney, *The Twelve Prophets*, Berit Olam Studies in Hebrew Narrative & Poetry (Collegeville, MN: Liturgical Press, 2000), 114, acknowledges the plausibility of the LXX's positive reference to Israel's return to Egypt, while at the same time admitting that verse 5 in the Hebrew may well be a reference to Israel not returning to Egypt.

[51] E.g., see Hans Walter Wolff, *Hosea* (Philadelphia: Fortress, 1974), 192, who sees that the pronoun *lô* either should be included at the end of verse 4 or that the particle *lō'* in verse 5a be taken in a positive asseverative manner; so also James Luther Mays, *Hosea*, Old Testament Library (Philadelphia: Westminster, 1969), 150, 154, and Douglas Stuart, *Hosea-Jonah*, Word Biblical Commentary, vol. 31 (Waco, TX: Word, 1987), 179, who prefer that the pronoun *lô* should be included at the end of verse 4. See David Allan Hubbard, *Hosea*, Tyndale Old Testament Commentary (Leicester/Downers Grove: Inter-Varsity, 1989), 190, and Francis I. Anderson and David Noel Freedman, *Hosea*, Anchor Bible Commentaries, vol. 24 (New York: Doubleday, 1980), 583–84, who cite *lō'* asseveratively ("surely"), the latter who cite others in agreement. See also Gary V. Smith, *Hosea, Amos, Micah*, NIV Application Commentary (Grand Rapids, MI: Zondervan, 2001), 159, 162, 164, who sees verse 5a as a rhetorical question expecting a positive answer. Cf. similarly Allen R. Guenther, *Hosea, Amos* (Scottsdale, PA/Waterloo, ON: Herald, 1997), 180, who takes the return to Egypt to be figurative for an entering into captivity in Assyria, on which see further Appendix 2 below.

I understand the expression to be a positive one: either "they will return to Egypt" or "will they not return to Egypt?," the latter expecting a positive answer. Since *lō'* can easily be taken in a positive sense, it is quite plausible that this is the force, especially since repeatedly throughout Hosea it is prophesied that Israel will reenter Egypt and that they will return from Egypt. If Hosea 11:5a were truly affirming that Israel would not reenter Egypt, it would be the lone reference in Hosea and, indeed, would contradict all the other positive references in the book, which is unlikely, especially since 11:11 ("they will come trembling like birds from Egypt") assumes that Israelites are already in Egypt, as well as in Assyria. Nevertheless, some still try to make sense of verse 5a as a negative reference within the context of Hosea.[52]

If *lō'* is not taken with a positive asseverate force or as a question expecting a positive answer, then it is just as possible that it forms the end of verse 4, so that the negative particle *lō'* is read as the third-person plural pronoun *lô* ("for him," corporately understood as "them"), which is the way the *Biblia Hebraica Stuttgartensia* takes it: "I [God] lifted the yoke from their neck, and gently fed *them* [literally "him"]," so that verse 5 begins with "They [he] will return to Egypt . . ." If this is correct, as the *NET Bible* thinks, then the textual confusion between the negative *lō'* and the pronoun *lô* occurred due to an error in hearing, since the two words sound identical, which is a scribal confusion found elsewhere in the Hebrew Bible (so see the note in the *NET Bible*).[53] The Septuagint essentially follows the Hebrew: "I will prevail with *him* [= corporate *them*]," and begins verse 5 by "Ephraim settled in Egypt." The Septuagint's expression, "Ephraim settled in Egypt," is either a reference to the past or, more probably, the past tense verb is like a Hebrew prophetic perfect, functioning to refer to the future.

But even if the original reading were "they will not return to Egypt," the LXX's positive rendering (which understood the Masoretic Text positively)

---

[52] E.g., Landy, *Hosea*, 139, and Macintosh, *Hosea*, 450–51. In this respect, Macintosh, among others, thinks that Hos. 11:5 reflects the historical situation of 2 Kings 17:1–6, where King Hoshea of Israel tried to make an alliance with Egypt against Assyria, but the alliance was thwarted by the Assyrian king, and Hoshea did not go to Egypt but went into Assyrian exile. However, this text may merely refer to an attempted alliance with Egypt by the Israelite king and not an actual attempt to go to Egypt. Perhaps Isaiah 20 is a better fit, where it is prophesied that Israelite refugees in Egypt will be delivered into the hands of "Sargon, the king of Assyria."

[53] It is difficult to know if this is the reasoning behind the positive renderings of Hos. 11:5 by the RSV, NRSV, JB, NLT, and NEB, since they have "them" at the end of verse 4, which, alternatively, could be the result of thinking that "them" is the implied meaning at this point (which is also read in as implied by NASB, KJV, ASV, Douay, HCSB, and Targum, which take verse 5 as "they will not return to Egypt") or whether they are actually implicitly reading the particle *lō'* at the beginning of verse 5 in an asseverate manner ("indeed," "assuredly"). The Jewish Publication Society reads the negative particle *lō'* as beginning verse 5, but still takes the first part of the verse positively: "No! They return to the land of Egypt," seeing the "no" as a sinful response to God's offer of sustenance to them at the end of verse 4.

would have become part of the exegetical tradition in the first century AD, of which Matthew may have been aware and would have appreciated in light of the other positive references elsewhere in Hosea to a future return to Egypt (perhaps comparable to Paul's view of Ps. 68:18 in Eph. 4:8, where he changes "He received gifts" to "He gave gifts," likely in order to understand the overall notion elsewhere throughout the psalm of God bestowing gifts to Israel). And, even if Matthew were aware of only a negative reference in Hosea 11:5, we have seen earlier that there are repeated references to Israel's future return to Egypt in chapters 7–9 of Hosea, which lead up to chapter 11, from which Matthew could well have derived the theme of Israel's future return to Egypt and woven it into his typological understanding of chapter 11.

Appendix 2: Is the Reference to "Egypt" in Hosea 11:5a and 11:10–11 Literal or Figurative?

Douglas Stuart[54] and Allen R. Guenther[55] are among those who take the return to Egypt to be figurative for an entering into captivity in Assyria. Hans Walter Wolff,[56] J. Andrew Dearman,[57] and Marvin A. Sweeney,[58] among others, contend that Egypt and Assyria are literal geographical places and that Egypt is not symbolic for Assyria. Limburg[59] enigmatically takes "Egypt" both as a literal land to which Israel will return and figurative for future captivity in Assyria. It is unlikely that "Egypt" is figurative for "Assyria" in Hosea 11:5, since "Egypt" is never used figuratively throughout the Old Testament outside of Hosea, except in Genesis 13:10, where it is part of an explicit simile comparing it to part of the Promised Land. It is not convincing that Hosea uses "Egypt" figuratively for "Assyria" elsewhere in the book and then uses it to refer to literal "Egypt" in 11:5 (as, e.g., argued by Thomas Edward McComiskey[60]).

As far as I can tell, in more than six hundred instances in the Old Testament, "Egypt" is used only once figuratively, which, as seen above, occurs in a formal simile: "Sodom and Gomorrah" was "like the garden of the Lord, like the land of Egypt" (Gen. 13:10). When the restoration from Assyria and Egypt are mentioned together elsewhere in the Old Testament,

---

[54] Stuart, *Hosea-Jonah*, 179.
[55] Guenther, *Hosea, Amos*, 180.
[56] Wolff, *Hosea*, 200, 202.
[57] Dearman, *Hosea*, 293.
[58] Sweeney, *The Twelve Prophets*, 114.
[59] Limburg, *Hosea-Micah*, 39.
[60] McComiskey, "Hosea," in *The Minor Prophets*, 184, 188.

it is clear that both are to be literally understood (from the Old Testament perspective) as geographical places, which are listed among other geographical places from which scattered Jews are to be gathered (Isa. 11:11, 15–16; Mic. 7:11–13; Zech. 10:8–11; apparently also Isa. 27:12–13, in light of 11:11, 15–16; see also Isa. 19:23–25, which refers to Egypt and Assyria themselves as returning to God in the eschaton). When "Egypt" and "Assyria" are mentioned together elsewhere in noneschatological contexts, they are also distinct literal geographical places (Gen. 25:18; 2 Kings 17:4; 23:29; Isa. 7:18; 20:3–4; Jer. 2:16–18, 36; Lam. 5:6). The references to "Egypt" and "Assyria" in Hosea appear to be best taken in the same way as elsewhere in the Old Testament, especially elsewhere in the Prophets. Hosea 7:11 (Israel "calls to Egypt, they go to Assyria") likely refers to distinct geographical regions, since 7:8 says "Ephraim mixes with the *nations* [plural]," apparently referring to more than the one nation Assyria. Hosea 9:3 ("Ephraim will return to Egypt, and in Assyria they will eat unclean food") should be taken similarly in light of 9:17 ("they will be wanderers among the *nations* [plural]"). Hosea 12:1 (Israel "makes a covenant with Assyria, and oil is carried to Egypt") apparently should be taken in the same way. The reference in Hosea 11:10–11 to Israel returning not only from "Egypt" and "Assyria," but also "from the west," would appear to indicate that a broader restoration is in mind than merely from Assyria, so that "Egypt" may be a literal reference among the various locations of the diaspora from which Israel is to be restored.

15

Is Inerrancy Inert? Closing the Hermeneutical "Loophole"

INERRANCY AND INTERTEXTUALITY

Abner Chou

Students have a knack for finding loopholes. As a professor, I see their clever attempts to bypass requirements and ask for extensions on assignments. I hear many professors say they wish students would put as much effort into their studies as they put into trying to get out of them.

However, students are not the only ones who find loopholes. Some of their teachers do so as well, especially in the area of inerrancy. Recently, certain scholars, who claim to be inerrantists, have undermined inerrancy in their interpretations of the Bible. Despite what the Bible says, they argue that Adam never existed (Gen. 1:26–28) and that certain details of Jesus's life are fictional (Matt. 2:1–23; 27:52–53).[1] How can they still be inerrantists? They point to inerrancy's fine print: hermeneutics and authorial intent. An error occurs only when an author affirms something false. The

---

[1] Craig Blomberg, *Can We Still Believe the Bible? An Evangelical Engagement with Contemporary Questions* (Grand Rapids, MI: Baker, 2014), 152–53, 165–73; Michael R. Licona, *The Resurrection of Jesus: A New Historiographical Approach* (Downers Grove, IL: IVP Academic, 2010), 185–86, 548–53.

loophole involves reinterpreting what he affirmed. If Moses *claimed* Adam was historical, then concluding he is a myth means the Bible is wrong. However, if the Bible never talks about a historical Adam, then concluding Adam is mythical does not imply the Bible is in error. By changing one's interpretation of what the author intended, one can apparently make any interpretation consistent with inerrancy. "The author never really meant . . ." are the magic words that vindicate any interpretation from contradicting inerrancy. With such a loophole, inerrancy is rendered inert, for it no longer affects how we understand the Bible.

How do we deal with that loophole? The solution is to understand how biblical writers really thought. Did they care about the precise meaning of the words of Scripture and what they entailed (e.g., historical claims)? Or was their concern solely with its general message?

This question of how the biblical authors interpreted and applied the Bible has to do with intertextuality.[2] Some appeal to intertextuality to show that the biblical authors were not hermeneutically precise and we shouldn't read them so exactly.[3] To these scholars, the biblical writers' hermeneutic reveals that the Bible is inerrant only in its intended message, but not in all that its statements affirm. Thus, we need to loosen our hermeneutic and understanding of inerrancy.

Conversely, upon further examination, we can see that the biblical writers maintained a high hermeneutical standard, and alleged "problem passages" do not prove otherwise. Under the inspiration of the Spirit, the biblical authors read Scripture with a literal grammatical-historical hermeneutic and upheld its truthfulness on every level (cf. John 16:13). Their use of Scripture exhibits their conviction that the Bible is accurate, unified, precise, authoritative, and inerrant. This is the way they wrote the Bible, and they demand we read it the same way. Inerrancy is not inert. No one can simply appeal to "But the author never intended . . ." as a loophole because intertextuality shows us the authors' intent to read every statement of God's Word as the truth, the whole truth, and nothing but the truth.

Literal Hermeneutics and God's Word as Truth

At the heart of literal interpretation is the matter of truth. Did the biblical writers abide in the original intent of earlier revelation and treat Scripture

---

[2] Intertextuality has to do with the way one text relates to another. Thus, it does not deal with how the apostles revealed new truths, but how they dealt with information that had been previously revealed. The New Testament use of the Old Testament would be a primary example of intertextuality in the Bible.

[3] Peter Enns, *Inspiration and Incarnation: Evangelicals and the Problem of the Old Testament* (Grand Rapids, MI: Baker, 2005), 158–63.

as God's authoritative, unchanging, consistent truth? Or did their use of Scripture show they viewed it as less than that?

I initially offer three major observations about how the New Testament writers handled the Old Testament:

1. *The apostles viewed the Old Testament as truth* (John 17:17; 2 Tim. 2:9–15; cf. 2 Tim. 3:16; 2 Pet. 1:21). That is no small observation. The term *truth* refers to that which is factual (Acts 26:25), the nature of God (Rom. 3:4), and the words of Christ (John 8:31–32). This means the apostles believed Scripture to be accurate and to reflect God's character. In fact, John uses a phrase from Isaiah 65:16 about God's truthfulness and applies it to God's Word in Revelation 22:6.[4] This is a case of the New Testament's use of the Old Testament that shows how Scripture possesses God's own truthful nature. Accordingly, the apostles introduce Scripture as both the words of the prophets (Matt. 4:14) and the words of God (Matt. 1:22). They believed God's message was exactly what the Old Testament writers communicated, nothing more or less (cf. 2 Pet. 1:20–21).

2. *The apostles claimed to remain consistent with the Old Testament.* When citing Scripture, the apostles used phrases such as "in accordance with the Scriptures" (1 Cor. 15:3–4), "as it is written" (Mark 1:2; Luke 2:23; Rom. 8:36), "for [followed by a Scripture quotation]" (1 Cor. 6:16; Gal. 3:11; Heb. 7:17), "for it is written" (Gal. 3:10), and "in order to fulfill" (John 15:25; Acts 1:16; 3:18; James 2:23 AT). The apostles appealed to the Old Testament as the *foundation* of their message, the *basis* of comparison, and the *reason* for their argument. They also understood that their message *worked out* what the Old Testament stated. Accordingly, they viewed the Old Testament as authoritative and claimed to be faithful to what it said. They believed the Old Testament intended to point to the New Testament and Christ (Luke 24:24–27; 1 Pet. 1:10–12).[5] Their message was the fulfillment of the Old Testament, not the undoing of it (Matt. 5:17; Rom. 3:21; Heb. 1:1–2).

3. *The apostles used the Old Testament in context.* They did so when discussing the place of Christ's birth (Matt. 2:6; cf. Mic. 5:2), the importance of faith (Rom. 4:3; Gen. 15:6), the atoning death of Christ (1 Pet. 2:24; Isa. 53:5), and God's holiness (1 Pet. 1:16; Lev. 19:2).[6] Their reading

---

[4] See G. K. Beale, "Can the Bible Be Completely Inspired by God and Yet Still Contain Errors? A Response to Some Recent 'Evangelical' Proposals," *Westminster Theological Journal* 73, no. 1 (March 1, 2011): 1–22.

[5] D. A. Carson, *Collected Writings on Scripture* (Wheaton, IL: Crossway, 2010), 281–83.

[6] See list in Robert L. Thomas, "The New Testament Use of the Old Testament," in *Evangelical Hermeneutics*, ed. Robert L. Thomas (Grand Rapids, MI: Kregel, 2002), 243–47.

of the Old Testament was so contextual that they even knew how Old Testament passages related to each other. Paul, in his discussion on sin, continues the way that Isaiah develops Psalm 14 (Rom. 3:10–19; cf. Ps. 14:1; Isa. 59:7).[7] Mark continues Malachi's discussion of the messenger in Isaiah 40 (Mark 1:2–3; cf. Isa. 40:3; Mal. 3:1).[8] Even more, their thoroughly contextual hermeneutic led them to read and apply Scripture the exact same way. For example, various New Testament writers appealed to Isaiah 53 to describe Christ's sacrifice (Mark 10:45; Rom. 4:25; 1 Pet. 2:24) and used Leviticus 19:18 ("Love your neighbor as yourself") as a basis for Christian morality (Matt. 19:19; Gal. 5:14; James 2:8). The apostles consistently had a hermeneutic that was faithful to the text.

In sum, the apostles declared that the Old Testament is the truth, asserted that they used it accordingly, and actually did so. All of this affirms a high view of Scripture in proclamation and practice.

At this point, scholars counter that the apostles occasionally seem to use the Old Testament out of context. We now turn our attention to those passages.

The above paragraphs should give us pause before immediately casting judgment on the apostles. After all, they have a significant track record of interpreting Scripture carefully. Furthermore, they claimed to rely upon and remain consistent with the meaning of the Old Testament. Shouldn't we take that assertion seriously? Shouldn't we give them the benefit of the doubt and see if it is possible they did what they said?

As we consider their claims, we should think through two important factors the above discussion points out. First, we should distinguish between meaning and significance (implication). The apostles were not always commenting on the meaning of Old Testament texts as much as making inferences from those texts to support their arguments. This is clear in their introductory formulas. We should be careful of condemning the apostles for "reading into the text" when they were actually drawing very legitimate implications.

Second, we need to consider the full Old Testament context the apostles were working with. As discussed, the apostles understood and followed the way the prophets used the Old Testament. Put differently, the prophetic hermeneutic continued into the apostolic hermeneutic. We should

---

[7] Hans-Joachim Kraus, *Psalms 1–59*, Continental Commentary (Minneapolis: Fortress, 1993), 224; Thomas R. Schreiner, *Romans*, Baker Exegetical Commentary on the New Testament (Grand Rapids, MI: Baker, 1998), 165.

[8] R. T. France, *The Gospel of Mark: A Commentary on the Greek Text*, New International Greek Testament Commentary (Grand Rapids, MI: Eerdmans, 2002), 63.

be careful of concluding the apostles did not understand the context when we may have failed to see the full context they were working with.

With those two factors in mind, we can work through some major examples of the apostles' supposed misuse of the Old Testament. Although I cannot provide exhaustive argumentation or address every problem passage, the initial observations made in this chapter show how to resolve these issues and how the apostles interpreted Scripture in a way that affirmed its authority and accuracy.[9]

One type of supposed misuse occurs when a New Testament writer uses an Old Testament text as a prophecy when it was not one originally.[10] Matthew's use of Hosea 11:1 is a primary example of this. How can Matthew use Hosea 11:1 as a prophecy of Jesus's journey to Egypt when it originally referred to Israel's exodus?[11]

To be sure, Hosea 11:1 *refers* to Israel's escape from Egypt. However, that does not explain how Hosea *used* the idea in context. That question becomes quite important when we consider why Matthew used Hosea in the first place. A lot of passages talk about the exodus (Ex. 4:22–23; Num. 24:8; Deut. 4:34; Ps. 106:10–12). If Matthew just wanted to talk about the event, why not use a more prominent text? Matthew thought Hosea's mention of the exodus was significant, and we need to investigate why.

Hosea's mention of the exodus follows a pattern set by his predecessors: the first exodus is the basis for a greater deliverance (cf. Ps. 74:10–15; 77:14–15; 80:16). Maintaining that logic, the context of Hosea 11:1 discusses how God's love for Israel in the exodus will drive him to deliver the nation in the future (v. 11). Throughout the book, the prophet has described that deliverance, when the Messiah will lead his people home from exile in a second exodus (1:11; 3:5). In context, Hosea 11:1 does not merely discuss history, but history as the precedent for God's future workings. This greater prophecy is the point of the text, which is picked up and echoed by other prophets (Mic. 7:14–15; Isa. 43:1–21).[12]

Matthew continues this line of thought. God saved Jesus from Herod in his own personal exodus to demonstrate that God loves Jesus as much

---

[9] For further comprehensive argumentation, see *Commentary on the New Testament Use of the Old Testament*, ed. G. K. Beale and D. A. Carson (Grand Rapids, MI: Baker, 2007); Abner Chou, *The Prophetic, Apostolic, and Christian Hermeneutic: Learning Biblical Interpretation from the Writers of Scripture* (Grand Rapids, MI: Kregel, forthcoming).
[10] See list in Thomas, "The New Testament Use of the Old Testament," 247–51.
[11] For a more extensive treatment of this question, see chapter 14 in this volume, "The Use of Hosea 11:1 in Matthew 2:15: Inerrancy and Genre" by G. K. Beale.
[12] See Duane A. Garrett, *Hosea, Joel*, The New American Commentary, vol. 19A (Nashville: Broadman & Holman, 1997), 220–21; K. L. Barker and W. Bailey, *Micah, Nahum, Habakkuk*, The New American Commentary, vol. 20 (Nashville: Broadman & Holman, 1998), 131.

as he loved his son, Israel. This proves Jesus is Israel's true representative and King, who will lead them in a new exodus. He is the messianic individual about whom Hosea prophesied (cf. Hos. 1:11; 3:5).[13] Thus, Matthew shows how God is fulfilling the *purpose of Hosea 11:1*. Hosea 11:1 in context discusses how the first exodus demands a new exodus led by the Messiah. The Gospel writer shows an important implication of that reality; namely, how Christ's life fits into and works to fulfill that biblical-theological theme.[14]

Another category of potential misuse concerns the matter of the law. Scholars point out that the apostles say we are no longer under the law (Rom. 6:14; James 2:8) and do not need to keep certain commands (Col. 2:13–23). Does this imply that the New Testament writers viewed the law as lacking authority or that it communicated something less than what is true, something that the New Testament later corrects? Once again, we need to examine the context. God designed the law to teach Israel about his character and his holy demands (Lev. 19:2). In fact, the term "law" (*tôrâ*) means "to teach" or "to point" (cf. Ex. 15:25–26).[15] Each command explained theological truth to Israel and the watching world (cf. Ex. 19:5–6).

The law not only taught about God, but also pointed to his goal of changing people from the heart (Deut. 30:1–6). This implied there would be a time when the law would accomplish its purpose and give way to something new. Later, Isaiah recognized that when the Servant would atone for and transform his people's hearts (Isa. 44:3; 52:13–53:12), the law would be fulfilled and not in force (Isa. 56:4).[16] The prophet accentuated what the law originally indicated. Thus, when the New Testament writers show the fulfillment of what Isaiah (and others) prophesied, they are not disregarding the authority of the Old Testament. Rather, by showing the fulfillment, they demonstrate that Scripture is infallible. The purpose of the law would not be thwarted, but would be fulfilled.

Moreover, even though the apostles do not require obedience to the letter of the law, they still use the law to discuss God's character (1 Pet. 1:16)

---

[13] Matthew compares Jesus with Moses throughout his Gospel. See Dale C. Allison, *The New Moses: A Matthean Typology* (Minneapolis: Fortress Press, 1993). Also involved is the recapitulation of Israel's history to show that Jesus is their kingly representative.

[14] D. A. Carson, *Matthew*, Expositor's Bible Commentary, vol. 8, ed. Frank Gaebelein (Grand Rapids, MI: Zondervan, 1979), 93–95. The idea of "fulfilled" has the idea of "worked out" primarily. For example, James 2:23 shows how Abram's faith (Gen. 15:6) is "fulfilled" in that it is worked out by his actions.

[15] Nahum Sarna, *Exodus*, JPS Torah Commentary (Philadelphia: Jewish Publication Society, 1991), 84.

[16] John N. Oswalt, *The Book of Isaiah, Chapters 40–66*, New International Commentary on the Old Testament (Grand Rapids, MI: Eerdmans, 1998), 458–60.

and his demands (Rom. 13:9; James 2:11). This shows the apostles believed the law teaches truth. The law's fulfillment in Christ and the new covenant does not change that reality. The New Testament writers' appeal to the law demonstrates that it is not only infallible, but also inerrant. It is true in its purpose and in what it propositionally claims about God and his standard.

What do we learn from all of this? The apostles handled God's Word carefully. They did not approach Scripture in a cavalier fashion. Rather, they affirmed Scripture as their final authority and understood it in context. Such reverence reflects the fact that they believed (as they say) that the Bible is God's authoritative and unalterable truth. Even in supposed problem passages, we observe they were not taking Scripture out of context, but knew of a greater context and rationale in the Old Testament. The problem is not that the apostles misunderstood Scripture, but that they knew it far better than we do.

The apostles' grasp of context underscores an important reality: the analogy of faith. The analogy of faith states that Scripture is absolutely harmonious, without contradiction. This is a key principle in traditional hermeneutics, one that is rooted in the inerrancy of Scripture. Some allege that we have forced the paradigm of inerrancy and the analogy of faith upon Scripture.[17] However, the above discussion shows we were not the first to view the Bible this way. The biblical writers practiced the analogy of faith in their extensive collation of Scripture. They believed Scripture is perfectly and authoritatively unified. In this way, the apostles' highly contextual hermeneutic affirms they believed the Bible is wholly consistent and thereby inerrant.

Grammatical Hermeneutics and God's Word as Whole Truth

The apostles handled Scripture in a way that reflects its truthfulness. How far, though, does that truthfulness extend? This raises the issue of grammatical interpretation. Did the apostles and prophets view every phrase and word of Scripture as truth? Or did they merely view its general ideas as the truth? Is the Bible the whole truth, words and all?

Our Lord asserts that every word of the Bible matters. He states that Scripture cannot be broken (John 10:35) and that not one letter of the law will pass away (Matt. 5:18). He also focuses upon the wording of "three days" in Jonah 1:17 (Matt. 12:40), "two becoming one flesh" in Genesis

---

[17] This is the logic of Peter Enns, "Inerrancy, However Defined, Does Not Describe What the Bible Does," in *Five Views on Biblical Inerrancy*, ed. J. Merrick and Stephen M. Garrett (Grand Rapids, MI: Zondervan, 2013), 83–88.

2:24 (Mark 10:7), "lord" in Psalm 110:1 (Matt. 22:44), and "gods" in Psalm 82:6 (John 10:34). These words become critical for his argument about his resurrection, the nature of marriage, and his divinity. Jesus claims every word of Scripture is important and reads the text that way. The Gospel writers follow his example. They exhibit equal concern for the details of the text. From Isaiah's prophecy that the Servant would heal (Matt. 8:17; cf. Isa. 53:4) to the details about the bones of God's chosen one (John 19:36; cf. Ex. 12:46; Ps. 34:20), the Gospel writers discuss the exact wording of Scripture.

Acts and the Epistles are just as precise. Luke sees the phrase "to the end of the earth" in Isaiah 49:6 as the basis for the church's mission to the Gentiles (Acts 1:8).[18] Peter appeals to "nor did his flesh see corruption" to prove Psalm 16 refers to the Messiah (Acts 2:31). He also focuses on terms such as *word* (Isa. 40:8; 1 Pet. 1:23–25) and *cornerstone* (Isa. 28:16; 1 Pet. 2:6–7) in his writings to make points about the gospel and the nature of Christ and the church. Paul applies Scripture similarly. He uses Isaiah 28:6 the same way Peter does—to show that Jesus is the "cornerstone" (Eph. 2:20). Paul also examines how the Old Testament utilizes the term *faith* in Abraham's life and in Habakkuk (Gen. 15:6; Hab. 2:4; Gal. 3:1–11). The author of Hebrews also pays attention to the words of Scripture when he focuses on the words *faith* (10:39–11:1) and *rest* (4:1–5; cf. Gen. 2:2; Ps. 95:11) in the Old Testament. James cares about the wording of Scripture as well. He concentrates on the phrase "give favor" in Proverbs 3:34 to show how God gives grace so that we can meet his demands (James 4:6).

Although this is a brief survey, our discussion demonstrates that the New Testament writers affirmed the veracity and authority of the words of Scripture. Though space does not permit a full discussion, that same exactness is also found in the Old Testament, which claims God's words are pure (Ps. 119:140) and that not one of all God's good words has failed (Josh 21:45). Both the prophets and apostles cared about what the words of the sacred text say.

Nevertheless, scholars raise objections. Some claim the apostles did not correctly understand the grammar of a text. For instance, in discussing the role of law and promise, Paul states that God made a promise to Abraham's singular offspring, who is Christ (Gal. 3:16). However, the original context

[18] Darrell Bock, *Acts*, Baker Exegetical Commentary on the New Testament (Grand Rapids, MI: Baker, 2007), 64, 464.

suggests the word *seed* or *offspring* refers to Abraham's collective descendants. Scholars argue the apostle bent the grammar to suit his purpose.[19]

In response, we again need to examine the greater context. In Genesis 3:15 and other passages (4:25; 22:17–18; 24:60), Moses uses pronouns and verbs in the singular to refer to *seed*. The grammar in these cases indicates "seed" discusses a person, not a group. This distinct usage of *seed* makes it a technical term for the messianic individual in 3:15.[20] So when God makes the promise of blessing to Abraham's "seed" in 22:18, that guarantee develops 3:15 and the Messiah. Psalm 72:17 confirms this reading when it says, "May people be blessed in him, all nations call him blessed!" (note the singular).[21] Paul's statement is correct. The noun *offspring* in the singular points back to the singular Seed who represents Abraham's offspring and will fulfill the promises. Paul reads the Old Testament both contextually and grammatically. He pays attention to whether a word is singular or plural.

Another objection concerns how the New Testament translates the Old Testament. Some argue that translations hindered the apostles' accuracy and even misled them. Scholars point to the use of Psalm 8:5 in Hebrew 2:7–9 as an example.[22] Psalm 8:5 states God made man lower than *'elohiym* (אֱלֹהִים), which could be translated as "God" or "angels." The author of Hebrews 2:7 translates this as "angels," which is important for his argument. Scholars, though, think "God" was originally intended.[23] Is this a case where bad translation made the apostles inaccurate?

As already noted, the word in Hebrew can be translated as "angels," and David intended this. The psalmists never directly talk to God and then immediately address God in the third person. If Psalm 8:5 was talking about someone being made less than God, we would expect "You made him lower than *yourself*," not "You made him lower than *God*."[24] The translation "God" does not fit in this verse. Furthermore, in other passages that directly address God and talk about *'elohiym* (אֱלֹהִים), the latter means

---

[19] Enns, *Inspiration and Incarnation*, 136–38.

[20] T. D. Alexander, "Genealogies, Seed, and the Compositional Unity of Genesis," *Tyndale Bulletin* 44 (1993): 255–70; Jack Collins, "A Syntactical Note (Genesis 3:15): Is the Woman's Seed Singular or Plural?" *Tyndale Bulletin* 48 (1997): 139–48.

[21] T. D. Alexander, "Further Observations on the Term 'Seed' in Genesis," *Tyndale Bulletin* 48 (1997): 365. In context, the "him" is David's ultimate offspring.

[22] Translations themselves do not impugn inerrancy unless they communicate a false idea. See Vern S. Poythress, "Problems for Limited Inerrancy," *Journal of the Evangelical Theological Society* 18, no. 2 (March 1, 1975): 96–97.

[23] Peter C. Craigie, *Psalms 1–50*, 2nd ed., Word Biblical Commentary (Nashville: Nelson Reference & Electronic, 2004), 108.

[24] Some examples of addressing God consistently in the second person include Ps. 4:1; 5:10; 10:12; 16:1; 43:2.

"angels" (cf. Ps. 138:1). By that pattern, *'elohiym* in Psalm 8:5 should mean "angels." The translation "angels" is the most linguistically consistent and defensible option. Far from being imprecise or erroneous, the New Testament writer shows care about the wording of Scripture, down to the term *angel*. He viewed every word as important.

Is the Bible the whole truth, words and all? The prophets and apostles handled it that way. They built their arguments based upon various terms and phrases in the text. They cared about the grammar of the text, and they show that precision is not lost in translation. Their linguistic focus demonstrates the Bible is true down to what the words communicate.

Historical Hermeneutics and God's Word as Nothing but the Truth

The Bible's precision extends to its wording. However, could it ever include something that is not true? Some scholars argue that the biblical writers wove fictional details and events into their portrayal of history.[25] This brings up a question: How did the biblical writers think through the Bible and history? Did they view Scripture as historically accurate, or did they think the Bible had history mixed with myth?[26]

The biblical writers categorically objected to myths. Moses warned against idolatry and embracing pagan concepts (Deut. 4:16–20). Paul and Peter denounced myths (1 Tim. 1:4; 4:7; 2 Tim. 4:4; 2 Pet. 1:16) *because they had nothing to do with the truth* (2 Tim. 4:4; 2 Pet. 1:16).[27] Such objections illustrate why the biblical authors never affirm myths. They rejected tales that made untrue claims. This speaks to their view of history.

Consistently, the biblical writers believed accurate history leads to accurate theology. The most obvious example of this is the resurrection. Paul argues that Christianity cannot be true without the historicity of Christ's resurrection (1 Cor. 15:14). In addition, Paul states that Christ's life and death are essential in securing atonement (Rom. 4:25) and demonstrating God's love for us (Rom. 5:8). Peter reasons that the flood was a precedent for God's future judgment (2 Pet. 3:6–7). God declares that his acts in the exodus distinguish him from everyone else (Deut. 4:31–36). In each of these cases, if the event did not take place, the theology discussed has no

---

[25] Licona, *The Resurrection of Jesus*, 182–86; John Walton, "A Historical Adam: Archetypal Creation View," in *Four Views on the Historical Adam*, ed. Ardel B. Caneday and Matthew Barrett (Grand Rapids, MI: Zondervan, 2013), 89–118.

[26] Traditionally, historical hermeneutics refers to the author's culture and background. What I am speaking of is a subset of that relative to whether Scripture provides its own historical background accurately.

[27] George W. Knight, *The Pastoral Epistles: A Commentary on the Greek Text*, New International Greek Testament Commentary (Grand Rapids, MI: Eerdmans, 1992), 72.

foundation. The biblical writers' logic binds the truthfulness of theology with the reality of history.

The authors' approach to history is pervasive in Scripture. The New Testament refers frequently to events in Old Testament history when discussing theology. This includes creation (2 Pet. 3:4), Adam (Rom. 5:14), Cain (Jude 11), Enoch (Jude 14), Abraham, Isaac, and Jacob (Matt. 22:32), Sodom and Gomorrah (Luke 17:28–29), David's wilderness wanderings (Luke 6:3–4), the queen of Sheba (Luke 11:31), Elijah and Elisha (Luke 4:26–27), Jonah (Matt. 12:39–41), and the Ninevites (Luke 11:29–32). The author of Hebrews also walks us through much Old Testament history in the "hall of fame of faith" (Hebrews 11). In all these passages, the authors do not doubt Scripture's historical accuracy. Rather, they base their argument upon its historical assertions. This even extends to the subject of authorship. For example, Jesus and the apostles assume that Isaiah wrote the entire book of Isaiah (John 12:38–41), Moses wrote the Pentateuch (Mark 7:10; Luke 5:14; Rom. 10:5), and Daniel wrote Daniel (Matt. 24:15). The apostles thoroughly affirmed the historical accuracy of the Old Testament in their writings.

The New Testament writers are not alone in this mentality. The Old Testament prophets recount past events as historical and as the basis for why Israel should obey the Lord (cf. Psalm 78; 104–6; Neh. 9:1–38; Dan. 9:4–13). This brings up another important observation about history in the Bible. History is what ties the Bible together. The Bible's storyline is redemptive history, the fleshing out of God's plan in creation, fall, Israel, exile, Christ, church, and final consummation when Christ returns. Accordingly, history is a key part of how the biblical writers thought and wrote. It is the basis of their theology, argument, and the message of Scripture as a whole. They were convinced that history and historical accuracy are necessary for the Bible's message.

Some scholars are skeptical. They point out that the apostles included parables in their writings. If they allowed for one form of fiction, why not another? But parables do not pose themselves as historical narrative. In fact, they are often introduced as parables (Matt. 13:3; Luke 5:36; 6:39) and take place *within* historical narratives, not *as* historical narratives. The apostles did not write parables because they wanted to fictionalize their writings, but because they were reporting what people said in space and time. Their use of parables actually supports historical accuracy.

Scholars also cite two passages to show the biblical writers were not concerned with historical accuracy. First, they appeal to 1 Corinthians 10:4, which speaks of a rock following Israel around in the wilderness. Some say Paul borrowed this idea from Jewish legend.[28] However, the Old Testament uses the "Rock" as the title of the God who led Israel in the wilderness (cf. Deut. 32:4; Ps. 78:35). Paul's statement is not based on legend but on the Old Testament itself. It actually illustrates how he examined the details of the Old Testament closely and affirmed their truthfulness.[29]

Second, scholars raise the issue of Paul's "allegory" in Galatians 4:21–31 to show historical accuracy was not central in the biblical writers' mind-set.[30] However, Paul affirms the details of what happened (vv. 21–23) and uses them to make an extended analogy about theology. That is the notion of "allegory" in this text.[31] History is again the basis for theology. Along that line, Paul's analogy is appropriate. In context, Abram's effort to have a child with Hagar (Gen. 16:1–4) contrasts his faith (Gen. 15:6). God's choice of Isaac shows that only God's provision through faith is acceptable. Isaiah alludes to these events to show God will fulfill his promise to restore his people apart from human effort (Isa. 51:2; 54:1–3). Paul continues that line of thought by showing how human effort will never obtain the promise (Gal. 4:28–31). The apostle not only affirms the historicity of the Sarah-Hagar story, but he also uses it appropriately.

The biblical writers' hermeneutic is immersed in history. They shunned fables, affirmed the historicity of Scripture, and linked the truthfulness of theology with the reality of history. This mentality bears out even in supposed cases to the contrary. With such a rationale, it is inconceivable that they would have incorporated myths into their portrayal of history. Rather, the hermeneutic of the biblical authors points to the fact that the Bible is nothing but the truth.

First Inerrantists and the Hermeneutics of Surrender

Is authorial intent the loophole that makes inerrancy inert? The answer is no. We have seen that the biblical writers affirmed inerrancy. They believed the Bible was the truth, the whole truth, and nothing but the truth. They were the first inerrantists. As such, they not only defined inerrancy, but they show us how it works in interpretation. They interpreted the Bible according to its original context, exact wording, and historical claims. They did this because they believed the Bible was true and consistent, precise to its

---

[28] Enns, *Inspiration and Incarnation*, 149–51.
[29] G. K. Beale, "A Surrejoinder to Peter Enns," *Themelios* 32, no. 3 (2007): 14–25.
[30] R. Longenecker, *Biblical Exegesis in the Apostolic Period* (Grand Rapids, MI: Eerdmans, 1975), 127.
[31] Ben Witherington, *Grace in Galatia* (Grand Rapids, MI: Eerdmans, 1998), 330.

very phraseology, and without fault in its affirmations of history. We do not merely derive inerrancy deductively, but also from the way the Bible works, the way its writers intended it to operate.

Authorial intent doesn't create loopholes; it closes them. Any interpretation that denies the truthfulness of Scripture's details or historicity also denies inerrancy. Such interpretations contradict the way the first inerrantists have shown inerrancy to operate in Scripture. Those conclusions also contradict their intent and claims. Rather, the biblical writers establish literal-grammatical-historical hermeneutics as the standard for scriptural interpretation. Inerrancy is not inert. It has bearing upon our interpretation.

That being said, we must recognize there is a difference between wrestling *with* the words and historical claims of the text and wrestling *against* them. A standard does not mean that we will always interpret the Bible correctly and that disagreements will cease. Differences will arise and can abide within the bounds of inerrancy. Nevertheless, the doctrine of inerrancy pushes us to work to get it right. It tells us there is a way to interpret Scripture, and our job is to align our interpretations with that standard. With patience and perseverance, we endeavor to understand and articulate the truth, the whole truth, and nothing but the truth.

In an age that talks about a hermeneutic of humility and love, the first inerrantists leave us with a hermeneutic of surrender. Intertextuality and inerrancy not only refute those who subvert God's Word, but also remind us how to be better interpreters of Scripture. We display our conviction about inerrancy when we teach the entire counsel of God's Word because it is wholly consistent and interconnected truth. We proclaim inerrancy when we study every word of the text and affirm its reality. We exhibit inerrancy when we do not pick and choose what we want to believe and practice, but surrender our lives to God's Word because it is the authority and we are not. That is what the prophets and apostles did, and they have shown us how to rightly divide the Word of truth. The prophetic and apostolic hermeneutic is our hermeneutic. May we continue the way the first inerrantists interpreted and lived out Scripture.

16

Can Error and Revelation Coexist?

INERRANCY AND ALLEGED
CONTRADICTIONS

William Barrick

In a court of law, the trustworthiness of a witness or even of a document rises to the level of primary importance.[1] If a witness lies or appears confused on one point, his or her trustworthiness becomes suspect or is destroyed outright. The trustworthiness of Scripture depends on an equally high standard, if not a higher one. The writers of Scripture claim that what they write came from God himself. Is their witness impeachable? If so, what does that imply about God's own testimony? Can error coexist with revelation originating with God?

The topic of biblical inerrancy is once again drawing the attention and scrutiny of evangelicals, not just theological liberals. Why has it returned to the forefront of theological discussion and debate? As recent commentators have attempted to resolve alleged biblical contradictions, some have found

---

[1] See a similar argument made by Gleason L. Archer, "Alleged Errors and Discrepancies in the Original Manuscripts of the Bible," in *Inerrancy*, ed. by Norman L. Geisler (Grand Rapids, MI: Zondervan, 1980), 59.

previous commentators' answers less than satisfactory. In addition, in an era dominated by postmodern thought, even some evangelical scholars have called absolute truth into question and have given in to a hermeneutic of doubt and skepticism regarding the inerrancy of Scripture.

No one could honestly claim that differences in the biblical text do not exist. To both unbelievers and believers alike, such differences might appear to be errors of fact.[2] However, we must clearly distinguish interpretive difficulties from errors. We must also be mindful of the fact that unresolved difficulties or alleged discrepancies do not automatically demand the denial of the Bible's truth and trustworthiness. As long as viable solutions exist, as they certainly do, it is neither wise nor necessary to deny the trustworthiness or accuracy of Scripture.

Although many different categories of difficulties might be identified and listed, opponents of biblical inerrancy tend to raise three major objections:

1. A variety of readings in different biblical manuscripts supposedly points to mistakes made by copyists. Thus, it appears that the current biblical text has been contaminated by error and might be, at least in part, untrustworthy.
2. Discrepancies involving Hebrew numbers and their interpretation appear to open the door to accusations of inaccuracy.
3. New Testament writers citing Old Testament texts seem to take liberties with those texts and so do not appear to consider the Old Testament inviolable.

Let us consider these objections more closely.

The Text of the Old Testament

Some evangelical scholars, such as Alfred Hoerth,[3] resort to textual emendation in order to explain historical references in difficult texts. For example, Hoerth cites scribal glosses in his treatment of the phrase "in the land of Rameses" in Genesis 47:11.[4] Such treatment seems at odds with the

---

[2] Cf. John H. Walton and D. Brent Sandy, *The Lost World of Scripture: Ancient Literary Culture and Biblical Authority* (Downers Grove, IL: IVP Academic, 2013), 307.
[3] Alfred J. Hoerth, *Archaeology and the Old Testament* (Grand Rapids, MI: Baker, 1998), 59.
[4] Ibid., 156n14, 166n1. The problem faced by interpreters relates to how the Egyptian city of Tanis could be called Rameses several hundred years prior to Pharaoh Rameses. My point is not that it does not comprise a legitimate problem, but that textual emendation (or scribal glosses) do not offer the preferred manner of dealing with the matter. The solution must also account for evidence of the existence of Rameses as an upper-class Egyptian name prior to the birth of Moses; Gleason L. Archer, "An Eighteenth Dynasty Rameses," *Journal of the Evangelical Theological Society* 17, no. 1 (Winter 1974): 49–50. See also the seemingly contrasting views of Charles F. Aling, "The Biblical City of Ramses," *Journal of the Evangelical Theological Society* 25, no. 2 (June 1982): 129–37, and Bryant G. Wood, "From Rameses to Shiloh: Archaeological Discoveries Bearing on the Exodus-Judges Period," in *Giving the Sense: Understanding and Using Old*

accusation he makes against critical scholars: "To accept the biblical account is now said to be naïve."[5] It also contradicts his own principle that it is not a sound practice to emend "the biblical text to make the identification fit."[6] Such practices run counter to a healthy approach to the biblical text, because the interpreter assumes that he has rightly obtained all information and personally attained all knowledge necessary to change the biblical text rather than retain its reading.

Conjectural Emendations

In many cases, adopting scribal glosses amounts to conjectural emendation (i.e., "the suggestion of new readings that are not transmitted in the witnesses of the biblical text"[7]). The burden of proof rests with the conjecturer. As Emanuel Tov so fittingly reminds his readers concerning conjectural emendations to the Hebrew Bible, "The emendation of the text pertains to all witnesses of the biblical text and not solely to" the Masoretic Text.[8] Just think what that implies. Is there really a high likelihood that a modern scholar (without any textual evidence for his emendation) might correctly impeach all extant ancient witnesses to the biblical text? If "a reading found in only one single translation, without any corroborating witnesses or original-language manuscripts, has an extremely small chance of possessing the correct reading found in the *autographa*,"[9] what are the odds of a reading without support in any ancient translation?

Three observations concerning conjectural emendation help to identify their nature: (1) a conjectural emendation exhibits a high degree of subjectivity; (2) with increased knowledge and evidence, most such emendations later prove to be unnecessary; and (3) scholars should consider conjectural emendation only as a last resort.[10] In other words, as long as there is any moderately reasonable explanation for the text as it stands, that option ought always to be preferred. Interpreters too often pursue textual emendations because they lack sufficient knowledge to make sense of the text as it stands. Ignorance, however, should never be an excuse to emend the text in order to make it understandable to the modern Western mind. Adhering

Testament Historical Texts, ed. David M. Howard Jr. and Michael A. Grisanti (Grand Rapids, MI: Kregel Academic & Professional, 2003), 260–62.
[5] Hoerth, *Archaeology and the Old Testament*, 215.
[6] Ibid., 225.
[7] Emanuel Tov, *Textual Criticism of the Hebrew Bible*, 3rd ed. (Minneapolis: Fortress, 2012), 328.
[8] Ibid., 328.
[9] Douglas Petrovich, "O.T. Textual Criticism Variant Reading Resolution: 1 Kings 6:1, https://www.academia.edu/5987760/Resolution_of_1_Kings_6_1_Textual_Variant (accessed Dec. 15, 2014).
[10] Tov, *Textual Criticism of the Hebrew Bible*, 330.

consistently to biblical inerrancy requires an admission of one's ignorance and inability to resolve every problem. Our ignorance, however, should never become the excuse for compromising the integrity of the Scriptures. Our first assumption should be that *we* are in error rather than applying the hermeneutic of doubt to the text. No native biblical Hebrew speaker lives today, and no scholar has lived in the era of the biblical writers. We all approach Scripture with huge gaps in our ability to understand the more difficult texts.

THE CLARITY OF SCRIPTURE

Our lack of ability to understand the biblical text with the same language, background, and knowledge of the ancient writers and readers should not cause us to ignore the fact that God intended his written revelation to be understood. The clarity of Scripture[11] depends upon an all-wise God who knows how to express his revelation in a way that can be understood by all people in all cultures and all eras. Any interpretation or emendation that depends mostly upon modern knowledge cannot be trusted to reflect a correct understanding. Why would an omniscient Author convey biblical content that only people living thousands of years later would be capable of understanding?

TRANSMISSION AND TRANSLATION MISTAKES

Most differences between translations (both ancient and modern) involve translational variations, not textual variations. Translators looking at the same Hebrew or Greek text can translate it quite differently, depending on their translation philosophy and their translation technique. Variation in translation does not automatically reveal that the translators are looking at different readings in the same biblical text. Due to the involvement of fallen men and women, errors do creep into the biblical text during its transmission (especially during scribal copying). One example within an English Bible is the continuous mistranslation of Psalm 14:4 in the New American Standard Bible (NASB). From the very beginning, "Lord" appears rather than "LORD" as the translation for "Yahweh." Even the updated (1995) version perpetuated the error until several reprints had been published. Such errors do not impugn the God-given text. They reflect the work of fallen people who make mistakes in either translating or editing the Bible versions.

---

[11] Rather than discuss this topic here, I leave it to other chapters in this volume. See especially chapter 18, "How the Perfect Light of Scripture Allows Us to See Everything Else: Inerrancy and Clarity" by Brad Klassen.

The doctrine of inerrancy applies to the original manuscripts and does *not* extend into scribal/textual transmission. By the sovereign will of God, the transmission process was not inerrant; consequently, there may be variations in the manuscripts of biblical books in which only one reading is correct. While these variations are statistically extremely small, they do present examples of apparent contradiction between parallel texts of Scripture.

Apparent, but Not Necessarily Real, Contradictions

Between 2 Samuel 24:13–24 and 1 Chronicles 21:12–25, we observe three major differences that appear to be contradictions.[12] First, 2 Samuel 24:13 reads "seven years" in the Hebrew text rather than "three years," as recorded at 1 Chronicles 21:12.[13] The Greek Septuagint in 2 Samuel 24:13 has "three years." The Samuel text asks a direct question with words not found in the Chronicles text. The Chronicles text also adds "take for yourself" to introduce the three alternatives. The former might well represent Gad's first words (a question about seven years of famine), while the latter might represent his final ultimatum, in which the alternatives are all threes.[14]

Second, 2 Samuel 24:24 says that David paid fifty shekels of silver for the threshing floor, while 1 Chronicles 21:25 speaks of six hundred shekels of gold. Note, however, that Samuel specifies the threshing floor and the oxen for the burnt offering, while Chronicles identifies the purchase as "the site" (or "plot of ground"). David evidently paid the larger figure for the entire property surrounding the threshing floor.[15]

Third, 2 Samuel 24 refers to Araunah as the owner of the land, while 1 Chronicles 21 calls him Ornan.[16] Ancient Hebrew personal names often occurred in different forms: e.g., Nebuchadnezzar and Nebuchadrezzar (the first spelling occurs twenty-five times in Kings, Chronicles, Ezra, Nehemiah, Esther, and Daniel, and seven times in Jeremiah; the second spelling occurs thirty-four times in Jeremiah and Ezekiel),[17] Adoram and Adoniram

---

[12] Some commentators ignore these issues, choosing instead to mention only the difference between the Chronicler's substitution of "Satan/adversary" for "Yahweh"; e.g., Joyce B. Baldwin, *1 and 2 Samuel*, Tyndale Old Testament Commentaries (Downers Grove, IL: InterVarsity Press, 1988), 294–98, esp. 294–95.

[13] Ronald F. Youngblood, *1, 2 Samuel*, in The Expositor's Bible Commentary, 12 vols., ed. Frank E. Gaebelein (Grand Rapids, MI: Zondervan, 1992), 3:1104.

[14] See Gleason L. Archer, *Encyclopedia of Bible Difficulties*, Regency Reference Library (Grand Rapids, MI: Zondervan, 1982), 189–90.

[15] Youngblood, *1, 2 Samuel*, 3:1103; J. Barton Payne, "Part I: The Validity of the Numbers in Chronicles," *Bibliotheca Sacra* 136, no. 542 (April 1979): 120.

[16] These distinct differences in names occur in the Hebrew text. However, many translations (e.g., a number of English and Russian versions) harmonize so that readers cannot observe the variations.

[17] Robert Dick Wilson, *A Scientific Investigation of the Old Testament*, rev. by Edward J. Young (1959; repr., Birmingham, AL: Solid Ground Christian Books, 2007), 68. Wilson suggests that the variations in

(2 Sam. 20:24 and 1 Kings 4:6), Bathsheba and Bath-shua (2 Sam. 12:24 and 1 Chron. 3:5), Berodach-baladan (in some versions) and Merodach-baladan (2 Kings 20:12 and Isa. 39:1). Some people even bore more than one name: Solomon/Jedidiah (2 Sam. 12:24, 25), Gideon/Jerubbaal (Judg. 7:1), Abram/Abraham, and Jacob/Israel.

THE OLD TESTAMENT'S DEPENDABILITY

While we may not possess any autographs of the books of the Old Testament, the state of our knowledge regarding the history of the text has made great strides since the discovery of the Dead Sea Scrolls in the mid-twentieth century. The Dead Sea manuscript discoveries support the integrity of the Masoretic Text nearly eight hundred years in advance of the Masoretes themselves.[18] Karen Jobes and Moisés Silva declare, "The remarkably faithful work of the Masoretes assures us that the form of their text takes us as far back as the late first century of our era."[19] Indeed, biblical texts from the Judean Desert prove that the Masoretic Text was already stable prior to the time of Jesus.[20]

Since God himself sovereignly controls the giving of his Scriptures, confidence in the Bible's teachings rests upon the belief that he also sovereignly preserves his written Word without undue alteration.[21] As Al Wolters points out, "The relative uniformity of the witnesses to the biblical text is far greater than its variety."[22]

Hebrew Numbers

As we saw with the comparison of 2 Samuel 24 and 1 Chronicles 21, parallel texts sometimes contain what, at first glance at least, appear to be contradictory readings. One subset of apparent contradictions involves

---

spelling are legitimate: "The writing in Daniel of Nebuchadnezzar for Nebuchadrezzar, involving the change of *r* to *n*, may be explained either by assuming that the former is the Aramaic for the latter, or that the *r* is changed to *n* as in the example given in Lidzbarski." He argues that proper names, even with variant spellings, were meticulously recorded and "transmitted with the most minute accuracy. That the original scribes should have written them with such close conformity to correct philological principles is a wonderful proof of their thorough care and scholarship; further, that the Hebrew text should have been transmitted by copyists through so many centuries is a phenomenon unequaled in the history of literature." Ibid., 71.
[18] Al Wolters, "The Text of the Old Testament," in *The Face of Old Testament Studies: A Survey of Contemporary Approaches*, ed. David W. Baker and Bill T. Arnold (Grand Rapids, MI: Apollos/Baker, 1999), 21; Tov, *Textual Criticism of the Hebrew Bible*, 107–10.
[19] Karen H. Jobes and Moisés Silva, *Invitation to the Septuagint* (Grand Rapids, MI: Baker Academic, 2000), 147.
[20] Ibid., 177.
[21] A full discussion of the topic of Scripture preservation is available in William D. Barrick, "Ancient Manuscripts and Biblical Exposition," *Master's Seminary Journal* 9, no. 1 (Spring 1998): 25–38.
[22] Al Wolters, "Text and Textual Criticism," in *Dictionary of the Old Testament: Historical Books*, ed. Bill T. Arnold and H. G. M. Williamson (Downers Grove, IL: InterVaristy Press, 2005), 960.

differences between large numbers cited in parallel texts. Chronicles and parallel texts agree on the numbers cited in 194 out of 213 instances[23]—a fairly low percentage (approximately 9 percent) of apparent contradictions. In texts containing such numerical differences, Chronicles uses a higher number in eleven places and a lower number in seven places. There are several possible explanations for these differences.

POTENTIAL SCRIBAL MISTAKES

The Hebrew text has "40,000" stalls for chariot horses at 1 Kings 4:26, while 2 Chronicles 9:25 has "4,000" stalls. Likewise, "700" charioteers are mentioned by 2 Samuel 10:18, whereas 1 Chronicles 19:18 gives the number as "7,000." In each of these cases, a simple mistake in copying the number in the early stages of writing and/or transmitting the Hebrew text might involve merely the addition or loss of a dot above a Hebrew letter representing the initial value.[24]

POTENTIAL VARIATION IN REPORTING

In some cases, the differences simply reflect a different basis for counting or reckoning. The historical heading for Psalm 60 refers to the events of 2 Samuel 8:1–14 and 1 Chronicles 18:1–13. "Abishai" appears in place of "Joab" in 1 Chronicles 18:12, whereas 2 Samuel 8:13 refers to David. The differences might reflect the chain of command: David as commander-in-chief, Joab as field commander, and Abishai as a subordinate to Joab. The figure of "12,000" in Psalm 60 occurs as "18,000" in 2 Samuel 8:13 and 1 Chronicles 18:12. The variation in number might reflect different methods of calculating and/or reporting casualties at separate levels in the chain of command. Perhaps the differences involve different battles within the military campaign. ("Edom" is "Aram" in 2 Sam. 8:13. Perhaps both Edomites and Arameans joined the campaign against David's forces.[25]) It is not unusual for such computations to vary in accord with different estimators.[26] My West Point graduate son, serving at one time with the United States Army's Central Command, confirmed this for casualty figures from Iraq and Afghanistan. In fact, according to him, such variations in the

[23] Payne, "Part I: The Validity of the Numbers in Chronicles," 125–26.
[24] R. Laird Harris, *Inspiration and Canonicity of the Scriptures* (Greenville, SC: A Press, 1995), 95; Archer, "Alleged Errors and Discrepancies," 60–61.
[25] C. F. Keil and F. Delitzsch, "The Books of Samuel," trans. by James Martin, in C. F. Keil and F. Delitzsch, *Commentary on the Old Testament*, 10 vols., C. F. Keil and F. Delitzsch (1880; reprint.; Peabody, MA: Hendrickson Publishers, 1996), 2:611.
[26] R. K. Harrison, *Introduction to the Old Testament* (1969; repr., Peabody, MA: Hendrickson, 2004), 1165.

biblical record regarding this particular situation give it the air of authenticity historically and militarily.

Rounding Numbers

Sometimes differences involve either rounding or not rounding numbers: 2 Samuel 5:5 ("seven years and six months") versus 1 Chronicles 29:27 ("seven years"), or 2 Samuel 24:9 ("500,000") versus 1 Chronicles 21:5 ("470,000"). It is possible in the latter instance that the book of Samuel included thirty thousand Benjamites not listed by the Chronicler,[27] or it could be that the author of 2 Samuel rounded the Chronicler's figure upward. A similar instance of rounding could explain the difference between the twenty-three thousand cited by the apostle Paul in 1 Corinthians 10:8, as compared to the calculation of twenty-four thousand for the same event in Numbers 25:9. Vern Poythress asks, "Was the precise number halfway between, at 23,500?"[28] In the common use of language, nearly every culture rounds numbers without the intent to contrast or provide different statistical data. As such, this variation does not amount to error in the biblical record.

J. Barton Payne's conclusion to his analysis of numbers in Chronicles deserves repeating: "The claims so often repeated about impossible numbers in Chronicles simply are not true. Those who join with Jesus Christ in affirming the inerrancy of the Scriptures have no need to modify or redefine that doctrine because of numerical phenomena occurring within these inspired books."[29]

New Testament Use of the Old Testament

Observing the role of Old Testament quotes within the New Testament leads to the impression that the New Testament comprises God's own commentary on key portions of the Old Testament. For example, passages such as Acts 2:23–36 and 13:34–37 demonstrate that the messianic interpretation of Psalm 16:10 arises out of the Old Testament text itself.

Apostolic interpretation of Old Testament texts, however, speaks to only one category of New Testament use of the Old Testament. For instance, G. K. Beale argues that the New Testament citations from a wide range of Isaianic prophecies prove that evangelicals are walking on thin ice

---

[27] Archer, *Encyclopedia of Bible Difficulties*, 189.
[28] Vern Sheridan Poythress, *Inerrancy and the Gospels: A God-Centered Approach to the Challenges of Harmonization* (Wheaton, IL: Crossway, 2012), 58.
[29] J. Barton Payne, "The Validity of the Numbers in Chronicles: Part II," *Bibliotheca Sacra* 136, no. 543 (July 1979): 220.

to side with those who hold to multiple authorship of the book of Isaiah.[30] He concludes that a careful study of the Isaiah authorship issue provides proof that Jesus did not err in his affirmations about Scripture.[31] Indeed, the same arguments might be applied to both Mosaic authorship of the Pentateuch and Davidic authorship of the psalms bearing superscriptions apparently indicating his authorship.[32]

An examination of the New Testament use of the Old Testament involves a large amount of material, as well as multiple interpretive approaches and methodologies.[33] The topic demands a much longer and more detailed study than this chapter can provide. I will cite just one example— the citation of Hosea 11:1 in Matthew 2:15,[34] which has been categorized as "notoriously thorny."[35] Scholars have taken a variety of approaches in an attempt to resolve Matthew's apparent noncontextual use. One of the more innovative is that taken by Walter Kaiser, who attempted to demonstrate that the context of Hosea 11:1 itself indicates a messianic meaning.[36] A simpler and more direct solution seems to be available, however.

Richard Longenecker takes the position that New Testament writers quote the Old Testament out of context.[37] He places Matthew 2:15 and the citation of Hosea 11:1 among the texts that he sees as inconsistent with the original meaning of the Old Testament passage. Taking a similar approach to that of Longenecker, Peter Enns claims that Matthew's interpretation "turns Hosea's retrospective observation into a prophetic utterance" and "is not constrained by Hosea's context."[38] However, Matthew's use must be understood within his presentation of Jesus as the legitimate representative of the nation of Israel. Jesus replicated Israel's national history in his own life.[39]

---

[30] G. K. Beale, *The Erosion of Inerrancy in Evangelicalism: Responding to New Challenges to Biblical Authority* (Wheaton, IL: Crossway, 2008), 123–59.

[31] Ibid., 158.

[32] Ibid., 159.

[33] See Rynold D. Dean, *Evangelical Hermeneutics and the New Testament Use of the Old Testament: "If the Bugle Produces an Indistinct Sound . . ."* (Iron River, WI: Veritypath, 2009); Kenneth Berding and Jonathan Lunde, eds., *Three Views on the New Testament Use of the Old Testament*, Counterpoints (Grand Rapids, MI: Zondervan, 2007).

[34] For a more extensive treatment of this question, see chapter 14 in this volume, "The Use of Hosea 11:1 in Matthew 2:15: Inerrancy and Genre" by G. K. Beale.

[35] G. K. Beale, *Handbook on the New Testament Use of the Old Testament: Exegesis and Interpretation* (Grand Rapids, MI: Baker Academic, 2012), 60.

[36] Walter C. Kaiser Jr., *The Uses of the Old Testament in the New* (1985; repr., Eugene, OR: Wipf & Stock, 2001), 43–53.

[37] Richard N. Longenecker, "'Who Is the Prophet Talking About?' Some reflections on the New Testament's Use of the Old," *Themelios* 13, no. 1 (Oct/Nov 1987): 4.

[38] Peter Enns, "Response to Professor Greg Beale," *Themelios* 32, no. 3 (May 2007): 10.

[39] Craig L. Blomberg, "Matthew," in *Commentary on the New Testament Use of the Old Testament*, ed. G. K. Beale and D. A. Carson (Grand Rapids, MI: Baker Academic, 2007), 8. Blomberg writes, "Moreover, Jesus will prove faithful where the nation had been faithless; in numerous respects he recapitulates the history of Israel as a whole." He cites W. Kynes, *A Christology of Solidarity: Jesus as the Representative of His People in Matthew* (Lanham, MD: University Press of America, 1991) as support for his statement.

God sent the Israelites into Egypt to preserve their lives; God also sent Jesus into Egypt with his parents to preserve his life. Subsequently, God brought Israel (God's "son") out of Egypt in the exodus; he now also brings Jesus (God's Son—the only messianic title in Matthew 2) out of Egypt. Matthew does not rip Hosea 11:1 from its context, nor does he make it mean anything different than Hosea intended. Hosea 11:1 speaks of Israel, not the Messiah.

Beale assigns this example to the category of indirect typological prophetic fulfillment.[40] Rather than understanding the typological reference to the qualifications of Messiah, he takes it to refer to another "exodus" of God's people out of the nations (not just Egypt).[41] Either way, the interpretation does not indicate a noncontextual use of Hosea.

Conclusion

Evangelical exegetes and expositors must accept the biblical text as the inerrant and authoritative Word of God. As noted above, adhering consistently to this declaration of faith requires us to admit our ignorance. That ignorance, however, is no excuse to compromise the integrity of the Bible or to avoid preaching it with authority. Whether the difficulty encountered in the biblical text falls into the category of potential textual critical issues, differences between texts involving Hebrew numbers, the apparent freedom of New Testament use of the Old Testament, or any of a number of other types of problems, Scripture proves dependable. We must not lose sight of the unique character of the Bible as God's own Word, superintended in its writing by the Holy Spirit (2 Pet. 1:20–21).

Some Scripture difficulties have sat for millennia without any other acceptable approach than simply trusting that God knows what he is talking about, even if we do not quite get it. Consider the belief that the Hittites were a figment of the Old Testament writers' imaginations, which was widely held until, in the late nineteenth century, archaeologists discovered their ancient capital city in Turkey and recovered a wealth of tablets and inscriptions documenting their existence, their history, and their culture. The discoveries unmasked the historical and biblical skeptics and the practitioners of a hermeneutic of doubt. They revealed the hubris of scholars who give up on finding a viable solution rather than holding tenaciously to the authenticity, integrity, and accuracy of the biblical text in spite of their own ignorance.

---

[40] Beale, *Handbook on the New Testament Use of the Old Testament*, 58.
[41] Ibid., 60–64.

The Sadducees sought to trap Jesus by their questions and to discredit him and his teaching. Jesus responded by rebuking them for not knowing either the Scriptures or God's power (Matt. 22:29–33). Those Sadducees had committed two basic errors: (1) they had assumed that the nature of the afterlife could be extrapolated from the nature of present life and (2) they had failed to consider God's power to transform an individual's state of being.[42] The tactics of present-day evangelicals who question biblical inerrancy reveal similar mistaken concepts. First, they conclude that the Scriptures must contain error by extrapolating from the fallen condition of mankind. Second, they fail to adequately consider the nature and power of the divine Author himself to superintend and preserve his written Word. The vast majority of apparent contradictions can be traced back to a Sadducee-like tendency to discredit the accuracy of Scripture in an attempt to make it a more human product, rather than to recognize the dominance of the divine Author.

---

[42] See David L. Turner, *Matthew*, Baker Exegetical Commentary on the New Testament (Grand Rapids, MI: Baker Academic, 2008), 531–32.

17

The Holy Spirit and the Holy Scriptures

INERRANCY AND PNEUMATOLOGY

Sinclair B. Ferguson

"Mystery is the life blood of dogmatics," wrote Herman Bavinck.[1] The veracity of his axiom is, of course, related to and rooted in the so-called Creator-creature distinction. God is not a man. He is a different kind of being, underived, independent, infinite, the great "I AM," one in three and three in one. As such, he relates to all things in a manner that is different from the creature, even the supreme creature, man—and, indeed, in an unimaginably different manner. Our concepts and language describe this distinction, but can never define it. Our language about God always has an accommodated, creaturely form, legitimated only by the fact that he has made all things to reflect his glory and has made man, male and female, in his image.

We recognize this to be true in all of our talk about God and in every

---

[1] Herman Bavinck, *Reformed Dogmatics*, 4 vols., ed. John Bolt, trans. J. Vriend (Grand Rapids, MI: Baker Academic, 2003–2008), 2:29.

sphere of theology. The relationship of the Creator to the creature always "surpasses knowledge," even if, through his self-revelation to us as appropriately created receptors, we are able to grasp it.[2]

God, for example, is omnipresent and eternal. But his presence (which is "omni") relates to the space-time continuum in a manner altogether different from my relationship to it. The fact that I occupy a specific "space" (say six feet by fourteen inches by five inches) does not delimit his omnipresence (as though it surrounded my space but was excluded from it). This would be a misconceptualization of reality and a misstep in theology. No; God-relationship is an altogether different kind of phenomenon from my creaturely relationship to any created reality. Because we are not God, there is an inevitability to our limited grasp of his being and actions, both within himself (*opera ad intra Trinitatis*) and beyond himself (*opera ad extra Trinitatis*). This is what we mean when, with Bavinck, we say that mystery is always the starting place, as well as the concluding point, of theology.[3]

Yet the wonder is that God is a revealer of mysteries. We do not fully comprehend them, but nevertheless we may grasp them within the limitations of our creatureliness.

The Holy Spirit

If this is an important general theological axiom, it is certainly true whenever we speak about the person of the Holy Spirit and his mode of operation and relationship to man. To use our Lord's analogy, "The wind [*pneuma*] blows where it wishes, and you hear its sound, but you do not know where it comes from or where it goes. So it is with everyone who is born of the Spirit" (John 3:8). If this is true of the *sine qua non* of seeing and entering the kingdom of God (John 3:3, 5), then it is surely correspondingly true of all of the Spirit's operations. Indeed, his very title ("Spirit") conveys an atmosphere somewhat distinct from that of either "Father" or "Son." These latter have points of connection with us in terms of human relationships. "Spirit" also has a connection, but a more mysterious one. If you doubt it, ask someone to define the terms *father* and *son*, and then to define the term *spirit*.

What becomes increasingly clear throughout Scripture, however, are

---

[2] This is a principle Paul employs in relationship to the love of God, but, *mutatis mutandis*, it is applicable to the whole, to every aspect of, the Creator-creature relationship. By parity of reasoning, this may be said about all divine "attributes," including those sometimes described as "communicable."

[3] In all of our theological thinking, we want simultaneously to be both "clothed and in [our] right mind" (Mark 5:15) and yet also "lost in wonder, love, and praise" (from the hymn "Love Divine, All Loves Excelling" by Charles Wesley, 1747).

(1) the rich and intimate relationships between the Spirit and the Father and the Spirit and the Son (he is the Spirit "of" both; Rom. 8:9) and (2) the role the Spirit characteristically plays in the external acts of the Trinity.

The fathers of the church insisted that the persons of the Trinity never act independently, nor should we ever think of one person abstracted from the others. Yet each person characteristically plays a distinct role: the Father plans, the Son mediates, the Spirit effects and completes. This is true in creation (e.g., Gen. 1:1–3), in providential governing (and restraint) (e.g., Gen. 6:3), in redemptive history,[4] in the incarnation,[5] and in the actual application of salvation to believers (1 Cor. 6:11).

The Spirit occupies a similar role epistemologically. God has acted and revealed himself in creation, providence, and history, culminating in his grand action in Jesus Christ. But how do we have *access* to the facts and to their true interpretation so that we may come to know God as he is and trust and love him because of what he has done? How does he become *our God* in this sense? According to Scripture, the final connecting links are made by the ministry of the Holy Spirit. In the postapostolic age, those connecting links are, in one form or another, ultimately related to the giving of Scripture.

The God-Breathed Word

The best-known New Testament text on Scripture, while having in view its *practical effects*, emphasizes the Spirit's originating role by stating that all Scripture is *theopneustos* (θεόπνευστος), or "breathed out by God" (2 Tim. 3:16).

As Benjamin B. Warfield demonstrated with copious references, the force of this *hapax legomenon* is passive.[6] It refers to Scripture's origin in God ("God-breathed") and not to its activity ("breathing-out God"). Even if there is a sense in which this is what Scripture does, that it does so is a function of its God-breathed quality.

While Paul's vocabulary is unique, it simply summarizes a claim evidenced throughout Scripture and confirmed in the New Testament. It can hardly have been accidental that his term is a compound of *theos* (θεός,

---

[4] This is seen perhaps most strikingly in Isaiah's commentary on the exodus, in which what God does (deliver his people from Egypt) is mediated through the angel of the Lord and executed by the Spirit—against whom, alas, the people rebelled. See Isa. 63:7–19.
[5] Jesus is conceived by the Spirit, anointed with the Spirit, led by the Spirit to defeat Satan, effects his miracles through the Spirit, offers himself as a sacrifice in the Spirit, is raised by the power of the Spirit, energizes his church by the Spirit, and will subdue all things by the power that is at work in him (presumably the Holy Spirit). See Matt. 1:18; 4:1; 12:28; Heb. 9:14; Rom. 1:4; Acts 2:33; Phil. 3:21.
[6] Benjamin B. Warfield, *The Works of Benjamin B. Warfield*, 10 vols. (New York: Oxford University Press, 1927), 1:229–80.

"God") and *pneuma* (πνεῦμα, "Spirit"), since the Spirit is the breath of God.[7] Scripture comes to us through the ministry of the Holy Spirit. This is a major element in its own teaching about itself.

Scripture "Claims"?

It is said that there is no point at which "Scripture as a whole" makes this claim about "Scripture as a whole."[8] After all, this would virtually necessitate that the last words of the Bible contain a dogmatic statement about the Bible as a whole (perhaps including a statement, akin to those found in a number of confessions of faith,[9] about what actually constitutes the Bible as a whole). But, in fact, in a wide variety of ways, the books of Scripture bear testimony—and, on occasion, a cross-fertilized testimony—to their divine origin. The claim of the editor of 2 Samuel that David's words constitute an "oracle of . . . the anointed of the God of Jacob" and his record of David's "last words"[10]—"The Spirit of the LORD speaks by me; his word is on my tongue . . ." (2 Sam. 23:1–2)—provide one of many illustrations of a Spirit-consciousness on the part of the authors of the Old Testament, an understanding that they constituted a line of individuals through whom God breathed out his Word. Thus, Hebrews summarizes the entire period of redemptive history until Christ: "Long ago, at many times and in many ways, God spoke to our fathers by the prophets" (1:1). The Word comes *from* God; it is spoken *through* the prophets. He is the origin, the ultimate Author; they are the speakers or writers through whom he breathes out his Word.[11]

It is noteworthy that when "God" speaks, he does so through the Spirit. This is the New Testament's understanding, as several references make plain:

> In those days Peter . . . said, "Brothers, the Scripture had to be fulfilled, which *the Holy Spirit spoke* beforehand by the mouth of David concerning Judas . . ." (Acts 1:15–16)

> "Sovereign Lord, who made the heaven and the earth and the sea and everything in them, who through the mouth of our father David, your servant, *said by the Holy Spirit* . . ." (Acts 4:24–25a)

---

[7] The parallelisms in Ps. 104:29–30 underscore this relationship within the context of Paul's mind-set being structured by the teaching and vocabulary of the Old Testament.

[8] Notably by Professor James Barr in his *Fundamentalism* (London: SCM, 1978), 78. "All this," writes Professor Barr, "is nonsense."

[9] E.g., the Gallic Confession, III (1559), the Belgic Confession, Article 4 (1561), the Thirty-Nine Articles, Article 6 (1562), the Irish Articles, I (1615), and the Westminster Confession of Faith, 1.2.

[10] In this context, presumably his last prophetic words, not his dying words.

[11] I have tried to illustrate this conscious awareness in Paul's letters in *From the Mouth of God: Trusting, Reading, and Applying the Bible* (Edinburgh: Banner of Truth, 2015), 28–30.

"*The Holy Spirit was right in saying* to your fathers through Isaiah the prophet . . ." (Acts 28:25)

The same perspective runs through the letter to the Hebrews:

Therefore, *as the Holy Spirit says*, "Today if you hear his voice, do not harden your hearts . . ." (3:7–8a)

But into the second [section of the tabernacle or temple] only the high priest goes, and he but once a year, and not without taking blood, which he offers for himself and for the unintentional sins of the people. By this *the Holy Spirit indicates* that the way into the holy places is not yet opened . . . (9:7–8a)

And *the Holy Spirit also bears witness to us, for after saying*, "This is the covenant that I will make with them . . . ," *then he adds*, "I will remember their sins and their lawless deeds no more." (10:15–17)[12]

It has been wisely observed that the strongest confirmation of any particular biblical doctrine is found not so much in the key "big" or "proof" texts, but in its pervasiveness throughout Scripture, especially in almost casual references in passages where the central burden is not that particular doctrine. The fact that God speaks by his Spirit is established by these several quotations. In none of them is the doctrine of biblical inspiration the central issue. Yet, *en passant* as it were, the role of the Holy Spirit in the giving of Scripture is "accidentally" highlighted—as is the conviction, occasionally evident, that through the Word that was written (past tense), God continues to speak (present tense).

This point—the reality of the ministry of the third person of the Trinity in the giving of Scripture—has often been neglected because the chief polemical issues surrounding the doctrine of Scripture have focused not on the agent in inspiration but on the more general issues of inspiration, authority, or reliability. Yet if the Spirit's role is hinted at in the use of the term *theopneustos* (2 Tim. 3:16), it is elsewhere made explicit:

Concerning this salvation, the prophets who prophesied about the grace that was to be yours searched and inquired carefully, inquiring what person or time the Spirit of Christ in them was indicating when he predicted the sufferings of Christ and the subsequent glories. It was

---

[12] The striking existential and contemporary nature of the Spirit's witness mentioned here will be discussed later.

revealed to them that they were serving not themselves but you, in the things that have now been announced to you through those who preached the good news to you by the Holy Spirit sent down from heaven, things into which angels long to look. (1 Pet. 1:10–12)

Four things should be noted here:

First, in view here is the central message of the Old as well as the New Testament. Peter's reference to the suffering and glory of the Messiah is reminiscent of Jesus's instruction in which he drew various lines from the Old Testament to show how they converged in himself and in his death, resurrection, and glory (Luke 24:25–27, 32, 44–49).[13]

Second, the revelation that was transmitted through the prophets, though not fully understood by them, was sourced in the ministry of the Holy Spirit, who is one and the same as "the Spirit of Christ."

Third, the ultimate source of old covenant (and therefore "Old Testament") written revelation[14] was one and the same as the source of the gospel, since the apostles preached the new covenant message "by the Holy Spirit sent down from heaven."

Fourth, the preached Word and the written Word are both attributed to the Holy Spirit. The written Word is simply the preached revelation written.

What is stated *en passant* elsewhere is here stated dogmatically, and indeed further elaborated by Peter:

No prophecy of Scripture comes from someone's own interpretation. For no prophecy was ever produced by the will of man, but men spoke from God as they were carried along by the Holy Spirit. (2 Peter 1:20b–21)[15]

Peter's choice of verb is significant. The authors of Scripture *wrote* (or dictated to an amanuensis) the text of Scripture. But Peter's verb is *spoke*. Here, speech and writing share a common character. In this communicative act, the authors were "carried along" by the Spirit.

This is a particularly striking statement since it refers not simply to the

---

[13] "Moses and all the Prophets" (v. 27); "in all the Scriptures" (v. 27); "the Law of Moses and the Prophets and the Psalms" (v. 44); "the Scriptures" (v. 45).

[14] The revelation was "written" because, as the text makes clear, the prophets understood they were to serve a future generation, not merely speak to their contemporary generation, implying the permanence of the revelation they received and passed on.

[15] The significance of verse 20 has been much discussed: does "no prophecy . . . comes from someone's own interpretation" refer to (1) the experience of the prophet who speaks the word or (2) the hearer who receives and understands the word. For (1), see R. Bauckham, *Jude, 2 Peter*, Word Biblical Commentary (Waco, TX: Word, 1983), 229–33; for (2), see Thomas Schreiner, *1, 2, Peter, Jude*, The New American Commentary (Nashville: Broadman & Holman, 2003), 322–23. Either interpretation is consistent with the point made here with reference to verse 21.

quality of the Scriptures as Spirit-given, or God-breathed, but refers also to the *mode* by which this giving took place. The Spirit "bore" the authors. The verb *pherō* (φέρω) is used four times in verses 17–18 (twice) and verse 21 (twice). The voice of God on the Mount of Transfiguration carried from heaven to earth (vv. 17–18); prophecy is not borne from the will of man, but "men spoke from God as they were carried along ["borne"] by the Holy Spirit." The same verb is used of a ship being carried along by the wind (Acts 27:15, 17). The ship "sails," but its ability to do so depends on and is resourced by the wind. There are analogies here to the manner in which Scripture is given: the penmen wrote, but in their writing they were "carried along" by the Spirit.

We inevitably ask further questions: How did this happen? What did the authors experience? But Peter's words are not porous at this point, and answers will not be found by dogmatic deduction from these texts, but only by a broader observation of the testimonies found in Scripture itself. The modes are varied (*polytropos*, πολυτρόπως), as the author of Hebrews notes (1:1).

In fact, some few parts of Scripture come to us by a form of divine dictation. This is not to claim the much-maligned "dictation theory" of inspiration—an analogy characteristically used to describe the *result* of inspiration (the very words God wished), but frequently abused as though it referred to the *mode* of inspiration. This misrepresentation notwithstanding, when God said, "Write," the biblical authors wrote what they were commanded (e.g. Ex. 34:27; Rev. 2:1, 8, 12; 3:1, 7)!

Scripture indicates a variety of modes were employed by the Spirit: visions, dreams, ongoing application of the covenant law, applications of earlier promises, meditations on God's glory, remembering what Jesus said, doing careful research, and so on. These phenomena alert us to the fact that the inspiration of Scripture is the fruit of the multidimensional activity of the Holy Spirit. It includes, but is not confined to, the existential moment of penning the original *autographa*.[16] In particular, we observe here a ministry of preparation of the authors and one of superintendence of their writing.

This should not surprise us, insofar as the giving of the Scriptures is an

---

[16] Two comments are in order here. It is recognized, of course, that the "original" of some parts of Scripture may predate their inclusion in a book of Scripture. The "faithful sayings" in the Pastoral Epistles predate the writing of these letters. Their "inspiration" is a function of their inclusion in the text Paul wrote or dictated. It should also go without saying that "inspiration" attaches to the *autographa*. Indeed, this is virtually a truism for the simple reason that it is the text undergirding our copies that constitutes the "divine original." Unfortunately, much unnecessary academic fussing has taken place over this concept—paradoxically by authors who might well be quick to point out to their publishers that they have found "errors" in the published versions of their manuscripts, such that the manuscripts do not represent *what they originally wrote!*

aspect of the overarching providence of God in history. In this respect, the classical term *inspiration* can prove to be more misleading than illuminating if it conveys the impression that inspiration is a kind of existentially experienced divine afflatus rendering the biblical authors wholly passive and in a virtually trancelike condition in relation to the actual composition of the text. Rather, inspiration has an organic as well as an immediate dimension. This is an important aspect of the doctrine of Scripture that has been emphasized especially by Reformed theologians.[17]

Inspiration—Two Dimensions[18]

When we say that Scripture is "inspired" as the result of the ministry of the Holy Spirit, we do not mean that the Spirit makes every sentence in it *inspiring*. Many are, but some are mundane; they are "inspiring" only when read within the larger context of Scripture's grand narrative. For instance, "I left Trophimus, who was ill, at Miletus" (2 Tim. 4:20b) is not particularly "inspiring," nor does it carry the weight of a statement such as "Christ Jesus came into the world to save sinners, of whom I am the foremost" (1 Tim. 1:15b). Yet, set within the larger context of the Pauline mission, it can "inspire." However, when Paul wrote that all Scripture is "inspired by God" (2 Tim. 3:16 NASB),[19] he was not thinking about its *effect on us* (inspiring), but about its *source in him* ("God-breathed").[20]

Warfield explains:

> It is very desirable that we should free ourselves at the outset from influences arising from the current employment of the term "inspiration."
> . . . This term is not a Biblical term, and its etymological implications[21] are not perfectly accordant with the Biblical conception of the modes of the divine operation in giving the Scriptures. The Biblical writers do not conceive of the Scriptures as a human product breathed into by the Divine Spirit, and thus heightened in its qualities or endowed with new qualities; but as a Divine product produced through the instrumentality of men. They do not conceive of these men, by whose instrumentality Scripture is produced, as working upon their own initiative, though energized by God to greater effort and higher achievement, but as

---

[17] Notably by Warfield, e.g., *Works*, 1:101, and especially Bavinck, *Reformed Dogmatics*, 1:435–48.

[18] I am following here, and employ, my discussion in *From the Mouth of God*, 9–17.

[19] Second Tim. 3:16 is the only text in which, strictly speaking, the Scriptures are described as "inspired."

[20] He describes its effect or usefulness *later* in the verse when he explains the ways in which Scripture is "profitable," or useful, in our lives—to "inspire" us to receive its teaching, feel its rebukes, be "corrected" and transformed, and to be equipped for service!

[21] The root meaning and significance of the word itself.

moved by the Divine initiative and borne by the irresistible power of the Spirit of God along ways of His choosing to ends of His appointment.[22]

Warfield's reticence about the term is well founded. The Bible is not a book *into which* God breathed, *breathing into* ("in-spiring"[23]) what men had already written, but something that God himself "breathed out." "In-spiration" actually involved God *breathing out* his Word ("exspiration"). This is why, in the New Testament, the expressions "God says," "the Holy Spirit says," and "Scripture says" are seen as virtually interchangeable. If Scripture states it, then (since Scripture is God-breathed) we can say: God, through the Holy Spirit, has said it.[24]

But how does this take place?

Concurrence

Undoubtedly the human writers of Scripture were conscious that they were expressing their own thoughts as they wrote. But at the same time, they were under the sovereign direction of the Spirit. Theologians call this two-dimensional reality "concurrence."[25] It is a characteristic of divine providence. God acts to bring about his purposes, but he does so through human means in a way that maintains human activity and responsibility.[26] He is active in the event in a "God manner," while we are active in the same event in a "human manner."[27] We cannot collapse these two dimensions into one and apportion, say, 50 percent of the event to the action of God and 50 percent to man. While this is a common perception, it is a misapprehension that carries disastrous theological and practical implications.

There is mystery here, of course, but it is in the nature of the case. God is God; we are not. But while this is so, the concept of concurrence prevents us from employing mistaken logic and concluding that if God is active in an event, then, to that extent, man must be inactive. It is this fundamental *theological* error that leads people to an automaton view of inspiration, in

---

[22] Warfield, *Works*, 1:99.

[23] From the Latin verb *spiro*, "to breathe," and the preposition *in*, meaning "in or into."

[24] See Gal. 3:8 and Rom. 9:17, where "Scripture" is really the equivalent of "God"; and Matt. 19:4–5 (quoting Gen. 2:24), Heb. 3:7 (quoting Ps. 95:7), and Acts 4:24–25 (quoting Ps. 2:1), where what "Scripture says" is regarded as equivalent to what "God says."

[25] From the Latin verb *concurrere*, "to run together," from which we get our English word *concurrent*, that is, events that take place simultaneously.

[26] As the Westminster Confession of Faith notes, in relation to sovereign divine ordination, "nor is violence offered to the will of the creatures, nor is the liberty or contingency of second causes taken away, *but rather established*" (3.1).

[27] Outstanding illustrations of this principle are found in Gen. 50:20 and Acts 2:23.

which the Spirit is perceived as rendering the writer wholly passive, perhaps even wholly inactive at the cognitive level.

But only unthinking readers of Scripture have ever held this view.[28] And only prejudiced theologians imply that this is the "conservative" or "traditional" (or worse, "fundamentalist") view of divine inspiration. Paradoxically, these theologians sometimes commit the opposite error, concluding that if human authors were actively involved in the writing of Scripture, then it must by definition be fallible and errant. To make such an *a priori* claim is to imply that the divine action was limited by the human engagement.[29]

Here, the christological parallel proves to be helpful. The Son of God assumed real humanity in the womb of the (sinful) Virgin Mary. He was genuinely of the seed of David (and of Abraham, and ultimately of Adam; Matt. 1:1; Luke 3:23–38). Gabriel said to Mary, "*You will conceive* in your womb" (Luke 1:31), yet only because "*the Holy Spirit will come upon you*, and the power of the Most High will overshadow you" (v. 35). Thus, "that which is conceived in her is from the Holy Spirit" (Matt. 1:20), and "therefore the child to be born will be called holy—the Son of God" (Luke 1:35). Here is both concurrence (the Spirit overshadows; Mary conceives) and a Spirit-guaranteed holiness (the "child to be born will be called holy"—a moral "inerrancy"), preserving Jesus from the sinfulness that is characteristic of fallen humanity (but not definitive of humanity as such).

Rather than say, "The Spirit was 50 percent active, while Mary accomplished the other 50 percent," or, "If Mary conceived in her womb, the child must, by definition, have been fallen, sinful, and errant," Scripture teaches us that both deity and humanity were involved, and that the Spirit secured the moral inerrancy of the humanity of the Savior.

In a parallel way, the inspiration of the Bible is a special example of concurrence. God fulfilled his purpose by means of secondary causation.[30] The Spirit of God was 100 percent engaged in *breathing out* his Word; the human authors were 100 percent active in *writing out/dictating* that Word.

---

[28] A more careful reading of the theologians who have used metaphors—such as Scripture coming through the authors as music comes from a lute—usually indicates that, set in the broader context of the authors' work, the metaphors refer to the product of inspiration rather than to the mode.

[29] It is therefore inadequate to parrot, "To err is human, to forgive is divine," since, strictly speaking, erring is not a function of *human nature* as such but of *fallen people*.

[30] The Westminster Confession of Faith well expresses the idea: "Although, in relation to the decree of God, the first cause, all things come to pass immutably and infallibly; yet by the same providence, he ordereth them to fall out according to the nature of second causes, either necessarily, freely, or contingently" (5.2). The same principle can be seen in Paul's description of the process of sanctification in Phil. 2:12–13.

The Scriptures came from or by (*apó*, ἀπό) the Spirit, but also through (*diá*, διά) the human author.

The early church clearly understood this. Thus, for example, when they quoted from Psalm 2:1–2, they understood these words to entail God speaking by the Holy Spirit through the mouth of King David (Acts 4:24–26). David spoke/wrote, but as he did, the Spirit governed his life so that all David wrote was in keeping with God's purposes.

There were, therefore, two elements involved in the inspiration of the Scriptures. God (1) overruled the lives of those who wrote the Bible, in ways that would prepare them to write it, and (2) superintended them as they wrote.

Same Spirit, a Variety of Ways of Working

Scripture's claim to be Spirit-borne should not be seen to create any real tension with the diversity of styles, thought patterns, linguistic preferences, or descriptions of personal experiences in the authors. This diversity—it is hard to imagine Jeremiah preaching Isaiah's sermons, or the author of Chronicles writing the Song of Solomon, or Paul writing 1 John—is an illustration of Paul's principle that in the exercise of spiritual gifts, there is a diversity of operations, yet one and the same Spirit at work (1 Cor. 12:4–6). Again, Warfield pointedly (and in his day, somewhat controversially) described what this means:

> If God wished to give his people a series of letters like Paul's, he prepared a Paul to write them, and the Paul he brought to the task was a Paul who spontaneously would write just such letters.[31]

One result of this is that the nature of the Spirit's work in giving Scripture cannot be deduced from the mere statement of the fact that he does work. It must be expounded in terms of the nature of the Scriptures themselves. Its contents were composed in very different ways. A few parts of it came in the context of unusual mystical experiences. The book of Psalms was composed over an extended period of time. In places (such as the book of Job), it contains reflections on the activity and even the character of God that flow from the author's theological and spiritual malfunctions. "Inspiration" turns out to have been a complex phenomenon because it was embedded in the historical process.

---

[31] Warfield, *Works*, 1:101.

Take another New Testament example: how did the Spirit "inspire" Luke's Gospel? The author tells us:

> It seemed good to me also, having followed all things closely for some time past, to write an orderly account for you, most excellent Theophilus, that you may have certainty concerning the things you have been taught. (1:3–4)

Luke was not an eyewitness of the events he describes, nor was he the penman of a mystical revelation. Rather, he was a careful researcher. The Spirit shaped him with gifts and opportunities to do this, then superintended his activity.

The book of Revelation provides a further illuminating illustration of the Spirit's activity in the production of Scripture. No New Testament book sits closer to mystical experience. John received the revelation from Jesus when he was "in the Spirit on the Lord's day" (1:1, 10). Yet John himself frequently described what *he himself saw* (for example, 1:12; 5:1; 6:9; 7:1; etc.).[32]

It is clear that the lenses through which John "saw" were crafted according to a prescription filled with Old Testament imagery and language. He did not make up the vision. Yet he could not have described what he saw in the terms he did unless his mind was *already* deeply imbued with a profound knowledge of the Old Testament Scriptures.[33]

Here is a vivid, yet essentially simple and obvious, proof of Warfield's point. John "sees" the book of Revelation during the period he describes himself as being "in the Spirit on the Lord's day" (that is, within the time constraints of a Sunday!). But in order for him to "see" and be the penman of this part of Scripture, it was necessary for the Spirit to have prepared

---

[32] Thus, while there is some "dictation" in Revelation (chaps. 2–3), the dominant verb is "see" (vision), not "write" (dictation).

[33] Sometimes, in an effort to demonstrate connections to the Old Testament in the text of Revelation, commentators fall into the trap of describing the biblical allusions as though John were consciously piecing together the vision itself from the Old Testament. The more encyclopedic commentaries become in their inclusion of every intertextual hint, the more likely it is that this way of expressing things will occur. But— at least for those who hold to a biblical doctrine of the Spirit's work in inspiration—it is of considerable importance to make clear that John describes what was actually "there" in his vision; that is to say, it was because of his superlative knowledge of the Old Testament that he was able to describe the visions God gave him in their appropriate terms. Put otherwise, a person without John's knowledge of the Old Testament would have described the same things differently; without the appropriate categories in his mental equipment, he would not have been able to "see" and therefore "write" what was actually "there." Think of a child's answer to the question, "What do you see?" Answer: "A bird." "Describe it for me please." "It has a small head, a soft covering, two feet, two eyes, and wings with which it flies." Then contrast the answer a leading ornithologist would give to the same question. The ornithologist has the categories in his mental equipment to explain the significance of what the child sees, and so he does so more fully, in greater detail. Both "see" the same object, but they do not perceive the same things. That said, in describing what he sees, the ornithologist is not "making it up," but more fully exegeting the same perceived reality.

John in advance to see what he would see. His whole life, of necessity, had required the Spirit's superintendence of his lifelong study and absorption of the Old Testament in order to enable him both to recognize the imagery he would see and to describe it in terms of its Old Testament connections. The way in which the Spirit gave us the text of the book of Revelation thus provides an illustration of how inscripturated revelation as a whole comes to us, through long-term providential preparation and under the immediate superintendence of the Holy Spirit in the actual writing of the text.[34] In this sense, the Spirit has embedded, in the text he has "inspired," clues to how "inspiration" took place.

There is a further, and often neglected, dimension to the Spirit's work.

The apostles were empowered by the Holy Spirit to fulfill the Great Commission.[35] Insofar as this commission was originally given exclusively to the apostles (as Matthew specifically states; 28:16), a question arises: How were they to accomplish this? While it may not be a necessary deduction from Jesus's command, the apostolic band realized that a *de facto* requisite for this commission to be accomplished to the ends of the earth *and* to the end of the age was a written form of the gospel message—in a word, new Scriptures, what we know as "the New Testament."

If there is a hesitation to see this as a *necessary* logical conclusion of Christ's commission, it is important to realize that Christ gave such a responsibility to the apostles' in the context of his Upper Room Discourse (John 13:1—17:26).

Links in a Chain of Inspiration

The discourse begins with our Lord's dealings with Peter and Judas, and continues by explaining how the disciples will be helped and strengthened through the coming of the Spirit. This is set in the midst of Jesus's remarkable revelation of the interaction of the three persons of the Trinity. Here we find a strand of teaching that illuminates his specific purposes in sending his Spirit to the apostles:

> But the Helper, the Holy Spirit, whom the Father will send in my name, he will teach you all things and bring to your remembrance all that I have said to you. (John 14:26)

---

[34] If Charles H. Spurgeon could say of John Bunyan, "Prick him anywhere and he flows bibline," we can surely say of John, "Look into his eyes and you will see their color is Old-Testamentine!"

[35] John 20:21–23 contains parallels to what is also in view in Matt. 28:18–20. The responsibility of the apostles to teach others everything Christ commanded them, and the horizons of this task ("all nations" and "the end of the age"), seem to require something beyond the *vivae voces* of the apostles themselves.

When the Spirit of truth comes, he will guide you into all the truth, for he will not speak on his own authority, but whatever he hears he will speak, and he will declare to you the things that are to come. He will glorify me, for he will take what is mine and declare it to you. All that the Father has is mine; therefore I said that he will take what is mine and declare it to you. (John 16:13–15)

Here are three promises about what the apostles would experience through the coming of the Spirit. They would (1) remember the words of Christ, (2) understand the mystery of Christ, and (3) receive revelation regarding the future fulfillment of his kingdom.

All this would be the end result of a divine dynamic. In the discourse itself, this involves the Son receiving from the Father, and the Spirit in turn receiving from the Son and the Father, and taking that which he has received to the apostles (vv. 14–15).

This becomes even clearer when Jesus prays for the apostles and for all who will later come to faith:

- He had received the words he spoke from his Father. His words were his Father's words. The Father had granted him a "power of attorney" in the world to act and speak on the Father's behalf and with his authority (17:7–8).
- Jesus then had given these words to the apostles. They had received and believed them. Now, in turn, he grants them a "power of attorney." This will take place through the ministry of the Spirit, who, having received from Christ what he in turn has received from the Father, will communicate this to the apostles (v. 14).
- The apostles' task is now to give those words to others who will come to believe in Jesus (v. 20).

The new Word of God for the new age thus comes through these links:

Father → Son → Spirit → apostles → whole church

In this way, *inter alia*, the promise of Jesus will be fulfilled:

When the Helper comes, whom I will send to you from the Father, the Spirit of truth, who proceeds from the Father, he will bear witness about me. And you also will bear witness, because you have been with me from the beginning. (15:26–27)

Here, in the teaching of Jesus, we hear a striking prophecy of divine and human concurrence. The Spirit, who has been with Jesus "from the beginning" (i.e., from the beginning of the incarnation, and, in a deeper sense, from all eternity), and the apostles, who have, in a lesser sense, been with Jesus "from the beginning" (i.e., the beginning of his ministry), together will bear witness to him. We see this given a first fulfillment on the day of Pentecost. But Pentecost is not the *terminus ad quem*. As is clear from the extension of Jesus's prayer to those who believe in him through the apostles' word (17:20), this witness will be borne everywhere men and women come to believe through the apostolic testimony. By implication, the New Testament is in view. For if we ask, "Where do we find all these promises of the Spirit's ministry coalescing?" the answer, surely, is "In the New Testament!"

Here Jesus was specifically preparing his apostles through the coming ministry of the Spirit to give the New Testament to the church.[36] This was what he had in view when he promised that the Spirit would remind them of his words, lead them into the truth, and reveal the things that were still to come.

The apostles' "word" thus became the contents of the New Testament: Gospels (what Jesus said and did); Epistles (the truth about Jesus); and Revelation (the things still to come[37]). In these ways—memory of things said and done, understanding of the gospel, a sense of future things, and the ability to articulate the revelation—God would "breathe out" through them the New Testament Scriptures to add to the Old Testament, which they, with Christ, received as the Spirit-breathed Word of God.

Links in a Chain of Illumination

There is a further work of the Spirit, however, which Paul implies when he speaks about the communication of the Word of God (1 Cor. 1:18–2:16).[38]

Paul eschewed the style of the classical orators ("lofty speech or wisdom"). Instead, he employed the rhetoric of the cross. Neither was his disposition one of self-assurance based on his talents and training, but of "weakness . . . fear and much trembling." Yet his speech and message were

---

[36] It is worth noting here in passing, by way of *caveat*, the common modern tendency to apply Jesus's words in John 14:26 and 16:13 (especially the latter: "[The Spirit] will guide you into all the truth") directly to ourselves. But we were not present in the upper room. These words were not spoken to or about us. Their fulfillment is found in the ministry of the apostles. If they have any *application* to us, it involves our searching the Scriptures where the apostles recorded the truth into which the Spirit thus led them.

[37] One wonders if the apostle John reflected on what he had written in John 16:12–15 after he had completed the book of Revelation!

[38] Here it is a safe assumption that whether the Word is spoken or written, the same dynamic is operative.

"in demonstration of the Spirit and of power, so that your faith might not rest in the wisdom of men but in the power of God" (1 Cor. 2:3–5).

Here Paul is describing the Spirit's concursive operation: "my speech and my message . . . in demonstration of the Spirit" (v. 4). This wisdom of God had been "*revealed* . . . through the Spirit" (v. 10), but God had also given him the Spirit so that he "might *understand* the things freely given us by God" (v. 12). Paul experienced the Spirit's work of superintending the "inspiration" of the apostolic word as illumination. The communication of this revelation led, in turn, to the hearers' illumination.

Notice that the dynamic pattern here is reminiscent of that in the Upper Room Discourse: the Father had given the Son his words; he, through the Spirit, had given the words to the apostles; and they had received them and would go on to speak them with the authority of the Father and the Son. This they would be enabled to do only when the Father and the Son sent the Spirit to them. The Spirit who gave the revelatory Word is the same Spirit who illumines the hearer's or reader's understanding by saving and transforming reception of the Word.

The Spirit has now come with a full divine power of attorney. He "searches everything, even the depths of God" (v. 10). Paul has been commissioned into this "chain of revelation and illumination," for the wisdom of God has been "revealed to [him] through the Spirit" (v. 10). Now he can impart it to others "in words . . . taught by the Spirit" (v. 13). The result is a "demonstration of the Spirit and of power, so that your faith [the Corinthians', but surely ours also] might not rest in the wisdom of men but in the power of God" (v. 4).

The Spirit gave Scripture to us through his servants. There was concursive activity in the *donation*. But there also needs to be concursive activity in the *reception*, for apart from the Spirit's work, "the natural person does not accept the things of the Spirit of God, for they are folly to him, and he is not able to understand them because they are spiritually discerned" (v. 14).

In the presence of the inscripturated Word, we are by nature in the same position as was Nicodemus in the presence of the incarnated Word—we can neither see nor enter the kingdom (John 3:3, 5). We are spiritually dead, blind, and deaf. How, then, can we receive the Word of the gospel contained in the Scriptures? We can do so only when the Spirit works in us with and by the Word itself to open our eyes and ears to see, hear, and respond to the illumined Word. In Paul's words to Timothy, when we "think over" the apostolic word, "the Lord will give . . . understanding" (2 Tim. 2:7).

This is exactly what the Thessalonians experienced. The people "received the word of God . . . [and] accepted it not as the word of men [merely] but as what it really is, the word of God, which is at work in you believers" (1 Thess. 2:13). How so? Because the "gospel came . . . not only in word, but also in power and in the Holy Spirit and with full conviction" (1:5). The joint testimony of the Spirit with the Word reaches into the hearts of hearers/readers with the result that they are enabled to see the kingdom although they have been blind, and to hear the voice of Christ although they have been deaf.

In this way, in a Lazaruslike phenomenon, it is the word that Christ speaks in the power of the Spirit that makes those who are in fact deaf actually hear! Herein lies the mystery: words that Lazarus was not able to hear effected in him the ability to hear those very words! Similarly, illumination takes place not by the apostolic word *apart from the Spirit*, nor by the Spirit *apart from the apostolic word*, but through the Spirit and the Word operating together, concursively.

Thus, as in our understanding of *inspiration*, so in our understanding of *illumination* we find an analogy in Christ. His Word enables the deaf to hear, the blind to see, the lame to walk, the leper to be cleansed, and the dead to live (Matt. 11:4–5). He spoke to those who were "foolish" and "slow of heart," and his words caused their hearts to burn (Luke 24:13–35). He later "opened their minds to understand the Scriptures" (v. 45). He still does. And the point he underlines in the Upper Room Discourse is that what he did during his earthly ministry will be continued by *allos paraklētos* (ἄλλος παράκλητος), "another Helper" like himself, who will come in his place to continue and consummate his ministry (John 14:16).[39]

What Christ did, then, through his personal presence on his resurrection day, he now does throughout the last days by the Spirit's illumination of the Word. Thus, in the words of William Cowper (1731–1800):

The Spirit breathes upon the word,
And brings the truth to light.[40]

Of course, Cowper was describing the experience of illumination from the perspective of appearance and experience—it seems as if something has

---

[39] The distinction between the Greek words for "another"—*allos* (ἄλλος), another of the same kind, and *heteros* (ἕτερος), another of a different kind—may not always have been sustained, but certainly in this context Jesus is underlining for the disciples the intimacy of the relationship between himself and the Spirit and his presence and that of the Spirit.
[40] The opening line of the hymn "The Light and Glory of the Word," in *Olney Hymns* (1779; repr., Olney, UK: The Cowper and Newton Museum, 1979), Book II, hymn LXII, 255.

happened to the Bible. But it would be both inconsistent and anachronous to think he was adopting a neoorthodox view of Scripture![41] Theologically, of course, it would be truer to say that it is on the reader/hearer that the Spirit breathes through and with the Word, thus giving illumination of the Word through the Word itself. We *hear* something that has been there all the time—in his Word, the Father is always "addressing" us (*present* tense) (Heb. 12:5).

This is the ministry that John Calvin well described as the *internum testimonium Spiritus Sancti*, and we can do no better than listen to his words:

> The highest proof of Scripture derives in general from the fact that God in person speaks in it. . . . We ought to seek our conviction in a higher place than human reasons, judgments, or conjectures, that is in the secret testimony of the Holy Spirit. . . .
>
> The testimony of the Spirit is more excellent than all reason. For as God alone is a fit witness of himself in his Word, so also the Word will not find acceptance in men's hearts before it is sealed by the inward testimony of the Spirit. The same Spirit, therefore, who has spoken through the mouths of the prophets must pentrate into our hearts to persuade us that they faithfully proclaimed what had been divinely commanded. Isaiah very aptly expresses this connection in these words: "My Spirit which is in you, and the words that I have put in your mouth and of the mouths of your offspring, shall never fail" (Isa. 59:21). Some good folk are annoyed that a clear proof is not ready at hand when the impious, unpunished, murmur against God's Word. As if the Spirit were not called both "seal" and "guarantee" (2 Cor. 1:22) for confirming the faith of the ungodly; because until he illumines their minds, they ever waver among many doubts![42]

This, then, is how we *hear* the Word of God as the Word of God. This is how the Father addresses us and how the Son speaks to us—when the Spirit engages us through Scripture.

Implications for Inerrancy?

These pages have provided something of an overview of the role Scripture *specifically* attributes to the Holy Spirit in relationship to Scripture. Insofar

---

[41] That is, that Scripture is not so much in itself the Word of God, but "becomes the Word of God" to us existentially.

[42] John Calvin, *Institutes of the Christian Religion*, ed. John T. McNeill, trans. Ford Lewis Battles, Library of Christian Classics, vols. 20–21 (Philadelphia: Westminster John Knox Press, 1960), 1:78–80.

as the Spirit is in some senses the executive person of the Trinity, what can be said about inerrancy in general can also be said of the Spirit and his ministry. But within the confines of this particular study, several implications for inerrancy can be derived *specifically* from the exposition above.

1. *The possibility of inerrancy.* In his ministry of sanctifying believers, the Spirit clearly works in and though sinful humanity without as yet perfecting it. Few Christians have doubted that they remain sinners and continue to err, although indwelt by the Spirit. But the Spirit is not constrained by our sinfulness. Mary was sinful, yet she bore the inerrant Son of God; the humanity of Christ was derived from Mary, yet "sanctified, and anointed with the Holy Spirit above measure."[43] In the same way, Scripture is sanctified and preserved by his power.

2. *The theological argument for inerrancy.* When God speaks, what he says is expressive of his character and is by implication therefore inerrant. Since Scripture comes to us through the work of the Spirit, we may say that it is the special work of the Spirit to accomplish this. He is himself divine and also the person of the Trinity who effects in the world the purposes of God. Consistently in the New Testament, the new Word and words that accompany and interpret the incarnation of Christ are said to be the fruit of the Spirit's ministry. This divine testimony bears its own divine character, namely, inerrancy. Men and women may lie to the Holy Spirit, and do so (cf. Acts 6:3). But he does not lie to them.

3. *The integrity of the Spirit.* Whenever the Holy Spirit is mentioned in relation to Scripture, the absolute integrity of what he says there is implied and assumed, never doubted, and certainly never contradicted or accused of error. The ease with which this truth is recognized carries with it the assumption that the verbal integrity characteristic of the person of the Spirit is manifested in the Scriptures the Spirit gives. Thus, it is no aberration when Luke virtually concludes the Acts of the Apostles with a quotation from Isaiah 6:9–10 introduced by Paul's comment, "The Holy Spirit was right in saying . . ." (Acts 28:25).[44]

4. *The reliability of the Spirit's work.* Peter attributes God's carrying of the prophetic Word to its divinely intended destiny specifically to the Holy Spirit. This implies that we are given in Scripture precisely the revelation God intended us to receive. Again, therefore, it is to be received as expres-

---

[43] Westminster Confession of Faith, 8.2.

[44] Paul uses *kalōs* (καλῶς) here in the sense of "correct, in a manner free from objection"; literally, "Right was the Holy Spirit . . ."!

sive of his character. This is not to adopt a naive view of inerrancy,[45] but to say that the Spirit who gives Scripture expresses his holy character in it in a manner analogous to the way he sanctified the human nature assumed by God's Son.

In this sense, we can have the same confidence in the Spirit's ministry in relationship to Scripture as we have in relationship to his Son. In both, he commits himself to historical realities, indeed to the historical process; in both, he preserves the integrity of his gracious gifts.

The inerrancy of Scripture is a confession of faith. In the very nature of the case, we are not able to prove *a posteriori* that every statement in the Bible is error-free. Nor can we have absolute confidence in Scripture unless it is confirmed by an authority equal to or greater than itself. In this, too, the Spirit who has given us Scripture remains faithful by giving his own testimony to Scripture by the way he illumines it to us in its true light. He who carried the Word of Scripture into history continues to minister to us in our place in that same history so that as we read the Word he has brought to us, we recognize it for what it really is—the inerrant Word of the inerrant God, breathed out to us through the One who is to him as his own breath, the Holy Spirit.

Thus, when it is said, "This is the Word of the Lord," we know we can trust it without reservation, and therefore we say, "Thanks be to God!"

---

[45] One of I. H. Marshall's criticisms of the concept is that there are statements in Scripture in which to ascribe inerrancy is, essentially, a category mistake. For instance, whereas John 11:18, "Bethany was near Jerusalem, about two miles off," may be true or false, inerrant or errant, Jesus's command, recorded later in the chapter, "Take away the stone" (v. 39), can be neither inerrant nor errant. *Biblical Inspiration* (Grand Rapids, MI: Eerdmans, 1982), 54. But the point of claiming inerrancy is not to suggest that all biblical statements are truth claims, but that God has breathed out his Word in a way that preserves its truthfulness and integrity. In addition, clearly there are "errors" in Scripture. We meet one as early as Gen. 3:4, in the lie of the Serpent. The point, however, is that it is indeed true that this was the form the first temptation took.

18

How the Perfect Light of Scripture Allows Us to See Everything Else

INERRANCY AND CLARITY

Brad Klassen

In December 1520, Martin Luther published a work that became famous more for the controversy it created than for its contents. Part of the storm that ensued centered on the genre of the book, which was represented by the first word of its title—*Defense*—a word that appropriately described Luther's confidence in his theological convictions amid growing opposition from the Roman Catholic Church.[1] What evoked particular anger was the basis Luther claimed for making his defense: "Scripture is by itself so certain, simple, and accessible," he argued, "that it interprets itself, testing, judging, and illuminating everything else."[2] This declaration set the stage for one of the most famous debates in all of church history over the nature of God, revelation, and authority.

---

[1] The work was written in Latin under the title *Assertio omnium articulorum M. Lutheri, per Bullam Leonis, X. novissimam damnatorum* (*Defense of All the Articles of M. Luther Condemned by the Latest Bull of Leo X*). It is included in D. *Martin Luther's Werke: Kritische Gesamtausgabe* (Wiemar, Germany: 1883–1929), 7:94–151.
[2] Ibid., 7:97.

Luther's chief opponent was the Roman Catholic scholar Desiderius Erasmus. His most direct disagreement was with Luther's assertion that the unbeliever is completely enslaved to his sinful nature. In response, Erasmus published his own work in 1524, entitled *On the Freedom of the Will: A Diatribe or Discourse.*

But more than a defense of free will, Erasmus's work dealt with a subtle point of epistemology (the nature and grounds of human knowledge). Erasmus's opening sentence immediately identified his fundamental presupposition: "Among the difficulties, of which not a few crop up in Holy Scripture, there is hardly a more tangled labyrinth than that of 'free choice.'"[3] For Erasmus, Scripture's teaching on the human will was ambiguous, so the making of any assertions on the issue solely on the basis of the Bible was intellectually and morally dangerous. In fact, Erasmus's reluctance to see sufficient clarity in Scripture extended far beyond the issue of the human will. He admitted openly that "so far am I from delighting in 'assertions' that I would readily take refuge in the opinion of the Skeptics."[4] While some of his dislike was due to the arrogance with which some made assertions, his fundamental reason sprang from his conviction concerning the nature of the Bible itself and its ability to impart knowledge. Erasmus explained:

> For there are some secret places in the Holy Scriptures into which God has not wished us to penetrate more deeply and, if we try to do so, then the deeper we go, the darker and darker it becomes, by which means we are led to acknowledge the unsearchable majesty of the divine wisdom, and the weakness of the human mind.[5]

For Erasmus, doctrinal assertions could not be made on the basis of the Bible alone, since the Bible did not provide the necessary clarity. The Bible's purpose was to inspire man to worship, which was to be done most often in mystic silence and not in irreverent inquisitiveness. And while there were specific things in the Bible that were indeed clear, these were limited to moral teachings related to "the good life."[6] To go beyond this and claim the Bible as the sufficient and decisive authority for establishing doctrines was a grave mistake, for the Bible on its own was not sufficiently clear.

[3] Desiderius Erasmus, *On the Freedom of the Will*, in *Luther and Erasmus: Free Will and Salvation*, trans. and ed. E. Gordon Rupp and Philip S. Watson, Library of Christian Classics, vol. 27 (Philadelphia, PA: Westminster Press, 1969), 35.
[4] Ibid., 37.
[5] Ibid., 38. For evidence that Erasmus also allowed for error in Scripture, see "Letter 844 (May 15, 1518)," in *Collected Words of Erasmus*, vol. 6, *The Correspondence of Erasmus, Letters 842–992, 1518–1519*, trans. R. A. B. Mynors and D. F. S. Thomson (Toronto: University of Toronto Press, 1982), 28, 30.
[6] Erasmus, *On the Freedom of the Will*, 39–40.

Not to be misunderstood, Erasmus nonetheless affirmed the need for Scripture. "The same Scriptures," he stated, "are acknowledged and venerated by either side. Our battle is about the *meaning* of Scripture."[7] By denying Scripture's clarity while still affirming its importance, Erasmus argued for the necessity of an additional authority—the Roman Catholic Church—whose duty it was to make Scripture's authority real by clarifying its obscurities. Consequently, doctrinal discussions were to be conducted under the direction of the pope and his bishops; it was not "proper to prostitute them before common ears," as Luther had done with his publications.[8] Untrained common folk could not be trusted to apply the nuanced methods of allegorical interpretation or grasp the complexities of centuries of church tradition, which itself was viewed as a conduit of divine revelation.

The following year, in 1525, Luther countered Erasmus with *On the Bondage of the Will*. While focused on the debate over human freedom and sovereign grace, the book powerfully articulated many of the fundamental principles that powered the Reformation.

Aiming at Erasmus's distaste for assertions, Luther stated:

> For it is not the mark of a Christian mind to take no delight in assertions; on the contrary, a man must delight in assertions or he will be no Christian. And by assertion—in order that we may not be misled by words—I mean a constant adhering, affirming, confessing, maintaining, and an invincible persevering.[9]

In contrast to the misery caused by uncertainty, Luther described true Christianity as a life of confidence in divinely revealed truth: "The Holy Spirit is no Skeptic, and it is not doubts or mere opinions that he has written on our hearts, but assertions more sure and certain than life itself and all experience."[10]

The basis for Luther's certainty was not a naive enthusiasm regarding human reason; his position on the intellectual abilities of fallen man was evident. Rather, certainty was established by the nature of the Bible itself. God had given a *clear, accessible Word* that could be read and understood

---

[7] Ibid., 43 (emphasis added).
[8] Ibid., 40. The Reformers' drive to translate the Bible into the vernacular languages of their day and distribute tracts and written sermons to the public—even in the face of martyrdom—was based on their belief that the average person could and must understand the contents of Scripture. It is said that William Tyndale stated to an opponent of his effort to translate the Bible into English, "If God spare my life, ere many years I will cause a boy that driveth the plough shall know more of the Scripture than thou dost." David Daniell, *William Tyndale: A Biography* (New Haven, CT: Yale University, 1994), 1.
[9] Martin Luther, *On the Bondage of the Will*, in *Luther and Erasmus*, 105.
[10] Ibid., 106.

on its own merits. For the Christian to respond with skepticism and doubt, or to appeal to other authorities for more sure answers, was not Christlike humility but immoral disbelief—the same kind that marked mankind's plunge into depravity in the first place.

This did not mean that Luther denied the reality of mystery or divine incomprehensibility. To affirm that God's Word was clear was not to suggest that it exhaustively revealed everything about God. Man's responsibility, however, was to not trespass beyond the text into speculation. What God had decided to make known to man was essentially clear, and the suggestion that it remained obscure was nothing less than a satanic tool to keep men from reading Scripture, portray Scripture as deficient, and open the church's doors to the plagues of philosophy.

Luther was also careful to distinguish between *external* and *internal* clarity. Regarding external clarity, Luther taught that all of Scripture's truth "has been brought out by the Word into the most definite light, and published to all the world."[11] Scripture needed no improvement to be presented to all men. Regarding internal clarity, "the Spirit is required for the understanding of Scripture, both as a whole and in any part of it."[12] Man's inability to understand was not due to Scripture's obscurity, but to the moral obstruction that was introduced by the fall, an obstruction that could be broken only by a special work of the Spirit. Like the sun that is bright in itself, Scripture's external clarity shone whether or not it was acknowledged. But that light could not be appreciated by the blind man's eyes until the Spirit performed his surgery. And even for the Christian, who now saw yet still struggled with understanding portions of the Bible, such difficulty was not due to an inherent obscurity in Scripture, but to the believer's own ignorance or immaturity. With careful study, he was able to understand difficult texts with increasing ease, particularly as he studied them in light of those he understood more easily.

Ultimately for Luther, if the Bible was not clear, there was no hope. Man could not establish knowledge by other means if God himself had failed to deliver it accessibly in his Word. "Are we not obscure and ambiguous enough," he asked, "without having our obscurity, ambiguity, and darkness augmented for us from heaven?"[13] Luther would have no part of that: "Let miserable men . . . stop imputing with blasphemous perversity the darkness and obscurity of their own hearts to the wholly clear Scriptures

---

[11] Ibid., 112.
[12] Ibid.
[13] Ibid., 162.

of God."[14] The Bible was clear enough to serve as both the first source and final arbiter for human knowledge—and it was clear enough to make that knowledge certain.

While Luther and Erasmus debated Scripture's clarity half a millennium ago, the issue remains as relevant as ever. More than just an interesting Reformation idea, the clarity of Scripture is a doctrine that is essential if we wish to make any sense of this world in which we live.

Defining Clarity

Biblical clarity has been defined as "that quality of the biblical text that, as God's communicative act, ensures its meaning is accessible to all who come to it in faith."[15] Clarity is an *inherent quality* of divine revelation—just like Scripture's necessity, sufficiency, authority, and veracity—and not simply a hermeneutical principle, denominational stance, or personal posture toward the Bible. We do not *ascribe* clarity to God's Word as a result of first determining for ourselves that it is clear. Scripture *is* clear by its very nature, whether that fact is recognized or not. In other words, God's verbal revelation was given not in a secret code or with the intent to confuse man's understanding of his nature and intentions, but in forms and with words that are comprehensible to its audience and successful in making God and his ways knowable. God is a revelatory God, a God of light. Because he himself is clear, his revelation automatically reflects that clarifying quality. God is also a missionary God. Because he desires to be truly known by his creation, his revelation is automatically successful.

As with any doctrine, the doctrine of clarity must be defined on the basis of Scripture's own witness. And when read carefully, Scripture presents no shortage of testimony. From the very beginning, the Bible emphasizes that God is a God of words, a Creator who speaks first and whose words successfully accomplish exactly what he intends (Gen. 1:3; Heb. 11:3; 2 Pet. 3:5–7). Created in God's image, man is able to use language and communicate successfully with his Creator (Gen. 1:26–30). Even after man's rebellion against God's words at the fall (Genesis 3), verbal revelation remains God's primary means of communicating his lordship, immanence, and goodness to man. That revelation becomes vitally important for the plan of redemption, for only through God's words comes the offer of the gospel (Rom. 10:13–17). Scripture testifies that God's Word is light

---

[14] Ibid., 111.

[15] Mark D. Thompson, *A Clear and Present Word: The Clarity of Scripture*, New Studies in Biblical Theology (Downers Grove, IL: InterVarsity Press, 2006), 169–70.

(Ps. 19:8; 119:105; Prov. 6:23; 2 Pet. 1:19), is intended for the common people (Lev. 1:2; Eph. 1:1), makes the young and ignorant wise (Deut. 6:6–8; Ps. 119:130; Prov. 1:1–6), effectively reveals God's expectations (Deut. 30:11–14; 2 Tim. 3:16–17), communicates most precisely his name and character (Ex. 34:5–8), serves as the standard to assess and reward obedience or disobedience (Deut. 11:26–28; Heb. 4:12–13), always accomplishes its purposes (Isa. 55:10–11), and is essential for enabling saving faith (Gen. 15:4–6; Rom. 10:17; 2 Tim. 3:15).

Scripture also testifies that its message is not simplistic, nor will every part of it be equally clear to those who do believe (2 Pet. 3:15–16). Believers are called to grow in their understanding through appropriate effort (Heb. 5:11–14; 2 Tim. 2:7, 15; 2 Pet. 3:17–18) and to discern Scripture's meaning in the context of the believing community (Acts 17:11). To assist in this process, God has given his Spirit (1 John 2:20–21, 27), as well as pastors and teachers (Acts 8:30–31; Eph. 4:11–12). At the same time, Scripture emphasizes that the unbeliever does not recognize its clarity (1 Cor. 2:14; 2 Cor. 4:4) and that God himself can choose to conceal the plain message of his Word as an act of judgment (Isa. 6:8–13; Matt. 13:11–16).

Scripture sets the limits on its own clarity. Though clear about what it reveals, it affirms the reality of secret things outside of its contents that remain a mystery (Deut. 29:29) and warns against the attempt to intrude into what God has kept hidden (Deut. 18:9–14; 1 Cor. 4:6).

Ultimately, as Luther argued, the clarity of Scripture is essential for making doctrinal assertions. Without clarity, one cannot truly "do theology," much less believe it. Those who try, while downplaying the clarity of Scripture, simply presuppose the clarity of some other source of knowledge, such as religious tradition, reason, or personal experience. Noting the essential role clarity plays, D. A. Carson observes:

> One can talk endlessly about the centrality of Scripture, the authority of Scripture, the truthfulness of Scripture, and so forth, but none of this has more than theoretical interest unless some form of responsible doctrine of *claritas scripturae*—what the English speaking world often refers to as the perspicuity of Scripture—can be sustained.[16]

The same conclusion can be drawn with respect to the Trinity, justification, the definition of marriage, or the fate of the unbeliever after

---

[16] D. A. Carson, "Is the Doctrine of *Claritas Scripturae* Still Relevant Today?" in *Collected Writings on Scripture*, compiled by Andrew David Naselli (Wheaton, IL: Crossway, 2010), 179.

death. All truly evangelical assertions of doctrine assume the doctrine of perspicuity.[17]

Clarity's Twilight

As essential as the doctrine of clarity is, it does not always receive its due recognition. While Protestants historically have considered clarity to be a core attribute of Scripture,[18] many evangelical theologies written in the past one hundred years have not even devoted a section to the subject.[19] Distortions and abuses have caused some to avoid it, while the current climate of pessimism toward truth and certainty makes clarity an unpopular discussion. This neglect has had significant ramifications.

First, neglect has allowed revisionist versions of the doctrine's history to take root. While some have contended that Luther invented it to advance his cause, others have claimed that clarity—together with inerrancy—are modernist inventions crafted only in the nineteenth century. Since we've now grown wise to the naïveté of modernist thinking, they assert, we must leave clarity behind "in favor of a better approach to Christian truth and authority."[20]

Second, neglect of the doctrine has led to a growing surrender to interpretive pluralism. Words such as *multivocality* and *polysemy*—terms used to indicate that words or statements contain multiple meanings—are now part of the exegete's vocabulary. Interpreters increasingly advocate a plurality of related or even contradictory meanings for any given text, taking no responsibility before their audiences to validate one over any of the others. Texts are said to contain "surpluses of meaning" that were not discernible to the writers themselves and are further expanded by the readers. Rather than being encouraged to discern "if these things were so" (Acts 17:11) or to look to the writer as the authority for his text (Acts 8:34), Christians are called to embrace interpretive diversity not only as an undeniable reality but as a divine blessing. The Godhead, it is argued, has multiple voices—so why not the biblical text?[21] In fact, does the text even have a voice? Is not the only voice heard that of the

---

[17] Larry D. Pettegrew, "The Perspicuity of Scripture," *The Master's Seminary Journal* 15, no. 2 (Fall 2004): 209–10.

[18] See Herman Bavinck, *Reformed Dogmatics*, 4 vols., ed. John Bolt, trans. John Vriend (Grand Rapids, MI: Baker Academic, 2003), 1:449–94.

[19] Gregg R. Allison, *Historical Theology: An Introduction to Christian Doctrine* (Grand Rapids, MI: Zondervan, 2011), 139.

[20] Christian Smith, *The Bible Made Impossible: Why Biblicism Is Not a Truly Evangelical Reading of Scripture* (Grand Rapids, MI: Brazos, 2012), 3, 145.

[21] John R. Franke, *Manifold Witness: The Plurality of Truth* (Nashville: Abingdon, 2009), 7–8.

reader?[22] The only clarity that matters in such a climate is what is clear *to me*.

Related to the advance of pluralism is the return to Erasmus's assertions of ambiguity. Words such as *obscure* and *enigma* are increasingly common in describing biblical texts.[23] There is a popular conception that for Scripture to be inspired and profound, it must defy plain language and confuse. The Bible is said to raise more questions than it answers since God has intentionally embedded obscurity into his revelation. Or it is argued that limited human language is simply unable to communicate divine truth successfully. Attempts to explain perceived discrepancies or harmonize parallel accounts in Scripture are scorned, and interpreters are called to adjust their basic belief about the Bible to one that allows for factual contradictions and regularly unresolvable ambiguities.[24]

The neglect of clarity also leads to the sacrifice of literal interpretation. The allegorical method—and its emphasis on the Magisterium as the only authoritative interpreter—rose to dominance in the medieval period in correlation with the growing belief that Scripture was obscure. Conversely, the Reformers' recovery of the doctrine of clarity—and their return of the Bible to the common people—went hand in hand with their recovery of literal interpretation.[25] This transformation was captured vividly by the Reformation's motto—*Post tenebras lux*, "After the darkness, light." Yet for many today, the momentum toward literal interpretation initiated by the Reformation is too naive. As one evangelical argued, "In our understanding of inspiration, we have probably erred on the side of a fixed, unambiguous, straightforward, descriptive text that we can defend objectively."[26] The

---

[22] For example, David J. A. Clines writes: "Today, since I think that we have moved into a post-modern age, I would be much more careful in speaking of meaning. I would not now be speaking of '*the* meaning' of the Pentateuch . . . as if there was only one meaning for the Pentateuch. Nowadays I tend rather to believe that texts do not have meaning in themselves, and that what we call meaning is something that comes into being at the meeting point of text and reader. If that is so, then meaning is reader-dependent and reader-specific, and there are in principle as many meanings as there are readers." *The Theme of the Pentateuch*, 2nd ed. (Sheffield: JSOT, 1997), 131.

[23] This is not, of course, to deny the use of figures of speech and wordplays in Scripture. Scripture makes abundant use of the rich diversity of human language. However, in order to label a text as figurative, it must be identified as such on the basis of established rather than arbitrary categories. Moreover, such designations must be legitimized on the basis of verifiable evidence from the author—from the signals he himself has left in his text to alert the reader to his intentional play on words—and not on the basis of the reader's imagination or theological preference.

[24] For example, see Peter Enns, "Inerrancy, However Defined, Does Not Describe What the Bible Does," 99–104, and Michael F. Bird, "Inerrancy Is Not Necessary for Evangelicalism outside the USA," 148–49, in *Five Views on Biblical Inerrancy*, ed. J. Merrick and Stephen M. Garrett (Grand Rapids, MI: Zondervan, 2013).

[25] Luther insisted that "we must everywhere stick to the simple, pure, and natural sense of the words that accords with the rules of grammar and the normal use of language as God has created it in man." *On the Bondage of the Will*, 221.

[26] D. Brent Sandy, "The Inerrancy of Illocution," a paper presented at the 2004 annual meeting of the Evangelical Theological Society (San Antonio, TX), 8.

amount of Scripture considered to be "nonliteral" is again vastly expanding, with complex critical methods being promoted as the only responsible means for protecting the Bible from simplicity, while at the same time making its message respectable to the academy. If the straightforward, plain interpretation of a text does not measure up to academic sensibilities, it can be rejected and the text considered "poetic" or "midrashic" instead—even if it lacks the verifiable features to support such conclusions.[27] As one scholar admitted, "The willingness *not* to take a text at face value is the essence of critical scholarship."[28]

Stumbling in Obscurity

As neglect of the doctrine of clarity leads to its rejection, serious practical consequences follow. First, evangelicalism's embrace of the concept of an obscure Bible necessitates the establishment of its own Magisterium—the higher critics—while simultaneously degrading the doctrine of the priesthood of all believers.[29] As Gerhard Maier warned, this leads to a new "Babylonian captivity":

> The representatives of the higher-critical method have given sharp opposition to the orthodox thoughts concerning the *perspicuitas* (clarity) and *sufficientia* (sufficiency) of the Scriptures. They have obscured the clarity by their "proof" of contradictions in the Bible, and they have clung to and deepened the obscurity by means of their fruitless search for a canon in a canon. They have undermined the sufficiency of the Scriptures by claiming that the historical-critical work was necessary in order to comprehend the Scriptures. To the degree that their views asserted themselves, a division set in between Scripture and congregation.[30]

Second, the demise of clarity leads to a significant expansion of the *adiaphora* of the Christian faith—the things Christians are to treat

---

[27] For example, Michael R. Licona, *The Resurrection of Jesus: A New Historiographical Approach* (Downers Grove, IL: IVP Academic, 2010), 548–53, sees the account in Matt. 27:51–53 of the resurrection of certain saints at the time of Jesus's resurrection as "a strange little text" more akin to poetry or legend than historical fact.

[28] Michael V. Fox, *Character and Ideology in the Book of Esther*, 2nd ed. (Eugene, OR: Wipf & Stock, 2010), 148–49.

[29] For a helpful survey on this development, see Keith D. Stanglin, "The Rise and Fall of Biblical Perspicuity: Remonstrants and the Transition toward Modern Exegesis," in *Church History: Studies in Christianity and Culture* 83, no. 1 (March 2014): 38–59.

[30] Gerhard Maier, *The End of the Historical-Critical Method*, trans. Edwin W. Leverenz and Rudolph F. Norden (St. Louis, MO: Concordia, 1977), 48–49.

indifferently.[31] The body of beliefs that the Bible compels man to embrace becomes increasingly limited as believers are given liberty to decide for themselves on a wide array of theological and moral issues, ranging from the nature of the atonement to homosexuality. Consequently, engaging in debate and calling on others to validate their views from Scripture is considered divisive and arrogant.[32] Without clarity, nothing can be duly judged as *error* or *sin*. The outcome is a Christianity that is defined on the basis of culture, tradition, or individualism. The church then is no longer doctrine-driven, but motivated and moved by a host of factors *other than* Scripture.[33]

Third, as clarity is denied, God's Word loses its right as both first principle and last court of appeal. In response, some embrace *traditionalism*, retreating back to Roman Catholicism to find the necessary authority to establish conviction and practice.[34] For postconservatives and Emergents, *communitarianism* is the solution, believing there to be no more effective authority for resolving what is ambiguous in Scripture than one's community of shared experience.[35] For others, *subjectivism*—in the forms of rationalism and mysticism—is the preferred response.[36]

The question of authority is "the most fundamental problem that the Christian Church ever faces."[37] The Westminster Confession of Faith expressed the implication of biblical clarity when it stated:

> The Supreme Judge, by which all controversies of religion are to be determined, and all decrees of councils, opinions of ancient writers, doctrines of men, and private spirits, are to be examined, and in whose

---

[31] See Smith, *The Bible Made Impossible*, 112. Ironically, those who, like Smith, reject the doctrine of clarity because it supposedly leads to religious anarchy by establishing the "right to private judgment," in the end advocate the same right by vastly expanding the spectrum of doctrines over which Christians can freely disagree.

[32] As John Piper has noted, "'Arrogance' is the condemnation of choice in the political and religious arena for anyone who breaks the rules of relativism." *Brothers, We Are Not Professionals: A Plea to Pastors for Radical Ministry*, rev. and exp. (Nashville: B&H, 2013), 193. Or, conversely, in the words attributed to G. K. Chesterton, "Tolerance is the virtue of the man without convictions."

[33] David F. Wells, *No Place for Truth or Whatever Happened to Evangelical Theology?* (Grand Rapids, MI: Eerdmans, 1993), 245–55.

[34] See Christian Smith, *How to Go from Being a Good Evangelical to a Committed Catholic in Ninety-Five Difficult Steps* (Eugene, OR: Cascade, 2011), 29–32. Smith joins other notable evangelical converts to Roman Catholicism in recent years, including former Evangelical Theological Society President Francis J. Beckwith.

[35] Franke, *Manifold Witness*, 81, 116; Brian D. McLaren, *A New Kind of Christianity: Ten Questions That are Transforming the Faith* (New York: HarperCollins, 2010), 103, 105, 111.

[36] Gregory A. Boyd, *Benefit of the Doubt: Breaking the Idol of Certainty* (Grand Rapids, MI: Baker, 2013), 163–66.

[37] J. I. Packer, *"Fundamentalism" and the Word of God* (Grand Rapids, MI: Eerdmans, 1958), 42.

sentence we are to rest, can be no other than the Holy Spirit speaking in the Scripture. (1.10)[38]

Fourth, the denial of clarity has significant implications for our understanding of the character of God. Francis Turretin recognized this in the era following the Reformation, when he argued that God, as the Father of lights and the Giver of all good gifts (James 1:17), "cannot be said either to be unwilling or unable to speak plainly without impugning his perfect goodness and wisdom."[39] The same argument holds true in today's context, with every attack on the clarity of revelation "ultimately an attack on the character of God—his goodness, his power, and his ability to communicate clearly to his people."[40] If Scripture leaves man without excuse, with God deciding his eternal fate on the basis of his response to Scripture's message, then to call Scripture ambiguous "is to charge God with dealing with us in a spirit at once disingenuous and cruel."[41] God is then no longer the missionary God who seeks, but a god who delights to hide himself from man in the darkness.

Finally, the denial of biblical clarity is often nothing less than an expression of prideful human autonomy, as man—despite the supposed obscurity of truth—declares his success in finding truth nonetheless. This is illustrated no better than by the eighteenth-century German philosopher Gotthold Lessing, who was instrumental in advancing the famous "quest for the historical Jesus." Lessing stated:

> For it is not the possession but the search for truth which expands man's powers and in which consists his ever-growing perfection. . . . If God would conceal all truth in his right hand, and in his left only the continuous drive for truth, though with the stipulation that I would always and forever go astray in the search, and would say to me, "Choose!," I would with humility fall into the left hand and say: "Father, give me this one! The pure truth is but for you alone."[42]

---

[38] The Reformers argued that because Scripture is clear, it is its own interpreter (*Scriptura sacra sui ipsius interpres*). It needs no higher authority to determine its meaning and is therefore to function as the ultimate authority. Confessions of faith, meanwhile, were not drafted to *clarify* Scripture, but to *systematize* and *summarize* it. Confessions such as the Westminster Confession of Faith are possible for the very reason that Scripture is clear. Subsequent generations, however, have not always been that consistent, sometimes treating the confessions as *more clear* interpretive grids through which to read *less clear* Scripture.

[39] Francis Turretin, *Institutes of Elenctic Theology*, trans. George M. Giger, ed. James T. Dennison Jr. (Phillipsburg, NJ: Presbyterian & Reformed, 1992), 1:145.

[40] Wayne Grudem, "The Perspicuity of Scripture," *Themelios* 34, no. 3 (Nov. 2009): 303.

[41] A. A. Hodge, *Outlines in Theology*, rewritten and enlarged (Grand Rapids, MI: Eerdmans, 1949), 85–86. Because God's *general* revelation—creation—is also "clear" (*phaneros*, φανερός), it leaves man without excuse for the particular knowledge it reveals (Rom 1:18–20).

[42] Gotthold Ephraim Lessing, *Anti-Goetze: Eine Duplik* (1778) in *Werke*, vol. 8, ed. H. Göpfert (Munich: Carl Hanser Verlag, 1979), 32–33.

In response, Abraham Kuyper rightly noted:

Thus for Lessing, the search for truth is more glorious than the posses-
sion of truth. But let no one be misled by this pithy saying. . . . Lessing's
statement runs perfectly parallel in the intellectual domain to work-
righteousness in the moral domain. To want to earn one's own salvation and not receive it by grace is perfectly on a par with the desire to
seek all truth by oneself and spurn any revelation of higher light. To
prefer to dispense with nine-tenths of the truth rather than to receive
the light of truth humbly and gratefully from God's hand is to want to
pick from the tree of knowledge in order to be like God and to owe
one's knowledge to no one but oneself and to own it thanks solely to
one's own effort.[43]

Nothing Left to Say

Ultimately, the denial of clarity—if held consistently—directly undercuts
the validity of any theological assertion and leads to the devastating loss
of doctrinal certainty.[44] For instance, if Scripture is not clear, how can the
"central tenets" of the Christian faith—those supposedly few, undisputable
core canons, such as the love of God—even be ascertained and expressed?
Granted, some try by imposing so-called "Christological frameworks" to
serve as a "canon-determining canon,"[45] but any careful reading of such
interpretive grids reveals much heat but little light. If the Bible—including
the Gospels—becomes clear only by reading it through a knowledge of
Christ, from where does one draw this authoritative knowledge of Christ?
In the end, such frameworks take on the same pliability as a wax nose.

The rejection of clarity inevitably leads into a dark, silent abyss. By denying clarity, we are left with no positive response to the Serpent's repeated
question, "Did God actually say?" (Gen. 3:1). As Maier stated: "Since
through Scripture we meet God and learn to know him, therefore by invali-
dating the clarity and sufficiency of Scripture, they have also destroyed the
certainty of faith. If it is uncertain *where* the living God is speaking, then I
no longer know *who* is speaking."[46] And in the same way that a denial of
the historical inerrancy of the Gospels leads to the invalidation of our faith
(1 Cor. 15:12–19), the denial of scriptural clarity empties the gospel of its

[43] Abraham Kuyper, *Scholarship: Two Convocation Addresses on University Life*, trans. Harry Van Dyke
(Grand Rapids, MI: Christian's Library Press, 2014), Kindle ebook, loc. 505.
[44] John MacArthur, "Perspicuity of Scripture: The Emergent Approach," *The Master's Seminary Journal*
17, no. 2 (Fall 2006): 144.
[45] Smith, *The Bible Made Impossible*, 93–126; Boyd, *Benefit of the Doubt*, 155–93.
[46] Maier, *The End of the Historical-Critical Method*, 49.

message and power.[47] The missionary, theologian, and preacher will have nothing left to say, for to continue to speak if the Bible is indeed obscure would be the height of human arrogance. As Luther argued, "Take away assertions and you take away Christianity."[48]

Conclusion

In the summer of 1522, several years prior to the publication of Luther's *On the Bondage of the Will*, Swiss Reformer Huldrych Zwingli declared his own position on the clarity of Scripture to an audience of nuns in a sermon entitled "Of the Clarity and Certainty of the Word of God." He concluded that sermon with this exhortation:

> And now finally, to make an end of answering objections, our view of the matter is this: that we should hold the Word of God in the highest possible esteem—meaning by the Word of God only that which comes from the Spirit of God—and we should give to it a trust which we cannot give to any other word. For the Word of God is certain and can never fail. It is clear, and will never leave us in darkness. It teaches its own truth. It arises and irradiates the soul of man with full salvation and grace. It gives the soul sure comfort in God.[49]

Submission to Scripture as the clear and inerrant Word of God leads to one conclusion: it must be *believed* in its entirety and without reservation, and *proclaimed* to the world with all sincerity and courage. Indeed, "The secret things belong to the LORD our God, but the things that are revealed belong to us and to our children forever, that we may do all the words of this law" (Deut. 29:29). With the clarity of Scripture comes the necessity of assertions, and with the necessity of assertions comes the obligation for belief and proclamation. We are left without excuse. The fate of men's souls hangs in the balance.

---

[47] Grudem, "The Perspicuity of Scripture," 289.
[48] Luther, *On the Bondage of the Will*, 106.
[49] Huldrych Zwingli, "Of the Clarity and Certainty of the Word of God," in *Zwingli and Bullinger*, ed. G. W. Bromiley, Library of Christian Classics, vol. 24 (London: SCM, 1953), 93.

19

Words of God and Words of Man

INERRANCY AND DUAL AUTHORSHIP

Matt Waymeyer

The words of Scripture are consistently presented as both the words of God and the words of man. Commonly known as *dual authorship*, this fundamental reality has profound implications for how one views the trustworthiness of the biblical text.

For those who reject the inerrancy of the Bible, the human element in Scripture plays a prominent role. According to Bruce Vawter, "A human literature containing no error would indeed be a contradiction in terms, since nothing is more human than to err."[1] The human authorship of Scripture, in other words, guarantees that the Bible contains errors.

In contrast, for those of us who defend the doctrine of biblical inerrancy,[2] the divine authorship of Scripture provides compelling evidence for its absolute trustworthiness. Because God is the Author of Scripture (2 Tim.

---

[1] Bruce Vawter, *Biblical Inspiration* (Philadelphia: Westminster, 1972), 169.
[2] This chapter will assume the definition of biblical inerrancy articulated in the Chicago Statement on Biblical Inerrancy and summarized by John D. Feinberg: "Inerrancy means that when all facts are known, the Scriptures in their original autographs and properly interpreted will be shown to be wholly true in everything that they affirm, whether it has to do with doctrine or morality or with the social, physical, or life sciences." John D. Feinberg, "The Meaning of Inerrancy," in *Inerrancy*, ed. Norman L. Geisler (Grand Rapids, MI: Zondervan, 1980), 294.

3:16)—and because he always speaks the truth (Titus 1:2; Heb. 6:18)—the Bible must be true in everything it says. As R. Albert Mohler Jr. writes, "The God who is completely trustworthy has given his people a book that is equally trustworthy."[3] In this way, the divine authorship of Scripture is proof that the Bible is completely free from error.

In the simplest of terms, the two views can be distinguished like this:

Errantist view: human authorship guarantees an errant Bible.
Inerrantist view: divine authorship guarantees an inerrant Bible.

The difference between the two positions, however, is not simply a matter of emphasizing one side of dual authorship over the other. The real difference is found in the views of the *relationship* between the two authors in the writing of Scripture.

In this chapter, I will address the implications of dual authorship for the trustworthiness of the Bible. In the process, I will demonstrate that *the relationship between the human and divine authors, as presented in the Bible itself, ensures that the text of Scripture is completely trustworthy in all that it teaches.* But first I need to frame the issue by summarizing and briefly critiquing the way human authorship is used as an argument for errors in the biblical text.

Divine Accommodation of Human Error?

Among confessing evangelicals, the most common way to deny biblical inerrancy is to say that the divine Author accommodates the errors of the human authors in the writing of Scripture. In the recent publication *Five Views on Biblical Inerrancy*, three of the contributors appeal to human authorship as the reason for the errors they see in the Bible. Peter Enns claims that the biblical writers "shaped history creatively for their theological purposes"[4]; Michael Bird describes them as storytellers who were "given to creativity"[5] and "flexible on the details"[6]; and John Franke argues that God accommodated their limited human capacities[7] and therefore that the

---

[3] R. Albert Mohler Jr., "When the Bible Speaks, God Speaks: The Classic Doctrine of Biblical Inerrancy," in *Five Views on Biblical Inerrancy*, ed. J. Merrick and Stephen M. Garrett (Grand Rapids, MI: Zondervan, 2013), 45.
[4] Peter Enns, "Inerrancy, However Defined, Does Not Describe What the Bible Does," in *Five Views on Biblical Inerrancy*, 101.
[5] Michael F. Bird, "Inerrancy Is Not Necessary for Evangelicalism outside the USA," in *Five Views on Biblical Inerrancy*, 168.
[6] Ibid., 169.
[7] John R. Franke, "Recasting Inerrancy: The Bible as Witness to Missional Plurality," in *Five Views on Biblical Inerrancy*, 267–69.

words of Scripture "remain subject to the limitations of their creaturely character."[8] This, says Franke, makes it impossible for the Bible to communicate absolute truth.[9]

This appeal to divine accommodation is not a new argument against biblical inerrancy. In fact, when Vawter insisted on the inevitability of human error a generation ago, the broader context of his assertion included the same line of reasoning. According to Vawter, speaking through human authors required that God include the various errors that these fallible writers introduced into the biblical text. In the words of Vawter, "To conceive of an absolute inerrancy as the effect of inspiration was not really to believe that God had condescended to the human sphere but rather that He had transmuted it into something else."[10] Similar reasons led Clark Pinnock to describe the Bible as "a human text beset by normal weaknesses."[11]

In more recent years, self-identified evangelical Kenton Sparks has made the same argument. Sparks, who insists that his view is "compatible with a robust, evangelical faith,"[12] claims that divine accommodation explains how and why "the one true God, who does not and cannot err, [spoke] through human discourse that includes human error."[13] According to Sparks, when God used fallen human beings to communicate his Word, he refused to run roughshod over their humanity by protecting their words from the normal limitations of human fallenness. Instead, in an act of divine accommodation, he adopted the viewpoints and perspectives of these finite human authors, including all of the limitations, foibles, and lapses in ethical judgment that were characteristic of their fallen humanity.[14] The

---

[8] Ibid., 269.

[9] Ibid., 266–70.

[10] Vawter, *Biblical Inspiration*, 169.

[11] Clark H. Pinnock, *The Scripture Principle: Reclaiming the Full Authority of the Bible*, 2nd ed. (Grand Rapids, MI: Baker Academic, 2006), 126.

[12] Kenton L. Sparks, *God's Word in Human Words: An Evangelical Appropriation of Critical Biblical Scholarship* (Grand Rapids, MI: Baker Academic, 2008), 255.

[13] Ibid., 227.

[14] Ibid., 55, 171, 224–59. According to Sparks, "Scripture's words are truly informed by and convey revealed truths from God, but these truths were received by and communicated through the finite, fallen horizon of a human author" (246). Sparks likens this accommodation to providing an overly simplistic answer to children when they ask what clouds are: "This misinformation will have to stand until their minds mature and become capable of understanding a fuller, more detailed answer" (249). In his most recent book, however, Sparks goes far beyond this portrayal of divine accommodation to speak of the "dark side" of the Bible, which he describes as "a great and holy book that admittedly includes many unsavory elements." *Sacred Word, Broken Word: Biblical Authority and the Dark Side of Scripture* (Grand Rapids, MI: Eerdmans, 2012), 11. In discussing this "dark side," Sparks claims that the Bible "stands within the fallen order" (22); it contains values that are "troublesome" and that "strike us as truly sinister and evil" (37); it contains "errant and diverse perspectives" (39); it is "a product of and evidence for the fallen world that it describes" (46); it "stands in need of redemption" (46–47); it "includes evil" (47); it contains "errant and even sinful viewpoints" (53); it "speaks the truth through perceptive yet warped human horizons" (103); it conveys "ideas that verge on what we would call vice" (103); it is "warped and broken" by human influence (111); it was written by "finite and fallen men, each with his own weaknesses and blind spots" (115); and it contains things that are

result, says Sparks, is that "the Bible contains more fictional literature than some evangelical readers can stomach,"[15] and thus it "does not fare so well when judged by the yardstick of divine perfection."[16]

It is certainly true that God accommodated himself to mankind in the Scriptures, namely by revealing truth in a way that human beings are able to comprehend. As Norman Geisler writes, "Historically, most evangelical theologians have adopted a form of divine condescension to explain how an infinite God can communicate with finite creatures in finite human language."[17] But there is a vast difference between accommodating Scripture to the *finitude* of mankind by making the truth understandable and accommodating it to the *fallenness* of mankind by adopting the errors of the human authors. The inerrantist believes that God always speaks truth and does so at a level his children can understand (accommodation to human *finitude*), but the errantist insists that God sometimes speaks falsehood because of the fallible nature of his human instruments (accommodation to human *fallenness*):

> Errantist view: accommodation to human fallenness
> Inerrantist view: accommodation to human finitude

This distinction highlights the difficulty with the accommodationist argument. According to Sparks, the fallen nature of the human authors inevitably results in errors in the biblical text: "Human beings err, and this accounts in part for the errant and diverse perspectives that sometimes appear in Scripture."[18] Elsewhere he writes, "It is precisely because the Bible is genuine human discourse that it also participates in the fallible horizons of its human authors."[19] But the simple problem with this argument is that it assumes that because human beings are fallible, therefore all human communication must be tainted by error. As John Feinberg explains, "For the human element in the Scripture to necessitate errors in the text of the Bible it must be shown that errancy is essential to humanity."[20] But this cannot

---

"ungodly" (47), "bad" (54), "unrighteous" (54), "dangerous" (69), "contradictory" (103), and "incoherent" (106). Furthermore, according to Sparks, "We can no more offer a full-orbed, detailed explanation and solution for the ethical problems in Scripture than we can offer a thorough and sensible explanation for the Nazi physicians who tortured Jewish children" (49). At the same time, Sparks believes that "God infallibly achieves his redemptive aims through the fallible words of human authors" (49).

[15] Sparks, *God's Word in Human Words*, 214.

[16] Sparks, *Sacred Word, Broken Word*, 61.

[17] Norman L. Geisler, "A Review of *Five Views on Biblical Inerrancy*," *The Master's Seminary Journal* 25, no. 1 (Spring 2014): 72.

[18] Sparks, *Sacred Word, Broken Word*, 39.

[19] Sparks, *God's Word in Human Words*, 227.

[20] Feinberg, "The Meaning of Inerrancy," 282.

be done, for if error were essential to humanity, then Adam was not human until he erred, and believers will not be human in the glorified state, since they will no longer sin or err.[21]

The fact that human beings are finite and fallen does not mean they are always in error. As D. A. Carson explains, "Human beings who in the course of their lives inevitably err and sin do not necessarily err and sin in any particular circumstance."[22] Because error is not essential to humanness or finitude, the humanity of the biblical authors did not necessitate the presence of falsehood in what they wrote, and God did not compromise their humanness by safeguarding their writings from error when they composed Scripture. The fallibility of human nature does not necessitate that all human communication is tainted by error, which is evident from the simple reality that everyone makes dozens of statements every day that are completely true.[23] The dual authorship of Scripture no more necessitates errors in the biblical text than the two natures of Christ mean that Jesus must have sinned.[24]

But the more serious problem with this view concerns the divine authorship of Scripture. Because the Bible is the Word of God, the accommodationist argument for errors in the biblical text simply cannot escape the charge that it makes God the Author of falsehood. Stated more bluntly, it makes God a liar. In contrast, Scripture repeatedly declares that God is true (John 3:33; Rom. 3:4), that all of his words are true (2 Sam. 7:28; Ps. 12:6; 18:30; 19:7, 9; 119:43, 140, 142, 151, 160; Prov. 8:8; 30:5; Luke 24:25; John 10:35; 17:17; Rev. 21:5), and that it is impossible for him to speak anything but the truth (Num. 23:19; 1 Sam. 15:29; Titus 1:2; Heb. 6:18). The simple reality is that God always speaks words that are true and he never speaks words that are false.

Consequently, the errantist view of divine accommodation undermines the very nature of God as revealed in his Word. As Wayne Grudem explains:

---

[21] Ibid.

[22] D. A. Carson, "Recent Developments in the Doctrine of Scripture," in *Hermeneutics, Authority, and Canon*, ed. D. A. Carson and John D. Woodbridge (Eugene, OR: Wipf & Stock, 1986), 28.

[23] Wayne Grudem, *Systematic Theology: An Introduction to Biblical Doctrine* (Grand Rapids, MI: Zondervan, 1994), 98.

[24] Herman Bavinck, *Reformed Dogmatics*, 4 vols., ed. John Bolt, trans. J. Vriend (Grand Rapids, MI: Baker Academic, 2003), 1:435; Kevin DeYoung, *Taking God At His Word: Why the Bible Is Knowable, Necessary, and Enough, and What That Means for You and Me* (Wheaton, IL: Crossway, 2014), 37; article II of the Chicago Statement on Biblical Inerrancy. According to Sparks, the main problem with this analogy is that Scripture does not consist of a hypostatic union of divinity and humanity, because none of the biblical authors were both divine and human: "They were human beings only—good men, perhaps, but also fallible sinners in need of redemption, who wrote texts that the church has nevertheless embraced as God's word." *Sacred Word, Broken Word*, 28–29. Unfortunately, Sparks completely misrepresents the analogy, for it is not the human writers who have two natures but rather Scripture itself, having both a human author and a divine Author. For this reason, the words of Scripture are thoroughly human and thoroughly divine.

Yes, God does condescend to speak our language, the language of human beings. But no passage of Scripture teaches that he "condescends" so as to act contrary to his moral character. He is never said to be able to condescend so as to affirm—even incidentally—something that is false. If God were to "accommodate" himself in this way, he would cease to be the "unlying God." He would cease to be the God the Bible represents him to be.[25]

It is one thing for God to adapt the teaching of truth to the capacity of human understanding, but it is quite another for him to adopt human errors and present them as divinely revealed truth.[26] In the former, God enhances effective communication; in the latter, he acts contrary to his nature.

To avoid this charge, Sparks claims that "any errant views of Scripture stem, not from the character of our perfect God, but from his adoption in revelation of the finite and fallen perspectives of [human beings]."[27] According to Sparks, "Scripture was written by godly but fallen human authors who sometimes thought and wrote ungodly things," but God is no more the Author of these errors than he is the Author of sin itself.[28] For this reason, "flaws in Scripture should not be blamed on God but rather on humanity and its sinful, fallen state,"[29] for the Bible "speaks the truth through . . . warped human horizons."[30] This could be likened to a master musician playing a concerto on a piano that is out of tune: no matter how perfectly he plays the piano, the music will reflect the imperfection of his instrument, even though he himself makes no errors.[31] For Sparks, this kind of divine accommodation is the best explanation for errors in a book that was written by a perfect God.

The problem with this reasoning is that it betrays an unbiblical understanding of the dual authorship of Scripture. To say that the Bible errs, but that God is not the one speaking falsehood when it does, is to drive a wedge

---

[25] Grudem, *Systematic Theology*, 97.

[26] Rolland McCune, *A Systematic Theology of Biblical Christianity, Volume 1: Prolegomena and the Doctrines of Scripture, God, and Angels* (Detroit: Detroit Baptist Theological Seminary, 2008), 101. As John Frame writes: "Accommodation does not mean, as some have claimed, that God speaks error to us. Rather, it means that he speaks truth in such a way that we can understand it, insofar as it can be understood by human beings. Theologians often compare divine accommodation to a parent's accommodation to his young children. But a wise parent, while choosing simple language to use with his children, does not lie to them." *The Doctrine of the Word of God* (Phillipsburg, NJ: P&R, 2010), 175. This is why Article IX of the Chicago Statement on Biblical Inerrancy denies "that the finitude or fallenness of these writers, by necessity or otherwise, introduced distortion or falsehood into God's Word."

[27] Sparks, *God's Word in Human Words*, 256. According to Sparks, "To attribute error to God is surely heresy, but to deny the errant human elements in Scripture may verge on a kind of docetism." Ibid.

[28] Sparks, *Sacred Word, Broken Word*, 46–47.

[29] Ibid., 47

[30] Ibid., 103.

[31] This illustration is not provided by Sparks, but rather is my own summary of his view.

between the human and divine authors so that some words in the biblical text have their origin in God while others have their origin in man. But understood biblically, dual authorship means not only that all the words of the biblical text are both the words of God and the words of man, but also that God is the ultimate Author of Scripture—the divine Author who spoke *through* the human authors—so that everything in the Bible is what he himself has said.[32] This leads to two inescapable conclusions: (1) the argument for errors in the Bible ascribes falsehood to the God who cannot lie, and (2) the relationship between the human and divine authors guarantees that the text of Scripture is completely trustworthy in all that it teaches. This can be seen clearly by taking a closer look at the dual authorship of Scripture.

The Dual Authorship of Divine Revelation

Although dual authorship most directly concerns the actual writing of the biblical text, it can only be understood properly within the larger framework of God's sovereignty. God did not merely select certain individuals to write the Bible—he providentially fashioned them throughout their lifetimes to become the very men who were perfectly suited to compose his written revelation at specific points in time. As Benjamin B. Warfield so eloquently stated, "God is Himself the author of the instruments He employs for the communication of His message to men and has framed them into precisely the instruments He desired for the exact communication of His message."[33] This is often referred to as *providential preparation*.

THE PROVIDENTIAL PREPARATION OF THE HUMAN AUTHOR

The human authors of Scripture possessed characteristics common to everyone who is created in God's image, as well as distinct features unique to each one of them.[34] But because the prophets and apostles lived and moved and had their being in the realm of divine sovereignty (Acts 17:28), these unique features were not left to chance—they were ultimately determined by the One who works all things according to the counsel of his will (Eph. 1:11). In the outworking of his sovereignty, God not only determined the ancestral line of each human author—along with the time and place of his birth—but also set him apart as a divine spokesman even before he

---

[32] Bavinck refers to God as "the primary author" and the human writers as "the secondary authors." According to Bavinck, an accurate view of biblical inspiration depends "on putting the primary author and the secondary authors in the right relationship to each other." *Reformed Dogmatics*, 1:428.

[33] Benjamin B. Warfield, *The Inspiration and Authority of the Bible* (Philadelphia: Presbyterian and Reformed, 1948), 92.

[34] Gordon R. Lewis, "The Human Authorship of Inspired Scripture," in *Inerrancy*, 249.

was born (Jer. 1:5; Gal. 1:15). God's providence also extended to all of the countless variables that influenced the human writer throughout his lifetime: his immediate family, his cultural context, his social environment, his personal relationships, his educational training, and all of his various life experiences from birth to the time of writing (Acts 7:20–38). God used each of these factors to prepare all of his chosen vessels to communicate his Word in precisely the way he intended when the appointed moments arrived.

At the same time, the sovereign hand of God was equally involved in the *heart* of each human writer, not only providentially guiding his innumerable responses to his life experiences (Prov. 16:1, 9), but also forming the different aspects of his personality—his emotions, his personal interests, his natural gifts and abilities, his distinct vocabulary and writing style, and his individual patterns of thought and reasoning. The entirety of this process shaped the human author into an instrument uniquely prepared to set forth the revelation of God in the pages of Scripture. As Gordon R. Lewis writes:

> Unlike a human editor of the writings of a number of different men, God did not have to wait helplessly to see what would come in. He could do far more than issue guidelines for the production. God, as an editor *par excellence*, could providentially bring into being the types of individuals, styles, and emphases He wanted.[35]

In addition to preparing the human authors, God also orchestrated all the intricately related events of human history to bring about the specific circumstances that precipitated and shaped the writing of the biblical text. Even such events as the revolt of Absalom against David (2 Samuel 15–18), the rise of heresy in Galatia (Gal. 1:6–7), and the persecution of Paul in Thessalonica (Acts 17:1–10) were ultimately ordained by God to lead to the writing of Psalm 63, Galatians, and 1 Thessalonians, respectively. Something similar could be said about almost any book in the Bible.

The result of this intricate process, including both the preparation of the authors and the orchestration of the various historical backgrounds of their writings, "was to bring the right men to the right places at the right times, with the right endowments, impulses, acquirements, to write just the books which were designed for them."[36] Thus, a proper understand-

---

[35] Ibid., 250.
[36] Warfield, *The Inspiration and Authority of the Bible*, 155. In cases where human research was involved prior to the writing of the biblical text (e.g., Luke 1:1–4), God providentially guided the entire investigative process of the human author.

ing of dual authorship requires a robust confidence in the sovereignty of God.[37]

At the same time, however, the role of the divine Author in the writing of Scripture went far beyond mere providence. In other words, when the human author sat down to write the actual words of the biblical text, the divine influence exerted upon him transcended the everyday providence of God that determines the words of all men at all times (Prov. 16:1). Instead, it consisted of a unique influence upon the biblical writer by which God ultimately revealed his own words through the pen of the human author. This divine influence is sometimes referred to as *superintendence*.

THE SUPERNATURAL SUPERINTENDENCE OF THE HUMAN AUTHOR

While providential preparation took place in the life of the human author *prior* to the writing process, supernatural superintendence occurred in the heart of the human author *during* the writing process. The clearest description of this superintendence of the biblical author is found in 2 Peter. In this epistle, the apostle exhorts his readers to be diligent in their pursuit of holiness (1:1–15; 3:11–14) in spite of the false teachers who had infiltrated their churches (2:1–22; 3:17–18). Among their many errors, these deceivers denied that Christ will return to bring judgment to the wicked and final deliverance to the righteous, insisting instead that life will continue on as always (3:3–7). Because the second coming is one of the primary motivations to be holy in the sight of God (3:14), Peter was determined to refute this error and reaffirm the certainty that Jesus will come again in judgment to establish new heavens and a new earth (3:4–13).

To reaffirm the trustworthiness of these promises, Peter seeks to strengthen his readers' confidence in the testimony of the prophets and apostles over against the novel teachings of the heretics (3:1–2). In 2 Peter 1:16–21, he substantiates his claim that Jesus will come again by pointing to these same two sources of divine authority: the eyewitness testimony of the apostles (vv. 16–18) and the written revelation of the prophets (vv. 19–21). After presenting the apostolic testimony of the transfiguration as evidence for the second coming in verses 16–18, he reminds his readers of the trustworthy testimony of the prophetic revelation in verses 19–21:

---

[37] As Warfield writes, "When we think of God the Lord giving by His Spirit a body of authoritative Scriptures to His people, we must remember that He is the God of providence and of grace as well as of revelation and inspiration, and that He holds all the lines of preparation as fully under His direction as He does the specific operation which we call technically, in the narrow sense, by the name of 'inspiration.'" Ibid., 156.

We also possess the completely reliable prophetic word, to which you do well to pay close attention as to a light shining in a dark place until the day dawns and the morning star rises in your hearts, knowing this above all, that no prophecy of Scripture arises from the prophet's own interpretation, for no prophecy was ever produced by the will of man, but men moved by the Holy Spirit spoke from God. (AT)

In this passage, Peter uses three interchangeable terms—the "prophetic word" (v. 19), "prophecy of Scripture" (v. 20), and "prophecy" (v. 21)—to shift his focus to the reliability of the written revelation of the Old Testament.[38] Because false teachers were denying the future return of Christ, Peter's immediate purpose in verse 19 is to direct his readers to pay close attention to Scripture as a completely trustworthy source of truth,[39] as a light shining in a world of darkness throughout the present age.[40] Confidence in the reliability of the written Word, along with the discernment that comes from a devotion to its message, would protect them from error that might otherwise undermine their pursuit of holiness.

To motivate his readers to give careful attention to the prophetic word,[41] Peter emphasizes the *source* of biblical revelation, reminding them in verse 20 "that no prophecy of Scripture arises from the prophet's own interpretation." In other words, in contrast to the claims of the false teachers, the revelation of the Old Testament did not originate in the personal insight or individual reflection of the prophet himself. The prophetic word does not have a human origin, Peter says, because it did not ultimately come from the mind of man, and therefore we can trust in the certainty of its eschatological promises.

When Peter speaks of the prophet's own "interpretation" (v. 20), this

---

[38] Peter's use of the word *Scripture* (*graphē*) in verse 20 indicates a reference to written rather than oral prophecy, and his terminology "*no* prophecy of Scripture" (v. 20) and "*no* prophecy" (v. 21) expands this reference to the entirety of the Old Testament rather than simply prophecies about the second coming. In addition, what Peter says here about the Hebrew Scriptures can be applied by extension to the New Testament writings as well (2 Pet. 3:15–16).

[39] The Greek adjective *bebaioteron* is comparative in its form—and thus translated "more sure" in the New American Standard Bible—but the context suggests it is used with an elative sense. For this reason, it would be better to translate it "very sure" or "completely reliable" in reference to the absolute reliability of the prophetic word, rather than to its comparative reliability in relation to the eyewitness testimony of the apostles in verses 16–18.

[40] Verse 19 says the light will continue to shine in a dark place "until the day dawns and the morning star rises in your hearts." According to Douglas J. Moo, "The dawning of the day refers generally to the eschatological climax, whereas the rising of the morning star in the heart refers to the effects of that climax in the life of the believer." *2 Peter, Jude*, The NIV Application Commentary (Grand Rapids, MI: Zondervan, 1996), 76.

[41] The participle *ginōskontes* at the beginning of verse 20 is most likely *causal* and therefore introduces the reason why Peter's readers are to pay close attention to the prophetic word: because they know it did not originate in the mind of man (vv. 20–21a), but rather in the mind of God (v. 21b).

may refer to the prophet interpreting what was revealed to him by God.[42] If so, Peter is emphasizing that the words written by the prophet did not arise from his own fallible and quite possibly mistaken notions about the meaning of the vision or revelation he received.[43] Alternatively, it may simply refer to the prophet interpreting reality from his own individual perspective.[44] In this case, Peter is denying that Scripture arose from the prophet's own contemplation of current affairs or his own personal insight into what would happen in the future.[45] But either way, his point is clear: the truth of the Old Testament did not emerge from the mind of the human author. Scripture did not originate in the contemplation of the prophet himself, and if God's people are to give due attention to his Word, they must never lose sight of this.

To further clarify the source of biblical revelation,[46] Peter continues in verse 21 by once again denying the human origin of Scripture, stating that "no prophecy was ever produced by the will of man." According to Peter, the writing of Scripture was never an act of human volition, as if the prophet spoke on his own and simply wrote what he himself had decided. Unlike the false prophets, who proclaimed "the deceit of their own minds" (Jer. 14:14; cf. 23:26; Ezek. 13:2–3, 17), the human authors of Scripture were not autonomous in their proclamations, and they did not prophesy on their own initiative. As Robert Reymond observes, "Peter totally excludes the human element as the ultimate originating cause of Scripture."[47]

---

[42] This is the view of Richard L. Bauckham, *2 Peter and Jude*, Word Biblical Commentary (Dallas: Word, 1983), 229–33; Peter H. Davids, *The Letters of 2 Peter and Jude*, Pillar New Testament Commentary (Grand Rapids, MI: Eerdmans, 2006), 211–13; John Sherwood, "The Only Sure Word," *The Master's Seminary Journal* 7, no. 1 (Spring 1996): 71–72; Gene L. Green, *Jude and 2 Peter*, Baker Exegetical Commentary on the New Testament (Grand Rapids, MI: Baker, 2008), 231–32; Moo, *2 Peter, Jude*, 77–78; D. Edmond Hiebert, *Second Peter and Jude: An Expositional Commentary* (Greenville, SC: Unusual Publications, 1989), 81–83.

[43] Moo, *2 Peter, Jude*, 77.

[44] This is the view of Frame, *The Doctrine of the Word of God*, 127; Robert L. Reymond, *A New Systematic Theology of the Christian Faith* (Nashville: Thomas Nelson, 1998), 38; John Murray, "The Inspiration of Scripture," in *Collected Writings of John Murray* (Carlisle, PA: Banner of Truth, 1982), 4:46; McCune, *A Systematic Theology of Biblical Christianity*, 83; and R. C. Sproul, *1–2 Peter*, St. Andrew's Expositional Commentary (Wheaton, IL: Crossway, 2011), 239.

[45] Reymond, *A New Systematic Theology of the Christian Faith*, 38. A third possibility is that verse 20 refers not to the *prophet's* interpretation, but rather to the interpretation of his prophecy by those who read it later. According to this view, Peter is correcting the false teachers who impose their own interpretation on the prophetic word rather than embrace its proper interpretation as given by the apostles. Although this view is possible (see Thomas R. Schreiner, *1, 2 Peter, Jude*, New American Commentary, vol. 37 [Nashville: Broadman & Holman, 2003], 322–23), it faces several significant difficulties. First, in the immediate context of this verse, Peter is specifically arguing for the trustworthiness and authority of the Old Testament, not for its apostolic interpretation. Second, the verb *ginomai* ("arise" or "come about") plus the genitive of *epilysis* ("interpretation") in verse 20 most naturally indicates the source from which something arises and therefore describes Scripture's origin rather than its interpretation. Third, this view has difficulty explaining how verse 21 provides an explanation of (or reason for) what is stated in verse 20. In contrast, these three points offer support for both views articulated above.

[46] The conjunction *gar* at the beginning of verse 21 introduces a further explanation of verse 20.

[47] Reymond, *A New Systematic Theology of the Christian Faith*, 38.

This brings us to the clearest biblical description of the relationship between the human and divine writers in the dual authorship of Scripture. In contrast to the claim that Scripture was ultimately produced by the volition of the human prophet, Peter writes that "men moved by the Holy Spirit spoke from God" (2 Pet. 1:21b). "From God" (*apo theou*) means that the words of the biblical authors ultimately had their *source* in God. This is Peter's way of recognizing the human authorship of Scripture ("men . . . spoke") and yet emphasizing the divine origin of what these human authors wrote ("from God"). In contrast to the false prophets—who "speak visions of their own minds, not from the mouth of the LORD" (Jer. 23:16)—the biblical authors proclaimed the message of God himself, for their words were ultimately his words.

According to verse 21, the prophets were able to speak forth the very words of God because they were "moved by the Holy Spirit,"[48] who is repeatedly described as "the Spirit of truth" (John 14:17; 15:26; 16:13). The verb *moved* means "to cause to follow a certain course in direction or conduct,"[49] and it describes the divine influence of the Holy Spirit on the human authors of Scripture as they wrote the biblical text. As Kevin DeYoung writes, "It suggests an assured outcome, one that is carried out and guaranteed by another."[50] According to 2 Peter 1:21, then, the human authors of the Bible wrote the very words of God because the Holy Spirit was at work within them, causing them to follow the specific course of writing what they did.

Peter does not explain how the Holy Spirit guided this process, but it is clear that the human authors were not mere secretaries, passively and mechanically writing whatever was dictated to them.[51] Instead, without suspending, suppressing, or negating their individual freedom and personalities, the Holy Spirit superintended the biblical writers in such a way that they wrote precisely what he was pleased to reveal through them, and

---

[48] The participle *moved* introduces either the reason or the means by which these men were able to speak from God. Either way, the influence of the Holy Spirit upon the human authors was the compelling factor that enabled them to speak, with God as the source of their words.

[49] Walter Bauer, Frederick W. Danker, William F. Arndt, and F. Wilbur Gingrich, *A Greek-English Lexicon of the New Testament and Other Early Christian Literature*, 3rd ed., rev. and ed. Frederick W. Danker (Chicago: University of Chicago Press, 2000), 1051. When used passively, as it is in 2 Peter 1:21, the verb is best translated "moved" or "driven" (ibid.).

[50] DeYoung, *Taking God At His Word*, 37.

[51] It is true that certain portions of Scripture were dictated by God (e.g., Ex. 17:14; 24:4; 34:1, 27–28; Deut. 10:2, 4; Isa. 8:1; Jer. 36:4; Revelation 2–3), but these occasions were clearly the exception and not the rule. At the same time, although the language of dictation is completely inappropriate to describe the *mode* of inspiration, it describes well the *results* of inspiration, for the end product was nothing less than the very words of God. See Carson, "Recent Developments in the Doctrine of Scripture," 29; Frame, *The Doctrine of the Word of God*, 142.

300 Inerrancy in Theological Perspective

yet in words of their own choice and in the style they were accustomed to using. In this way, the Spirit was not simply standing by, ready to correct or supplement any inadequacies in the human authors as they composed the biblical text.[52] Rather, he was actively working within them, supervising and guiding the process so that they freely composed the Scriptures in their own words—words that simultaneously were nothing less than the very words of God.[53]

THE ULTIMATE AUTHORSHIP OF DIVINE REVELATION

Scripture further clarifies the relationship between the two authors by consistently presenting God as the ultimate Author of what is written and man as the human instrument through whom he has spoken. In this way, the divine and human authors were both active in the writing of Scripture, but they did not play corresponding roles in the process.

More specifically, Scripture describes divine revelation as a process by which God puts his words "in the mouth" or "on the tongue" of the prophet (Num. 22:38; 23:5; Deut. 18:18; 2 Sam. 23:2; Jer. 1:9), who then speaks forth precisely those words and no others (Num. 22:35, 38; 23:5, 12, 16; Deut. 18:20–22; Jer. 26:2).[54] For this reason, not only does God describe the prophets as "my mouth" (Jer. 15:19), but he repeatedly commissions them to speak forth "my words" (Jer. 23:22; Ezek. 2:7; 3:4; cf. Jer. 26:2) and to preface their message with the proclamation, "Hear the word of the LORD" (Isa. 1:10) or "Thus says the Lord GOD" (Ezek. 2:4).[55] To ensure faithfulness to this commission, the Holy Spirit came upon the prophets and enabled them to prophesy the words of God (Num. 11:25–26, 29; 24:2–3; 1 Sam. 10:6, 10; 19:20, 23; 2 Chron. 20:14–15; Ezek. 11:5; Luke 1:67; Acts 19:6). This is what Peter describes as the prophets being "moved by the Holy Spirit" (2 Pet. 1:21; cf. Neh. 9:30; Matt. 22:43; Mark 12:36; Eph. 3:4–5). In contrast to false prophets, who do not speak "from the mouth of the LORD" (Jer. 23:16), the message of the divine spokesman is "the word of the LORD [that] came" to the prophet (1 Chron. 17:3; Ezek. 1:3; Mic. 1:1).

---

[52] Warfield, *The Inspiration and Authority of the Bible*, 95.
[53] Carson, "Recent Developments in the Doctrine of Scripture," 29, 45.
[54] Warfield, *The Inspiration and Authority of the Bible*, 86–87.
[55] The formula, "Thus says the Lord"—or one similar to it—is used 349 times in the Old Testament. As Grudem explains: "When the prophets say, 'Thus says the Lord,' they are claiming to be messengers from the sovereign King of Israel, namely, God himself, and they are claiming that their words are the absolutely authoritative words of God. When a prophet spoke in God's name in this way, every word he spoke had to come from God, or he would be a false prophet (cf. Num. 22:38; Deut. 18:18–20; Jer. 1:9; 14:14; 23:16–22; 29:31–32; Ezek. 2:7; 13:1–16)." *Systematic Theology*, 74.

This relationship between the divine and human authors is seen even more clearly in the biblical descriptions of how God spoke through the mouths of his prophets. Throughout Scripture, Old Testament prophecy is variously described as the words that God *said* through the prophets (Acts 4:25; Heb. 4:7), *spoke* through the prophets (1 Kings 14:18; 16:12, 34; 2 Kings 9:36; 14:25; Jer. 37:2; Luke 1:70; Acts 3:21; Heb. 1:1), *proclaimed* through the prophets (Zech. 7:7), *sent* through the prophets (Zech. 7:12), *foretold* through the prophets (Acts 3:18), *announced beforehand* through the prophets (Acts 7:52), *promised beforehand* through the prophets (Rom. 1:2), and *predicted* through the prophets (1 Pet. 1:10–11). In each of these descriptions, God is the One who is speaking; he is the ultimate Author who proclaimed his words through the human agency of his prophetic spokesmen.[56]

This same relationship can also be seen in Matthew 1:22 and 2:15, where the words of Isaiah 7:14 and Hosea 11:1 are described as having been "spoken by the Lord through the prophet" (AT). In this description, Matthew not only names both the human and divine authors of the Old Testament—"the Lord" and "the prophet"—but he also reinforces the previously described relationship between the two in the act of writing Scripture. When the Greek prepositions *hupo* ("by") and *dia* ("through") introduce two persons who perform the action of a passive verb—in this case, "spoken"—*hupo* introduces the *ultimate* agent of that action and *dia* introduces the *intermediate* agent. The ultimate agent is the person who is *ultimately* responsible for the action, whereas the intermediate agent is the one who is used by the ultimate agent to carry out this action on his behalf.[57]

Therefore, when Matthew describes Scripture as having been "spoken by [*hupo*] the Lord through [*dia*] the prophet," he identifies the Lord as the ultimate agent of these words and the prophet as the intermediate agent. Consequently, the Lord is ultimately responsible for the words that were spoken in the Old Testament, but he used the prophet as the one to speak forth those words on his behalf. Put another way, the prophet is the immediate author of Scripture—the one whose pen directly wrote the words—but the Lord himself is the ultimate Author of what was written. The words of the human authors are the very words of God himself.

---

[56] In each case, intermediate agency is introduced by the Hebrew preposition *b-* or the Greek prepositions *dia* or *en*.

[57] Daniel B. Wallace, *Greek Grammar beyond the Basics: An Exegetical Syntax of the New Testament* (Grand Rapids, MI: Zondervan, 1996), 431–34; Bavinck, *Reformed Dogmatics*, 1:428.

This reality is also reflected in the way the Bible describes its dual authorship. For example, Jeremiah 36:6–11 uses "the words of the LORD" and "the words of Jeremiah" interchangeably; Mark 7:9–13 describes the same Old Testament passage as "the commandment of God" (v. 9), what "Moses said" (v. 10), and "the word of God" (v. 13); Paul describes his own words to the Corinthians as "a command of the Lord" (1 Cor. 14:37),[58] and Peter refers to the words of the apostles as "the commandment of the Lord" (2 Pet. 3:2). In addition, when citing Old Testament passages, sometimes the New Testament writers attribute those words to the human author, introducing them as what "Moses says" (Rom. 10:19), what "Isaiah says" (Rom. 10:16), or what "David says" (Luke 20:42). But at other times, they attribute those words to the *divine* Author, introducing them as what *God* says (Matt. 15:4; 19:4–5; Acts 2:16–17; 4:24–25; 13:34–35; Rom. 9:15; 2 Cor. 6:2; Heb. 1:5–7; 4:3; 5:6; 8:5, 8; 12:26; 13:5) or what the *Holy Spirit* says (Acts 1:16; Heb. 3:7; 10:15–16). In each of these cases, the words of the human authors are simultaneously viewed as the words of God.

Conclusion

Any view that downplays the role of the divine Author simply cannot be sustained. Scripture teaches that all the words in the Bible are both the words of God and the words of man, but that God is the ultimate Author of everything that was written (2 Tim. 3:16). The same God who providentially prepared his human instruments also superintended these authors in such a way that when they composed the biblical text, they wrote the very words that he was communicating through them (2 Pet. 1:20–21). In the process, God did not accommodate the errant views of the human authors and begrudgingly attach his name to the final product, like a seasoned editor who defers to the poor decisions of an amateur writer rather than running roughshod over his humanity. God was the Author himself, the One who breathed out the very words of the biblical text.

Those who insist on the inevitability of error in Scripture drive an unbiblical wedge between the human and divine authors, attributing some words to the former and others to the latter. In the process, they end up

---

[58] Some point to 1 Corinthians 7 as evidence that the Bible itself distinguishes between the words of God (v. 10) and the words of the human authors (v. 12) in Scripture. But when Paul refers to himself (rather than the Lord) as the source of some of his instruction (v. 12)—and to the Lord (rather than himself) as the source of other instruction (v. 10)—he is simply pointing out that some of his teaching has been said before by Jesus during his earthly ministry, whereas he himself is the vehicle of new revelation in other parts of his teaching. Therefore, as Feinberg explains, "The distinction is not between revelation and nonrevelation, infallible and fallible, but is a distinction *within* revelation (the infallible) between what is repeated by Paul and what is original with him." "The Meaning of Inerrancy," 303.

denying either the ability of an all-powerful God to communicate truth through fallible human instruments or the integrity of a trustworthy God to communicate only truth in the pages of divine revelation. Neither is an option for the one who believes in the perfection of God's character.

If the words of Scripture are the words of God—and if it is impossible for God to lie—it is therefore impossible for Scripture to communicate anything but truth. Put another way, if the words of biblical revelation originated with God rather than man, and if God always speaks the truth, how can these words possibly contain any falsehood? The voice of Scripture and the voice of God are one and the same,[59] and therefore the Bible must be entirely true and reliable in every respect. For this reason, in contrast to those who are "foolish" and "slow of heart to believe all that the prophets have spoken" (Luke 24:25), those who defend the inerrancy of Scripture must boldly insist that the Bible is just as trustworthy as the One who ultimately wrote it.

---

[59] Mohler, "When the Bible Speaks, God Speaks," 39.

20

Do We Have a Trustworthy Text?

INERRANCY AND CANONICITY, PRESERVATION, AND TEXTUAL CRITICISM

Michael J. Kruger

Inerrancy is not a popular concept in the world of biblical studies today. A. E. Harvey, in his book *Is Scripture Still Holy?*, captures the modern academic sentiment quite well: "Inerrancy . . . is both theologically and philosophically indefensible and rightly rejected by the majority voice of a generation which has, in this respect, genuinely 'come of age.'"[1] The reasons for this scholarly rejection of inerrancy are many. Indeed, this volume has been written, at least in part, to respond to some of these objections. Prior chapters have dealt with the claims that inerrancy is a novelty in the history of the church, that it is insensitive to the complexities of the biblical genres, or that it ignores obvious contradictions. While each of these objections is weighty in its own right, in this chapter we shall address one of the most influential—and, to many, the most persuasive—objection to inerrancy, namely, that *the Word of God has not been reliably transmitted down to us.*

---

[1] A. E. Harvey, *Is Scripture Still Holy? Coming of Age with the New Testament* (Grand Rapids, MI: Eerdmans, 2012), 9.

This particular objection has manifested itself in two ways. The first is the problem of canonicity. It is argued that there was no reliable process by which the church could be assured it possessed the right books. Over thousands of years, new books were written, some books were forged, and others were forgotten. Even the church did not agree on which books were Scripture. The second is the problem of textual criticism. It is said that there was no reliable process by which the church could transmit the text of Scripture. Even if the church possessed the right books, the text was corrupted over thousands of years through both accidental and intentional scribal changes.

The implications of these objections for inerrancy are immediately clear. If the concept of inerrancy applies only to the inspired words of God, and we no longer possess these words (either because we have the wrong books or because the text has been corrupted), then the concept of inerrancy is meaningless.[2] We have no grounds to claim the Scriptures are inerrant when we have no reason to think that we actually possess the Scriptures. So, the critics argue, the concept of inerrancy is merely hypothetical—it applies to a situation that does not exist.

Of course, each of these subject areas—the development of the canon and textual criticism—is vast and complex. Our purpose in this chapter, then, is to give a broad overview of the major issues involved and to provide some reasons why we can trust the transmission of God's Word over the millennia.

The Development of the Canon

The Bible is not like most books. It was not formed in one place, at one time, by a single author. Instead, it is a collection of many individual books, composed by more than forty different authors over many centuries and in various locations in the ancient world. And each author brought his own perspective, historical context, and theological contribution. Such a scenario raises obvious questions regarding the canon. Why these sixty-six books and no others? Why not sixty-five or sixty-seven? What process brought them all together? And why should that process be trusted? What do we do with the so-called "apocryphal" literature that has been discovered? And what do we make of the disputes in the early church over these books?

---

[2] For an example of this argument, see B. D. Ehrman, *Misquoting Jesus* (San Francisco: HarperCollins, 2005), 7.

These are too many questions to answer in one chapter. But there are a number of considerations that can give us confidence in the canon we possess.

THE QUALITIES OF CANONICAL BOOKS

One key factor, not to be overlooked, is that the books themselves can provide evidence of their divine origins. As Richard Muller has noted, "There must be some evidence or imprint of the divine work of producing Scripture in the Scriptures themselves."[3] The idea that God's special revelation would possess such divine qualities should not be surprising; after all, God's natural revelation (the created world) also bears evidence of being from God (Ps. 19:1; Rom. 1:20). If natural revelation has qualities about it that display its divine origins, then how much more would we expect this to be true of special revelation? John Murray makes this precise argument: "If the heavens declare the glory of God and therefore bear witness to their divine creator, the Scripture as God's handiwork must also bear the imprints of his authorship."[4]

But what, in particular, are these divine qualities that identify a book as being from God? Some examples would include Scripture's beauty and excellency (Ps. 19:8; 119:103), its power and efficacy (Ps. 119:50, 98, 105, 111; Heb. 4:12–13), and its unity and harmony.[5] These sorts of qualities would have been evident in the books that were genuinely from God, allowing God's people to rightly recognize them.

THE INTERNAL TESTIMONY OF THE HOLY SPIRIT

Even if these qualities of canonical books are objectively present, one might still ask how we can be sure the church is rightly recognizing them. How can we be sure that the church has been correct in its assessment of these books? And if these qualities are really there, then why don't more people recognize them? The answer is that people's ability to assess the divine qualities of these books is limited by their spiritual condition. Because people are fallen and corrupted by sin, they must have the *internum testimonium Spiritus Sancti*, the "internal testimony of the Holy Spirit," if they are to

---

[3] R. A. Muller, *Post-Reformation Reformed Dogmatics* (Grand Rapids, MI: Baker Academic, 1993), 2:270.
[4] John Murray, "The Attestation of Scripture," in *The Infallible Word* (Philadelphia: P&R, 1946), 46. Similar arguments can be found in Francis Turretin, *Institutes of Elenctic Theology* (Phillipsburg, NJ: P&R, 1992), 1:63; John Owen, "The Divine Original: Authority, Self-Evidencing Light, and Power of the Scriptures," in *The Works of John Owen* (Edinburgh: Banner of Truth, 1988), 16:297–421.
[5] For more on these divine qualities, see Michael J. Kruger, *Canon Revisited: Establishing the Origins and Authority of the New Testament Books* (Wheaton, IL: Crossway, 2012), 125–59.

rightly recognize the qualities of scriptural books.[6] The *internum testimonium* is not private revelation, but the powerful work of the Spirit to overcome the noetic effects of sin and to help a person see the qualities of Scripture that are objectively present.

It is the *internum testimonium* that gives us confidence that the church has rightly recognized the books God has given. The church, as God's corporate people, is filled with the Holy Spirit, and thus we have every good reason to think that the consensus of the church is a key indicator of which books are canonical.[7] The response of the church informs our understanding of canon not because the church is infallible or because it somehow creates the canon, but because the church rightly responds to the powerful divine qualities of scriptural books through the help of the Holy Spirit.[8]

HISTORICAL CONFIRMATION

The divine qualities present in the canonical books, and the consensus of the church through the work of the *internum testimonium*, already give us good grounds for thinking we have the right books in our canon. But we have additional confirmation of this reality through solid historical evidence about how the canon developed.[9]

In regard to the Old Testament, we have good reasons to think that the contours of the canon were well established by the time of Jesus. The first-century Jewish historian Josephus plainly lists the books of the Old

---

[6] John Calvin, *Institutes of the Christian Religion*, ed. John T. McNeill, trans. Ford Lewis Battles, Library of Christian Classics, vols. 20–21 (Philadelphia: Westminster Press, 1960), 1.7.4–5; 3.1.1–3; 3.2.15, 33–36. The role of the *internum testimonium* in the establishing of the canon has been acknowledged by a number of Reformed confessions, including the Belgic Confession, the French Confession of Faith, the Scots Confession, and the Helvetic Confession. Helpful treatments of the *internum testimonium* include Bernard Ramm, *The Witness of the Spirit* (Grand Rapids, MI: Eerdmans, 1959); Alvin Plantinga, *Warranted Christian Belief* (New York: Oxford University Press, 2000), 241–89; R. C. Sproul, "The Internal Testimony of the Holy Spirit," in *Inerrancy*, ed. Norman Geisler (Grand Rapids, MI: Zondervan, 1980), 337–54; and John M. Frame, "The Spirit and the Scriptures," in *Hermeneutics, Authority, and Canon*, ed. D. A. Carson and John D. Woodbridge (Grand Rapids, MI: Zondervan, 1986), 217–35.

[7] C. Stephen Evans, "Canonicity, Apostolicity, and Biblical Authority: Some Kierkegaardian Reflections," in *Canon and Biblical Interpretation*, ed. Craig Bartholomew, et al. (Carlisle: Paternoster, 2006), 155; J. W. Wenham, *Christ and the Bible* (Downers Grove, IL: InterVarsity Press, 1972), 162–63; R. Nicole, "The Canon of the New Testament," *Journal of the Evangelical Theological Society* 40 (1997): 199–206.

[8] H. N. Ridderbos, *Redemptive History and the New Testament Scripture* (Phillipsburg, NJ: P&R, 1988), 37.

[9] For an overview of the Old Testament canon, see R. T. Beckwith, *The Old Testament Canon of the New Testament Church, and Its Background in Early Judaism* (Grand Rapids, MI: Eerdmans, 1986); Andrew E. Steinmann, *The Oracles of God: The Old Testament Canon* (St. Louis, MO: Concordia Academic, 1999); and E. Earle Ellis, *The Old Testament in Early Christianity: Canon and Interpretation in Light of Modern Research* (Grand Rapids, MI: Baker, 1992). For an overview of the New Testament canon, see Kruger, *Canon Revisited*, 195–287; B. M. Metzger, *The Canon of the New Testament: Its Origin, Development, and Significance* (Oxford: Clarendon, 1987); and H. Y. Gamble, *The New Testament Canon: Its Making and Meaning* (Philadelphia: Fortress, 1985). For volumes that deal with both, see F. F. Bruce, *The Canon of Scripture* (Downers Grove, IL: InterVarsity Press, 1988), and L. M. McDonald, *The Biblical Canon: Its Origin, Transmission, and Authority* (Peabody, MA: Hendrickson, 2007).

Testament canon[10]—which seems to match the thirty-nine books in our canon today[11]—and he does so in a manner that suggests the canon was "universal, clearly defined, and long settled."[12] Also in the first century, the Alexandrian Jewish thinker Philo indicates that the Jewish canon seems to have been divided into an established threefold division when he refers to "the laws and the sacred oracles of God enunciated by the holy prophets . . . and psalms."[13] Philo's threefold division is remarkably similar to Jesus's; speaking of the Old Testament, he refers to "the Law of Moses and the Prophets and the Psalms" (Luke 24:44).[14] This threefold division also finds an echo in much earlier texts such as the Jewish work Ben Sira (Ecclesiasticus)[15] and the fragment 4QMMT from Qumran.[16] Such evidence led Stephen Chapman to suggest that "by the turn of the millennium, a Jewish canon of Scripture was largely in place, if not absolutely defined and delimited in scope."[17]

Such a conclusion is confirmed by the fact that the New Testament is completely silent regarding any canonical disagreements amongst the various factions of first-century Judaism. While the Pharisees, Sadducees, and Jesus disagreed about the interpretation of Scripture, they never disagreed about which books were Scripture—a stunning silence if the canon was entirely in dispute at this point, as some critical scholars argue.[18] Moreover, when it comes to New Testament citations of Old Testament Scripture, there is not a single instance of a book being quoted as Scripture that is not in our current Old Testament.[19]

In regard to the New Testament, we have strong evidence that there was a "core" collection of books functioning as Scripture by the end of the second century.[20] This core collection would have consisted of the four Gospels, thirteen epistles of Paul, Acts, 1 Peter, 1–2 John, Hebrews, and Revelation. The rapidity with which this collection developed tells us that

[10] Josephus, *Against Apion*, 1.38–42, http://penelope.uchicago.edu/josephus/apion-1.html.
[11] Bruce, *Canon of Scripture*, 33.
[12] Ellis, *Old Testament*, 39.
[13] Philo, *On the Contemplative Life or Suppliants*, http://www.earlychristianwritings.com/yonge/book34.html. Philo also mentions "other books" used by the Therapeutae, which is likely a reference to noninspired books they still valued as useful. For more discussion, see Steinmann, *Oracles of God*, 80; Beckwith, *Old Testament Canon*, 117.
[14] Ellis, *Old Testament*, 9.
[15] See discussion in Beckwith, *Old Testament Canon*, 110–11.
[16] Stephen B. Chapman, "The Old Testament Canon and Its Authority for the Christian Church," *Ex Auditu* 19 (2003): 137.
[17] Ibid. See similar arguments in Stephen G. Dempster, "Torah, Torah, Torah: The Emergence of the Tripartite Canon," in *Exploring the Origins of the Bible: Canon Formation in Historical, Literary, and Theological Perspective*, ed. E. Tov and C. A. Evans (Grand Rapids, MI: Baker Academic, 2008), 87–127.
[18] Chapman, "Old Testament Canon," 139.
[19] Jude 14–15 cites the book of Enoch, but never refers to it as Scripture.
[20] J. Barton, *The Spirit and the Letter: Studies in the Biblical Canon* (London: SPCK, 1997), 1–34.

there was substantial unity around the core books from a very early time. Moreover, it also tells us that most of the disputes within early Christianity centered on only a small number of books, such as James, 2 Peter, 3 John, and Jude.[21]

The earliest evidence for a new canon of Scripture comes from the New Testament writings themselves, where 2 Peter 3:16 tells us that Paul's letters were already viewed as Scripture on par with the Old Testament, and 1 Timothy 5:18 contains a possible citation of Luke 10:7 as "Scripture." Both of these texts suggest that a canonical consciousness was already present in the first century.[22] It should also be noted that the New Testament writings often present themselves as authoritative documents for the church.[23] For instance, Paul regularly presents his words as the very words of God (e.g., 1 Cor. 14:36–38; Gal. 1:1; 1 Thess. 2:13; 2 Thess. 3:6, 14), and asks that his letters be read in the public worship of the church (2 Cor. 10:9; Col. 4:16; 1 Thess. 5:27; cf. Rev. 1:3).

This trend continues into the second century as Papias (writing ca. 125) receives Matthew and Mark, as well as 1 Peter, 1 John, Revelation, and perhaps even some of Paul's letters. Justin Martyr (writing ca. 150) appears to adopt all four Gospels[24] and declares that they are read publicly in worship alongside the Old Testament.[25] Irenaeus (writing ca. 180) adopts quite a full canon, including the four Gospels, Acts, the entire Pauline collection (minus Philemon), Hebrews, James, 1 Peter, 1 and 2 John, and Revelation.[26] Our earliest canonical list, the Muratorian fragment, which dates from about the same time period as Irenaeus, affirms the canonicity of the four Gospels, Acts, the thirteen epistles of Paul, 1 and 2 John (and possibly 3 John), Jude, and Revelation.[27]

In sum, the core of the New Testament canon was already in place by the early second century. Although the boundaries of the canon were not solidified until about the fourth century, this core collection was sufficient

[21] Kruger, *Canon Revisited*, 269–80.
[22] D. Meade, "Ancient Near Eastern Apocalypticism and the Origins of the New Testament Canon of Scripture," in *The Bible as a Human Witness: Hearing the Word of God through Historically Dissimilar Traditions*, ed. Randall Heskett and Brian Irwin (London: T&T Clark, 2010), 318.
[23] Michael J. Kruger, *The Question of Canon: Challenging the Status Quo in the New Testament Debate* (Downers Grove, IL: InterVarsity Press, 2013), 119–54.
[24] See C. E. Hill, *Who Chose the Gospels? Probing the Great Gospel Conspiracy* (Oxford: Oxford University Press, 2010), 123–50.
[25] Justin Martyr, *First Apology*, 47.3, http://www.earlychristianwritings.com/text/justinmartyr-firstapology.html.
[26] See discussion in Graham Stanton, *Jesus and Gospel* (Cambridge: Cambridge University Press, 2004), 105–6; and Metzger, *Canon of the New Testament*, 154–55.
[27] For a defense of the second-century date of the Muratorian fragment, see J. Verheyden, "The Canon Muratori: A Matter of Dispute," in *The Biblical Canons*, ed. J.-M. Auwers and H. J. de Jonge (Leuven, Belgium: Leuven University Press, 2003), 487–556.

to establish the stability and theological trajectory of early Christianity for years to come.

The Transmission of the Text

Even if we have good reasons to think the right books have been reliably passed down to the church (as we have just argued), there is still the question of whether we have the right *text*.[28] In the ancient world, texts could be transmitted only when they were copied by hand, and scribes, being human, sometimes made mistakes. At other times, scribes made intentional changes to the text.[29] Given the thousands of years during which manuscripts have been copied over and over again, what assurances do we have that we actually possess what was originally written? Scholars such as Bart Ehrman argue that we have no reason to think we have the original text. He declares: "What good is it to say that the autographs (i.e., the originals) were inspired? We don't *have* the originals! We have only error-ridden copies, and the vast majority of these are centuries removed from the originals and different from them . . . in thousands of ways."[30] Similarly, Frank Moore Cross claims that textual criticism has "broken the back of doctrines of inerrancy and . . . inspiration."[31]

Despite the overly skeptical approach of scholars such as Ehrman and Cross, textual critics over the years have expressed a good deal of confidence that the text we possess very much approximates what was originally written—or at least sufficiently close to it. Let us examine some reasons for this confidence.

Manuscript Resources

One of the fundamental reasons scholars believe we have a reliable biblical text is the wealth of manuscript evidence at our disposal. In the quest to ascertain the original text, there are two things on every text critic's wish list: numerous copies and some of them with an early date. Numerous

---

[28] What is meant by the term "original text" is complicated and much debated in modern scholarship. For more discussion, see E. J. Epp, "The Multivalence of the Term 'Original Text' in New Testament Textual Criticism," *Harvard Theological Review* 92 (1999): 245–81, and C. E. Hill and M. J. Kruger, eds., *The Early Text of the New Testament* (Oxford: Oxford University Press, 2012), 3–5.

[29] Bart D. Ehrman, *The Orthodox Corruption of Scripture* (New York: Oxford University Press, 1993).

[30] Ehrman, *Misquoting Jesus*, 7 (emphasis original).

[31] Frank Moore Cross, "The Biblical Scrolls from Qumran and the Canonical Text," in *The Bible and the Dead Sea Scrolls*, ed. J. H. Charlesworth (Waco, TX: Baylor University Press, 2006), 73. For an additional critique of inerrancy from the basis of textual criticism, see John J. Brogan, "Can I Have Your Autograph? Uses and Abuses of Textual Criticism in Formulating an Evangelical Doctrine of Scripture," in *Evangelicals and Scripture: Tradition, Authority and Hermeneutics*, ed. Vincent Bacote, Laura C. Miguelez, and Dennis L. Okholm (Downers Grove, IL: IVP Academic, 2004), 93–111.

copies are critical because they can be compared with one another, giving us assurance that the original text is preserved somewhere in the manuscript tradition. Thus, the more copies the better. But it is not just a high quantity of manuscripts that is desirable for the textual critic, but manuscripts that date as close as possible to the time of the original writing of that text. The less time passed between the original writing and our earliest copies, the less time there was for the text to be substantially corrupted, and therefore the more assured we can be that we possess what was originally written.

The Old Testament raises unique challenges because it was written long ago and over a great span of time.[32] But in comparison to other ancient texts from that time period, we have an impressive number of manuscript resources at our disposal. Of particular relevance are the Dead Sea Scrolls, which contain portions of every Old Testament book except Esther, and are dated approximately between the third century BC and the first century AD.[33] These manuscripts provide access to the Old Testament text multiple centuries before the coming of Christ—earlier than any other manuscripts of the Old Testament. Additional early Hebrew manuscripts include the Nash Papyrus (ca. 169–137 BC)[34] and the scrolls discovered at Masada (before ca. AD 73)[35] and at the Wadi Murabba'at site south of Qumran (ca. AD 135–137).[36] We also have Hebrew manuscripts that contain nearly all of the Old Testament, such as the Aleppo Codex (ca. AD 925) and the Leningrad Codex (ca. AD 1008).

Given the later date of the New Testament, it is not surprising that we have even better manuscript evidence available.[37] But even during this time period, it is not unusual for ancient texts to be preserved in only a handful of manuscripts. For example, the writings of the Roman historian Tacitus, dated from the first century, survive in only three manuscripts (not all are complete),[38] and the earliest, the Codex Mediceus, is from the ninth cen-

---

[32] For an introduction to Old Testament textual criticism, see E. Tov, *Textual Criticism of the Hebrew Bible* (Minneapolis: Fortress, 1992), or Ellis R. Brotzman, *Old Testament Textual Criticism: A Practical Introduction* (Grand Rapids, MI: Baker, 1994).

[33] For a general introduction to the scrolls, see J. C. VanderKam, *The Dead Sea Scrolls Today* (Grand Rapids, MI: Eerdmans, 1994), or R. A. Kugler and E. M. Schuller, eds., *The Dead Sea Scrolls at Fifty: Proceedings of the 1997 Society of Biblical Literature Qumran Section Meetings* (Atlanta: Scholars Press, 1999).

[34] W. F. Albright, "A Biblical Fragment from the Maccabean Age: The Nash Papyrus," *Journal of Biblical Literature* 56 (1937): 145–76.

[35] Y. Yadin, *The Ben Sira Scroll from Masada* (Jerusalem: Israel Exploration Society, 1965).

[36] Julia M. O'Brien, "Wadi Murabbaat: Texts," in *Anchor Bible Dictionary*, 6 vols., ed. D. N. Freedman (New York: Doubleday, 1992), 6:864.

[37] For an overview of New Testament textual criticism, see B. M. Metzger and B. D. Ehrman, *The Text of the New Testament: Its Transmission, Corruption, and Restoration* (Oxford: Oxford University Press, 2005).

[38] L. D. Reynolds, ed., *Texts and Transmissions: A Survey of the Latin Classics* (Oxford: Clarendon, 1983), 406–11.

tury, nearly eight hundred years after it was originally written. In contrast, we possess more than fifty-seven hundred copies of the New Testament in Greek alone.[1] And a number of these manuscripts are dated as early as the second century, only a short time after the originals were written.[2]

Eldon Epp highlights the significance of this wealth of manuscripts when he observes, "We have, therefore, a genuine embarrassment of riches in the quantity of manuscripts we possess. . . . The writings of no Greek classical author are preserved on this scale."[3] Then he clarifies why this matters: "The point is that we have so many manuscripts . . . that surely the original reading *in every case* is somewhere present in our vast store of material."[4]

The Nature of Scribal Changes

The above discussion has shown that the wealth of manuscripts gives us good reason to think that the original text is still preserved somewhere in the manuscript tradition. However, in addition to possessing the original text, we also have a vast number of textual variants. Textual variants are simply differences between the manuscripts. Such differences arise over time due to changes made by scribes, whether accidental or intentional. Thus, scholars are not lacking in information (as if the original text were lost), but actually have *too much* information (the original text plus variants). The issue is not whether we possess the original text in our manuscript tradition, but how to separate that text from the variants. Needless to say, the latter situation is much preferred over the former.

Naturally, this situation raises a number of questions. How significant are these textual variants? And how many are there? How different are the manuscripts we possess? One might think these questions could be answered simply by counting variants. Ehrman has taken this approach. In regard to the New Testament, he says, "Some say there are 200,000 variants known, some say 300,000, some say 400,000 or more!"[5] He then declares, "There are more variations among our manuscripts than there are words in the New Testament."[6]

---

[1] The official numbers are kept at the *Institut für neutestamentliche Textforschung* (Institute for New Testament Textual Research) in Münster, Germany.
[2] E.g., P52 (John), P66 (John), P98 (Revelation), and P104 (Matthew). The letter/number combinations are the papyrus numbers of the manuscript fragments, which are held at various libraries around the world.
[3] Eldon Jay Epp, "Textual Criticism," in *The New Testament and Its Modern Interpreters*, ed. Eldon Jay Epp and George W. MacRae (Atlanta: Scholars Press, 1989), 91.
[4] Ibid (emphasis added).
[5] Ehrman, *Misquoting Jesus*, 89.
[6] Ibid., 90.

Ehrman may well be right about these numbers—we are not exactly sure how many variants there are in the biblical text. However, numbers are not the whole story. The fundamental issue is not the number of variants, but the *kind* of variants. It is not just an issue of quantity, but of quality. And when it comes to the biblical text, it is important to realize that most textual variations are insignificant.[7] By the term *insignificant* we mean that these variants have no bearing on our ability recover the original text.[8] In regard to the Old Testament, Bruce Waltke has even observed that textual criticism can often be "boring because the differences are inconsequential."[9]

Examples of such insignificant textual variations[10] include: (1) spelling (orthographical) differences: this is one of the most common variations, as scribes often spelled words differently or made spelling mistakes; (2) meaningless word-order changes: scribes sometimes flipped the order of words accidentally, often not changing the meaning at all; (3) use of synonyms: scribes sometimes accidentally substituted one word for a synonym, with little effect on the meaning; (4) nonsense readings: some scribal mistakes are so obvious that they are quickly identified as errors and therefore not possibly the original reading; and (5) singular readings: some changes occur only in a single manuscript and have little claim to be original.

The fact that so many variants are insignificant shows that one cannot impugn the integrity of the biblical text merely by citing the quantity of the variants. Indeed, we cannot forget that we know about the high quantity of the variants only because we possess so many copies of the biblical text that we can compare. If we possessed fewer copies, we would know about fewer variants. Thus, the high number of variants has less to do with the integrity of the biblical text and more to do with the fact that so many manuscripts have been copied and preserved.

An example of how most textual variations are insignificant can be found in the Isaiah Scroll (1QIsa[a]) from Qumran. The scroll is nearly a millennium older than our previous copies of Isaiah (the Masoretic version)

---

[7] In regard to the New Testament, Daniel B. Wallace estimates that insignificant variants would constitute approximately 80 to 90 percent of known textual changes. See J. Ed. Komoszewski, M. James Sawyer, and Daniel B. Wallace, *Reinventing Jesus, How Contemporary Skeptics Miss the Real Jesus and Mislead Popular Culture* (Grand Rapids, MI: Kregel, 2006), 63.

[8] Eldon Jay Epp, "Toward the Clarification of the Term 'Textual Variant,'" in *Studies in the Theory and Method of New Testament Textual Criticism*, ed. Eldon Jay Epp and Gordon D. Fee (Grand Rapids, MI: Eerdmans, 1993), 57.

[9] Bruce K. Waltke, *The Dance between God and Humanity* (Grand Rapids, MI: Eerdmans, 2013), 161.

[10] For a survey of the kind of mistakes scribes made (both significant and insignificant), see Brotzman, *Old Testament Textual Criticism*, 107–21; Tov, *Textual Criticism of the Hebrew Bible*, 236–85; or Metzger and Ehrman, *Text of the New Testament*, 250–71.

and demonstrates that the text was remarkably well preserved. James VanderKam observes that the earlier and later copies "were nearly identical except for *small details that rarely affected the meaning of the text*."[11] The Isaiah scroll led Eugene Ulrich to speak more broadly about the reliability of the text at Qumran:

> A large number of manuscripts display impressive agreement with particular books of what emerged in the middle ages to be called the Masoretic text. . . . So we can be assured that our present biblical text is a copy, preserved with amazingly accurate fidelity.[12]

The Ability to Recover the Original Text

Of course, not all textual variations in the biblical manuscripts are insignificant; some are more substantial. In regard to the Old Testament, it is well known that manuscripts at Qumran reveal a variety of different textual types.[13] For instance, Qumran attests to a copy of the book of Jeremiah (4QJer[b]) that is substantially shorter than the Jeremiah preserved in the later Masoretic text.[14] On the New Testament side, there is the famous long ending of Mark (16:9–20) and the pericope of the adulterous woman (John 7:53–8:11), which seem to have been added at later times.[15]

Do these more substantial textual variations challenge the integrity of the biblical text? They would be a problem if we had no methodology to determine which readings were original and which were not. Put differently, variations like these would pose challenges if we assumed they were all equally viable. However, such an assumption runs contrary to the entire history of textual criticism, which has consistently maintained that not all readings are equally viable and that our text-critical methodologies are able, in most cases, to determine the original (or at least the earliest) reading with a reasonable level of certainty.[16] Kurt and Barbara Aland even insist that "we proceed on the premise that in every instance of textual variation

[11] VanderKam, *Dead Sea Scrolls*, 126 (emphasis added).
[12] E. Ulrich, "The Scrolls and the Study of the Hebrew Bible," in *The Dead Sea Scrolls at Fifty*, 31.
[13] For a broad overview of the Hebrew text at Qumran, see E. Ulrich, *The Dead Sea Scrolls and the Origins of the Bible* (Grand Rapids, MI: Eerdmans, 1999).
[14] E. Tov, "The Literary History of the Book of Jeremiah in the Light of Its Textual History," in *Empirical Models for Biblical Criticism*, ed. J. H. Tigay (Philadelphia: University of Pennsylvania Press, 1985), 211–37.
[15] For an overview of these two textual variants, see D. A. Carson and D. J. Moo, *An Introduction to the New Testament* (Grand Rapids, MI: Zondervan, 2005), 187–90, 273–74.
[16] For an overview of text-critical methodologies, see Metzger and Ehrman, *Text of the New Testament*, 300–343, or Tov, *Textual Criticism*, 293–350.

it is possible to determine the form of the original text."[17] If so, then these more substantial variations do not threaten the integrity of the biblical text because we can identify them as variations.

Even given the Alands' optimism that we can always recover the original text, it should be noted that a small number of variants remain where our methodology is unable to reach any definitive conclusion one way or the other. In these situations, there are two (or more) possible readings, and the evidence for each reading (whether external or internal) is relatively equal, or at least close enough that it is reasonable to think that either reading could have been original. But such situations are exceedingly rare. And even when they do occur, they do not materially affect the theology or teaching of the biblical text. So even though we do not have absolute certainty about every single textual variant, we do have a text that is so well-preserved that it is essentially what was written by the original authors.

These three considerations about textual criticism—the vast quantity of manuscripts, the fact that most textual variants are insignificant, and the fact that we have the ability to determine which readings are original—provide solid reasons for us to be confident that the text we possess is accurate and trustworthy. We are reminded, then, that we do not need the original manuscripts (the autographs) of the New Testament in order to possess the original text of the New Testament. Although the autographs *contained* the original text, we should not confuse the original text with a physical object—as if the autographs themselves *were* the original text. The original text can be preserved without the autographs, namely, through a multiplicity of manuscripts. Even though any given copy may not contain (all of) the original text, God has preserved it across a wide range of manuscripts.

Conclusion

This chapter has been about whether the Bible has been reliably transmitted down to us through the ages—in terms of which books and in terms of which text. Theoretically, such issues would not have arisen if God had delivered his Word in another fashion—perhaps dropping it straight from heaven on golden tablets. But God chose to deliver his Word through normal historical channels, making it subject to the normal challenges of transmission over long periods. Nevertheless, we have argued here that

---

[17] K. Aland and B. Aland, *The Text of the New Testament: An Introduction to the Critical Editions and to the Theory and Practice of Modern Textual Criticism* (Grand Rapids, MI: Eerdmans, 1989), 294.

there are excellent reasons for thinking that the right books have made it into the canon, and that the text has been sufficiently preserved to faithfully deliver its message.

But our confidence does not lie merely in historical evidences, as strong as they may be. Rather, throughout the many years of transmission, Christians ultimately have relied on the *providence of God*. If God intended his people to have his Word, then it is reasonable to think that he providentially oversaw the entire process so that his Word was faithfully delivered. The Westminster Confession of Faith affirms this principle when it says that the Scriptures "being immediately inspired by God, and by his singular care and providence kept pure in all ages, are therefore authentical" (1.8). And if God has faithfully and sufficiently delivered his Word to his people, then there is nothing problematic about affirming its inerrancy.

Part 4

INERRANCY IN
PASTORAL PRACTICE

Applying to Life

21

The Invincible Word

INERRANCY AND THE POWER OF SCRIPTURE

Steven J. Lawson

The inspired pages of the infallible Bible constitute the inerrant Word of God. Every ancient word on these pages is part of a timeless, transcendent testimony, one without fault or error. The Bible is not the word of man, but divine revelation that has proceeded from the mouth of God. From cover to cover, the Bible makes this emphatic assertion.

In the Old Testament, David declared, "The words of the LORD are pure words; as silver tried in a furnace on the earth, refined seven times" (Ps. 12:6).[1] This is to say that Scripture is absolutely pure, as though it had been refined in a furnace to the point where it is without alloys. An anonymous psalmist maintained, "Your word is very pure" (Ps. 119:140). This states that the Bible, the very Word of God, is entirely perfect in all it states. Solomon concurred with this assertion: "Every word of God," he said, "is tested" (Prov. 30:5). In other words, there is no impurity of worldly opinion, no amalgam of man's wisdom, within God's Word. It is the unadulterated truth of the living God.

In the New Testament, Jesus stated, "Your word is truth" (John 17:17). "Truth" means reality, the way things really are. It is the self-disclosure of God himself, of all that is consistent with his holy being. Truth is not what culture or society say it is. Neither is it what the majority of a population claims it to be. It is not how we perceive or define reality. Truth is whatever God says it is. Sin is whatever God says it is. Salvation is whatever God says it is. Heaven and hell are whatever God says they are. Paul writes, "Let God be found true, though every man be found a liar" (Rom. 3:4).

Truth is woven into God's trinitarian nature. Scripture tells us that God is the "God of truth" (Ps. 31:5). The Son of God is "the truth" (John 14:6). The Spirit of God is "the Spirit of truth" (John 14:17). The Word of God is "the word of truth" (2 Cor. 6:7). Everything about God—his nature, his person, and his Word—is truth. There is no disjunction between God and truth.

Scripture is the "perfect law" (James 1:25), *perfect* indicating that Scripture is the unadulterated record of divine truth. The Bible is also "pure milk" (1 Pet. 2:2), the word *pure* meaning unmixed with any human impurities. The Bible says, "It is impossible for God to lie" (Heb. 6:18). If Scripture is the Word of God, which it is, and if God cannot lie, which he cannot, then it must be concluded that the Bible cannot lie. Paul asserts this when he writes, "God . . . cannot lie" (Titus 1:2). There are certain things that God cannot do. He cannot act contrary to his own holy nature. Thus, God can never misrepresent the reality of any matter in his Word.

Affirming this fact, Charles Haddon Spurgeon said, "If I did not believe in the infallibility of Scripture—the absolute infallibility of it from cover to cover, I would never enter this pulpit again."[2] So it should be for everyone who ministers the Word. Those who do not believe in the inerrancy of the Word of God should never again enter a pulpit. But those who *do* believe it should proclaim the Bible's truth from the highest housetop.

The Inseparable Connection

Because the Bible is what it claims to *be*—the inerrant Word of God—it is able to do what it claims to *do*. Because the Word of God is inerrant, it is, therefore, invincible. Because the Word of God is impeccably pure, the logical necessity is that it is explosively powerful. The flawless Scriptures are incapable of being conquered. The inerrant Word of God is a superior weapon that is entirely able to carry out the purposes of God.

---

[2] Charles H. Spurgeon, *The Metropolitan Tabernacle Pulpit* (Pasadena, TX: Pilgrim Publications, 1974), 36:9.

No one symbol of the Bible can communicate the whole of its soul-saving power. Many metaphors are necessary to convey the comprehensive nature of its divine force. In its pages, the Bible uses a vast array of symbols to reveal its life-changing power, but there are seven in particular that represent its extraordinary force: a sword, a mirror, a seed, a milk, a lamp, a fire, and a hammer.

A Sword That Pierces

First, the Word of God is pictured as a sword, a sharp blade that can pierce and plunge into the depths of the human heart. Hebrews 4:12–13 asserts: "For the word of God is living and active and sharper than any two-edged sword, and piercing as far as the division of soul and spirit, of both joints and marrow, and able to judge the thoughts and intentions of the heart. And there is no creature hidden from His sight, but all things are open and laid bare to the eyes of Him with whom we have to do." These two verses state four truths regarding what the Bible *is* and four truths concerning what the Bible *does*. Let us first consider what they say the Bible *is*.

Fundamentally, this text tells us that Scripture is the *divine* Word. In no uncertain terms, it states that it is "the word of God." Though recorded by human authors, Scripture does not claim to be the mere word of man. Neither does it present itself as the best wisdom an ancient culture can offer. It does not maintain that it contains the long-held traditions of any religious institution. To the contrary, Scripture claims to be the very Word of God. The worldview recorded in this sacred book has come down from the mind of God.

Moreover, this passage states that the Bible is the *living* Word. It continues, "For the word of God is living . . ." That is to say, Scripture is a living book, ever speaking in every generation. In the previous chapter of Hebrews, the author writes, "The Holy Spirit says" (3:7), then quotes Psalm 95:7. What the Spirit "says" is what was recorded in Scripture. Furthermore, the verb is in the present tense. That means this psalm, written long ago, is what the Spirit says in the present through his Word. Though recorded thousands of years ago, the Bible is alive and is still speaking to mankind. This is precisely the emphasis that the author of Hebrews is making. The order of the words in the original language is "living for the Word of God is." "Living" is placed as the first word in the sentence, known as the emphatic position. This prominent placement is intended to draw attention to its importance. Simply put, the Word of God is living, ever speaking, and ever imparting spiritual life to those who receive its message.

Recognizing the living nature of Scripture, Martin Luther said: "The Bible is alive. It speaks to me. It has feet; it runs after me. It has hands; it lays hold of me."[3] This German Reformer claimed that this ancient book speaks to modern man in a soul-arresting fashion. Jesus said, "The words that I have spoken to you are spirit and are life" (John 6:63). The words that he speaks are full of life and give life. Every other book contains the futile words of man; as such, every other book is a dead book. But the inerrant Word of God is a living and life-giving book. Consequently, Scripture is the most relevant book ever written. This living book communicates to every person on every continent in every age. This book is constantly speaking, transcending times and cultures, addressing the real issues of every age. Many preachers today want to have a contemporary ministry. If so, they should preach the Bible. It is the most pertinent book ever written.

This text also says Scripture is the *active* Word. This means it possesses supernatural energy to perform the work of God in the world. The word *active* indicates that Scripture is most energetic. It is always full of divine energy, and thus is always at work. The Bible is never listless or flat. This dynamic book is never tired. It never drags itself into the pulpit. Many times when I step into the pulpit, I am physically, emotionally, and mentally drained. But when I open the pages of the Bible and preach its truths, this high-octane book surges through my soul and revives me. This divinely charged book never suffers burnout. It never takes a day off, never goes on sabbatical, and never needs a rest. This indefatigable book is always working in the world. After I proclaim the Word, I may be exhausted and may go home to rest. But long after the sermon, Scripture continues its work in the hearts of people, performing God's work in them.

What is more, this verse teaches that the Word of God is *sharp*, saying it is "sharper than any two-edged sword." In truth, it is the sharpest weapon in any arsenal in the world. No surgeon's scalpel can compare with its cutting power. This book is incomparably sharper than any manmade instrument. There is not a dull part in the Bible. No matter where it is opened, it is all edge. In fact, this sword is "two-edged," meaning it cuts both ways. It both convicts and converts, both softens and hardens, both saves and damns. There is not a flat passage in the entirety of Scripture. There is neither a rounded-off chapter nor a blunt verse in its whole. Every word, every

---

[3] Martin Luther, *The Table Talk of Martin Luther*, ed. Thomas S. Kepler (1952, repr.; Mineola, NY: Dover Publications, 2005), 207.

verse, every chapter, and every book in the Bible is razor-sharp. When this sword is wielded, it does not pierce skin, flesh, and bone. Rather, it cuts to the depth of a person's innermost being. No preacher should ever go into the pulpit without this divinely given weapon.

Having seen what the Bible *is*, the question remains: What does the Bible *do*? Hebrews 4:12–13 gives a fourfold mission statement for what the sword of Scripture, when wielded properly, accomplishes.

As a matter of its first use, the Word of God *pierces the soul*. This passage says Scripture "[pierces] as far as the division of soul and spirit" (v. 12b). This divinely inspired book is so sharp that it can penetrate the thickest facades that a person erects. Like a hot knife through butter, the Bible can cut through the strongest excuses a man can offer. The Word of God can plunge into the core of a person's being and address the deepest issues of his or her life. A human message addresses merely the felt needs of an individual. But the sword of Scripture descends into the deepest places of the soul. It gets beneath the surface of a person's life and penetrates into one's vital spiritual organs, where no other book can reach.

Further, the Word of God *judges the thoughts*. This text says it is "able to judge the thoughts and intentions of the heart" (v. 12c). The word *judge* (*kritikos*) means to critique, to be or act as a critic. This is to say that Scripture is able to accurately audit a person's life and size it up for what it is. The Word of God is able to examine the unseen attitudes and motivations, expose the secret ambitions and desires, and then render the divine verdict. Man looks on the outward appearance, but God looks upon the heart (1 Sam. 16:7). This sharp, two-edged sword is able to penetrate into the hidden crevices of the heart and judge what only God can see. The Word makes known what we alone know about ourselves—and often what we do not yet know of ourselves. Scripture plunges deep into the unseen places of the human spirit and judges the private matters of the heart. Only the razor-sharp Word of God can do this.

Moreover, the Word of God *exposes the heart*. Hebrews 4:13a adds, "And there is no creature hidden from His sight, but all things are open." This statement refers to those who are on the operating table, under the cutting force of this two-edged sword. God is omniscient and knows all things. He sees into the inner, private life of every person. Under the Word, all things are open for a man to see what God sees. The soul-piercing Word peels back the layers of a man's heart, enabling that person to peer into himself from God's divine vantage point. The attitudes, thoughts, intentions, and motives are exposed when the Word is wielded. Hidden closets within the human soul are brought out in the open. The ministry of the Word of God exposes everything.

This word *open* is the Greek word *gymnos*, from which we derive the English words *gymnasium* and *gymnastics*. In the first century, an athlete in training would go into a gym and strip down in order to exercise without any restrictions. No article of clothing would be allowed to hinder him. So it is in a spiritual sense. When rightly administered, the Word of God strips bare the soul. Scripture leaves one standing naked before a holy God. Exposed, a person sees himself as he is, as God sees him. Scripture removes all pretenses and excuses that men use to cover their flaws before God. The Word leaves the human soul stark naked before God.

Further, the Word of God *slays the life*. Scripture leaves one "laid bare" (*trachelizo*) before God (v. 13b). The English word *tracheotomy* is traced back to this Greek word. It represents the act by which one would seize the neck of a victim and expose his throat for the deathblow. In ancient times, the priest would take hold of the sacrificial lamb, pull its head back to expose its neck, then slit its throat. This is precisely what the Word of God does to self-centered ego and inflated pride. Scripture mortifies self-righteousness and kills self-sufficiency under its soul-piercing power.

The sin-slaying Word lays bare the heart before "the eyes of Him with whom we have to do" (v. 13c). This can be read, "to whom we must give an account." More literally, it can be rendered "to whom is our word." The idea is that the Word brings a person before the One to whom we must give an answer. This means the Word of God cuts into the depths of a person's soul and puts to death the old life. It crushes the old man by giving the conviction of sin and revealing one's desperate need for saving grace. The Word alone can perform such a dramatic open-heart surgery.

At the birth of the church, Peter wielded the sword of Scripture on the day of Pentecost. The apostle unsheathed this deadly sharp instrument, and those present "were pierced to the heart" (Acts 2:37a). In his sermon, Peter quoted Joel 2:28–32, Psalm 16:8–11, and Psalm 110:1. The apostle used passage after passage to penetrate to the hearts of those present that day. They were "pierced" (*katanusso*), a word meaning stabbed as with a knife. Under deep conviction, they cried out, "Brethren, what shall we do?" (Acts 2:37b).

Every preacher must take up this sharp, two-edged sword and thrust it with the power of the Holy Spirit. We must never enter the pulpit unarmed. The weapons of our warfare are not of the flesh but of the Spirit, "divinely powerful for the destruction of fortresses" (2 Cor. 10:4). I say to every preacher, put down all plastic forks of worldly wisdom. Put down all butter knives of religious tradition. Put away an ear-tickling, back-slapping message. Put down all ego-massaging preaching. Unsheathe "the sword of the Spirit, which is the word of God" (Eph. 6:17). You must be a soldier of the cross who wages war for the souls of men with this invincible weapon.

A Mirror That Reveals

Second, Scripture is represented as a mirror that reveals the human heart. James 1:23–24 reads, "For if anyone is a hearer of the word and not a doer, he is like a man who looks at his natural face in a mirror; for once he has looked at himself and gone away, he has immediately forgotten what kind of person he was." The idea here is that the Word of God is like a mirror that provides an accurate reflection.

What is the purpose of a mirror? It is intended to enable a person to see himself as he truly is. A mirror gives knowledge of self. It gives an exact representation of what a person looks like. This is precisely what the Word of God does. It is a spiritual mirror that reveals what a person looks like on the inside. Every person has a flawed self-awareness until the Word of God gives true knowledge of self. Scripture makes known to us who and what we are before God. In addition, the Word also shows our need for the grace of God.

I have experienced this reflecting power of God's Word. Indeed, I never truly knew myself until I began to read the Word of God. I was a firstborn child in the baby boomer era. My mother and father loved me, and my mother especially doted on me. My mother's sister lived with us, which gave me two indulgent women who praised me. I played football in high school, where I attended numerous pep rallies. I stood in front of the student body and was given awards and trophies. The cheerleaders cheered for me, and my teachers and classmates applauded me. I went to college to play football, and it was more of the same as fans and friends affirmed me.

In college, I began to read my Bible seriously, and I discovered that what God was saying about me was not what everyone else was saying. The New Testament was revealing things about me that I was not hearing elsewhere. This book was not flattering me, but confronting me. It was giving me a painfully accurate picture of myself. God's Word fostered an uncomfortable self-awareness that brought conviction to my heart. This mirror gave me the true knowledge of myself that had been lacking in my life. This self-realization proved to be the necessary means for my growth in grace.

Every preacher who stands in a pulpit must be constantly holding up the mirror before his listeners. As he expounds the Bible, it is as though he is standing behind the mirror of the Word. His listeners should not see him, but instead should be looking directly into this mirror, seeing God and themselves accurately.

Often, after I preached in my church, I stood in the lobby, greeting the congregation. Sometimes I would see a man standing in the corner, and I would sense that he was waiting for everyone to exit so that he could approach me privately. On such occasions, the man would nervously speak to me, asking, "Have you been talking to my wife?" In each instance, I had not spoken with his spouse. What had happened? The Word preached had exposed his heart and revealed his inner secrets. He was convinced I knew him so well only because I had spoken with his wife, the person who knew him closely. In reality, it was the Word of God that had revealed his heart to him, a shocking disclosure.

On one occasion, I was preaching through 1 Corinthians 13 and came to verse 4, which begins, "Love is patient . . ." In my mind, I was almost apologizing for bringing what I thought was a relatively benign sermon. I had sadly convinced myself that this sermon was not going to have an effect on anyone.

At the end of this message, I explained that Christ is the perfect embodiment of patient love, as the One who has perfectly loved us. Then, as soon as I finished the service, a visitor bolted to the pulpit in a state of near-panic. He explained that he had come to church by himself because no one in his family could bear his impatience, which, at times, made him demanding and overbearing. He confided that as I had spoken of God's patience toward us in Christ, his heart had been convicted. He confessed that he needed this patience. The Word of God had revealed this man to himself, and he saw his need for grace. There, on the front pew of the church, this broken man was born again.

If I had simply addressed the culture that day, if I had merely given a book review or cited a movie, if I had only critiqued a new television program, this man would never have been converted. It was because the Word of God was held up as a mirror that he saw his urgent need for grace, leading him to put his trust in Christ.

No one will be converted to Christ until he sees himself as God sees him. No one will grow in the grace of God without looking into the perfect law of liberty and beholding the holy character of God. It is there that people see their true need of him. This self-revealing law possesses sanctifying power to transform believers from one level of glory to another.

A Seed That Germinates

Third, Scripture identifies the Word of God as a seed that generates eternal life in spiritually dead souls. First Peter 1:23 says, "You have been born again not of seed which is perishable but imperishable, that is, through the living and enduring word of God." This verse addresses those who have been regenerated by the instrumentality of the divine Word. Scripture is represented as a seed that possesses the powers of reproduction. Regeneration happens passively—"born again" is a passive verb. God alone is active in regeneration. The new birth is monergistic, meaning there is only one active agent, namely, God. In this sovereign work, God acts upon the spiritually dead soul. He imparts spiritual life, so that men and women are raised to a new existence. The one born again becomes a new creature in Christ. The old things instantly pass away and new things come (2 Cor. 5:17). The one who is regenerated receives new life unlike anything he has experienced. Abundant life enters and energizes the once-dead soul.

In this verse, Peter first emphatically asserts how a person is *not* born again. He states that eternal life is not the result of a perishable seed being planted in one's life. Every seed reproduces life after its own kind. An apple seed does not produce a peach tree. Instead, it can produce only an apple tree, which, in turn, produces apples. A fundamental principle in life is this—like produces like. A seed can germinate for the propagation of the exact same kind of life. A seed reproduces after its own kind.

When Peter says that we have been born again of "imperishable seed," he means eternal life is given "through the living and enduring word of God." An eternal seed is necessary to produce eternal life. The seed of the Word is "living" and "enduring." Eternal life is imparted when an imperishable seed is sown in the heart. An "enduring" seed produces life that endures forever. It would be easier to grow oak trees by planting marbles than for someone to be saved by the planting of the perishable seed of the philosophies and religions of this world. In the parable of the soils, Jesus taught, "The seed is the word of God" (Luke 8:11). This divine seed possesses and produces divine life that never perishes. Jesus said, "He who believes in Me will live even if he dies" (John 11:25). It is exclusively through the inspired Word of God that the new birth comes.

In pulpit ministry, the preacher reaps what he sows. If he sows a worldly message, he will reap a worldly church. If he sows secular humanism and pop psychology, he will reap a shallow church. If he sows large handfuls of cultural trends and religious traditions, he will reap a fleshly church. If he sows generous portions of business principles and secular philosophy, if he sows personal experiences and political commentary, he will reap an unconverted church. But if a preacher sows the living and enduring Word, God will germinate the seed, resulting in a regenerate church.

Concerning the power of the Word, Spurgeon maintained: "I would rather speak five words out of this book than fifty thousand words of the philosophers. If we want revivals we must revive our reverence for the word of God. If we want conversions we must put more of God's word into our sermons."[4] I agree with the Prince of Preachers. We need more of God's Word in our preaching, not less.

A Milk That Nourishes

Fourth, the Word of God is portrayed as a milk that nourishes the soul. Once someone has been regenerated by the Word, his spiritual growth must be nurtured, which is accomplished by the milk of the Word. First Peter 2:2–3 says, "Like newborn babies, long for the pure milk of the word, so that by it you may grow in respect to salvation, if you have tasted the kindness of the Lord." The apostle is teaching that believers must always be like infants, constantly craving the pure milk of the Word. They must never assume that they will outgrow this need. Instead, they should always desire this milk. Every believer must cry out to be fed more of the Word. They must possess an unquenchable thirst in their souls for the Word.

Milk is a primary source of nutrition for human life and development. Babies are able to digest milk before they can digest solid food. Likewise, those who are born again should desire and devour spiritual milk. Milk contains antibodies that provide protection from disease. It is a potent stimulant for physical growth. In like manner, the Word of God protects believers and stimulates their spiritual growth. No child of God will be protected from sin or grow spiritually beyond his or her necessary intake of the Word of God.

The Word of God is the primary means of spiritual growth. As Peter makes clear, the intake of Scripture causes believers to "grow" in personal godliness. Biblical truth nurtures Christian character and causes believers

---

[4] Charles H. Spurgeon, *The Metropolitan Tabernacle Pulpit* (Pasadena, TX: Pilgrim Publications, n.d.), 38:114.

to advance "in respect to salvation," that is, progressive sanctification. As a baby needs milk often, the Word must be savored and swallowed on a daily basis. Quoting Deuteronomy 8:3, Jesus said, "Man shall not live on bread alone, but on every word that proceeds out of the mouth of God" (Matt. 4:4). In like manner, believers must live by the milk of the Word. This spiritual diet produces strong hearts, strong faith, and a strong immune system that fights off sin.

This sanctifying power of the Word is taught. The psalmist writes: "How can a young man keep his way pure? By keeping it according to Your word. . . . Your word I have treasured in my heart, that I may not sin against You" (Ps. 119:9, 11). When a believer treasures the Word in his heart, it enables him to resist the powerful lures of temptation and remain pure. This was seen in the life of the Lord Jesus Christ. When he was in the wilderness, our Lord faced multiple temptations from Satan. In response to each attack by the Devil, Jesus resisted by saying, "It is written . . ." Jesus unsheathed the sword of the Spirit and repelled the advances of Satan.

Every preacher must preach the Word and equip his flock to stand strong in their pursuit of holiness. Tragically, many pastors feed their people spiritual junk food that has no nutritional value for their spiritual development. Sad to say, there is a famine in the land for the hearing of the Word of the Lord (Amos 8:11). However, when a preacher expounds the Word of God, he is feeding his people the pure milk they need. By preaching the Word, expositors are nourishing their congregations to resist the advances of the world, the flesh, and the Devil.

A Lamp That Shines

Fifth, the Word of God is pictured as a lamp that shines in a dark world. The psalmist testifies, "Your word is a lamp to my feet and a light to my path" (Ps. 119:105). Importantly, this imagery implies that believers live in a fallen world of spiritual darkness. Many dangers, toils, and snares threaten the safety of all followers of Christ who are traveling the narrow path that leads to life. Many pilgrims have strayed from this trail and fallen into moral disaster, to their great harm. The path is sometimes hard to detect. Every believer needs divine light to be shed before him or her in order to avoid the dangers lurking on every side. In this dark and dangerous world, the Word of God is a shining torch that enables travelers to see their way home.

When the psalmist writes, "Your word is a lamp to my feet," the emphasis is not on the traveler's head and what he thinks. The attention is not on his ears and what he hears. Neither is the focus on his affections and what he feels. Instead, the stress is on his feet. The light that has shined into the mind, ears, and heart must not stop there. The lamp of God's Word must govern the direction our feet take. The goal of the Word is not merely to inform, but to direct and transform. What people learn with their heads must be lived out with their feet. James Montgomery Boice writes, "We do not know how to live our lives, but the Bible shines on the path before us to expose the wrong, dangerous ways we might take and light up the right way."[5] The inerrant Word gives infallible direction to our lives as we traverse this darkened world.

The Bible elsewhere confirms that the Word of God is a light that shines into the lives of believers, guiding them. David writes, "The commandment of the LORD is pure, enlightening the eyes" (Ps. 19:8). Solomon reinforces this: "The commandment is a lamp and the teaching is light" (Prov. 6:23). Peter adds, "We have the prophetic word made more sure . . . a lamp shining in a dark place" (2 Pet. 1:19). The lamp of divine, written revelation reveals the will of God for the believer. Whether it is expressed by biblical command or precept, by scriptural example or principle, the Word illumines the path every believer must take. This divine light in Scripture is not a mere option, but an absolute necessity for every follower of Christ.

Every preacher should be like a torchbearer, holding forth the light of truth in Scripture. Rather than bemoaning the present, decadent times, let us remember that the light shines brightest in the darkest hour of the night. This lamp of God's Word has never been more desperately needed than in this midnight hour. This sinful, adulterous generation is virtually unprecedented in the recent history of Western civilization. It has never been more necessary for the Word of God to shine from pulpits, revealing the way we must go. God's servants must hold forth the light of truth so that believers can avoid disastrous harm. Preachers must not hide their light under a bushel, but let it shine for all to see.

One who faithfully held forth the torch of truth in a dark world was Spurgeon. This Reformed Victorian voice said: "Everything in the railway service depends upon the accuracy of the signals: when these are wrong, life will be sacrificed. On the road to heaven we need unerring signals, or the catastrophes will be far more terrible."[6] There is only one divine standard that gives infallible signals in life. This inerrant guide is the lamp of the

---

[5] James Montgomery Boice, *Psalms, Vol. 3: Psalms 107–150* (Grand Rapids, MI: Baker, 1998), 1026.
[6] Spurgeon, *The Metropolitan Tabernacle Pulpit*, 36:167.

Word of God. Every pulpit must be shining brighter than the sun at high noon. As this age grows darker, every pulpit must blaze with the truth that pierces the darkness.

A Fire That Consumes

Sixth, the Word of God is represented as a fire that consumes whatever is false. The Word of God is a powerful instrument that destroys all that is contrary to its message. The weeping prophet, Jeremiah, recorded the words of God: "'Is not My word like fire?' declares the LORD" (Jer. 23:29). This is a rhetorical question, the answer being so obvious that it does not need to be answered. Any rational person knows the answer. The divine Word *is* like a fire. There are many positive uses for fire—it gives light, yields warmth, and cooks food. However, God intends to convey the negative sense in which his Word is like a fire—it consumes that with which it comes in contact.

In Jeremiah's day, those in danger of being consumed with divine fire were the false prophets and all who followed their lies. God rebukes these men for prophesying falsely out of the deception of their own hearts (v. 26); for making the people forget his name (v. 27); for speaking their dreams (v. 28); for stealing his Word (v. 30); and for leading the people away from the truth (v. 32). God will abandon all who refuse his message (v. 33). In the end, he will punish these false prophets and all who follow their words (v. 34).

Earlier in Jeremiah's prophecy, God said, "Behold, I am making My words in your mouth fire" (Jer. 5:14b). This is to say that the Word of God is like a fire that will consume all unbelievers. The flames of divine judgment will come upon all who do not turn to the Lord. God is represented as a "consuming fire" (Heb. 12:29) who will damn all unbelievers in the eternal incineration of hell. God, who is fire, and his fiery Word are inseparable. God will ignite the fires of eternal punishment upon all who have not built upon the solid rock of his Word.

This weighty message of divine vengeance must be proclaimed by every preacher. This flaming message will cause listeners to be either blessed or burned. There is no middle ground. In this hour, we need bold men who will declare that divine fire will consume all that is false. At the same time, we preach the grace and the mercy of God. But this must not preclude the message of divine wrath. God will burn up all who refuse his message. When rightly preached, the Bible is a red-hot book. The Scriptures sizzle with the leaping flames of divine judgment. The Word contains the hottest message this world has ever heard. When any man preaches, he is called to start and spread this consuming fire.

A Hammer That Shatters

Seventh, the Word of God is pictured as a hammer that shatters the hardest hearts. In this same Jeremiah passage, where God is the speaker, and Jeremiah is mouthpiece, God says, "Is not My word . . . like a hammer which shatters a rock?" (23:29). Here is another rhetorical question, the answer being a strong affirmative. There is no force in the world that compares with the soul-crushing power of the Word of God. It comes with such devastating impact that it smashes all who resist God in unbelief.

In this context, the rock refers to sin-hardened hearts that embrace the message of the false prophets. These false teachers and their followers were hardheaded and hard-hearted. They were stiff-necked people. Their foreheads were like flint. Their lives were cemented in their defiance to the truth of God. By repelling truth, they rejected God. They had cold, lifeless hearts of stone that were resistant to the truth of God.

How will such hardness of heart be humbled before the Lord? The submission that leads to salvation comes when the invincible hammer of the Word of God is wielded by the preacher. This powerful weapon is able to break down all resistance in the day of God's power. This divine instrument is harder than the hardest heart. It is stronger than the thickest forehead. It is harder than the stoniest soul. It can dash into pieces the most resistant heart. This hammer can bring a man or a woman to the place of unconditional surrender, the place where he or she will call upon God's name for saving grace.

But if a man will not repent, this hammer will inflict the judgment of God. If the Word will not soften a heart, it will further harden it. Upon hearing the Word, no heart ever remains the same. Under the blows of this hammer, every heart is either becoming softer or harder, either receptive or more resistant.

Frail men, in pulpits with the Bible, have a sledgehammer in their hands. As they expound Scripture, they bring a great force to bear upon the hearts of their listeners. They bring the power of the Word of God upon the lives of their congregation. This pounding tool shatters pride into the dust of humility. It smashes self-righteousness into the smallest of pieces, leading to humble submission before God.

Conclusion

These seven symbols represent the invincible power of the inerrant Word. The Bible is able to do what it does because it is what it claims to be—the unadulterated Word without any mixture of human error. The purity and power of the Word are inseparably bound together. Because Scripture is flawless, it is therefore forceful. Because it is trustworthy, it is consequently triumphant.

I call every preacher to wield the sword, to hold up the mirror, to scatter the seed, to serve the milk, to shine the lamp, to spread the flame, and to swing the hammer. Stop with the secular wisdom in the pulpit. Cancel the entertainment in the church. Fire the drama team. Get rid of the shtick. Unplug the colored lights. Put the pulpit back in the center of the building. Stand up like a man. Open the Bible. Lift it up, let it out, and let it fly. It is the inerrant Word, and it is full of invincible power.

22

The Mandate and the Motivations

INERRANCY AND EXPOSITORY PREACHING[1]

John MacArthur

A generation ago, in October 1978, nearly three hundred evangelical scholars and pastors signed the Chicago Statement on Biblical Inerrancy. It was
a sweeping affirmation of the truthfulness of God's Word and an important
witness to the watching world. Liberal Protestants, and even some within
broader evangelicalism, were openly questioning the accuracy and trustworthiness of Scripture. In light of their skeptical attacks, it was necessary
for Bible-believing Christians to take a strong stand, rallying around cardi-
nal doctrines such as the inerrancy, inspiration, and authority of Scripture.

The church today must take that same stand. A commitment to God
and his Word must be reaffirmed in every generation. I am grateful for
those men who have taken that stand in the past. I am equally thrilled to

[1] In this chapter, I have incorporated material from two articles written for *The Master's Seminary Journal*,
both of which can be found on the seminary's website, http://www.tms.edu. The articles are as follows:
"The Mandate of Biblical Inerrancy: Expository Preaching," *The Master's Seminary Journal* 1, no. 1 (Spring
1990): 3–16; "Preach the Word: Five Compelling Motivations for the Faithful Expositor," *The Master's
Seminary Journal* 22, no. 2 (Fall 2011): 163–77. For a corresponding exposition of 2 Timothy 3–4, see my
chapter entitled "Preach the Word," in *The Shepherd as Preacher*, ed. John MacArthur (Eugene, OR: Harvest House, 2015), 9–28. For a book-length treatment of the topic of expository preaching, see *Preaching:
How to Preach Biblically*, MacArthur Pastor's Library (Nashville: Thomas Nelson, 2005).

see a new generation of Christian leaders being raised up who will carry the baton of faithfulness forward.

But how is a commitment to biblical inerrancy fleshed out in practical ministry? The answer is seen, first and foremost, by the way in which the Word of God is proclaimed from the pulpit. Evangelical preaching ought to reflect our conviction that God's Word is unfailing and without error. Too often, it does not. Over the past few decades, in many so-called evangelical churches, there has been a discernible trend *away* from biblical preaching and a drift *toward* an experience-driven, pragmatic, audience-centered approach.

But if we believe that "all Scripture is inspired by God," we should be equally committed to the reality that every part of divine revelation is "profitable for teaching, for reproof, for correction, for training in righteousness; so that the man of God may be adequate, equipped for every good work" (2 Tim. 3:16–17).[2] This requires that the focus of our preaching be the accurate exposition of the biblical text. After all, the power to save sinners and to transform lives lies not in human cleverness or oratorical skill, but in the Spirit-empowered truth of God's Word (Heb. 4:12).

The Mandate for Expository Preaching

For the biblical expositor, 2 Timothy 4:2 majestically stands out as sacred ground. It is precious territory for every pastor who, following in the footsteps of Paul, desires to faithfully proclaim the Word of God. In this verse, the apostle defined the primary mandate for God-honoring church ministry, not only for Timothy, but for all who would come after him. The minister of the gospel is called to "preach the word." This call summarizes biblical ministry in one central directive. Any form of preaching that ignores this intended purpose and design of God falls short of the divine plan.

Significantly, Paul's directive comes after his emphasis on the inspired, inerrant, and sufficient nature of Scripture (3:16–17). Because it is God's Word, and because it comes with his very authority (4:1), it must be proclaimed faithfully. Like the herald of a king, the biblical preacher has been charged by his heavenly Sovereign to declare the royal message with *accuracy* and *completeness*. Anything less constitutes a dereliction of duty.

Accordingly, the preacher's responsibility is to convey the meaning of each biblical passage *entirely* and *exactly* as it was intended by God. This is the very essence of *expository* preaching—to explain the meaning and

[2] Scripture quotations in this chapter are from *The New American Standard Bible*®. Copyright © The Lockman Foundation 1960, 1962, 1963, 1968, 1971, 1972, 1973, 1975, 1977, 1995. Used by permission.

implications of the text with clarity and conviction so that God's people can understand and obey his Word. Because every word of Scripture is inspired and inerrant, every word must be preached.

The doctrine of inerrancy derives from the simple reality that God is true (cf. Ex. 34:6; John 14:6) and that he speaks in harmony with his nature (cf. Prov. 30:5; Isa. 65:16; James 1:18). Thus, he cannot lie (cf. Titus 1:2; Heb. 6:18). The Word of God, then, is a Word that is free from any error or falsehood. It is absolutely and wholly true. As Jesus declared to his Father, "Your word is truth" (John 17:17).

A commitment to biblical exposition follows from the fact that God gave his true Word to be communicated *entirely* as he gave it, that is, the whole counsel of God is to be preached (Matt 28:20; Acts 5:20; 20:27). Moreover, God gave his true Word to be communicated *exactly* as he gave it. It is to be dispensed precisely as it was delivered, without any alteration of the message. Thus, faithful preaching must be both comprehensive and precise. It must encompass all portions of Scripture and it must interpret the details of the text with accuracy and precision.

The New Testament provides numerous examples of this kind of Scripture-oriented preaching. The Word of God is what Jesus preached (Luke 5:1). It is the message the apostles taught (Acts 4:31; 6:2). It is the word the Samaritans received (8:14), as given by the apostles (v. 25). It is the message the Gentiles received, as preached by Peter (11:1). It is the word Paul preached on his missionary journeys (13:5, 7, 44, 48, 49; 15:35–36; 16:32; 17:13; 18:11; 19:10). It was the focus of Luke in the book of Acts, in that it spread rapidly and widely (6:7; 12:24; 19:20). Paul was careful to tell the Corinthians that he spoke the Word as it was given from God, that it had not been adulterated, and that it was a manifestation of truth (2 Cor. 2:17; 4:2). He readily acknowledged that God's Word was the source of his preaching (Col. 1:25; 1 Thess. 2:13).

As it was with Christ and the apostles, so preachers today are to deliver Scripture in such a way that they can say, "Thus says the Lord." Their responsibility is to proclaim the text as it was originally given and intended. That is the only way they will faithfully fulfill their God-given mandate to *preach the Word*.

The Motivations for Expository Preaching

In the verses surrounding 2 Timothy 4:2, Paul provided his protégé with much-needed motivation to stand firm and persevere to the end. For Timothy, the command was clear—*preach the Word*—and the calling was deadly serious: souls were at stake. In order to equip him for the task, Paul gave Timothy five compelling reasons to persevere in ministry faithfulness. These motivations, found in 2 Timothy 3:1–4:4, are as applicable today as they were two millennia ago.

MOTIVATION 1: THE DANGER OF THE SEASONS (2 TIM. 3:1–9)

In 3:1, Paul warns Timothy "that in the last days difficult times will come." As used here, the phrase "the last days" refers not merely to the end of the church age, but to the entirety of it, from the day of Pentecost to the parousia. Paul's point is that, until the Lord comes back, the church will continually experience difficult times. The phrase "difficult times" does not refer to specific points of chronological time, but rather to seasons or epochs. And the term *difficult* carries the meaning of "savage" or "perilous."

Paul is expressing the reality that, throughout the church age, there will be seasons when believers are savagely threatened. With his execution imminent, the apostle certainly knew a great deal about the difficulty that Christians might face. He also understood that Timothy was facing persecution and hostility, and that his young apprentice would be tempted by sins of cowardice and compromise. But that was exactly why Timothy needed to preach the Word. The looming threat made his ministry mandate all the more necessary and urgent.

In 3:13, Paul writes, "Evil men . . . will proceed from bad to worse." Such men are "lovers of self, lovers of money, boastful, arrogant, revilers, disobedient to parents, ungrateful, unholy, unloving, irreconcilable, malicious gossips, without self-control, brutal, haters of good, treacherous, reckless, conceited, lovers of pleasure rather than lovers of God" (vv. 2–4). They are externally religious, "holding to a form of godliness, although they have denied its power," as they "enter into households and captivate weak women weighed down with sins, led on by various impulses, always learning and never able to come to the knowledge of the truth" (vv. 5–7). Being of a depraved mind, they are filled with sin, error, and destruction. They oppose sound doctrine and reject the faith.

Significantly, based on Paul's description, it is clear that the greatest threat to the church comes not from hostile forces without, but from false teachers within. Like spiritual terrorists, they sneak into the church and leave a path of destruction in their wake. They are wolves in sheep's clothing (Matt. 7:15). It is their treachery that makes the "difficult times" of the last days so perilous.

The church has been threatened by savage wolves and spiritual swindlers from its earliest days (cf. Acts 20:29). Satan, the father of lies (John 8:44), has always sought to undermine the truth with his deadly errors (1 Tim. 4:1; cf. 2 Cor. 11:4). It is not surprising, then, that church history has often been marked by difficult times—seasons in which falsehood and deception have waged war against the pure gospel.

Those attacks have continued in our own day, which is why expository preaching is just as needed now as it has ever been. In light of the dangers that constantly threaten the church, preachers must equip God's people with the sword of the Spirit, which is the Word of God (Eph. 6:17).

The church today is a hodgepodge product of the accumulated errors of church history—from sacramentalism to subjectivism to syncretism. The "difficult times" that Paul spoke of certainly characterize the contemporary situation. Yet, in the midst of this chaos and confusion, faithful ministers are still required to carry out the very task that Paul gave to Timothy. In fact, the only solution for the church today is for pastors to diligently fulfill their God-given responsibility to *preach the Word*.

Motivation 2: The Devotion of the Saints (2 Tim. 3:10–14)

The faithful preacher is also motivated by his love and appreciation for those believers who have gone before him. Like a great cloud of witnesses, the steadfast spiritual leaders from generations past, by means of their examples, spur the biblical expositor on toward greater commitment and ministry effectiveness.

In Paul's case, he reminded Timothy of his own example and urged him to follow suit. Thus, he says in 3:10–11, "Now you followed my teaching, conduct, purpose, faith, patience, love, perseverance, persecutions, and sufferings, such as happened to me at Antioch, at Iconium and at Lystra; what persecutions I endured, and out of them all the Lord rescued me!"

The gospel Paul taught, Timothy was to continue preaching. The conduct, confidence, and Christlikeness that marked the apostle's ministry were likewise to characterize his son in the faith. Even the suffering that Paul endured, Timothy was to embrace as well. The young pastor was to stay the course and follow in the path of his mentor.

The integrity of Paul's ministry had been obvious to Timothy. In their travels together, Timothy had witnessed the consistency between Paul's public teaching and his private practice. The testimony of the apostle's life was one of unwavering conviction—a fact that Timothy knew firsthand. Thus, Paul was able to commend himself to Timothy and encourage him not only to preach faithfully, but also to follow the same God-centered purpose: to passionately pursue faithfulness in his own life.

Throughout his missionary journeys, Paul had suffered greatly for the sake of the gospel. Even as he wrote this letter, he was suffering for Christ. Timothy surely felt the weight of Paul's words when the apostle added, "Indeed, all who desire to live godly in Christ Jesus will be persecuted" (v. 12). Yet, Paul is clear, such tribulation is no reason to shy away from following the way of faithfulness.

Paul warned that the world would continue to grow darker: "Evil men . . . will proceed from bad to worse, deceiving and being deceived" (v. 13). Nonetheless, Timothy must not capitulate or be deceived. His task was not easy, but it was simple: to stay true to the Word of God and preach it carefully and consistently. Thus, Paul challenged Timothy with these words: "You, however, continue in the things you have learned and become convinced of, knowing from whom you have learned them" (v. 14).

In exhorting Timothy to hold fast and endure, Paul called on his disciple to remember his own example. Timothy did not need a new strategy. He simply needed to follow the pattern of faithfulness he had observed in the man of God who had gone before him.

Paul understood that uniqueness and novelty in ministry are deadly. The right approach is not to reinvent the paradigm, but simply to follow in the well-worn paths of those who have gone before.

The faithful preacher appreciates his spiritual heritage—recognizing that he is linked to a long line of godly men from whom there can be no separation. Moreover, he understands that it is his responsibility, as part of the current generation of church history, to guard the truth that has been entrusted to him so that, one day, he can pass it on to the those who come after him.

That this was Paul's expectation for Timothy is clear from his instruction in 2:2: "The things which you have heard from me in the presence of many witnesses, entrust these to faithful men who will be able to teach others also." Four ministerial generations are described in that verse: Paul, Timothy, faithful men, and others also. From generation to generation, the truth was to be safeguarded by each generation and then passed on without innovation or deviation.

The brash folly of young men today tempts them to disregard the wisdom of previous generations and to glory in their own cleverness or originality. Those who scorn the faithful examples of saints now in heaven, and instead prize their own self-styled, inventive approaches to ministry, do so at their peril.

But, as evidenced by Paul's instruction to Timothy, the faithful preacher is motivated by the heritage left by prior generations of church history. And like the spiritual giants of past centuries, he is committed to the same ministry mandate they were. He has the privilege of standing on their shoulders. But he also bears the responsibility to carry on their legacy. Therefore, through both his life and his lips, he must *preach the Word*.

Motivation 3: The Dynamic of the Scriptures (2 Tim. 3:15–17)

The faithful expositor is motivated, thirdly, by the nature of the Bible itself. He understands that Scripture is no ordinary book; it is the inspired revelation of God himself. If the pastor desires to honor the Lord in his ministry or to see the Holy Spirit's work unhindered in the lives of his people, he has no alternative but to preach the Word faithfully.

Timothy had experienced the power of God's Word from a young age. Paul reminded him of that reality with these words: "From childhood you have known the sacred writings which are able to give you the wisdom that leads to salvation through faith which is in Christ Jesus" (3:15). It was clear to Timothy where the power and authority in ministry lay.

The term Paul used for "childhood" refers to an infant. From the time Timothy had been a baby in the arms of his mother, he had been exposed to the Word of God. And it was through the Scriptures that he had come to saving faith in Jesus Christ.

The apostle appealed to Timothy's past, essentially asking, "Why would you do anything other than preach the Word when you know, from your own personal testimony, that it alone is the wisdom that leads to salvation?" When the mission is to present the message of salvation in all its Spirit-empowered fullness, the only option is to faithfully proclaim the truth of God's Word.

Having already appealed to Timothy's upbringing, Paul reinforced his point by emphasizing the Bible's true nature and dynamic effectiveness: "All Scripture is inspired by God and profitable for teaching, for reproof, for correction, for training in righteousness; so that the man of God may be adequate, equipped for every good work" (vv. 16–17). This sacred book is "inspired by God" or, more literally, *God-breathed*. And, as these verses indicate, it is powerful not just to save (v. 15), but also to sanctify.

The Word of God is *profitable*, or useful toward sanctification, in four ways. First, as the sole source of divine truth, it provides the doctrinal content for *teaching*. Second, it is the authority for admonition and *reproof*, because it confronts sin and error. Third, it provides the vehicle for *correction*. The Scriptures not only expose wrongdoing, they also show transgressors how to be restored to an upright position. Finally, after the truth of God's Word has torn down sin and error, it builds up the believer through *training in righteousness*. Clearly, the function of the Scriptures in the life of the believer is a comprehensive work.

The result of this all-encompassing work is that the man of God and everyone under his influence is made mature, whole, complete, and equipped for every good work (v. 17). The first student of the Word is the preacher, who himself must be impacted. He is the primary beneficiary, and his ministry to others flows out of the Word's transforming work in his own heart.

With such a comprehensive work of both salvation and sanctification available through the power of the Scriptures, why would anyone be tempted to preach anything else? The pastor who cares about the spiritual growth of his people must make God and his Word the centerpiece of his ministry. In order to do that, he must *preach the Word*.

MOTIVATION 4: THE DEMAND OF THE SOVEREIGN (2 TIM. 4:1–2)

Paul prefaced his command to preach by warning Timothy about the dangerous seasons that would come and by pointing to his own example and to the supernatural power of Scripture. But in 4:1, the apostle escalated his exhortation to an even greater level. Invoking God himself, Paul expressed the seriousness of the situation in explicit terms: "I solemnly charge you in the presence of God and of Christ Jesus, who is to judge the living and the dead, and by His appearing and His kingdom . . ." Those piercing words should strike holy fear into the heart of every preacher. They stand as the apex of Paul's previous statements, and should serve as the most compelling motivation in the life of the expositor.

The Scottish Reformer John Knox certainly understood this reality. Upon being commissioned to preach, and feeling the weight of that responsibility, Knox "burst forth in most abundant tears and withdrew himself to his chamber."[3] He was completely overwhelmed by the awesome accountability of that duty. Timothy's call to preach came not simply from Paul, but from the sovereign King by whom he was commissioned and before whom he would one day give an account. Jesus Christ is the one who will judge the faithfulness of his ministers. As men of God, they are under holy scrutiny from the Lord himself.

This is nowhere made clearer than in Revelation 1:14, where Christ is portrayed as surveying his church with penetrating eyes of fire. Those who are called to preach are under inescapable divine observation (cf. Prov. 15:3). There is no relief from his gaze, no hiding from his evaluation (cf. Ps. 139:7–12).

It is for this reason that James exhorted his readers to refrain from becoming teachers, as theirs is a greater judgment (James 3:1). It is why the apostle Paul said in 1 Corinthians 4:3–4 that it was a small thing to him what men thought of him, and even what he thought of himself, because he was accountable to God. Hebrews 13:17 plainly states that leaders "will give an account" for their ministry. The most dominant force in the preacher's life and ministry is the realization that he will one day give an account to God (cf. 2 Cor. 5:10).

Consider the following anecdote from Charles Spurgeon's ministry:

> A young preacher once complained to Charles Spurgeon, the famous British preacher of the 1800s, that he did not have as big a church as he deserved.
>
> "How many do you preach to?" Spurgeon asked.
>
> "Oh, about 100," the man replied.
>
> Solemnly Spurgeon said, "That will be enough to give account for on the day of judgment."[4]

Serious ministry is motivated by that weighty reality. Popularity with people, recognition from peers, winsomeness in the pulpit—these are not the standards of success. God's opinion is the only one that ultimately matters. And his measure of success is *faithfulness* (cf. Matt. 25:21, 23). Knowing this, the biblical expositor is driven to carefully, clearly, and consistently *preach the Word*.

---

[3] Marion Harland, *John Knox* (New York: G. P. Putnam, 1900), 16. Prior to this reaction, a fellow preacher named John Rough read Knox a charge very similar to Paul's words in 2 Tim. 4:1.

[4] Cited from Warren W. Wiersbe, *The Bible Exposition Commentary: New Testament* (Colorado Springs: Cook, 2001), 2:254.

MOTIVATION 5: THE DECEPTIVENESS OF THE SENSUAL (2 TIM. 4:3–4)

Having reminded Timothy of the ultimate accountability, Paul continued by warning him that *faithful* preaching will not necessarily be *popular* preaching. As the apostle explained, "For the time will come when they will not endure sound doctrine; but wanting to have their ears tickled, they will accumulate for themselves teachers in accordance to their own desires, and will turn away their ears from the truth and will turn aside to myths" (4:3–4).

Sinners refuse to heed the truth that saves and sanctifies. Instead, hardening their hearts, they seek out soft-peddled messages that accommodate their sin. Thus, they search for preachers who make them feel good, not guilty. And false teachers are happy to oblige, tickling the ears of their audiences with man-centered messages and false hopes.

In the process, the seriousness of sin is downplayed and disregarded; greed is promoted with promises of prosperity; worship is reduced to vain emotionalism; and felt needs are highlighted while the true gospel is ignored. These false teachers are the same people who, according to 2:16, pursue worldly, empty chatter that leads to further ungodliness. Their worldly message may be popular, but, like gangrene, its spread is actually deadly.

Paul's words certainly describe the scene in contemporary American Christianity. *Doctrine* has become a bad word; truth is viewed as relative; and numbers have been made the measure of ministry effectiveness. The temptation to tickle ears is great, since the preachers who attract the largest crowds are deemed the most successful. But to pervert the truth by watering down the gospel is a deadly form of wickedness. The minister who caters his message to the whims of the world, telling unregenerate hearts only what they want to hear, has sold out.

By contrast, the faithful minister is willing to speak the whole truth boldly, even when it is not popular to do so. The only way to see lives transformed from sensuality to salvation is to faithfully proclaim the message of the gospel. If those who wish to have their ears tickled are to be radically transformed, they must be confronted with the truth. To that end, the faithful expositor will not cease to *preach the Word*.

Faithful to the End

Paul was under no delusions that the commission would be easy for Timothy, or for the faithful men coming after him. It had not been easy for Paul either. Yet, in spite of the many trials he had faced, the apostle had remained true to the end. As a result, he could say: "I am already being poured out as a drink offering, and the time of my departure has come. I have fought the good fight, I have finished the course, I have kept the faith" (4:6–7).

In this, his last appeal to Timothy, he invited the young pastor to likewise run the race with endurance (cf. Heb. 12:1–2). But Paul went to his grave not knowing how the story would end for Timothy. He had to trust that the Lord would preserve his young son in the faith. Would Timothy remain faithful to the end?

The book of Hebrews offers an initial answer to that question. In 13:23, the author told his readers, "Take notice that our brother Timothy has been released, with whom, if he comes soon, I will see you." These words, likely written after the death of Paul, indicate that Timothy had been in prison, but was soon to return to the work of ministry. The implication is clear: Timothy had been persecuted for the sake of the gospel. Yet, like Paul, he had remained faithful and steadfast in spite of the suffering he faced.

Church history provides a later glimpse into Timothy's legacy of faithfulness. According to *Fox's Book of Martyrs*:

> Timothy was the celebrated disciple of St. Paul, and bishop of Ephesus, where he zealously governed the Church until A.D. 97. At this period, as the pagans were about to celebrate a feast called Catagogion, Timothy, meeting the procession, severely reproved them for their ridiculous idolatry, which so exasperated the people that they fell upon him with their clubs, and beat him in so dreadful a manner that he expired of the bruises two days after.[5]

To his dying day, Timothy courageously confronted the culture around him with the truth of the gospel. That unwavering commitment cost him his life. Like Paul, he was martyred for his faithfulness. At the end of Timothy's life, he too was able to look back on a ministry that had been devoted to honoring Christ through the preaching of his Word.

In the same way that Timothy had received a legacy of faithfulness, he passed it on to the next generation of Christian leaders. Bible expositors today, though removed by many centuries, are the recipients of that faithful heritage. The motivations that drove Paul and Timothy ought to compel the current generation of preachers and teachers. God is still delivering his divine mandate to faithful men: *preach the Word*.

---

[5] John Fox, *Fox's Book of Martyrs*, ed. William Byron Forbush (Grand Rapids, MI: Zondervan, 1967), 7.

Conclusion

Like Timothy, the faithful expositor will make it his lifelong aim to preach the mind of God as he finds it in the inerrant Word of God. He understands it through the disciplines of hermeneutics and exegesis. He exposits the Scriptures as the message that God spoke and commissioned him to deliver.

To cite Spurgeon once more:

> It is blessed to eat into the very soul of the Bible until, at last, you come to talk in Scriptural language, and your spirit is flavoured with the words of the Lord, so that your blood is Bibline and the very essence of the Bible flows from you.[6]

Inerrancy demands an exegetical process and an expository proclamation. Only the exegetical process preserves God's Word entirely, guarding the treasure of revelation and declaring its meaning exactly as he intended it to be proclaimed (cf. 1 Tim. 6:20–21; 2 Tim. 2:15). Expository preaching is the result of the exegetical process. Thus, it is the essential link between inerrancy and proclamation. It is mandated to preserve the purity of God's originally given inerrant Word and to proclaim the whole counsel of God's redemptive truth.

---

[6] Charles Spurgeon, cited in John R. W. Stott, *The Preacher's Portrait* (Grand Rapids, MI: Eerdmans, 1961), 31.

23

Putting Scripture Front and Center

INERRANCY AND APOLOGETICS

Michael Vlach

In June 1886, Charles Haddon Spurgeon addressed the issue of apologetics and the Bible from his pulpit at the Metropolitan Tabernacle in London. Early in the sermon, he stated, "I believe the best way of defending the Gospel is to spread the Gospel!" He then offered an analogy involving a lion in a cage:

> Suppose a number of persons were to take it into their heads that they had to defend a lion. There he is in the cage, and here come all the soldiers of the army to fight for him. Well, I should suggest to them, if they would not object, and feel that it was humbling to them, that they should kindly stand back, and open the door, and let the lion out! I believe that would be the best way of defending him, for he would take care of himself; and the best "apology" for the gospel is to let the gospel out. . . . Let the Lion out, and see who will dare to approach him. The Lion of the tribe of Judah will soon drive away all his adversaries.[1]

---

[1] Charles H. Spurgeon, "Christ and His Co-Workers," in *The Metropolitan Tabernacle Pulpit* (London: Passmore, 1896), 42:256.

For the English preacher, the Bible and the gospel did not need to be defended by others as much as they needed to be freed to defend themselves. On another occasion, Spurgeon reputedly exclaimed: "Defend the Bible? I would as soon defend a lion! Unchain it and it will defend itself."[2] The message: don't keep the lion caged up. Let him out!

Over a century later, debate continues concerning the role of God's inerrant Word in apologetics. The purpose of this chapter is to highlight the relationship between the Bible, inerrancy, and Christian apologetics.[3] It also will address the connection between inerrancy, and what is called presuppositional apologetics. This chapter asserts that the best starting point and basis for apologetic encounters is the unerring Bible—the Word of God, which comes from the God without whom nothing would exist. Inerrancy, therefore, is important for Christian apologetics.

This truth should encourage all Christians. Any Christian who knows the Bible can present the Christian faith in a bold manner since the authority of God and his Word is behind him. He never needs to worry that the Bible is in error. Inerrancy also means that apologetics is not just for the brightest of the bright, the academic elite, or those who have spent years studying philosophy. It is for all Christians.

We certainly are grateful for expert Christian apologists who have devoted much of their lives to providing answers to non-Christian objections, showing the flaws of other worldviews, and establishing that there are no errors in the Scriptures. We not only learn from their work, but we encourage more of it. Yet as we affirm the importance of Christian scholarship on this issue, we also assert that the success of the apologetic encounter is not ultimately based on cleverness, quick wit, debating skills, or years of studying the classic arguments for God's existence, but on the power of God and his Word. It is the Bible, through the power of the Spirit, that saves people. Thus, the proclamation of the inerrant Scriptures and the worldview they present should be front and center in our encounters with a lost world. This does not mean that the first words we use must always be Scripture verses or that we don't use other evidences, but the inerrant Word should not be held back, concealed, or brought up later, only after "other things" have been established. The Bible is the sword of the Spirit (Eph. 6:17), a mighty offensive weapon that we bring to the encounter. We don't fight with one

---

[2] This appears to be a paraphrase of a message Spurgeon offered to the Bible Society in 1875.

[3] "At the heart of contemporary evangelical Bibliology and apologetics is the question of Scriptural inerrancy—in particular, the most appropriate and effective method of its exposition and defense." Greg L. Bahnsen, "Inductivism, Inerrancy, and Presuppositionalism," in *Journal of the Evangelical Theological Society* 20 (1977): 289.

hand tied behind our backs. We don't cage the lion. We let the lion out of the cage to win the battle!

Defining Inerrancy

Inerrancy is the view that the entire Bible is true in all it affirms. There are no errors in the Scriptures. Whatever topic the Bible addresses, it does so accurately, with no mistakes.

Often, defenses of inerrancy focus on refuting claims that the Bible has errors. This should occur, since false claims need to be refuted. For example, the fact that some Gospel writers include details about the resurrection that other writers don't is not an error. Differing details are not necessarily contradictory details. Also, a New Testament writer's paraphrase of an Old Testament passage rather than a verbatim quotation is not an error. A paraphrase can be accurate, even if it is not a word-for-word quotation. To use another example, a person who rejects the manuscript evidence of the New Testament (fifty-six hundred manuscripts) but accepts the accuracy of Plato's writings (seven manuscripts) should be shown the foolishness of this conclusion.

Yet while addressing objections to inerrancy is important, there is an even bigger issue: worldview and a correct view of God. If God is real and possesses the attributes ascribed to him in the Bible, and if this God is personal and desires to communicate with those whom he created, then he is able to reveal himself without error. Making the case for inerrancy, therefore, is not simply about putting out individual fires that the skeptic of inerrancy starts. The Christian does not have to play an endless game of "Bible whack-a-mole," where answering one objection only leads to multiplying objections from a skeptic. The defense of inerrancy is rooted in a proper view of God and this God's ability to communicate with his creatures.[4] The Christian can rest assured that God's Word is true in all it affirms. As Paul stated, "Let God be found true, though every man be found a liar" (Rom. 3:4).[5] Thus, the inerrancy of Scripture is not a presupposition with no context. The apologist can assume the inerrancy of Scripture because of who God is.

---

[4] "Few can maintain this balancing act with intellectual honesty. Either the Bible is from God or it is not. If it is from God, why does God not know how to tell the truth about science and history?" John Jacob Tollefsen, "An Apologetic Approach to Hermeneutics and Inerrancy," http://phc.edu/UserFiles/File/_Other %20Projects/Global%20Journal/11-2/Tollefsen%20for%20GJCT%20vol%2011%20no%202.pdf (accessed Nov. 28, 2014).

[5] Unless otherwise indicated, Scripture quotations in this chapter are from *The New American Standard Bible*®. Copyright © The Lockman Foundation 1960, 1962, 1963, 1968, 1971, 1972, 1973, 1975, 1977, 1995. Used by permission.

Defining Apologetics

Our term *apologetics* is derived from the Greek term *apologia*, which was used in pagan writings, Christian literature, and the New Testament. For example, Plato's account of Socrates' trial is called *The Apology of Socrates*. Justin Martyr wrote his *Apology* to defend Christianity from heretical ideas. When standing before a mob in Jerusalem, Paul declared, "Hear my defense [*apologia*]" (Acts 22:1). In the New Testament, *apologia* refers to making a defense of something.[6] In the context of Christianity, apologetics is a rational defense of the Christian faith.[7]

Apologetics can take different forms. First, there is *proof*, which involves providing various evidences for the Christian faith. The emphasis here is on offering a positive case why Christianity should be accepted. Second, there is *defense*. This involves shielding Christianity from attacks made against it. This also includes answering criticisms and objections from opponents of Christianity. Third, there is *refutation* of competing worldviews. Here the goal is to show that non-Christian belief systems are internally inconsistent and unable to offer a coherent explanation of reality.

A robust apologetic should include all three elements. All three can be used by the Spirit of God. In our world, there is truth and error. The Christian addresses both. He actively promotes what is true and refutes what is contrary to the truth (Titus 1:9). Thus, apologetics is multidimensional, involving positive reasons for the Christian faith along with negative critiques of competing worldview beliefs.

The concept of apologetics is explicitly found in 1 Peter 3:15. Peter declares, "But sanctify Christ as Lord in your hearts, always being ready to make a defense to everyone who asks you to give an account for the hope that is in you, yet with gentleness and reverence." The word translated as "defense" here is *apologia*. The context of Peter's statement involves giving a reasoned defense of the hope within Christians who are facing persecution. Peter addresses the framework and spirit in which apologetics must be done. Apologists must "sanctify Christ as Lord in [their] hearts," which means the Christian's commitment to the Lord Jesus Christ must be established. Also, Peter says the apologetic encounter must be done

---

[6] According to Richard L. Pratt, "'Apologetics' is the study which pertains directly to the development and use of defense." *Every Thought Captive: A Study Manual for the Defense of Christian Truth* (Phillipsburg, NJ: P&R, 1979), 2.

[7] Norman Geisler, "Apologetics, Need for," in *Baker Encyclopedia of Christian Apologetics* (Grand Rapids, MI: Baker, 1999), 37. Steven B. Cowan notes, "Apologetics is concerned with the defense of the Christian faith against charges of falsehood, inconsistency, or credulity." "Introduction," in *Five Views on Apologetics*, ed. Steven B. Cowan (Grand Rapids, MI: Zondervan, 2000), 7.

with "gentleness and reverence." This involves a right attitude and a right character. Apologetics is not about pride or winning, but about presenting Jesus to a lost world in the right manner. Peter does not say the Christian must be exceptionally intelligent or well-acquainted with philosophical arguments. What matters is his commitment to Jesus and right character. The challenges to Christianity will vary throughout the ages, but one thing remains constant: every Christian is called to offer a reasoned defense of his or her faith in the right way with the right character.

Inerrancy and Presuppositional Apologetics

There are various apologetic approaches—classical, evidential, presuppositional, and Reformed epistemological.[8] Adherents of inerrancy can be found in all four camps.

The classical approach often stresses the necessity of beginning with natural theology to establish theism as the correct worldview. Then, after God's existence has been proven, there is a move to historical evidences to show and distinguish Christianity as the true religion.[9] The classical view has a long history and is held by many Christian apologists.

Evidentialism is similar to classical apologetics in that it utilizes various positive and negative arguments, including philosophical and historical evidences. The key difference between the two approaches concerns the use of miracles. With evidentialism, miracles do not presuppose God's existence (as classical apologists often assert), but they serve as one sort of evidence for God. Thus, evidentialists argue for both theism and Christian theism at the same time.[10] Like classical apologetics, the evidential approach emphasizes various evidences as the basis for believing the Christian faith.

Reformed epistemology is a more recent approach. It is a reaction against the Enlightenment emphasis on providing reasons for everything we believe. Thus, it is perfectly rational for a person to believe many things without evidence—including belief in the existence of God. Reformed epistemology holds that belief in God is properly basic and does not require the support of evidence or argument in order for it to be rational.[11] Believing

---

[8] For an excellent discussion and comparison of the various approaches to apologetics, see Cowan, *Five Views on Apologetics*.

[9] William Lane Craig states, "The methodology of classical apologetics was first to present arguments for theism, which aimed to show that God's existence is at least more probable than not, and then to present Christian evidences, probabilistically construed, for God's revelation in Christ." "Classical Apologetics," in *Five Views on Apologetics*, 48.

[10] See Cowan, "Introduction," in *Five Views on Apologetics*, 16–17.

[11] See ibid., 20.

in God is somewhat like believing in the existence of other people or trusting our senses. It comes naturally to human beings and needs no rational defense in order to be accepted. With this approach, positive arguments for Christianity are not necessary for rational faith.

So what is presuppositional apologetics and why is this approach especially tied to the doctrine of inerrancy? Presuppositional apologetics is a school of Christian apologetics that presents a rational basis for the Christian faith. It does so by defending the Christian faith against objections and exposing the flaws and inconsistencies of other worldviews and religions. With this perspective, Christianity is seen as not just a viable worldview or the best of several good options, but as the only worldview that is true. All other worldviews are inherently contradictory and unable to account for reality. Christianity must be true since the God of the Bible is the precondition to all aspects of reality, including rationality, beauty, and existence. If God did not exist, nothing would exist, and there would be no such things as laws of logic, mathematics, or anything else. Neither would there be any people in position to reason or experience anything. Thus, attempts to use reason or experience to defeat Christianity are self-refuting since the God of the Bible is the precondition for reason or experiencing anything at all.

One key distinctive of the presuppositional approach is that the Christian worldview as found in the Bible must be assumed to understand the world. There are no "neutral" assumptions from which to reason with a non-Christian, whether it be historical evidences or experience. Inerrancy, therefore, is a crucial and nonnegotiable part of presuppositional apologetics. Many adherents of other apologetic approaches can and do hold to inerrancy, but there is an inherent link between inerrancy and presuppositionalism. As Steven West points out: "In many ways, the presuppositional approach to the role of the Scripture in apologetics is very straightforward. Since the Christian is defending Christianity, and since Christianity is a full system, the entire system needs to be presupposed for the defense."[12] Also, "Since presuppositionalism depends on the inerrancy of the Scriptures, it will be a rather obvious observation that, if presuppositionalism is granted its maximum force, then the doctrine of inerrancy is vindicated."[13]

---

[12] Steven D. West, *Resurrection, Scripture, and Reformed Apologetics: A Test for Consistency in Theology and Apologetic Method* (Eugene, OR: Pickwick, 2012), 172.

[13] Ibid., 184. "Thus human investigation does not demonstrate the inerrancy of Scripture; on the contrary, the inerrancy of Scripture is taken to be necessary to ground the legitimacy of human thought and investigation. While this position is, to put it mildly, controversial, if it is sound then the Reformed doctrine of inerrancy is secured." Ibid.

Inerrancy is not established because reason deems it to be so, although reason properly working will come to this conclusion. The basis for accepting inerrancy is the statements of Scripture affirming its inerrancy. As Greg Bahnsen points out: "The self-referential statements [in Scripture] are and must be primary in our approach to the nature of Scripture and the question of its authority. The question of Biblical inerrancy must be resolved presuppositionally."[14]

Presuppositionalism is not against using empirical evidences in defense of the Christian faith. Such evidences can and should be used, but the apologist needs to go further. Bahnsen notes: "Not only must one utilize inductive empiricism but he must press beyond this and examine the foundations of science and inductive method. That is, we must not stop short in our philosophical analysis but rather inquire into the presuppositions necessary for an intelligent and justified use of empiricism."[15] Thus, one should not stop with "facts." One should press on to a "philosophy of facts." What is the precondition for the facts we are observing? The precondition for empirical data is the God of the Bible. An exploration of empirical evidence cannot rightly be done apart from the One who makes empirical data possible. So data can be understood rightly only in light of God and his inerrant Word.

The Context for Apologetics

ONTOLOGY (BEING)

Apologetics does not occur in a vacuum. The setting for an encounter with an unbeliever involves several matters that must be considered. First, in regard to *ontology*, or being, God is the Creator and starting point for reality—including all reason, experience, and laws, whether mathematical, scientific, or logical. All facts are God's facts. Every square inch of the universe belongs to the Lord. Thus, no fact can be rightly understood apart from the Creator. As Psalm 24:1 states, "The earth is the LORD's, and all it contains, the world, and those who dwell in it." Second, man is a creature who lives in God's world. So there is a Creator-creature distinction; the creatures are here to serve the Creator. Since man is a creature with the imprint of the image of God, he instinctively knows that he is to serve the Creator. God's revelation in nature also constantly testifies to man that God exists (Rom. 1:18ff.). Man knows the God of the Bible by internal and

---

[14] Bahnsen, "Inductivism, Inerrancy, and Presuppositionalism," 302.
[15] Ibid., 294.

external witness. To deny that God exists is foolish—"The fool has said in his heart, 'There is no God'" (Ps. 14:1).

DEPRAVITY

Sin and depravity corrupted all aspects of man's being, including his ability to reason accurately. All men are darkened in their understanding apart from God's intervention (Eph. 4:17–18). But man is still expected to obey the Creator and live in light of what God says. The doctrine of total depravity must be considered when it comes to an apologetic approach. The unbeliever is not a neutral arbiter of facts, but a truth suppressor (Rom. 1:18) who can be won only by the powers of God's Word and Spirit.

EPISTEMOLOGY (KNOWING)

Apologetics is related to *epistemology*, the study of knowing. All knowledge stems from God; thus, true knowledge comes from understanding God's world in God's way. When a Christian engages in apologetics, he or she asserts that Christianity is true and that competing worldviews are wrong. Biblical Christianity is exclusive in that it alone is the true philosophy that leads to salvation, and it alone has the correct understanding of reality. Christianity makes truth claims and, in doing so, declares that competing truths claims are false.

Before the fall, Adam and Eve relied entirely upon God for their knowledge of the world. But when they sinned, they started with themselves instead of God for understanding the world. They took their eyes off what God had revealed ("Did God actually say . . . ?"; Gen. 3:1 ESV) and decided to interpret the world on their own, with disastrous consequences. Every person since who has interpreted the world from his own perspective apart from God has repeated what was at the heart of the first sin—the pursuit of autonomy and rejection of the Creator. The difference between a Christian and a non-Christian is that the Christian once again looks to God and his Word as the starting point for knowledge. The non-Christian starts with himself and what he thinks is right. He is acting as Adam did in the garden.

Much debate has occurred over what the starting point should be for an apologetic encounter with an unbeliever. Should the starting point be reason? Should it be experience? Or should it be Scripture itself? Since whatever one uses as a starting point functions as an ultimate authority, some Christian apologists have rightly argued that Scripture must be this starting point. If one starts with human reason for understanding reality, then reason becomes ultimate and the Bible becomes subject to it.

The Enlightenment of the eighteenth century insisted that human reason is superior to revelation. It asserted that reason must be the starting point for knowledge and that the ideas of revelation must be subject to human reason. Enlightenment thinkers put the doctrines of Christianity through the meat grinder of human reason. As a result, Christianity was distorted—no more deity of Christ, depravity of man, inerrancy of the Bible, or accuracy of the prophetic Scriptures. Later, postmodernism declared that there is no objective truth and that every person has a right to decide what is true for him or her. The human person is left as king. He gets to use his own reason as the authority (Enlightenment rationalism) and he gets to decide for himself what is true (postmodern subjectivism).

But if this is God's world ("This is my Father's world . . ."[16]), why should the Christian have to play by the rules of the Enlightenment or postmodernism? Why should he cater to the unbeliever's worldview? To use a football analogy, why play a road game when you can play at home? The world and all that's in it is the Father's turf.

For the Christian, Scripture should be the starting point for understanding reality. In an apologetic encounter, Christians are calling on non-Christians to submit to what the Bible says about reality. But if another source becomes the standard for determining whether the Bible is true, then the battle is lost at step one. We cannot rightly tell people that they must submit to what the Bible says while also affirming their autonomy to judge the Bible by their reason or experience. The unbeliever is called to obey the Word of the Creator, not sit in judgment over it.

Inerrancy is not established because reason deems it to be so (although reason properly working will come to this conclusion). The basis for inerrancy is found in the statements of Scripture affirming its own inerrancy.

Many think that starting with the Bible and assuming its authority is a bad idea. They believe such an approach is *petitio principii* (circular reasoning or "begging the question")—the fallacy of assuming as a premise a statement that has the same meaning as the conclusion. But the circular argument claim must be understood in the context of the ultimate starting point for knowledge. An ultimate starting point by nature cannot have an authority over it or it would not be an ultimate point of knowledge. This is true whether one believes reason, experience, or Scripture is the begin-

---

[16] From the hymn "This Is My Father's World," by Maltbie B. Babcock, 1901.

ning point. If one starts with reason, what reason is given for this starting point? The same is true for experience or sense perception. So the issue is not who is assuming an ultimate staring point and who is not; the issue is which starting point is correct. Everyone is being circular at some point. The Christian who assumes the inerrant Word of God from the God who makes all things possible is no more circular than the person assuming human reason or experience. The main difference is that the Christian's assumption is based on God, without whom nothing would exist.

In addition, some believe that starting with God and Scripture for knowledge is fideistic in the sense that people are called to believe in something without reason. But John Frame has rightly argued that faith in God is not divorced from rationality. As he puts it: "The rational basis for faith is God's own rationality. The sequence is: God's rationality → human faith → human reasoning. The arrows may be read 'is the rational basis for.'"[17] Such an approach is consistent with Augustine's assertion, "I believe in order that I may understand," and Anselm's concept of "faith seeking understanding."

Spiritual Tools and Weapons

The Christian apologist must use the right weapons and tools in apologetic encounters. This includes the Holy Spirit and the Bible. New birth or regeneration is a work of the Spirit of God (John 3:5–8; Titus 3:5). No one can be saved apart from his work. And it is belief in the Word of God that brings salvation. Paul declared, "So faith comes from hearing, and hearing by the word of Christ" (Rom. 10:17). Peter stated, "For you have been born again . . . through the living and enduring word of God" (1 Pet. 1:23). The Word of God is able to pierce the inner man and reach his soul: "For the word of God is living and active and sharper than any two-edged sword, and piercing as far as the division of soul and spirit, of both joints and marrow, and able to judge the thoughts and intentions of the heart" (Heb. 4:12).

It is the Word of God that is most powerful when it comes to confronting unbelievers. Why would any Christian not bring the power of the Word of God to an encounter? The non-Christian might resist it and deny it, but when Scripture is proclaimed, he is hearing the Word of his Creator. God's Word does not return to him void (Isa. 55:11). It always accomplishes something—whether faith for salvation or accountability for judgment.

---

[17] John Frame, "The Presuppositional Method," in *Five Views on Apologetics*, 210.

Biblical Examples

We have argued that Scripture should be up front in apologetic encounters. There are examples in the Bible for this.

ACTS 14:15–17

In Acts 14, Paul and Barnabas addressed a crowd in Lystra that had no access to God's special revelation in Scripture. Yet the apostles appealed to what Scripture had to say about God as Creator:

> Men, why are you doing these things? We are also men of the same nature as you, and preach the gospel to you that you should turn from these vain things to a living God, WHO MADE THE HEAVEN AND THE EARTH AND THE SEA AND ALL THAT IS IN THEM. In the generations gone by He permitted all the nations to go their own ways; and yet He did not leave Himself without witness, in that He did good and gave you rains from heaven and fruitful seasons, satisfying your hearts with food and gladness. (vv. 15–17)

As Paul and Barnabas addressed an audience with no Bible knowledge and a different worldview, they quoted Psalm 146:6, which picks up on Genesis 1:1 and its depiction of creation. The authoritative Scriptures and the worldview they affirm were front and center of their message to these people.

2 PETER 3

A connection between the inerrant Scriptures and apologetics is seen also in 2 Peter 3, when Peter is dealing with scoffers who mock the idea of God's judgment and the return of Jesus. Peter tells his readers, "You should remember the words spoken beforehand by the holy prophets and the commandment of the Lord and Savior spoken by your apostles" (v. 2). Here Peter explicitly draws his readers' attention to the written Scriptures. "Holy prophets" is a reference to the Old Testament Scriptures. "Apostles" is a reference to New Testament Scripture. Later in this chapter, Peter refers to Paul's letters as "Scripture" (v. 16), so he clearly has written Scripture in mind.

Then, starting in verse 3, he refers to mockers who deny Jesus is coming back: "Where is the promise of His coming?" they exclaim (v. 4a). Their skepticism is based on their experience, as revealed when they declare, "For ever since the fathers fell asleep, all continues just as it was from the beginning of creation" (v. 4b). In other words, these nonbelievers are denying the second coming of Jesus and the final judgment based on the authority of their own experience. They look at past history from their perspective and project into the future that all things will continue just as they have been and are now; there will be no cataclysmic judgment of God that intervenes in human history. They are appealing to their view of uniformity—that the future will be like the past. If the past has no judgment, the future will not as well. These scoffers are using their own experience and understanding of history to mock the Christian faith.

Yet Peter meets this false belief and false authority with what Scripture states, both for the past and the future. He argues that it is not true that "all continues just as it was from the beginning of creation." He notes that God once sent a flood to destroy wicked men—"the world at that time was destroyed, being flooded with water" (v. 6). Then he appeals to a coming day of the Lord that the Old Testament prophets predicted: "But by His word the present heavens and earth are being reserved for fire, kept for the day of judgment and destruction of ungodly men" (v. 7; see 3:10). For Peter, what the Word of God reveals about the flood of Noah's day is more authoritative than the perception of uniformity the mockers have. Also, what God's Word reveals about a coming Day of the Lord is to be trusted as opposed to the projections of the scoffers. In sum, Peter appeals to what Scripture says about the past global flood of Noah's day and the coming Day of the Lord. These scriptural teachings trump the experiences of the scoffers.

It is noteworthy that Peter presupposes the accuracy of Scripture in two areas here. First, he asserts the accuracy of what the Bible says about a past historical event—the global flood. And he affirms the truth of prophecy—specifically, prophecy about the coming Day of the Lord. The inerrant Scriptures speak to both history and prophecy.

LUKE 16:19–31

In the parable of the rich man and Lazarus in Luke 16, Jesus tells of a certain rich man who died and found himself in the fiery torment of Hades. After pleading for relief that was denied, his mind darted to his five living brothers. Perhaps they could avoid the torment he was experiencing if warned. He begged Abraham to send the also-deceased Lazarus to appear from the dead to his brothers:

> And he [the rich man] said, "Then I beg you, father, that you send him [Lazarus] to my father's house—for I have five brothers—in order that

he may warn them, so that they will not also come to this place of torment." (vv. 16:27–28)

This request seemed like a good one. Perhaps a dramatic visit from the grave would be enough to sway the rich man's brothers to repent and avoid the path that he had taken. Yet Abraham did not agree:

But Abraham said, "They have Moses and the Prophets; let them hear them." (v. 29)

Abraham responded that the five brothers already had access to the words of Moses and the prophets. This was enough. But not convinced by Abraham's reply, the rich man again pleaded his case:

But he said, "No, father Abraham, but if someone goes to them from the dead, they will repent!" (v. 30)

For the rich man, the words of God through the prophets were not sufficient. Certainly, an astounding post-grave appearance from Lazarus would convince his brothers. An undeniable experience from beyond would get their attention and convince them. Yet Abraham again denied the request and the idea behind it:

But he said to him, "If they do not listen to Moses and the Prophets, they will not be persuaded even if someone rises from the dead." (v. 31)

This encounter between the rich man and Abraham carries helpful instruction about the use of Scripture in apologetics. The rich man in Hades requested an after-death appearance to convince his brothers to repent. Yet Abraham did not agree. Why? The brothers already possessed the special revelation of Moses and the prophets. These words from God were superior to any miracle or experience—so much so that Abraham could say, with full confidence, that if the brothers did not heed the words of Moses and the prophets given through Scripture, then they would not be convinced by a beyond-the-grave encounter. It is the Word of God that is primary. It must be heeded.[18] This account reveals an important apologetic truth: the Word of God is primary for those needing to be saved. It is more important than experience and more vital than outside evidence.

---

[18] This is consistent with Peter's words that the "prophetic word" is "more sure" than experience, even his own personal encounter with Jesus on the Mount of Transfiguration (2 Pet. 1:16–19).

Conclusion

Inerrancy intersects with many key issues. One of them is apologetics. The Christian apologist should not just present theism in general. Neither should he argue only for the probability of Christianity. He is to present the God of the Bible and the Christian faith with certainty. The foundation for these claims is self-attesting Scripture, which is inerrant. It is also based on the character of God, who cannot lie and is able to give his Word to man without error. This should be a comfort to the Christian apologist. He can rest confident that the God who created all things speaks truthfully on all matters he addresses. Whether it is salvation, history, or geography, the Bible is true in all that it affirms. Since the God of the Bible is the precondition for everything that exists, the apologist does not need to worry that some discovery or fact will surface that defeats the Christian faith.

24

"All That I Have Commanded"

INERRANCY AND THE GREAT COMMISSION

Miguel Núñez

I was given the task of showing how vitally important the doctrine of inerrancy is to the Great Commission. The assignment proved to be harder than I anticipated since I could not find any piece of literature directly addressing the topic. The authorities in the fields of mission and New Testament stated that they were not aware of any writing covering that particular issue. Nevertheless, I thought that the inerrancy of Scripture is such a vital doctrine that there must be not only a connection but an important connection between it and the Great Commission.

I selected a well-known passage of the Bible to deal with the topic assigned to me. It is found at the very end of the Gospel of Matthew:

Now the eleven disciples went to Galilee, to the mountain to which Jesus had directed them. And when they saw him they worshiped him, but some doubted. And Jesus came and said to them, "All authority in heaven and on earth has been given to me. Go therefore and make disciples of all nations, baptizing them in the name of the Father and of the Son and of the Holy Spirit, teaching them to observe all that I have commanded you. And behold, I am with you always, to the end of the age." (28:16–20)

As we all know, this is the ending of Matthew's Gospel, but it is the beginning of Christ's global mission. As one would expect, a universal mission was going to require a universal authority, and a universal and constant presence of the person in command of the mission. That is what we see in the Great Commission text. The disciples are given all authority to go and the promise that "I am with you always [all the time], to the end of the age." All authority, all nations, all obedience, all the time. This portion of Scripture sounds as absolute as anyone can state it. Certainly this is not a postmodern declaration.

As some have pointed out, verse 18 of this passage contains the highest christology of the New Testament.[1] The authority (*exousia*, ἐξουσία) that Jesus received after his resurrection was not so much new as it was wider.[2] And with that expanded authority, Jesus sent his disciples into a new mission.

As the Lord commissioned his first missionaries, he passed to them not only a message, but also a conviction, a passion, a hope, a certainty. It is hard to imagine all of that being transmitted through a corrupted Word. He gave them a commandment with an authority that couldn't fail, because behind those words was the integrity of his name. A mission as monumental as the one announced by Christ before he ascended into heaven would need a solid, unquestionable, unshakable, and unchallengeable authority. And such the disciples received in his Word.

If we did not believe in an inerrant Word, it would be very difficult to deal objectively even with the passage at hand, since the wording of Matthew is so different from the endings of the rest of the other evangelists. Do these differences in the Gospel narratives represent errors on the part of the authors? Or did God purposely inspire them as complementary, but not discordant?[3]

Let's keep in mind that if parts of the Bible are in error, as critics state, any part of it can be found in want, and that includes the Great Commission texts found in the New Testament. Furthermore, if we are not certain about the inerrancy of the original message we have inherited, we

---

[1] Grant R. Osborne, *Matthew,* Zondervan Exegetical Commentary on the New Testament, ed. Clinton E. Arnold (Grand Rapids, MI: Zondervan, 2010), 1078–79.

[2] Daniel M. Doriani, *Matthew, Vol. 2,* Reformed Expository Commentary (Phillipsburg, NJ: P&R, 2008), 531.

[3] For a better understanding of this topic, see Vern Sheridan Poythress, *Inerrancy and the Gospels, A God-Centered Approach to the Challenges of Harmonization* (Wheaton, IL: Crossway, 2012).

cannot be sure of what the gospel is and we cannot repeat the words of
the apostle Paul:

> Now I would remind you, brothers, of the gospel I preached to you,
> which you received, in which you stand, and by which you are being
> saved, if you hold fast to the word I preached to you—unless you be-
> lieved in vain. For I delivered to you as of first importance *what I also
> received."* (1 Cor. 15:1–3a)

That last phrase, "what I also received," is very important. We pass on
to others the same gospel message we received, being certain that we are
handing to the next generation a trustworthy Word in its entirety.

For the purpose of seeing how vitally important the doctrine of inerrancy is in evangelism and missions, I will divide the Matthean Great Commission text into four parts:

1. "Go Therefore"
2. "To the Ends of the World"
3. "Make Disciples"
4. "Teach Them to Obey All That I Have Commanded You"

"Go Therefore"

Jesus was sending his eleven disciples and their followers on a worldwide
mission where they would encounter all kinds of opposition, obstacles,
and uncertainties. That is the very reason why he was so emphatic when
he said, "All authority . . . has been given to me." He was commissioning
his evangelists on the basis of his expanded authority and delegating his
authority to these men he had personally trained. At the same time, he was
delegating a certain level of authority to everyone who would carry his
Great Commission. But that authority was invested in his Word.

The people being sent needed complete confidence in the sender, but
also in the message to be shared. Any degree of doubt in either one, Christ
or his Word, would create doubtful or hesitant disciples, fearful and incapable of embracing a task as encompassing as reaching the entire world.
Can we imagine going to the ends of the world with a corrupted message
or with portions of it considered uninspired, altered by human intervention,
or mixed with errors or myths? The men of old risked their lives, going and
preaching the Word to evangelize the heathen, because they were convinced
that "no prophecy was ever produced by the will of man, but men spoke
from God as they were carried along by the Holy Spirit" (2 Pet. 1:21).

They had absolute confidence in the power and trustworthiness of the message they preached. They knew full well that if men spoke from God, they spoke in his name, and therefore, the preaching of a fallible message would bring into question the trustworthiness not only of his Word, but also of his name—the very name to be used in baptizing converts. Indeed, the questioning of his Word or his name would immediately bring into question God's very nature, for they both represent who he is. This is how the psalmist expresses this truth: "You have exalted above all things your name and your word" (Ps. 138:2b).

When disciplemakers go into the mission field believing that the Word being shared is not totally reliable, they have a tendency to retreat when the message is challenged. Some say, for instance, that we cannot believe the cosmology of the Bible, especially in the first three chapters of Genesis, because it doesn't square with today's understanding of science. These critics would argue that the writers of the Bible quite frequently described the cosmos or historical accounts according to the mythological understanding of their day.[4] If the critics are correct in their assessment, then there is no way to argue against the cosmological understanding of the false religions in the mission field, since both understandings (theirs *and* ours) would reflect basically "mythological" descriptions of the origin of the universe, or "mythologized history," as some would call it.[5]

Why should anyone abandon his flawed understanding of life and the world (*weltanschauung*) for another defective religious view? Many do not understand how vast are the implications of denying the inerrancy of the Bible. J. I. Packer is so right when he states, "When you encounter the view of Holy Scripture, you are encountering the source, criterion, and control of all Evangelical theology and religion."[6]

If those who are being sent to proclaim the gospel cannot be sure about the message to be shared, will they go passionately? Will they risk their lives? Will they engage in apologetic evangelism? Will they confront the lies of the cultures? If the revealed Word they carry is inaccurate, what will be their moral authority to challenge the beliefs of those being evangelized? The Great Commission will become the impossible mission.

If one loses confidence in the gospel to attract and transform lives, it is

---

[4] For a defense against these critics, see G. K. Beale, *The Erosion of Inerrancy in Evangelicalism: Responding to New Challenges to Biblical Authority* (Wheaton, IL: Crossway, 2008), 161–218.
[5] Peter Enns, "Inerrancy, However Defined, Does Not Describe What the Bible Does," in *Five Views on Biblical Inerrancy*, ed. J. Merrick and Stephen M. Garrett (Grand Rapids, MI: Zondervan, 2013), Kindle version, Loc. 1578 of 5903.
[6] J. I. Packer, *Engaging the Written Word of God* (Peabody, MA: Hendrickson, 1999), 4.

only natural to resort to ancillary methods. This is what drove the introduction of gimmicks and strategies to attract unbelievers at the peak of the
church-growth movement in the United States in the 1990s. As the "senders
and goers" lost trust in the inerrancy of the Bible, the church became skeptical about the effectiveness of biblical evangelism, and as a consequence,
there was a new interest in the social sciences within the church:

- Sociology became attractive as a way to study communities to discern what kind of church the population really wanted.
- Psychology became the preferred field of knowledge with which to
  do biblical counseling.
- Marketing became so appealing that articles and books were
  published at the end of the century explaining how to market the
  church.[7]

In his critique of this phenomenon, Os Guinness quoted a church-
growth consultant, who claimed, "Five to ten million baby boomers would
be back in the fold within a month if churches adopted three changes:
(1) 'advertise'; (2) let people know about 'product benefits'; and (3) be 'nice
to new people.'"[8] You would have to ask yourself whether these people
read the same Bible evangelicals read.

Soon this movement began to go beyond American frontiers. Is it any
wonder that one of the gurus of this movement was C. Peter Wagner, professor of church growth at Fuller Theological Seminary's School of World
Missions? This institution began to abandon the doctrine of the inerrancy
of the Bible in the 1960s and finally changed its doctrinal statement in
1971.[9]

All of these new ideas were introduced with the "good intention" of
building the church in fulfillment of the Great Commission. But the wrong
church was being built in many cases. It is not an accident that many of the
people involved in the development of these trends were not and are not
believers in the inerrancy or the sufficiency of the Bible. The church allowed
modernity to impact its theological understanding, and it is now suffering
the consequences of such a clash. Modernity questioned the inerrancy of
God's Word and the sufficiency of God's work.

---

[7] See George Barna, *A Step-by-Step Guide to Church Marketing: Breaking Ground for the Harvest* (Ada,
MI: Baker, 1992).
[8] Os Guinness, "Sounding Out the Idols of Church Growth," http://www.gospel-culture.org.uk/guinness.htm
(accessed Dec. 5, 2014).
[9] Gregg L. Allison, *Historical Theology: An Introduction to Christian Doctrine* (Grand Rapids, MI: Zondervan, 2011), 116.

Jesus told the disciples, "The harvest is plentiful, but the laborers are few; therefore pray earnestly to the Lord of the harvest to send out laborers into his harvest" (Matt. 9:37b–38). How is that for a marketing strategy? People who don't believe in the Bible would rather pay than pray. You can either pay a consultant or you can pray to God. That decision will determine the quality of the church that is built.

The disciples were further instructed about waiting for power from above, and when they waited, they preached the Word boldly (Luke 24:49; Acts 1:8; 4:13). Jerusalem was filled with the apostles' teaching (Acts 5:28). Samaria was filled with joy (Acts 8:8). Ephesus was in turmoil (Acts 19:23). All of this transformation took place without any of the social sciences of today and without the use of the new teaching on evangelism, which I will mention later.

"To the Ends of the World"

Some have declared that inerrancy is an American construct that resulted from the clash between fundamentalism and modernity. Based on this observation, many have concluded that the concept of inerrancy is unnecessary outside the American church. Some have noted that this doctrine has not been an issue in the Global South, where there have been no classic debates about inerrancy such as have been known in American history.[10] However, to affirm such an idea is to ignore what else has taken place in the Global South and to overlook the doctrine of inerrancy throughout church history.[11]

It would be unthinkable to undertake a mission encompassing the entire world with truths related to God's revelation that are important in one place and not in the other. If the inerrancy of the Bible is important in North America, it must be important in South America. Why? Because inerrancy is about truth, and truth is universal; it is about God, the revealer of truth.[12] Likewise, the Great Commission is universal: it involves all nations.

We only need to ask how and why inerrancy is important here and there. The inerrancy of the Bible is important in North America given the

---

[10] Michael Bird, "Inerrancy Is Not Necessary for Evangelicalism outside the USA," in *Five Views on Biblical Inerrancy*, 145–73.
[11] John D. Woodbridge, *Biblical Authority, A Critique of the Rogers / McKim Proposal* (Grand Rapids, MI: Zondervan, 1982). In this book, Woodbridge demonstrates that inerrancy has been the doctrine of the Christian church throughout history.
[12] Norman Geisler, "Truth, Nature of," in *Baker Encyclopedia of Christian Apologetics* (Grand Rapids, MI: Baker, 1999), 741–45.

attacks on the Bible that this book has detailed. And it is important in the other hemisphere given the proliferation of alleged extrabiblical revelation there, revelation that is said to supplement what we already have. The doctrines of inspiration, inerrancy, sufficiency, and completion of the canon are bound up together. These truths represent a unified whole. If one of these foundational truths is removed, the whole building suffers with it.

It is true that in the Global South, modernity did not clash with fundamentalism the way it did in the United States.[13] For this reason, the loss of confidence in the Bible in the South did not come through the front door of challenges to inerrancy, but through the back door of alleged extrabiblical revelation, which represents a denial of the sufficiency and finality of the canon. In many cases, the introduction of supposed extrabiblical revelation came as a consequence of the animistic worldviews of the nations being evangelized.

But once we yield to extrabiblical revelation, the denial of the inerrancy of the Bible is simple. Extrabiblical revelation presupposes an open canon and therefore an incomplete Bible, which someone needs to complete. Moving from a Bible in need of completion to a Bible in need of correction (the denial of inerrancy) is only one step.

In the Global South, the reputed prophets and apostles are trying to complete the Bible with their new revelations. In the North, the critics are trying to correct the Bible with their new research. There is new revelation in the animistic hemisphere and new research in the rationalistic world. The South does it through mysticism. The North does it through rationalism.

A Word that is in error cannot be sufficient; its sufficiency would depend upon the authority of those who pretend to correct it. A complete and closed canon is a sufficient Word, and a sufficient Word is an inerrant Word. The supposed prophets and apostles in the North and South have never been defenders of the inerrancy of the Bible; they cannot be. Their "completion" of the revelation of God fits better with an errant Bible.

I mentioned earlier that during the 1990s, many in the church-growth movement in America attempted to use the social sciences to improve evangelistic efforts. In the mission field, a similar phenomenon was taking place, but instead of using social sciences, the churches in the Global South were being taught how to do spiritual warfare. The problem, according to the new teachers, was that demons opposed the evangelization of the pagan

---

[13] Daniel Salinas, *Latin American Evangelical Theology in the 1970s: The Golden Decade* (Boston: Brill, 2009), 103.

regions; therefore, the church needed to get rid of them through power encounters before effective preaching could take place.[14]

A new spiritual-warfare movement was launched. The result was that the church neglected the preaching of the Word and began rebuking demons. However, Christ's command was "[teach] them to observe all that I have commanded you." He wanted the disciples to teach obedience to his word. Later, Paul instructed Timothy, "Preach the word; be ready in season and out of season" (2 Tim. 4:2), and his premise was that the gospel is the power of God unto salvation for all who believe (Rom. 1:16). Today we have exchanged the confident preaching of the Word for new approaches, bringing into question the power of the Word of God in evangelism.

At the center of both controversies (the church-growth and spiritual-warfare movements) was Wagner from Fuller Theological Seminary, the institution already mentioned in connection with the denial of the inerrancy of the Bible since 1971. Once we stop believing in the inerrancy of the Bible, we chip away at the authority and the sufficiency of that same Bible.

As part of the spiritual-warfare movement, some speak of what have been called prophetic acts, the remitting of the sins of nations, the tearing down of strongholds, and other new ideas.[15] These terms were unheard of before the 1990s.[16] Evidently, according to this new teaching, the church has been largely ineffective until now, not understanding how to carry out the Great Commission through evangelism and mission.

Others have spoken about training the goers to perform signs and wonders so that they might carry out the mission of the church through what has been called power evangelism.[17] In the New Testament, the ability to perform signs and wonders was a "gift," not an ability that one could learn through training. Giving seminars to train people how to perform signs and wonders? How far many have drifted away!

While Christ spoke about preaching and teaching the Word to the ends of the world, we now speak of all kinds of power displays. Wagner says, "The key elements of this power boost that have so far emerged, are strategic-level spiritual warfare, spiritual mapping, and identificational

---

[14] For more information on this topic, see C. Peter Wagner, *Territorial Spirits: Insights on Strategic-Level Spiritual Warfare from Nineteen Christian Leaders* (Shippensburg, PA: Destiny Image, 2012).

[15] C. Peter Wagner, *Spiritual Warfare Strategy: Confronting Spiritual Powers* (Shippensburg, PA: Destiny Image, 1996), 15.

[16] Ibid.

[17] For more details on this topic, see John Wimber and Kelvin Springer, *Power Evangelism*, rev. and updated ed. (Ventura, CA: Regal, 2009).

repentance."[18] Spiritual mapping refers to the ability to determine what kinds of spirits (spirits of lust, addiction, etc.) are occupying certain territories, so that they can be expelled. Identificational repentance speaks about the identification of sins of previous generations that require confession by the present generation so that evangelism will be effective. Where in the Bible do we find teachings of this sort?

All of this is nothing more than the result of a lack of confidence in the power of the Word to evangelize the world. When inerrancy goes, the confidence in the Bible goes with it. The introduction of new ideas follows. The words of Timothy Pierce are very pertinent at this point:

> The "hermeneutic of suspicion" that characterizes so much of [the] scholarship and that has infiltrated the church is a dangerous undertaking because it undermines the principle of trust. When we as creatures begin to view God and His revelation through the lens of doubt and suspicion, it becomes easy not only to question the content of the message but the intent as well.[19]

Because the Word came from God, the Word is self-authenticated. We do not sit in judgment over the revelation of God; it is the other way around.

"Make Disciples"

The phrase "make disciples" summarizes the last commandment of Christ. In the original language, this phrase is only one word (*mathēteuō*, μαθητεύω), and it is the only verb in the imperative in this passage. The others, "go," "baptize," and "teach," are subordinate participles that take imperative force.[20] The task is about making disciples, not simply about evangelizing. The command was not to "make professions" (of faith), but to preach in order to see men and women totally committed to the lordship of Christ.

Those who were going to make disciples needed certain assurance in order to go into uncharted territories. That is precisely what Christ provided. He gave them two guarantees: (1) "All authority in heaven and on earth has been given to me. Go therefore . . ."; and (2) "Behold, I am with you always, to the end of the age." These phrases served as bookends, pro-

---

[18] Wagner, *Spiritual Warfare Strategy*, 45.

[19] Timothy M. Pierce, *Enthroned on Our Praise: An Old Testament Theology of Worship* (Nashville: B&H, 2008), 33.

[20] Donald A. Hagner, *Matthew 14–28*, vol. 33B, Word Biblical Commentary, ed. Bruce M. Metzger, Ralph P. Martin, and Lynn Allan Losie (Nashville: Thomas Nelson, 1995), 886.

viding full support to the disciples by promising them complete authority and continuous presence.

In the Sermon on the Mount, we have a perfect illustration of how Christ assured his disciples about the truthfulness of his revelation from beginning to end: "For truly, I say to you, until heaven and earth pass away, not an iota, not a dot, will pass from the Law until all is accomplished" (Matt. 5:18). There is the word *all* again. In others words, the disciples could count on the integrity of the revealed Word in its entirety until the consummation of time, and so can we. Until then, Christ promised to be with his disciples in the fulfillment of the Great Commission.

A similar assertion is found in John 10:34–35, where Christ quoted from Psalm 82: "Is it not written in your Law, 'I said, you are gods'? If he called them gods to whom the word of God came—and Scripture cannot be broken . . ." No, it cannot and it will not.

The assurance of texts of this sort is vital for the missionary enterprise. A pastor in a mission field can be anchored on that reality, and he can anchor his followers as well. However, the moment one admits the possibility of an errant Word, one could doubt the fulfillment of any prophecy, because one couldn't be sure if it was stated in the first place or if it was stated the way we have it today. If we deny the inerrancy of the Word, teaching converts the certainty of the fulfillment of the prophecies would be done on shaky ground.

The quality of the disciples we make depends in great measure on how those disciples receive the Word of God and what they believe about it. Paul said this about the disciples of the Thessalonian church: "You became an example to all the believers in Macedonia and in Achaia" (1 Thess. 1:7). Then he added, "And we also thank God constantly for this, that when you received the word of God, which you heard from us, you accepted it not as the word of men but as what it really is, the word of God, which is at work in you believers" (2:13).

First, Paul told them what a great testimony they had, then he explained the reason they had such a reputation. It was because they accepted Scripture "not as the word of men but as what it really is, the word of God." The Thessalonians were of a different opinion than the critics of the past two hundred years or so. Without a doubt, they were better witnesses than those who appeared nineteen hundred to two thousand years later.

In carrying out the Great Commission, we need to ask the following questions:

- What should we teach the disciples about the truthfulness of the Word they are receiving?
- Do we say that it is all reliable; partially reliable; or all reliable in some portions but partially reliable in other portions?
- What should we tell the disciples when they ask how we know which portions of the Bible are reliable and which are not?
- Should we say that the inerrancy of the Bible varies according to the interpreters (the critics)?

We either trust the entirety of the Word of God or the entirety of the word of the critics. There is no middle ground. One can predict what any teaching other than inerrancy will do: it will produce disciples who constantly question the authority of the Bible or portions of it. Certainly such disciples will never be of the same quality as the Thessalonians.

"Teach Them to Obey All That I Have Commanded You"

Finally, the Lord revealed to his disciples how to make new disciples: by teaching his Word, specifically, "all that I have commanded you." This instruction leaves out the possibility of selectively choosing portions of Scripture to be proclaimed and obeyed, while choosing others to be denied and ignored. Daniel Doriani adds a very poignant observation in his commentary about the Great Commission text in the Gospel of Matthew:

> The Greek expression that is translated "everything" ["all"] . . . is actually two terms. One means "all things" and the other means "as much as." The effect is to intensify the command. We must teach potential disciples to obey every last thing Jesus said.[21]

Why would the Lord give such an absolute command? Because all Scripture is God-breathed (2 Tim. 3:16), and it is therefore inerrant, absolute, authoritative, trustworthy, unbreakable, and worthy to be obeyed. Inerrancy is about truth and the source of truth, which is God.

I cannot imagine making disciples by telling them that they must obey all that Christ commanded and at the same time informing them, for example, that the discrepancies of the Gospel writers are due to errors on the part of the authors or the introduction of midrash, as some have claimed.[22]

---

[21] Doriani, *Matthew*, Vol. 2, 533.
[22] Robert H. Gundry, *Matthew, A Commentary on His Literary and Theological Arts* (Grand Rapids, MI: Eerdmans, 1982), 26–28.

Once we accept the possibility of midrash, myths, or errors, even the Great Commission text comes under suspicion.

If anyone is a believer in the Great Commission as depicted in Matthew 28:16–20, he needs to hold a high view of Scripture. Kevin Vanhoozer puts it this way:

> A high view of biblical authority that affirms its entire trustworthiness is necessary to preserve the integrity of the gospel, and other candidate terms (for example, infallibility) that have thought to capture this notion have become diluted over time. So while inerrancy is clearly not part of the substance of the gospel (union and communion with Christ), it is connected to the proclamation of the gospel: "Specifically, it is an outworking of the trustworthiness of Scripture."[23]

Yes, because Jesus's command was that his disciples teach others to obey all that he had commanded them. Our Lord wouldn't have commanded obedience to errors or midrash. A text with errors cannot command full obedience.

Some may argue that the "obey all" command refers to Jesus's words only, not to the Old Testament. But Christ treated the Old Testament as fully authoritative, as has been shown by many. And even after Jesus's death and resurrection, we find the apostle Paul making reference to the importance of teaching "the whole counsel of God" (Acts 20:27). The value of this statement from Paul about teaching the whole will of God can be called into question if we are dealing with a corrupted text.

Many are not aware that numerous heresies have been born in the mission field, and one of the reasons is the lack of confidence in the Word that quite frequently arises after the doctrine of inerrancy is abandoned. Certainly this has been the case in Latin America, where liberation theology was born.

The importance of a particular doctrine can be judged on the basis of three things:

1. The verdict from God found in the Bible itself (see Psalm 19 and 119).
2. The results seen when a particular doctrine, like inerrancy, is present.
3. The consequences produced in the absence of the same doctrine.

---

[23] Kevin J. Vanhoozer, "Augustinian Inerrancy: Literary Meaning, Literal Truth, and Literate Interpretation in the Economy of Biblical Discourse," in *Five Views on Biblical Inerrancy*, 203.

The history of the Reformation movement speaks well for the importance of embracing the doctrine of inerrancy. And the history of the liberal movement speaks forcefully about the consequences of the abandonment of inerrancy.

Conclusion

It is worth reconsidering the words of the apostle Paul to his young disciple Timothy:

> I charge you in the presence of God and of Christ Jesus, who is to judge the living and the dead, and by his appearing and his kingdom: preach the word; be ready in season and out of season; reprove, rebuke, and exhort, with complete patience and teaching. For the time is coming when people will not endure sound teaching, but having itching ears they will accumulate for themselves teachers to suit their own passions, and will turn away from listening to the truth and wander off into myths. As for you, always be sober-minded, endure suffering, do the work of an evangelist, fulfill your ministry. (2 Tim. 4:1–5)

Notice the connection between the charges "do the work of an evangelist" (v. 5) and "preach the word" (v. 2). We carry out the Great Commission by preaching God's inerrant and infallible Word. That is the way Christ did it, as seen in the Gospels. That is the way the apostles did it, as recorded in the book of Acts. That is the way the true church has always done it for two thousand years.

Let us not compromise at this time of ambivalence. Rather, let us stand together for the sake of God's Word and for the glory of his name. Let us go forth preaching this inerrant and unshakable Word to a drifting world.

Do not fear, for all authority has been given to Christ, and he promised to be with us always, to the end of the age.

Afterword

KEEP THE FAITH

John MacArthur

The authority and accuracy of Scripture have been attacked in every generation since Satan first spoke words of doubt to Eve: "Did God actually say . . . ?" (Gen. 3:1). From the dawn of human history until now, assaults on the veracity of God's Word have come in steady, ever-increasing waves, from every quarter. And if the epidemic of unbelief today seems more aggressive and more widespread than ever, that's because it is (2 Tim. 3:13; 2 Pet. 3:3).

Nevertheless, all the world's hostility to biblical truth would have little effect on the church if everyone who claims to be a Christian remained faithful to the Word of God. Opposition from the world has never posed a lethal or long-term threat to the spread of the gospel. Even the gates of hell cannot prevail against the church militant (Matt. 16:18).

The church has always managed to grow amid the fiercest worldly antagonism. It's a pattern that was established in the first generation of church history. Acts 12:1–2 records how James, the first apostolic martyr, was killed by direct order from Herod. That immediately launched a violent, systematic, worldwide persecution. But don't miss how Luke summarizes the impact of this persecution on the church. He ends that same chapter with this report: "The word of God increased and multiplied" (Acts 12:24). By the second century, Tertullian was saying that the blood of the martyrs is the seed of the church. The pattern continues even now. Just in the past half-century, the church has grown behind the communist Iron Curtain amid horrible persecution—while in free Western Europe, a fascination with theological novelties and a corresponding move away from Scripture has left churches moribund.

Survey all of church history and you will discover an unsettling fact: the most pernicious and spiritually devastating assaults on the church have always come from within—via subtle efforts to undermine the authority of Scripture. Artful deceit is more dangerous and more destructive than open rebellion. Wolves don sheep's clothing. Satan and his demonic minions disguise themselves as angels of light. False teachers robe themselves in pretended piety and decorate their walls with scholarly credentials from prestigious seminaries. They come under the pretense of being forward-thinking reformers or experts in evangelism and church-growth strategies. They say they just want to help the church be all that she can be. They always insist that the church must adapt her strategy and methodology or she will lose the next generation. That very claim is a subtle attack on the authority of Scripture.

But these are glib and likable trendsetters. They don't look anything like ravening wolves. And once they have gained entry and influence among the people of God, they can (and do) push whatever antibiblical agenda they please.

That has been the consistent pattern for centuries. Charles Spurgeon called it "the down-grade."[1] He carefully traced how the worst attacks on the Bible have always come from leaders *in the church* who want to be seen as progressive. They promise something fresher and more practical than any teaching or methodology previous generations of believers ever knew. But invariably, their "insights" are merely the same sterile, dubious doctrines that are trotted out and decked in cheap new clothes every quarter century or so. The same strategy has been followed for centuries by successive generations of Socinians, Deists, universalists, modernists, and other assorted proponents of theological liberalism.

The distinctive teachings of these "progressives" are always rooted in skepticism. The same basic set of ideas is marketed to the church in every generation through seemingly trustworthy channels—prestigious seminaries, popular church leaders, trendsetting movements, and best-selling books. The main allure is the promise of something fresh and revolutionary.

---

[1] See Appendix 1, "Spurgeon and the Down-Grade Controversy," in John MacArthur, *Ashamed of the Gospel: When the Church Becomes Like the World* (Wheaton, IL: Crossway, 2010), 233–59.

That is when faithful Christians should be most on guard and fully prepared to contend earnestly for the faith that was once for all delivered (Jude 3). The undiscerning Christian's instinct is to refrain from contradicting or contending with anyone who claims to be a Christian—especially those with impressive academic credentials, charismatic personalities, or large throngs of followers. To voice disagreement with someone who has gained a popular following in the evangelical community is automatically perceived as an egregious sin against Christian unity. (Progressives themselves liberally use that accusation as a defense against their critics.)

But the New Testament is full of exhortations for believers to defend the faith against self-styled prophets and false teachers who come *in Christ's name*. The apostle John wrote, "Beloved, do not believe every spirit, but test the spirits to see whether they are from God, for many false prophets have gone out into the world" (1 John 4:1). In Paul's farewell message to the Ephesian elders, he told them plainly: "I know that after my departure fierce wolves will come in among you, not sparing the flock; and *from among your own selves will arise men speaking twisted things*, to draw away the disciples after them. Therefore be alert" (Acts 20:29–31a). If that danger posed such a looming threat in the apostolic era, it is far more so in our era, in a postmodern culture where diversity, broad tolerance, and uncertainty are seen as high virtues.

It has been one scant generation since Harold Lindsell wrote *The Battle for the Bible* and ignited a major effort to defend the truth of biblical inerrancy. Most of the godly men who led the way in that skirmish are now in heaven. By any measure, they won a decisive victory and brought an end (for a very short time) to the overt attacks on the Bible's authority among mainstream evangelicals. But once it was clear that the battle was won, the evangelical movement seemed to lose interest in the very Book they had defended, and an era of runaway pragmatism ("seeker sensitivity" and "purpose-driven" ministry) ensued.

Today the evangelical movement is filled with (and, to a disturbing degree, *led* by) people who have little concern for Scripture. The average church member has a very superficial grasp of the Bible's content and a dangerously loose hold on biblical truth. Frankly, the typical evangelical congregation is loaded with people who simply "will not endure sound teaching" (2 Tim. 4:3). They want motivational talks, movie reviews, and messages designed to make them feel good. Oratorical skill and human cleverness are more highly regarded among church leaders than biblical convictions. The church is on the downgrade yet again, and (in Spurgeon's words) "We are going down hill at breakneck speed."[2]

The first decade of the new millennium saw the rise of the "Emergent church," a movement based on fluid postmodern values rather than the Bible's unchanging truths. The movement was skewed toward skepticism from the beginning, and it wasn't long before many key emerging figures were unashamedly parroting long-discredited liberal and Socinian doctrines. Some even veered into universalism, pantheism, and rank unbelief. Lacking any centralized leadership, the emerging church failed to emerge as a viable movement. It disintegrated suddenly and spectacularly, like a rocket that couldn't make it off the launchpad. But its low view of Scripture and left-leaning doctrines still linger and find regular expression among evangelicals—threatening to send a massive avalanche of churches and naive Christians barreling at record speeds into the darkness that lies at the end of the downgrade.

We who believe in the authority and inerrancy of Scripture must commit our souls in full earnest to the task of guarding the treasure with which we have been entrusted (2 Tim. 1:13–14). We must be willing to contend earnestly for the faith, even when—*especially* when—the authority of Scripture comes under attack from within the visible church.

Even today, though earthly courts and governments seem bent on censuring our faith, and popular culture is becoming militantly secular, treachery from within the church still poses a far greater danger than whatever persecution may come our way as hostility to the truth becomes more and more entrenched in the values of our society. If ecumenical efforts to reverse Supreme Court decisions on homosexuality and abortion have become more important to us than defending the truth within the household of faith, our priorities are seriously out of kilter, and we are not being faithful to our calling.

Judgment must always begin at the house of God (1 Pet. 4:17).

The cycle of downgrade disaster has replayed so frequently and so rhythmically because new generations of believers simply have not bothered to study the lessons of the past. People are naturally interested in what's new and stylish, and not particularly concerned with learning what we can from history. That is a serious mistake. It directly undermines our commitment to the timeless truth of God's ancient and everlasting Word.

My prayer is that this book has been an encouragement to you to "be

---

[2] From Charles Haddon Spurgeon's footnote in Robert Shindler, "The Down Grade," *The Sword and the Trowel* (March 1887), 122.

watchful, stand firm in the faith, act like men, be strong" (1 Cor. 16:13). It is absolutely true that we will not win the approval of the world by fighting for the truth of God's Word against the evil worldview of our age. But future generations of believers will scorn us if we give up the battle. And we know that our Lord will say "Well done" if we stand firm and keep the faith.

May each of us finally be able to say with the apostle Paul, "I have fought the good fight, I have finished the race, I have kept the faith" (2 Tim. 4:7).

Appendix

THE CHICAGO STATEMENT ON BIBLICAL INERRANCY

The authority of Scripture is a key issue for the Christian Church in this and every age. Those who profess faith in Jesus Christ as Lord and Savior are called to show the reality of their discipleship by humbly and faithfully obeying God's written Word. To stray from Scripture in faith or conduct is disloyalty to our Master. Recognition of the total truth and trustworthiness of Holy Scripture is essential to a full grasp and adequate confession of its authority.

The following Statement affirms this inerrancy of Scripture afresh, making clear our understanding of it and warning against its denial. We are persuaded that to deny it is to set aside the witness of Jesus Christ and of the Holy Spirit and to refuse that submission to the claims of God's own Word which marks true Christian faith. We see it as our timely duty to make this affirmation in the face of current lapses from the truth of inerrancy among our fellow Christians and misunderstanding of this doctrine in the world at large.

This Statement consists of three parts: a Summary Statement, Articles of Affirmation and Denial, and an Exposition. It has been prepared in the course of a three-day consultation in Chicago. Those who have signed the Summary Statement and the Articles wish to affirm their own conviction as to the inerrancy of Scripture and to encourage and challenge one another and all Christians to growing appreciation and understanding of this doctrine. We acknowledge the limitations of a document prepared in a brief, intensive conference and do not propose that this Statement be given creedal weight. Yet we rejoice in the deepening of our own convictions through our discussions together, and we pray that the Statement we have signed may be used to the glory of our God toward a new reformation of the Church in its faith, life, and mission.

We offer this Statement in a spirit, not of contention, but of humility and love, which we purpose by God's grace to maintain in any future dialogue arising out of what we have said. We gladly acknowledge that many who deny the inerrancy of Scripture do not display the consequences of this denial in the rest of their belief and behavior, and we are conscious that we who confess this doctrine often deny it in life by failing to bring our thoughts and deeds, our traditions and habits, into true subjection to the divine Word.

We invite response to this statement from any who see reason to amend its affirmations about Scripture by the light of Scripture itself, under whose infallible authority we stand as we speak. We claim no personal infallibility for the witness we bear, and for any help which enables us to strengthen this testimony to God's Word we shall be grateful.

A Short Statement

1. God, who is Himself Truth and speaks truth only, has inspired Holy Scripture in order thereby to reveal Himself to lost mankind through Jesus Christ as Creator and Lord, Redeemer and Judge. Holy Scripture is God's witness to Himself.

2. Holy Scripture, being God's own Word, written by men prepared and superintended by His Spirit, is of infallible divine authority in all matters upon which it touches: it is to be believed, as God's instruction, in all that it affirms; obeyed, as God's command, in all that it requires; embraced, as God's pledge, in all that it promises.

3. The Holy Spirit, Scripture's divine Author, both authenticates it to us by His inward witness and opens our minds to understand its meaning.

4. Being wholly and verbally God-given, Scripture is without error or fault in all its teaching, no less in what it states about God's acts in creation, about the events of world history, and about its own literary origins under God, than in its witness to God's saving grace in individual lives.

5. The authority of Scripture is inescapably impaired if this total divine inerrancy is in any way limited or disregarded, or made relative to a view of truth contrary to the Bible's own; and such lapses bring serious loss to both the individual and the Church.

Articles of Affirmation and Denial

ARTICLE I

We affirm that the Holy Scriptures are to be received as the authoritative Word of God.

We deny that the Scriptures receive their authority from the Church, tradition, or any other human source.

ARTICLE II

We affirm that the Scriptures are the supreme written norm by which God binds the conscience, and that the authority of the Church is subordinate to that of Scripture.

We deny that Church creeds, councils, or declarations have authority greater than or equal to the authority of the Bible.

ARTICLE III

We affirm that the written Word in its entirety is revelation given by God. We deny that the Bible is merely a witness to revelation, or only becomes revelation in encounter, or depends on the responses of men for its validity.

ARTICLE IV

We affirm that God who made mankind in His image has used language as a means of revelation.

We deny that human language is so limited by our creatureliness that it is rendered inadequate as a vehicle for divine revelation. We further deny that the corruption of human culture and language through sin has thwarted God's work of inspiration.

ARTICLE V

We affirm that God's revelation in the Holy Scriptures was progressive. We deny that later revelation, which may fulfill earlier revelation, ever corrects or contradicts it. We further deny that any normative revelation has been given since the completion of the New Testament writings.

ARTICLE VI

We affirm that the whole of Scripture and all its parts, down to the very words of the original, were given by divine inspiration.

We deny that the inspiration of Scripture can rightly be affirmed of the whole without the parts, or of some parts but not the whole.

Article VII

We affirm that inspiration was the work in which God by His Spirit, through human writers, gave us His Word. The origin of Scripture is divine. The mode of divine inspiration remains largely a mystery to us.

We deny that inspiration can be reduced to human insight, or to heightened states of consciousness of any kind.

Article VIII

We affirm that God in His work of inspiration utilized the distinctive personalities and literary styles of the writers whom He had chosen and prepared.

We deny that God, in causing these writers to use the very words that He chose, overrode their personalities.

Article IX

We affirm that inspiration, though not conferring omniscience, guaranteed true and trustworthy utterance on all matters of which the Biblical authors were moved to speak and write.

We deny that the finitude or fallenness of these writers, by necessity or otherwise, introduced distortion or falsehood into God's Word.

Article X

We affirm that inspiration, strictly speaking, applies only to the autographic text of Scripture, which in the providence of God can be ascertained from available manuscripts with great accuracy. We further affirm that copies and translations of Scripture are the Word of God to the extent that they faithfully represent the original.

We deny that any essential element of the Christian faith is affected by the absence of the autographs. We further deny that this absence renders the assertion of Biblical inerrancy invalid or irrelevant.

Article XI

We affirm that Scripture, having been given by divine inspiration, is infallible, so that, far from misleading us, it is true and reliable in all the matters it addresses.

We deny that it is possible for the Bible to be at the same time infallible and errant in its assertions. Infallibility and inerrancy may be distinguished, but not separated.

ARTICLE XII

We affirm that Scripture in its entirety is inerrant, being free from all falsehood, fraud, or deceit.

We deny that Biblical infallibility and inerrancy are limited to spiritual, religious, or redemptive themes, exclusive of assertions in the fields of history and science. We further deny that scientific hypotheses about earth history may properly be used to overturn the teaching of Scripture on creation and the flood.

ARTICLE XIII

We affirm the propriety of using inerrancy as a theological term with reference to the complete truthfulness of Scripture.

We deny that it is proper to evaluate Scripture according to standards of truth and error that are alien to its usage or purpose. We further deny that inerrancy is negated by Biblical phenomena such as a lack of modern technical precision, irregularities of grammar or spelling, observational descriptions of nature, the reporting of falsehoods, the use of hyperbole and round numbers, the topical arrangement of material, variant selections of material in parallel accounts, or the use of free citations.

ARTICLE XIV

We affirm the unity and internal consistency of Scripture.

We deny that alleged errors and discrepancies that have not yet been resolved vitiate the truth claims of the Bible.

ARTICLE XV

We affirm that the doctrine of inerrancy is grounded in the teaching of the Bible about inspiration.

We deny that Jesus' teaching about Scripture may be dismissed by appeals to accommodation or to any natural limitation of His humanity.

ARTICLE XVI

We affirm that the doctrine of inerrancy has been integral to the Church's faith throughout its history.

We deny that inerrancy is a doctrine invented by Scholastic Protestantism, or is a reactionary position postulated in response to negative higher criticism.

ARTICLE XVII

We affirm that the Holy Spirit bears witness to the Scriptures, assuring believers of the truthfulness of God's written Word.

We deny that this witness of the Holy Spirit operates in isolation from or against Scripture.

ARTICLE XVIII

We affirm that the text of Scripture is to be interpreted by grammatical-historical exegesis, taking account of its literary forms and devices, and that Scripture is to interpret Scripture.

We deny the legitimacy of any treatment of the text or quest for sources lying behind it that leads to relativizing, dehistoricizing, or discounting its teaching, or rejecting its claims to authorship.

ARTICLE XIX

We affirm that a confession of the full authority, infallibility, and inerrancy of Scripture is vital to a sound understanding of the whole of the Christian faith. We further affirm that such confession should lead to increasing conformity to the image of Christ.

We deny that such confession is necessary for salvation. However, we further deny that inerrancy can be rejected without grave consequences, both to the individual and to the Church.

General Index

Cambridge University, 52
Cameron, Nigel, 96
Cameron, Peter, 166
canon, 124, 139, 142, 304–16, 366
Carson, D. A., 49, 84, 280, 292
certainty, 48–51, 281, 361
Chapman, Stephen, 308
character, 109–12, 285, 359
Chicago Statement on Biblical Hermeneutics,
    205, 206
Chicago Statement on Biblical Inerrancy (CSBI),
    174–76, 180, 181, 198–99, 203–5, 288n2,
    378–83
China, 157
Christian maturity, 79
Christian theism, 350
christology, 361
chronology, 144
church councils, 127–28, 380
church fathers, 116–29
church-growth movement, 12–13, 364
Church of Scotland, 161–62, 163
church tradition, 128, 129–31
circular reasoning, 354
clarity, of Scripture, 35–36, 247, 275–87
classical theism, 145
cleanness, 36–37
Clement of Rome, 117
cleverness, 340
Clines, David J. A., 282n22
Coleridge, Samuel Taylor, 96
commitment, 105
communitarianism, 284
completeness, 335
completion, 77
compromise, 372
concurrence, 263–65
condescension. *See* divine accommodation
confessions of faith, 258, 274
conjectural emendation, 246–47
"contained in" the Scriptures, 162–63, 167
context, 180, 185–86, 233–34
contradictions, alleged, 244–54
convenience, 53
copyists, 245
cornerstone, 238
correction, 98
cosmology, 96, 363
Council of Constance, 137
Council of Nicaea, 127
Council of Trent, 133
courage, 287
covenant document, 194–95
Cowan, Steven B., 349n7
Cowper, William, 271–72
Craig, William Lane, 350n9
creation, 27
Creator-creature distinction, 255–56
Cross, Frank Moore, 310
cults, 12, 13–14
Cyprian, 127, 131
Cyril of Jerusalem, 125–26
Cyrus, 19

Dale, R. W., 153
darkness, 329–31
Davids, Peter H., 298n42
Dead Sea Scrolls, 249, 311
Dearman, J. Andrew, 227n50, 229
deception, 159, 160–61, 191, 374
declension, 176
defense, 349
Deism, 374
deliberateness, 53
deliverance, 68
demons, 159n25, 168
Denney, James, 159n25, 163, 164n33
dependability, 249
depravity, 353
depression, 34
Derrida, Jacques, 202
desertion, 102
Dever, Mark, 92, 100
Devil. *See* Satan
DeYoung, Kevin, 299
dia, 301
dialectical theology, 9
dictation, 44–46, 139, 140, 261, 266n32
Dionysius of Alexandria, 125
discernment, 32, 67
disciples, 368–70
discipleship, 75, 78, 86–87, 91
discrepancies, 245
disobedience, 78, 189
diversity, 375
divine accommodation, 289–94, 382
divine vengeance, 331
doctrine
    of clarity, 279
    of God, 145, 186–87
    importance of, 371–72
    pervasiveness of, 259
    of Scripture, 97–98, 137
    sound, 99–100, 107, 124, 128, 343
Dods, Marcus, 151, 152, 155
donation, 270
Donatists, 123
Doriani, Daniel, 370
doubt, 48, 278, 362
Downgrade Controversy, 172
dreams, 261
Driver, Christopher, 156
dual authorship, of Scripture, 41, 288–303
Durham University, 147

Eastern University, 207
Ebionism, 14
Eck, Johann, 116, 137
Egypt, 214–30, 235, 252–53
Ehrman, Bart, 310, 312–13
electability, 64
'elohiym, 239–40
emotionalism, 343
empiricism, 352
Enlightenment, 13, 134, 141, 142, 149, 201, 350
Enns, Peter, 46, 177, 180–81, 207–8, 211n2,
    211–12n8, 237n17, 252, 289

Sadducees, 254, 308
salvation, 68, 93, 158, 196, 197
sanctification, 99, 341
Sandy, Brent, 176
Sangster, W. E., 105
Satan, 12, 26, 64, 67, 140, 159–60, 168, 172,
    189, 338, 373, 374
Schleiermacher, Friedrich, 135, 200–201
Scholastic Protestantism, 383
science, 17–18, 88, 352, 363
scientific method, 173
Scopes Monkey Trial, 173
Scots Confession, 165, 307n6
Scottish Common Sense Realism, 134
Scottish Reformation, 162, 165
scribal changes, 247, 250, 305, 312–14
Scripture
    as active, 20–21, 322
    attacks on, 12–15, 26–27
    authority of, 15–17, 35, 76, 79, 277, 376,
        379
    certainty in, 48–51
    and Christians, 78–79
    claims of, 258–62
    clarity of, 35–36, 85, 139, 145, 247, 275–87
    cultural objections to, 177–78
    doctrine of, 97–98, 137
    dual authorship of, 41, 44
    as fire, 331–32
    as hammer, 332
    high view of, 89, 97, 115, 144
    and human agency, 41–44
    as its own interpreter, 285n38
    Jesus Christ on, 16–17, 74–78
    as lamp, 329–31
    as light, 67
    low view of, 153
    metaphors for, 321–33
    as milk, 328–29
    as mirror, 325–27
    organic nature of, 49–50
    perspicuity of, 35, 85, 139, 145, 275–87
    power of, 319–33
    preservation of, 304–16
    as profitable, 98–99
    as sharp, 322
    sufficiency of, 16, 25–39, 145, 366
    as sword, 321–25
Second Helvetic Confession, 145–46
Second Temple Judaism, 43
secondary causation, 263–65
seed, 239, 327–28
"seekers," 14
selective inspiration, 95
sensus plenior, 211, 212
Sermon on the Mount, 75, 85, 369
Seventh-Day Adventists, 13–14
Sherwood, John, 298n42
Sibbes, Richard, 103
significance, 234
signs and wonders, 367
Silva, Moisés, 249
simplicity, 283

Simpson, Patrick, 164
sin, 20, 36, 38, 66, 273, 284, 353
sincerity, 287
skepticism, 48, 278, 374, 376
Smeaton, George, 151
Smith, Christian, 284n31
Smith, George Adam, 151–52, 155, 163
Smith, Joseph, 13
Smith, William Robertson, 151, 152, 159n25
social sciences, 364
Socinianism, 145, 374
sociology, 364
sola Scriptura, 94, 116, 124, 129, 132–33, 198
soul, 30, 323
sound doctrine, 124
sovereignty, of God, 47, 217, 295–96
Sparks, Kenton, 290–91, 292n24, 293
special revelation, 27–28, 136, 306
Spencer, Herbert, 17
spiritual growth, 328–29
spiritual mapping, 367–68
spiritual-warfare movement, 367–68
spirituality, 108
spontaneity, 53
Sproul, R. C., 174–75
Spurgeon, Charles H., 101, 172, 267n34, 320,
    328, 330, 342, 345, 346–47, 374, 376
St. Andrew's College, Sydney, 166
Strauss, David, 154
strength, 68
Stuart, Douglas, 227n51, 229
Stuart, Moody, 155
stylistic distinctions, 42–44
subjectivism, 14, 200, 202, 284, 338
submission, 178, 179
suffering, 72, 110, 339
superintendence, 296–300
supernaturalism, 81
surrender, 242–43
Sweeney, Marvin A., 227n50, 229
syncretism, 14, 338
synecdoche, 29

Tacitus, 311
tâmîym, 29
Taylor, William M., 106
temptation, 66–67, 172
Ten Commandments, 45, 63, 192, 194
Tertullian, 118, 122, 373
testimony, 31, 296
textual criticism, 304–16
textual variants, 312–14
theism, 145, 350, 359
Theodoret of Cyr, 137
theology, 240–41, 280
theopneustos, 16, 40, 95, 96–97, 186, 257–58,
    259–60
thermodynamics, 18
Third Wave movement, 14
Thirty-Ninth Festal Letter (Athanasius), 119
Thomas Aquinas, 138
Thucydides, 43
Timothy, 92–95, 97, 102–12, 336–43, 372

Scripture Index

14 Classic Essays in Defense of Biblical Inerrancy

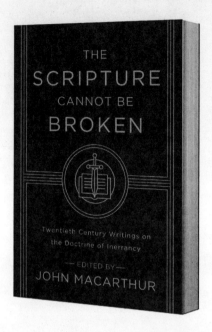

Biblical inerrancy is under attack. Now more than ever, the church needs to carefully consider what it stands to lose should this crucial doctrine be surrendered. Produced under the editorial oversight of pastor John MacArthur, this anthology of essays in defense of biblical inerrancy features contributions from a host of respected 20th-century evangelical leaders, including:

- John M. Frame
- Paul D. Feinberg
- Roger R. Nicole
- J. I. Packer
- B. B. Warfield
- Harold Lindsell
- John Murray

- Edward J. Young
- J. Barton Payne
- R. Laird Harris
- Alan M. Stibbs
- Robert Preus
- René Pache
- Gordon R. Lewis

The Scripture Cannot Be Broken is a call to stand alongside our spiritual forefathers with wisdom, clarity, and courage—resolute in our confidence that Scripture is the very Word of God.